Alexander Wallace

Notes on Lilies and Their Culture

Rewritten throughout, and embellished with numerous woodcuts; a reliable guide

for beginners; containing illustrations of all the chief lilies in flower; likewise of their

bulb growth

Alexander Wallace

Notes on Lilies and Their Culture
*Rewritten throughout, and embellished with numerous woodcuts; a reliable guide for
beginners; containing illustrations of all the chief lilies in flower; likewise of their bulb growth*

ISBN/EAN: 9783337212919

Printed in Europe, USA, Canada, Australia, Japan

Cover: Foto ©Andreas Hilbeck / pixelio.de

More available books at **www.hansebooks.com**

SECOND EDITION.

REVISED AND ENLARGED,

OF

NOTES ON LILIES AND THEIR CULTURE.

NOTES

ON

LILIES AND THEIR CULTURE:

SECOND EDITION,

REVISED, ENLARGED, RE-WRITTEN THROUGHOUT, AND
EMBELLISHED WITH NUMEROUS WOODCUTS;

A RELIABLE GUIDE FOR BEGINNERS;

CONTAINING

ILLUSTRATIONS OF ALL THE CHIEF LILIES IN FLOWER;
LIKEWISE OF THEIR BULB GROWTH;
AMPLE DIRECTIONS FOR THEIR SUCCESSFUL CULTIVATION;
A CHAPTER ON HYBRIDISATION;
VALUABLE LETTERS FROM FOREIGN CORRESPONDENTS
IN THE HIMALAYAS, JAPAN, AND NORTH AMERICA, ETC.;
MR. BAKER'S SYNOPSIS OF THE GENERA;
FALLACIES OF DUNEDIN;
INSTRUCTIONS TO COLLECTORS;
&c.,   &c.,   &c.,

BY

DR. WALLACE,

COLCHESTER.

1879.

TO BE HAD FROM
THE NEW PLANT AND BULB COMPANY, LION WALK, COLCHESTER.

TABLE OF CONTENTS.

INDEX.

For remainder of Woodcuts, *see* under head Lilium.

LIST OF

LILY NAMES MENTIONED IN THE SYNOPSIS,

CHAPTER IX.

The numbers refer to the species.   The names to which an asterisk (*) is attached are the adopted ones; the others are synonyms.

Abchasicum, 5
*Albanicum. 47
*Album, 18
*Alice Wilson, 26
*Alternans, 26
*Alutaceum, 26
Andinum, 20
Angustifolium, 46
*Armeniacum, 26
*Atrosanguineum, 23, 26
*Aurantiacum, 26
*Auratum, 19
Aureum, 24
Autumnale, 30
*Avenaceum, 36

Bartrami, 13
*Batemanniæ, 44
Batisux, 4
*Belladonnæ, 12
*Bicolor, 23, 26
*Biligulatum, 26
*Bloomerianum, 34
*Bloomerianum Ocellatum, 34
Bourgæi, 28
*Brevifolium, 26
Broussarti, 18
*Brownii, 8
*Bulbiferum, 23
Buschianum, 22

*Californicum, 28
*Callosum, 47
*Canadense, 28
Canadense Minus, 28
*Candidum, 11
*Candidum Foliis Aureo Var., 11
*Candidum Monstrosum, 11
*Carniolicum, 41

Carolinianum, Cat., 27
*Carolinianum, Mich., 30
Cattaneæ, 35
*Catesbæi, 27
*Chaixii, 25
*Chalcedonicum, 48
*Citrinum, 26
Colchicum, 38
*Columbianum, 33
*Concolor, 22
*Cordifolium, 1
*Coridion, 22
*Croceum, 24
*Croceum Tenuifolium, 25
*Cruentum, 19, 26

*Dalmaticum, 35
*Davidi, 22
*Davuricum, 25
Dexteri, 19

*Elegans, 26
*Emperor, 19
*Erectum, 23.
Excelsum, 42
*Eximium, Court., 5

Flavum, 47
*Fortunei, 16
*Fulgens, 26
*Fulgens Flore Pleno, 26

*Giganteum, 2
Glabrum, 35
Glehnii, 1
Gracile, 47

Hæmatochroum, 26
*Hansoni, 37
Hartwegii, 32
Hirsutum, 35

*Horsmanni, 26
*Humboldtii, 34
Humile, 23

*Immaculatum, 23
*Incomparabile, 23
Isabellinum, 42

Jama-juri, 5
*Japonicum Colchesterii, 8
Japonicum, Thunb., 9
Jucundum, 45

*Krætzeri, 18
*Kromeri, 9

Latifolium, 23
Ledebourii, 38
*Leichtlinii, 43
Leichtlinii Majus., 43
Linifolium, 50
Lishmanni, 16
Loddigesianum, 38
*Longiflorum, Thunb., 5
*Longiflorum, Wall., 4
*Lucidum, 31

*Maculatum, 21
*Madame von Siebold, 5
*Maritimum, 28
*Marmoratum, 26
*Marmoratum Aureum, 26
*Martagon, 38
*Martagon Album, 35
*Mawei, 26
*Maximowiczii, 45
*Medeoloides, 21
*Melpomene, 19
Metzii, 6
Michauxii, 30
Monadelphum, 38

NOTES

ON

LILIES AND THEIR CULTURE.

CHAPTER I.

INTRODUCTORY REMARKS.

Since the time when the Golden Banded Queen (*Lilium Auratum*), only a few years ago, burst upon us in her wondrous splendour—taking captive the startled senses of all, not merely horticulturists, but the public generally, by the enormous size and number of her flowers, their powerful fragrance, their elegant and graceful contour, their richness of ornamentation on a pure white ground, and by the general stateliness of the plant,—the cultivation of Lilies has received a great impetus.

Since that date, not only has Japan sent us Lily bulbs by tens of thousands, but America, both from her Eastern and Western Provinces, has contributed largely. India, Siberia, and the Caucasus, &c., &c., have furnished their quota, and Lily cultivators, who some ten or twelve years ago might almost have been counted on the fingers, are now to be numbered by the thousand.

About the same time, horticultural taste began to tire of the eternal sameness of red, yellow, and blue patterns, made up chiefly from Lobelias, Calceolarias, and Geraniums; foliage plants came into vogue, sub-tropical plants were utilised, herbaceous plants, old favourites, came again to the front, and with these, bulbous plants, especially the Iris family, Narcissi, and Lilies, found many admirers: and well they might, for few things are more graceful in outline, few things more useful for decoration, few things more fragrant than the pure white or richly coloured pendant bells of many a Lily and their congeners. There is also this much in their favour, that, with very few exceptions, all are perfectly hardy, and most easily grown out of doors in almost any garden in the British Isles (Scotland not excepted); and it is chiefly with a view to render this more easy, that these notes on Lilies and their culture have been penned.

In a Rhododendron bed, whether peaty or loamy, Lilies find a congenial soil, and what is most important, shade from scorching sun; and if planted on a slope, and well supplied at the roots with

B

moisture, they will, when the Rhododendron blooms are over, and the beds begin otherwise to look dull and uninteresting, astonish and delight their owner with stout vigorous stems, fine large well-coloured flowers, and glossy foliage.

One more point in their favour, from a decorative point of view, and I have done: What more truly beautiful than a pot of well-grown Lilies, whether it be *Szovitzianum* with its pendent canary-coloured bells, *Auratum* with its massive fragrant flowers, *Brownii* with its gracefully recurved tubes, richly browned outside, but pure white within, possessing a most delicate perfume, or *Speciosum* the loveliest of all; or among the smaller kinds, of the graceful *Pulchellum*, the taller but elegant *Tenuifolium*, or that pretty bright yellow star-like *Coridion?* yet it is not necessary that these should be grown from the beginning in a pot for this purpose, *see* page 9: trouble and labour may be spared by carefully lifting the plants from the border just when coming into flower, dropping them into a good sized pot, careful that no injury be done to the upper roots, watering well, and placing in the shade for a day or two; their blooms will open a little later on, without detriment to the bulb, and all their charms be displayed when and where required.

In order, therefore, to help former cultivators and interest new admirers in this very graceful section of flowers, and with a view to render their cultivation more easy, we shall be glad to offer in these jottings the result of our observations during the last few years: by no means supposing that we know everything about Lilies, but hoping, while imparting what we know, to extract from others further valuable information.

1. *As to the Hardiness of Lilies.*—There may be among the many imported forms a few Lilies, such as *L. Wallichianum* from India, *L. Catesbæi* from S. Carolina, and *L. Philippinense* from the Philippines, unable to stand a severe winter; but with these exceptions, we have found no Lily unable to endure the winter cold to which we are accustomed in England. It has been said that *L. Auratum* is quite hardy in Scotland, but that the *Lancifolium* section are killed by cold. It may be so, and in some districts it may be necessary either to protect certain Lilies in winter with ashes, cocoa-fibre, and other dry refuse, but, generally speaking, in England it is not necessary. One winter, after severe frosts with skating for several weeks, our *Auratum* bulbs planted out of doors three inches deep, were all examined; not one was damaged, and they came up and flowered as well as ever.* During the very severe winter of 1878-9 we do not think we have lost any out door Lilies from frost. Though I have no doubt that

---

* It is sometimes said of *L. Longiflorum* that, coming up as it does so early in the year, it is materially injured by spring frosts. This may be obviated by protecting the young growths with bracken or other dry litter.

winter frost alone will not damage Lily bulbs, I cannot, I fear, make the same statement respecting late spring (May) frosts. These have been very severe during the last few years, and falling with fierce fury upon the young tender growths, sometimes 18 to 24 inches long, of *L. Auratum* and *L. Speciosum* have demolished all hope of bloom for that season, and not only so, but have destroyed the foliage and materially injured the growth of the bulbs. Many forms, such as the *Umbellatum* section, the Caucasian and Siberian kinds, are, however, so hardy as to be unaffected even by this severe trial; we may therefore state, that no amount of ordinary frost in our climate will hurt the bulb in the ground, or the shoot just above ground before it has unfolded its tender leaves.

Wet, however, or rather stagnant moisture is more injurious than frost, such bulbs as *Brownii* with large open scales in a very wet winter, like that of 1876-77, in many places perished; this may be avoided : 1st by planting them in a place where good drainage will remove all superfluous moisture, protecting them further by a conical mound of earth, so as to throw the water off that particular spot : 2nd by adopting the Japanese custom, when planting, of placing the bulbs on their sides, instead of upright on their base; this will prevent the water lodging at the insertion of the scales, which in a wet summer is, I believe, the reason why so many tender bulbs decay just at that part. Wet, moreover, is injurious by setting the soil tight round the bulb, this must be met by a free admixture of sharp sand with the soil. Lastly, wet favours the attacks of slugs, deadly enemies to bulbs of all kinds and especially to Lilies : these pests must be kept at a distance by the use of lime, ashes, or sharp sand placed round the bulb, and by the use of traps, such as brewers' grains, lettuces, &c., to attract them to their destruction.

It is, indeed, a very simple matter to take up the bulbs in late autumn, and store them in some dry pit, shed, or cool cellar, where they would lie cool but protected from frosts; in that case, they should be stored in earth, sand, or cocoa-fibre, and an occasional drop of water is necessary during the winter months, to prevent the bulbs drying up too much. They may be planted out again in February or March; but for reasons which we will adduce further on, we do not recommend this plan, unless where absolutely necessary, owing to very wet soils. So much for hardiness.

2. *As to Soil.*—The Canadense section, to which belongs *Superbum, Pardalinum,* and *Puberulum* delight in moist boggy soil, *Parvum* the side of a running stream. *L. Humboldtii, Washingtonianum, Martagons* in general, the *Tiger* group and *Auratum* family delight in cool loam, and do well in peaty, moist soils. The *Umbellatum* section, *Thunbergianum* or *Elegans,* and *Speciosum* families will do exceedingly well on light soils, so also will *Longiflorum, Candidum,* and their allies; *Concolor* never did so well

with us on our light dry soil, as in one very rainy summer. So that each soil has its favourite Lilies, and each cultivator will no doubt for himself, by his own experience, determine the peculiarities of the soil and climate in his own garden, this will enable him better to follow the rules laid down by us. Of pure peaty soils we ourselves have had no experience, only of very light, loamy, and prepared mixed soils.

And here comes in the question of a disease* among the *Auratum* group, which has been closely observed by us during the past years, and to which we think we have found a clue. It may be recognised early by the curled, bent-over condition of the upper part of the stem, and discoloured black or brown foliage. Presently, after bright sunshine, the leaves shrivel and drop off, the stem withers, the flowers become abortive, the bulbs, when taken up, are found to be in a discoloured, decaying state, the upper set of roots are imperfectly developed and unhealthy, the lower roots scanty, brown, and discoloured, perhaps dead. This disease I have seen attacking not merely imported or newly planted bulbs, but also those that have been for several years unmoved. I have lost thousands of *Auratum* from this cause, as also bulbs of *Krameri, Umbellatum,* and, in a much less degree, *Thunbergianum* and *Speciosum.*

All these bulbs have two sets of roots, one set omitted from their base in autumn, the functions of which are to provide nourishment for the bulb, the other in early summer, from the base of the stem, to supply nourishment to the leaves and flowers. These roots in a healthy mature plant are very abundant, and may be described as forming a wig. If any one will examine a growing plant of *Auratum*, about 6 inches high, he will find at the junction of the stem with the bulb a double ring of stout white roots, whose functions evidently, from their appearance, must be an important one. Now if from any cause, such as being too near the surface, insufficient moisture, or want of pot room, these roots get dried up, scorched, or otherwise injured, it is clear that either the stem and leaves will be deprived of nourishment, or that they must obtain it from the bulb; in the former case I believe that the disease which I have described, makes its appearance; in the latter, the bulbs get smaller and deteriorate, a very common cause of complaint with people who cultivate Lilies in pots, or who do not allow a sufficient supply of water. I attribute, therefore, this so-called disease to a want of moisture experienced by the upper set of roots; it may be said that the lower roots may be supplied with moisture, though the upper ones are not—granted; in that case, the lower roots will be more healthy, and help to keep the bulb alive under the double burden laid upon it.

I may here remark that the wet season in Japan, lasting through-out the months of May and June, during which it rains more or less daily, coincides with the period of stem and foliage growth, and the

* By some called "sunstroke."

complete development of the upper wig of roots. A much longer interval for these purposes is thus afforded, before hot weather sets in, than ever we can hope for in this climate, and this throws, I think, much light on the premature scorching of the roots, so frequent with us, and points out the necessity for growing these Japanese Lilies in moist, shady, cool spots.

If a Lily stem be detached from the bulb, and planted with its roots undisturbed, it will flower and flourish vigorously, and may, perhaps, if there be time before autumn sets in, form tiny bulbs at the base of the stem to perpetuate itself, otherwise it dies, but not till the season is over; and if the transplanting has been carefully done, it is impossible to detect any check to the foliage and flowers. It dies in the natural course of Nature, and there is no bulb left to renew life the following year. Again: Lilies may get their stems eaten off, injured, or destroyed in various ways, or from some cause may lie over, as it is termed, and not emit shoots. But are the bulbs damaged? Not so, the roots at the base of the bulb are put forth, and the bulbs make their growth as usual; perhaps even the more so because there is no stem to draw nourishment from them.*

This, then, we submit, proves the independence of bulb and stem, the necessity for two sets of roots, and the true use of the bulb; one† set of roots serving for the nourishment of the stem, leaves, and flower alone, the other set for that of the bulb. And what is the bulb but a receptacle of stored-up force during the winter months to preserve life and perpetuate spring growth? If these views are correct, then it is clear that the leaves turned brown and died, as aforesaid, because the upper set of roots, being scanty and unhealthy, could no longer obtain the moisture necessary‡ to existence, the first hot sunshine scorched and withered leaves and stem. In no single instance in which these unhealthy Lilies were examined were the roots healthy and plentiful.

A recent writer on Lily Culture, under the pseudonym of Dunedin, has promulgated the remarkable statement that these upper or stem roots do harm (*Garden*, p. 371, *Oct.* 26, 1878). He says:—" A fruitful source of injury to the successional bulbs is the stem roots, which some actually encourage by top-dressing and heaping up the soil around the lower part of the stems. These stem roots are some of them of great length, they go down, and not only impoverish the

---

* We could relate an instance of this where no growth was made above ground, but the bulbs which had been supposed to have perished (having made no sign), were in the autumn found much finer than when planted the previous spring.

† Compare Mr. Miles' statement (chap. iv.) of Lilies flowering without any roots emitted from base of bulb.

‡ We have seen one or two Lilies in a clump thus turn brown and fail, while the others were in full vigour. Our explanation of this is, that the weakest has gone to the wall, and the roots of others have been more vigorous and obtained the necessary supply of moisture, those that failed to do so sickened.

soil, but they twine themselves in and out among the scales, suck out the sap, and destroy the bulbs for the next season's bloom. Rose growers wage war against suckers coming up, Lily growers should wage war against *suckers* going down. Every now and then remove the soil for 1 or 2 inches deep, and then carefully clip off every vestige of a stem root, returning the soil again. A professional writer says, ' As the flower stems advance in growth they put forth a number of young roots from the stem above the bulb, when that is perceived place round each stem some rough hard pieces of manure for these roots to strike into ; this will encourage the flower stems to grow strongly and flower firmly, besides increasing very much the size of the bulbs below.' Worse advice than this it is difficult even to imagine."

Those of my readers who have followed me so far will see that my ideas on this subject are totally opposed to those of Dunedin. Nature, who is never wasteful, would not have given these Lilies such a wig of roots were they not required for a purpose ; everything has its use, and that of these stem roots is, I have endeavoured to prove, to support, strengthen, and develope the stem, foliage, and buds.

To compare Rose suckers (which would if let alone form separate plants) with Lily roots, or, as he writes, *suckers* which can never form a separate plant, is ridiculous, and to recommend Lily growers to clip off the stem roots when such magnificent plants as those described (chap. iv.) at Oatlands, Weybridge, can be grown without any such meddling, would be simply an absurdity.

I have mentioned this fallacy of Dunedin's simply to caution my readers not to follow it.

But it is also possible for the bulb to be absorbed itself by the act of flowering. Of this we have seen many instances when, not knowing better, we potted *Auratum* bulbs in small pots, raising the bulbs above the soil, like a Hyacinth. In the autumn we saw our error. The flowers bloomed, but the bulbs dried up. The pots being small, the upper roots emitted could not obtain sufficient moisture from the soil, and the bulb was sucked dry to produce a flower.

We quote another instance in point. A friend lately informed us that some *Auratum* bulbs, planted in small pots, and plunged in cocoa-fibre, on the leads of his house, had flowered beautifully. Not a stem had turned brown, but the bulbs, on examination at the close of the season, had disappeared, though the roots were abundant and healthy. Here, as the pots were plunged in cocoa-fibre and watered well, there was plenty of moisture, but being small, nourishment could only be obtained by the roots by feeding upon the bulbs.

Such, therefore, we believe to be the cause of the disease referred to—deficient root action and insufficient supply of moisture. And we go further, convinced by our own experience, and say that the

Auratum and *Tiger* families will not do well generally in light soils and hot burning sunshine, because there is not sufficient moisture, and in proof we give our own experience. We have grown these bulbs planted both on light hot soil with sandy sub-soil, and on heavy loam, good corn land. On the former eight-tenths of the bulbs failed to flower, and had but few healthy roots; some died, few made any growth, notwithstanding heavy rains; while on the heavy land, bulbs planted at the same time, and picked out of the same lot, did admirably, flowered well, had enormous roots, and made good new growth. With regard to peaty soils we have no experience, but it should be remembered that Rhododendron beds, where it is recommended to plant *Auratum*, contain plenty of moisture, and the surface is protected from the scorching sun's rays by the overspread foliage of the Rhododendrons.

Hence we lay down the axiom that for these strong growing Lilies —and we think that the *Martagon* tribe generally, *L. Humboldtii, Brownii,* and others, must be put in the same category—a cool loamy soil with plenty of moisture is essential to their vigour.

Deep planting, say 4 to 6 inches, is for many reasons desirable.

1. It is a better security against frost.

2. There is more moisture below, and the upper set of roots lie protected from the sun's rays.

3. As the height of the stem is measured by feet, it matters little whether it has to shoot up a few inches more or less out through the soil.

4. We are told that M. Roezl finds some of the Californian Lilies 2 to 3 feet deep among rocks and stones.

We are therefore advocates for deep planting.[*]

We do not recommend pot culture generally. That Lilies can be grown to perfection in pots no one who has paid a visit to Mr. G. F. Wilson's (Weybridge) splendid collection can dispute, but it is not in the power of every amateur, however partial he may be to Lilies, to give the time, attention, and thorough knowledge of their culture that Mr. Wilson bestows upon his favourites, and unless this is done Lilies had far better be planted out-of-doors to take care of themselves. Our experience is that they get starved and dried up in pots, both in summer and winter. In fact some of our friends would have wintered their Lilies in pots in a dry corner without moisture had we not remonstrated; others dry off their Lilies for the winter, as they would Hyacinths, in July.

We believe this still to be a common custom: but against such treatment we protest most strongly. A Lily ought never to be dry. There is no time except, perhaps, when they have just flowered and the stems are dying down when the roots are inactive. Even in midwinter, dig up a Lily in the ground which has been undisturbed,

* Confer. Dr. Kellogg's letter, chap. iii.

its roots are full of vigour.   Therefore, we say, never move a Lily when it is doing well.   Never let it be out of the ground longer than necessary.   Never let it be dry.   All our experience goes to show that Lilies thrive best in pure fresh air, with a moderate share of sun light, and with a moist cool border for their roots.   In support of our view that Lilies would be generally grown out-of-doors in the open border to greater advantage than in pots, we will quote a few examples which have come under our observation.

(A.) *Lilium Thunbergianum Bicolor.*—We saw this grown in five different gardens in one year, a very rainy season.

1. In small pots, where it bloomed well, but the growth was stunted, and about 6 inches high; the bulbs, we will venture to add, when taken up would not be so large as when planted.

2. In our own and three other gardens without liquid manure—growth about 12 inches to 18 inches; flowers fine and well coloured; bulbs fine when taken up, with numerous small ones.

3. At Mr. Wilson's, both in pot and out-of-doors—growth very luxuriant, 2 to 3 feet high, fine trusses of flowers, richly tinted.

(B.) *Lilium Concolor.*—We had a patch of this charming Lily planted out in the open borders, and others in pots.   From the latter we scarcely obtained any flowers, and the bulbs when taken up were fewer in number and smaller than when planted; out-of-doors the bulbs flowered freely, doubled and trebled their size, and increased in quantity about 500 per cent.

Our experience with the *Thunbergianum* or *Elegans* group was of a similar nature.

(C.) *Lilium Tigrinum Fortunei.*—We have grown this Lily in pots, and the bulbs were smaller when taken up than when planted, and if not watered well in autumn, dried up under hot sunshine and died.

In all these cases no liquid manure was used by us, and only by experience did we learn that it was necessary to use far larger pots for Lilies than those generally in use.   Therefore, we conclude, that to grow Lilies successfully in pots, requires deep large pots, with a broad not a narrow pinched-in base, good stout loam and peat, mixed together with plenty of sharp sand, and a plentiful supply of water at all times,* in this way prize Lilies will be undoubtedly obtained; but ordinary amateurs having little time to give to flowers, will be amply repaid by planting out their bulbs in the open ground in suitable spots, bestowing upon them only the ordinary amount of attention, and leaving them to shift for themselves.

If our readers will patiently bear with us for a little further, we think they will prefer the latter mode, always excepting Mr. Wilson and those who can follow his example.   To our great surprise we

---

* Liquid manure in a diluted form may be given once or twice a week when growth is once fairly established, up to the flowering season, it must then be discontinued. *See* Mr. Smith's and Mr. Sheppard's letters, chap. iv.

found out by accident that our pets, the Lilies, were possessed of a special advantage not belonging, so far as we know, to any other garden flower, and one that, directly it was known, at once relieved us from all care or desire to grow Lilies in pots.

For after all, if the doubtful and special advantage of forcing Lilies into bloom before their season is excepted, what is the great advantage of pot culture; only that thus plants may be shifted from one place to another more suitable, viz., into conservatories, halls, drawing-rooms, flower shows, &c. Well, that may be had without trouble and without pot culture so far as Lilies are concerned. Plant out *en masse* Lilies in the quarters specially appropriated and made fit for each kind; then, when just coming into bloom, take up your plant carefully, roots and all, in a mass, and plunge into a large pot, ready crocked, and with some rough cocoa-fibre or sphagnum moss at bottom, water freely, and your Lily is now moveable and ready to be shifted where you like; stand for 24 hours in a shady spot and then you may put pot and Lily in hot sunshine without detriment, for if carefully moved no flagging will take place. Here is an advantage possessed by Lilies alone; the labour of watering your pots is at once done away with, except during the time when your plant is in flower, for after flowering you may replant your Lily. Space is economised, for only when the flower is ready is the pot wanted, and —what will gratify gardeners of show places—their Lily corner may thus be in bloom from June to November by successional transplant-ation as each sort comes on. Lilies so treated require to be watered freely. It might, perhaps, be asked, how are the bulbs, thus taken up and potted, affected by this treatment at the close of the season? In our experience, their roots are active, more so than usual; the bulbs firm and in no way inferior to those that have not been disturbed.

This successful result seems to be the one thing wanting to bring Lilies into general use and popular favour, and if by writing these notes, we help to bring into notice the most graceful of all flowers, the Lilies, to show how easily they may be cultivated out of doors, and when required for display brought readily into notice, our aim will be attained. What flower can be more elegant for the button-hole than some of the smaller Lilies, as, for instance, the bright scarlet *Concolor*, or that graceful star, the canary-tinted *Coridion*? What flower possesses more stately grace than the deeply reflexed *Brownii*? What in the distance is more striking than a tall stem of *Szovitzianum*, with its 20 or 30 straw-coloured bells, symmetrically poised? What for a lady's hair more becoming than a flower of the *Speciosum* section? How long a time will cut Lilies remain fresh for decoration! In very hot weather from two to three days, in cool weather a week at least. We have known *Concolor* to be worn all day in the button-hole without water, and placed drooping at night

in a specimen glass with water, in the morning it was as fresh as
ever.   Can anything be more pure or graceful for church decoration
than *Longiflorum, Brownii*, and their allies ?—for harvest homes than
the stately *Tiger*, the gorgeous and perfumed *Auratum*, and the
elegant *Speciosum* ?

The Lilies that we have found to do well with us on light soils are as
follows :—The *Umbellatum* section, including *Philadelphicum, Bulbiferum, Croceum, Davuricum*, and their varieties; *Concolor*, and *Coridion*;
The *Thunbergianum* or *Elegans* section, and their many varieties;
Candidum, Longiflorum, Chalcedonicum, Pyrenaicum, and the *Speciosum* group.   Those that in our experience do better on heavy soil,
are *Auratum*, the *Tiger* family, *Hansoni, Giganteum, Szovitzianum,
Washingtonianum, Humboldtii, Carniolicum, Testaceum*, and other
Martagons.   Those more especially suited for a peaty soil are *Krameri, Brownii, Pulchellum, Tenuifolium, Leichtlinii, Parvum*; the
Canadense group, including *Superbum, Puberulum*, and *Pardalinum*,
delight in a swamp; *Parvum* does best (like *Disa Grandiflora*) on the
banks of a running stream, roots in water, foliage in sunshine, *see*
chap. iii.   In planting Lilies, then, we advise that they should be
placed in the ground as soon as possible after flowering ; protected,
if necessary, from extreme wet and cold during the winter by a
mound of earth, with sloped sides, above them.   They may be
planted out from August to April or May, according to the season,
but it may be laid down as a rule, that all Lilies are best removed to
their allotted stations, as soon as the flowering season is over.   After
this time, the first rains that fall cause the emission of new roots, which
maintain their activity all the autumn and winter, and if these are
damaged by removal, it must cause a check to the due progress of
the plant, *see* chap. iv.   With regard to manure, it is generally held
by Lily growers of experience, that the application of fresh manure is
fatal to the bulbs.   We have found a mulching of thoroughly rotten
manure during the winter months advantageous : but we cannot
advise that manure, fresh or old, should be dug in when the bulbs
are planted, liquid manure may be freely applied during the growing
and blooming season.   The Japanese, great Lily growers, give their
bulbs a top-dressing of night soil in the winter months.   For pot
culture they should be looked over in October or November,
disturbed as little as possible about the roots, but the loose soil at
top, sides, and bottom should be crumbled away with a blunt-pointed
stick, fresh loam, or loam and peat, sharpened with a little sand
added, and the ball replaced.   The pots should be large, much larger
than those in general use, and the bulbs planted from two to three
inches below the surface, according to the size, so as to permit the
upper set of roots to be well covered by soil.   For planting out in a
border, choose an open spot, sheltered from wind, lest the stems be
knocked about and broken.   In moist soils, Lilies will grow well.

under trees in shrubberies and in the shade, but if roots of other plants rob the ground, and deprive it of moisture, the Lilies will be stunted, and cause disappointment. Give the larger growing kinds, such as *Giganteum, Humboldtii,* and the *Speciosum* tribe, plenty of room to display their beauty. Lilies like warmth and sunshine, but unless there is a cool bottom beneath, they cannot stand hot sunshine ; a border under a south wall would, we fear, prove too dry in many soils for good Lily growth. The common *Tigrinum Sinensis, Longiflorum,* the *Umbellatum* tribe, the *Pomponium* section, with *Bulbiferum, Croceum,* and *Candidum,* will, however, do well in shrubberies if not too much overhung.

Plant at least four inches deep—in light soils six inches will not be too deep ; give each bulb its own width at least on each side free from its neighbour's share. Do not plant in very wet or frosty weather ; in the first case the ground will set tight round the bulb, of which some kinds are impatient. In the second case the frost may penetrate the ground more readily when the upper crust is broken, and injure the bulb. In very wet soils plant the bulb on its side, but allow room in that case for the shoots to curve up. When a clump of bulbs has been some years planted in the same place, and increased much, it will be well to break them up separate and plant again single bulbs ; otherwise it is as well to leave the roots undisturbed in the winter, merely marking the spot with a stick, that the ground be not dug.

There is another way in which many tender delicate Lilies may be grown to perfection ; erect a frame with lights sloping towards the north, fill in with eighteen inches of prepared soil, one-third meadow loam, one-third peat, and one-third leaf mould well mixed together, and sharpened by sand (sea sand if possible), into such a compost that at any time the hand may be plunged readily deep down and bring up a bulb for examination without breaking the tender roots. In this plant such bulbs as *Pulchellum, Tenuifolium, Brownii, Japonicum, Colchesterii, Krameri, Coridion, Thunbergianum, Kamskatchense, Leichtlinii,* &c. (for the last add more loam). As the stems grow, lift up the frames by means of bricks placed on each side of the plate, air will be then admitted, and the effects of frost neutralised. In May after all danger from frost is over the frames may be entirely removed ; the bulbs flower earlier and are better ripened for the next year, while the heavy cold autumnal rains that do so much damage to unripened bulbs may be averted by replacing the frames.*

It may interest our readers to hear that in 1872 we bloomed our first Lily, *Thunbergianum Marmoratum,* var., *Aureo-pictum,* out-of-doors in a warm corner, on May 24th ; on 26th, *Thunbergianum*

---

* *Calochorti, Cyclobothras, Freesias, Nemastylis, Erythronium, Tigridias, Sparaxis,* and other Cape bulbs will thrive exceedingly well in such company, and well repay the slight cost of erection.

Marmoratum opened; on 28th, *Monadelphum*; on 30th, *Bulbiferum*. Our earliest *Auratum* opened out-of-doors, June 17th: on a light soil this species blooms early: in August our *Auratum*, planted on heavy land, came into bloom, and continued till December. Taken up and potted before being injured by the frost, *Auratum* might easily be bloomed up to Christmas under glass. A bed of 500 *Longiflorum* came into bloom July 12th, and remained with us a mass of beauty, the admiration of all beholding it, till Sept. 4th, when but three or four blooms were left. These bulbs (in light soil) increased 500 per cent. July 15th, *Concolor* came out with its charming red star shaped flowers; it also remained for about six weeks in bloom, admired by every visitor: *Auratum*, *Tigrinum*, and the *Speciosum* group then came into flower and continued through the autumn to afford us 50 or 60 flowers a day for decoration. The largest *Auratum* we opened measured 13 inches from tip to tip of petals when expanded to the full, but the extreme diameter of the cup as naturally open, was only 8 inches, the depth of the cup measured 5 inches, the length of a single petal 6¾ inches, breadth 2½ inches.

A few remarks about the growth of Lilies and their reproduction may be acceptable.

Lily seed, if sown directly it is gathered in the autumn may appear the next spring, but generally it requires two seasons to germinate when sown out-of-doors. The following directions by Mr. Falconer may be useful.

"Good flowering bulbs can be obtained from home-saved seed in three or four years; but for seed-producing the plants are better grown in pots. Sometimes they set freely without assistance, but it is perhaps the surest way to assist them by fertilization. The plants grown in borders also produce seed pods, but, unless in the extreme south of England, and a few other favoured localities, they commonly fail to ripen the seed. The seeds may be sown in pots or pans of peaty soil in early spring, the pots being placed on back shelves of a greenhouse, pit, or cold frame, and near the glass. In these pots the seedlings may be allowed to remain the first year. Next spring pot them singly in large sixties or forty-eight sized pots, according to the strength of the bulbs; keep them in the greenhouse or frame during the spring, but they may be placed outside on pieces of slate or beds of ashes in summer. After being wintered like the older ones, some may require another shift, and some may remain in their last year's pots, with the assistance of a top-dressing. Their summer treatment may be like the last. The next season some of the plants may flower; but if strong bulbs are the object, pick off the flower buds, and increase instead the vigour and strength of the leaves. They should be wintered as usual, and planted out in the reserve grounds in beds or in nursery lines on a dry day in February.*

* Perhaps better in October.

In planting, care should be taken not to destroy or injure the thick fleshy roots attached to the base of the bulbs; for, although the bulbs undergo a resting period and comparative dryness in winter, these fleshy roots retain their vitality, and are the great assistance of strength in spring. Under and over the bulbs strew a little sharp sand, and, after covering them about three inches, mulch the beds with two inches of half-decayed manure. In these beds they should remain throughout the summer, and in October or February any bulbs required for other purposes may be lifted."

Lilies are also increased by means of bulblets produced about the base of the large bulbs, and also about the neck of the stems. These should be removed in potting, and treated in precisely the same manner as seedlings, only they will be one, and in some cases two years' growth in advance of seedlings. The scales of bulbs, if well formed and uninjured, taken off separately and inserted into a pan of sandy peat, also become the progenitors of young bulbs.

It is well known that chips or scales detached from the bulbs by accident or otherwise, will, if planted out in a warm corner, form little bulbs at their base or side. We met with a curious instance of this one season. We had unpacked about one hundred cases of *Auratum*, and accumulated about three cartloads of dried soil in which they had been packed ; this was spread over the surface and dug in, and Potatoes planted. In digging these, when ripe, we came upon innumerable tiny bulbs, most of which had been formed by chips, which being either small or covered with dirt, had escaped our notice. It has even been recommended to detach the scales at the base, and plant them for reproduction of bulbs. Again, when a bulb has been cut or has been diseased, and the scales damaged, or when it breaks up naturally, a number of bulblets form about the base and sides, especially where there is any wounded scale, as if formed by exudation. We have counted over a hundred bulbs taken from a single parent, but this bulb was in the act of breaking up.

By breaking up we mean this: when a bulb, either from damage in coming over, or disease, or injury of any kind, is unable to make its new annual growth (which is the flowering bulb of the next season), the old scales seem to separate and get wider apart—perhaps some die away from between the others, or portions die, and in the interstices the little bulbs are seen, in most cases attached to the wounded, cut, or damaged part of the scale. In this state the bulb, for flowering purposes, is worthless, and may be set apart either to form small bulbs, or possibly to make new growth the next season, and become again a flowering bulb ; old scales may be known by their dirty discoloured look, young growth by its light-coloured fresh appearance. Importation seems to paralyse the growth of bulbs, and imported bulbs are generally later in starting than home-grown bulbs by at least the duration of the journey. Similarly, when bulbs have

been stored away for a long time out of the ground they are delayed
in their growth.

There is, however, another way in which bulbs increase, and that
too very rapidly. A bulb will send up two or more stems, at the
close of the season it will be found that each stem has acquired a
separate bulb, and that two, three, or more bulbs have been formed
out of the original parent. We have counted five good flowering
bulbs obtained in this way, all enclosed in the circumference of the
old part; this is especially the case in the *Longiflorum* section, the
Thunbergianum section, *Concolor*, &c.; less with *Speciosum* and
Auratum. Besides this increase there are generally three or four
tiny bulbs to be found about the base of each stem, so that it frequently happens that from one parent two or three flowering bulbs
and three or four small ones may be taken in a season. In such a
case it will be necessary every other year at least to take up the bulbs,
divide and plant out singly; the little bulbs will bloom the third
season. If not divided out thus, the mass will speedily become so
thick that individual bulbs will be starved of nourishment by their
neighbours. Among the *Auratum* and *Speciosum* families, it is common to find three to six small bulbs at the base of the stem; these
may be carefully detached and planted apart. The *Tigers* and
Bulbiferum form bulblets in the axis of their leaves; these, when
ripe, should be detached and planted out, where they may remain
undisturbed. Some of the *Umbellatum* and *Thunbergianum* will also
form bulblets where the flowers have been cut off.

Making New Growth.—We have constantly observed, when taking
up bulbs in the autumn, two sets of scales, the outer irregular discoloured portion, which represents all that is left of last year's bulb,
and an inner regular plump white set of scales, representing the
growth of the previous, and the inflorescence of the coming season,
this yearly increment of growth occurs in healthy Lilies in the interior
of the bulb, the outer and old scales are pushed further apart by the
new growth, and the bulb increases in size, more or less, according
to the nature and health of the plant. In choosing bulbs, therefore,
in addition to preferring a hard, weighty bulb, choose also one that
has a light-coloured plump interior, showing good recent growth for
next season's flowering. We were particularly led to these observations by noting some bulbs of *L. Brownii*, which had grown well one
season but had not flowered, the bulbs were half as large again as
when planted, the interior was filled up with light-coloured new
scales, outside which were a few outer discoloured scales, evidently
the last year's growth; the contrast was so great between the two as
to attract an inquiry into the cause, and further observations on other
kinds led to the inferences above quoted. Therefore, when it is said
that it often takes Lilies a year to recover themselves after importation, it really means that the journey has destroyed or impaired their

flowering power for that year, and that they require another season to make new growth in the interior of the bulb, from whence a flowering stem will emerge the following season. With regard to the rosy tint observable on many bulbs, it simply represents the amount of oxygenation consequent on exposure to the air, something similar to the greening of Potatoes. A light pale-coloured bulb, taken up and exposed for a few days to the sun's rays, changes tint, in *L. Concolor* to a lilac, in *L. Excelsum* to a pale mauve, in *L. Speciosum* to a deep rosy red. Conversely, a deeply-tinted bulb, if planted several inches below the surface for a year or two, will pale its tints.

CHAPTER II.

LETTERS ON LILIES FROM
FOREIGN CORRESPONDENTS.

We append a few notes about Indian, Japanese, and North American Lilies, received from reliable correspondents, interspersed with valuable remarks thereon from experienced Lily cultivators, which we believe will be acceptable to our readers, as enabling them to realise and imitate better the conditions under which some Lilies grow in their native habitats.

"*L. Wallichianum* grows only in the deep dells. The wear and tear in a temperature of 120°, and in glens full of malaria, is by no means inviting. We must climb 1000 feet, and more sometimes, and drop down again into the valley on the other side, before we can expect to find anything. It is no joke after such a day's pull to return home without more road than a sheep track, and without a single root into the bargain. *L. Thomsonianum* is abundant, but difficult to rear, as it grows here only in very finely comminuted limestone gravel. It is a weed on the lower limestone hills, and flowers abundantly in March and April, growing in very finely comminuted or crushed limestone, with a thin layer of good black vegetable mould above to the depth of 2 to 3 inches, the roots being in the limestone gravel, and thoroughly drained. The season at that time is warm, and showers only fall occasionally. After seeding, the plant dries and disappears. I have never been able to rear them in any other soil. I am waiting for a cool, shady day, when I shall descend and have a hunt; but until heavy rains fall (May 16) no Lilies will be found. *L. Wallichianum* is still dormant, except one in very light rich soil, which we planted last year. *L. Giganteum* is not found so low as this (6000 feet above sea level), but occurs higher up, and more in the interior. It is difficult to keep the bulb from rotting unless the soil is both good and light. If the earth cakes round the bulb it is sure to rot; it likes the cold, and is found on slopes shaded by trees and brushwood."—*Mussooree, from an Indian Correspondent.*

"·I am not a little surprised to see the allusion made to the native habitat of *L. Wallichianum.*   As I infer from the collector's notes, it flourishes only in deep dells, and the temperature stated, viz., 120°, would certainly lead any one to doubt its hardiness.   On this matter I am in a position to give an opinion, as it has been planted out in these gardens for above 16 years, and flowers every year.   It has never had any protection beyond the fact that its bulb is covered with about 6 inches of light peaty soil.   Although cultivated for so long, it is very shy of increase, possibly six or seven represents the plants that I have been in a position to distribute from it, and once I very nearly lost it through an endeavour to divide what appeared to be a perfectly formed offset.   This, as well as the scarceness in its native locality, must render it, I fear, for many years to come as rare in cultivation as it is beautiful.   Permit me to add, that hints from collectors are most valuable, and I trust—and it is a feeling which all cultivators of Lilies will heartily endorse—that all similar communications will be published.   Take, for example, the value of the hints as to *L. Thomsonianum,* with the culture of which I have never been successful, never dreaming of a limestone gravel being the *sine quâ non.*" —*James C. Niven, Hull Botanic Gardens.*

L. Thomsonianum.—"Permit me to say, in answer to Mr. Niven's remark about *L. Thomsonianum,* that flowering bulbs of this species can be easily produced even without the *sine quâ non* of limestone gravel. The bulb of this plant is annually formed anew, the old one entirely decays.   This latter serves for some time as nourishment and support for the shoot, which soon makes its growth independently from the decaying bulb, and so much so that it nourishes even a quantity of small bulbs that are produced between the scales of the newly forming and those of the decaying bulb.   These small bulbs are sometimes produced in such large quantities that they cannot keep their first position, which is next the root-stalk, but are driven onward, remaining, however, in connection with the root-stock by a sort of navel string, and deriving, as it appears, their nourishment from, and to the detriment of, the newly forming bulb.   Now, it is only necessary to look to the bulbs about now, or even later in the season, to scratch off the soil round the bulb, and to cut off the old still fresh scales, as well as the above described young bulblets, taking great care not to hurt the root-stock and the leaves.   This done once or twice the bulb must be left to itself.   In May begin to withhold gradually the water, and the result will be that out of ten plants operated upon at least five good flowering bulbs will be at hand, which, when the leaves get withered, must be taken up and kept dry for two months."—*Max Leichtlin, Carlsruhe, Baden.*

"In regard to elevation much depends upon latitude and longitude, as plants which are found in the North-Western Himalayas where the climate at 5,000 and 6,000 feet of elevation is temperate, will extend their range upwards to 8,000 and 9,000 feet in the warmer Eastern tracts of Nepaul and Sikkim.   First, then, as regards *L. Roseum (Thomsonianum).*   The elevation of its locality about Mussooree runs from about 5,000 to 6,000 feet on the outer or Southern spurs running down towards the plains. The latitude about 26° N.   The temperature of these slopes in March and

April, which is the flowering season of this species, is frequently very warm, and the earth from the rocky nature of the soil retains considerable heat. At this season refreshing showers are usually frequent. The plants are always, as a rule, found growing upon the slopes, and I might say never in flat ground; the surface soil to a depth of from 2 to 3 inches is a rich vegetable mould, composed of decayed leaves and grasses, acting like a top dressing; beneath this is a bed of small broken fragments of lime-stone, through which the flower stalk descends to the bulb, which is found in what may be termed a fine limestone sand; this becomes, from the bulb upwards to the surface, coarser and coarser, the bulb lying at various depths, sometimes near the surface and sometimes 4 to 5 inches deep. From the slope of the hill side and the porous nature of the soil, the drainage is perfect, but the sand is by no means so dry as to be devoid of moisture. I perceive that Professor M. Leitchlin is inclined to cavil at my saying these bulbs do not thrive well in earth, although, at the same time, he proves me to be correct by showing that his bulbs so treated are annually exhausted by rotting away and leaving only a number of small bulblets in their place. Now I did not mean to assert that this bulb can never be reared in earth, because I have myself sometimes succeeded in doing so, but then the soil was carefully kept from too much moisture.

"I can but record what I see to be the mode of treatment to which nature resorts, and I do not seek to improve upon or teach her.

"The natural soil is a fine, highly porous, limestone gravel, becoming a limestone sand as it descends; it is often hundreds of feet deep and beneath it usually runs a belt of greenstone, by which, when the hills were upraised, the limestone was crushed into fragments of every size, and in some places, instead of the limestone, we encounter our out-crop of green-stone or a deep bed of finely comminuted Lydian stone.

"Nature then points out that the proper soil for this species is a porous limestone gravel, with a top dressing of fine rich vegetable mould; but if, disregarding her instructions, we plant the bulb in a rich earth and on a flat surface, the moisture being greater than the plant requires, the bulb rots away and expands its strength in flowers and bulblets.

"This year I planted several roots of full size in good earth, and nearly the whole rotted away leaving plenty of offspring, but the flowers were poor; others planted in poor stony soil and sheltered, gave good flowers and all remained sound. Now they are all in limestone sand and for the future will remain so. In this soil they remain exposed to the full force of the wet Monsoon from the beginning of June to the end of September, and although the rain sometimes descends for a week together, in a perfect deluge, such is the porous nature of the soil, that the Lilies smile and thrive uninjured. When once they are found to thrive in their own soil let them alone, for I hold that the system of digging them up every year to be both injurious and puerile; they will stand any amount of cold, and are sometimes covered for a month or more with two feet of snow.

"Whom does nature employ to dig them up at stated seasons? Left in their natural soil and, if possible, on a slope among long coarse grass and dwarf shrubs, the bulbs, far from rotting, will annually increase in size until full grown, throwing off numerous bulblets, while the flowers produce an abundance of seed."

c

L. Wallichianum.—"In saying that these beautiful plants are found in deep dells, I find it is necessary to define what I mean by the word; for all is here on so vast and majestic a scale, that what you tarry-at-home travellers with your mole-hills would call a dell, we should regard as a mere nut-shell.

"Our Himalayan dells are, in truth, wide open valleys of considerable depth; and I have stood in younger days at the edge of a granite rock looking down into a valley where the river Sutledge ran like a silver thread at a perpendicular depth below me of 4,000 feet; yet this I call a deep glen. In some parts of these valleys the slopes are thickly studded with goodly forest trees, with an undergrowth of shrubs and various plants; in other parts they are only clothed with tall rank grass higher than the tallest man; while again, the sides of the valley are generally ribbed, as it were, with narrow sharp-backed ridges, running down from summit to base, and widening as they descend; these are pent-shaped, and usually covered with short grasses; these ridges are unwooded, and lie open to the sun from its rise to its setting.

"It is on the sloping sides of these edges that *L. Wallichianum* is generally found in the full blaze of the sun, with a temperature exceeding 120° Fahr.; I found one bed of these Lilies by scanning the slopes on the opposite side of the valley, at least half a mile wide, through a telescope, the white flowers being distinctly visible.

"In this spot we found nearly two hundred Lilies of various sizes—a fact which refutes the statement of one of your correspondents, that they are scarce in their natural habitats. The elevation at which we find them in this neighbourhood is usually about 5,500 feet, on a southern slope; and they are never found in a rich soil, but in a coarse stony soil, often passing at a little depth into limestone gravel. Indeed, I have always found that when grown in their natural soil they always grow stronger and flower better than when reared in a rich soil. The latter always forces them to a considerable extent, and exhausts the bulb, which is expended in throwing up a long thin flower-stalk without any flowers.

"Last year (1872) I had fifty of these Lilies in full flower, some with one, others with two, and even four flowers; the stalks were thick and healthy, and stood fully 4½ feet high. This year (1873) I was induced to try a light rich soil, and the result is thin sickly flower-stalks of half their usual height, and not the merest shadow of a bud. A few that are growing in their natural coarse soil are 4 feet high, healthy, and with flower buds.

"In future I shall follow nature in preference to all other guides.

"This Lily is decidedly a hardy species, enduring not only a temperature of 120° or more, but likewise the long continued heavy monsoon, and the frosts and snows of winter. From too much moisture they are protected in their natural localities by the sloping and stony nature of their soil, for they are never found in flat or level places, and the bulbs lie at a depth of from 6 to 8 inches. They certainly ought not to be dug up every year, if they flourish in the soil in which planted; for if left alone they are in root all the winter through, and prepared to shoot upwards as soon as the summer warmth and showers set in. With us they usually spring in June, and flower towards the end of August.

"Coming upon a bed of these Lilies, one is at first inclined to suppose they have been scattered abroad as seed, and yet I have never procured a single seed-pod either from wild or cultivated plants; they form at first, but never come to anything. The real mode of propagation is from the roots, one or two long roots being thrown out, from which at intervals small bulbs are formed, and after a time become independent plants. Suckers or offshoots are sometimes formed by the bulb, but it is rather a sign of weakness than of strength, and the original bulb suffers. Too much moisture is apt to produce offsets."

L. Polyphyllum.—"This I have only found in one locality as yet, and from that they have now been extirpated. The elevation was 6,500 feet, the locality a narrow shallow ravine covered over with trees and shrubs, so that the plants were well sheltered, and only got the forenoon sun; they were as usual growing on the sloping sides of the ravine, in good vegetable mould at the surface, but stony ground beneath. I see your Botanical works pronounce the flower to be *white*, which is incorrect; it is of a creamy or waxy white, the inside spotted with dull purplish dots, the ends of the petals reflexed, and the flower drooping. Height from 3 to 3½ feet. It is long since I saw the flower, but an old note-book tells me. 'Flower sweet-scented, waxy-white, irrorated inside with specks of purplish brown; flowers early in June, and affects shady moist shrubberies.' It does not appear to be a very hardy plant, and when in exposed situations without shelter it soon disappears. It thrives in damp shady shrubberies, with the sun on the locality until about 3 P.M."

"*L. Nepalense* is said to be found in Gurwhal, but I have not yet succeeded in procuring it."

L. Nanum.—"The flowers of a small low growing Lily were brought to me about two years ago from a spot not more than a mile from my house, but we have since searched in vain for the bulb. It was growing among fragments of rocks on the side of a cliff. Plants of this sort are often lost by the prevailing system of burning off the old grass to insure a fresh bite for cattle. I have referred the plant provisionally to *L. Nanum* until we can find it again."

"*L. Giganteum* is found farther in the interior, but not at any great elevation. I first procured it in 1837, four marches beyond Simla. It was in a deep sheltered valley, or rather glen, well clothed with trees and brushwood, where the sun could have exercised but little influence; the soil was a rich vegetable mould, but the slope was still great, and drainage perfect. It does not thrive on the outer Southern ranges, perhaps from too much warmth and too little attention to shelter; but whatever the cause, they are very liable to rot. It bears abundance of seed in favourable situations. I have seen them 5½ feet in height."

L. Macrophyllum.—"This is a beautiful species from Cashmere, and has a delicious odour. The flowers are in bunches of four or five, and pure white; altogether it resembles *L. Candidum* a good deal. Whether it grows in forest tracts, or in open, I know not, but there is certainly something wrong in its treatment, for it speedily disappears. I am now treating it like *L. Roseum*, and it looks bright and healthy."

"I agree with you, that Lilies which remain for a season without springing materially increase the size and strength of the bulb. But I object to the system of removing bulbs from the ground every autumn ; the process may answer as a part of the forcing system, but is quite unnatural, and weakens the plant by breaking off its nourishment. I object to all forcing, because it is a patent way of destroying the bulbs, which are compelled to over-exert themselves in the production of a good head of flowers, for all that appears above the surface is taken out of the bulb ; the rich soil does not compensate the bulb, it merely prompts it to make new efforts until it is exhausted. Cultivators should recollect that they cannot eat their apple and have it too ; and yet they force a bulb to expand itself in flowers, and at the same time expect it to grow strong and healthy, and increase in size. Your potting system I also abhor, for it is calculated to do much injury unless the pots are thoroughly protected from too much heat and too much cold ; for the pots being, I presume, *porous*, the roots extending to the sides will either be hardened and dried by the sun, or nipped by the frost; glazed pots are highly injurious, as stopping a circulation of air."—*Mussooree.*

From our Indian Correspondent at Landour :—

" *L. Polyphyllum* does not give us any trouble to flower up here, 7,000 feet above the sea level ; but *L. Wallichianum* often fails, being brought up to this altitude from the hottest valleys of these hills, and the low temperature up here does not suit it.

" I am afraid your *Polyphyllum* had too much of the hothouse treatment, which I should say they did not want at all in England ; they require to be planted deep, from 8 to 12 inches, in rather a rich soil and cold aspect, slightly shaded.

" The groundwork of its petals is greyish white, thickly covered or dusted over with small lilac spots ; it is powerfully sweet-scented, bearing from 1 to 20 flowers ; height of flower stem up to 7 feet.

" It is brought from the interior of India. They are found between 7,000 and 9,000 feet above the sea level, chiefly on the north face of the mountains, preferring the cold and shady nooks."

L. Neilgherrense.—" Three noble blooms are now (Sept. 9th, 1876) in full splendour at Heather Bank, and would form, as a group, a grand subject for an accomplished flower painter. The full and rich buff tone of the young flowers contrasts delicately and pleasingly with the light cream colour of the more mature blossoms, and the three blooms of the different ages now expanded, exhibit three distinct tones of colour. The flowers are larger and the tubes longer than in *L. Longiflorum*, from which this Lily is also distinguished by the glowing yellow of the interior of the cup, shading into rich creamy buff towards the ends of the petals ; it appears also to be of a more robust habit."—*Garden, vol.* 10, *p.* 254.

L. Neilgherrense.—" In 1876, a specimen, grown by G. F. Wilson, was awarded a First Class Certificate at South Kensington ; the flowers were trumpet-shaped, fully 9 inches in length, the gracefully shaped reflexed segments being of great substance and of a soft creamy yellow tint ; its height varies from 2 to 4 feet, its blossoms are delicately perfumed, and it undoubtedly deserves culture as one of the most noble of all the autumn-flowering Lilies."—*Garden, vol.* 10, *p.* 490.

L. Wallichianum.—" The bulb, a small one, was placed in a deep narrow pot used for Gladioli, the soil consisting of sandy turf, broken up, and mixed with a little coarse leaf-mould and bits of broken stone. It started into growth late in June, and when the foliage began to expand, was syringed overhead every day ; it bloomed in a common orchard house. I suppose the treatment suited it, as the bulb has increased considerably in size, and thrown up two strong stems this year."—*Rev. A. Rawson, Garden, vol.* 10, *p.* 480.

From Yokohama, Japan, Mr. Kramer writes to us in 1869 :—

" All Lilies, except *Auratum,* are cultivated in the gardens here, and must necessarily be dearer than a Lily found in the woods. *Auratum* is found in all the woods about this neighbourhood, but owing to large quantities having been shipped from here for several years, large bulbs are only to be found in more distant places, which makes the carriage more expensive, and in wet weather they are liable to rot if kept packed for four or five days. I have never known *Auratum* to rot in a garden here, nor have the native gardeners ; they leave them in the ground all the year round, and give them a top-dressing of nightsoil during the winter. Their treatment of other bulbs more valuable to them shows that they have suffered from disease. Their practice is as follows :—In autumn, soon after the stalk has withered, the bulb is taken out of the ground or pot, and all the old roots are removed. It is then exposed to the air about 10 to 15 days, but not in the sun, and replanted sideways, in order that the water may not lodge between the scales, which might be the case if the bulb were planted upright.

" The ground in which they grow the Lilies is generally black, 4 or 5 feet deep, very light and siliceous. I must, however, remark that I have never seen such fine Lilies here, as I have at home, and the native gardeners shake their heads in doubt, when I tell them that *Auratum* has had more than 100 flowers from one bulb.

" *Rubro-vittatum* is scarcely to be had, and I believe, at the present time, there are more in Europe than here. They have been exported by every one that fancied flowers, and especially by the Italian silkworm egg merchants, '*graineurs.*' They have also been sent to New York. *Virginale* is almost as scarce a variety of *Auratum* as *Rubro-vittatum.*"

In 1871 he writes :—

"The rain of last summer destroyed many bulbs, and the price has risen in consequence. *L. Auratum,* large bulbs, are getting very scarce here, and transporting them from a distance spoils about 25 per cent. of them. Lilies form no speciality here. In order to obtain them I have to go through more than 300 gardens, picking up six here, ten in another place, and rarely meeting with fifty bulbs of the same kind."

LILIUM AURATUM AT HOME.

" *L. Auratum* is found in great abundance on the steep partially-wooded hill sides that form the flanks of the well-known volcanic mountain, Fusi-Yama (Japan), and in smaller quantities throughout the district generally. The soil that covers, to a varying depth, the crumbling igneous rocks, consists of decomposed leaf soil, mixed largely with the detritus of this volcanic rock, that sparkles with particles of mica, and is excessively porous and friable.

"This Lily, then, grows on hill sides, where there is perfect drainage, in a soil free from lime, in a climate that is both hotter and wetter than our own in summer, and is in winter dry and bright, with occasional sharp frosts of a few days duration.

"Another point to be noticed is that this Lily abounds at the edges of woods, where the dwarf Bamboo, that in Japan takes the place of grass, effectually shields the stem and roots from the sun's rays, while the upper part of the stem with the broadest leaves rejoices in the sunshine. Sunstroke at the base of the stem is a fertile source of disappointment, and for this reason Lilies planted among Rhododendrons succeed well in warm localities in this country."—*E. H. W.*, *Garden*, *vol.* 14, *p.* 560.

Now leaving India and Japan, we will proceed *viâ* San Francisco, to the Western Straits of N. America.

CHAPTER III.

ON

CALIFORNIAN LILIES.

BY DR. BOLANDER. SAN FRANCISCO.

The Genus Lilium is represented in the State of California by the following distinct species, of which there are several well marked varieties :—1. *L. Washingtonianum* (Kellogg). 2. *L. Humboldtii* (Roezl), *L. Bloomerianum* (Kellogg). 3. *L. Canadense*[*](Linn.), var. *L. Parviflorum* (Hook.), var. *L. Pardalinum* (Kellogg), var. *L. Californicum* (Hort.). 4. *L. Parvum* (Kellogg).

Bulbs ovoid,[†] *outer scales largest, fleshy, imbricated, lanceolate.*

1. *L. Washingtonianum* (Kellogg).—" This occurs on the Cuyumaca Mountain in San Diego Co., its most southern limit, known at present ; northward along the western slope of the Sierra Nevada, between 3,500 and 6,000 feet altitude ; in Oregon to the Columbia River ; and on the coast ranges north of San Francisco, especially in the eastern parts of Mendocino and Humboldt Co. In all localities named, it occurs either on ridges, or on lightly shaded slopes of ridges, having a porous loose soil, resting on a gravelly sub-soil. At no time have I met with a plant of this species in a soil, the drainage of which was not perfect, and when found on a slope, did not face towards some point between east and south.

* The true *L. Canadense* (Linn.) is an Eastern, not a Western form.
† The Bulb of the true *L. Washingtonianum*, scarcely answers to this description ; its central axis is often horizontal and rhizomatous, but also sometimes vertical, and then the bulb assumes an ovoid form.

The pale loosely scaled ovoid bulb is generally found at a depth of from 12 to 20 inches. The height of the stem, the number of whorls and of flowers on a single stem, vary very much according to the soil, exposition, and age of the bulb. Much has been said about the difficulty of cultivating this beautiful species. I willingly confess that I have also met with many reverses, until I paid proper attention to its habits and habitats. If the bulb is planted at a depth of from 8 to 12 inches in a loose somewhat gravelly soil, having perfect drainage, there is no difficulty in obtaining satisfactory results. Although there is positively no specific difference between bulbs and plants collected either on the Sierras or on the coast ranges, yet I found that bulbs from the coast ranges would always bloom more readily in San Francisco (in cool-houses) than those from the Sierras. The reason is obvious, but it would be interesting to know if the same holds good at other places than San Francisco. The flowers are very fragrant, and change gradually from a pure white to various shades of purple or lilac, the purplish red spots are rather minute.[*] The figure in Mons. Louis Van Houtte's Flore (Vol. XIX.) is a very correct representation of this species."

2. *L. Humboldtii* (Roezl), *L. Bloomerianum* (Kellogg).

"This large species has apparently a far less wider range than the preceding. It occurs mainly on the more elevated portion of the foot hills of the Sierras, from 2,500 to nearly 3,500 feet altitude, evidently requiring a greater amount of heat to develope its full size and beauty than the first named species. The soils in which its bulbs are found are of a rather compact character, consisting of clay with an admixture of broken rocks, and a small portion of vegetable mould growing in open park land, or land entirely cleared off, and therefore exposed to a hot and burning sun, and surrounded by a dry and exsiccating air; we find its bulb also at a considerable depth. Its ovoid bulbs are very large and strongly built, its outer scales are the largest, imbricated, lanceolate, tinged with purple, and very fleshy, well calculated to hold a large supply of moisture. A short time ago, this species was also found by Mr. Harford on the Island of Santa Rosa,[†] opposite Santa Barbara. As far as I know it has not been found on any part of the coast ranges belonging to the mainland. The plant found on Santa Rosa Island, differs but slightly from that on the foot hills of the Sierras. Its leaves are of a brighter green, accuminate, and its whorls are dense and more regular; while the leaves of plants from the Sierras are rather spathulate, and terminating with a blunt point; their green is also of a less vivid colour. The former is exposed to sea breezes and fogs; the latter to a dry exsiccating air. It may be stated in connection with the above remarks, that bulbs from Santa Rosa Island do far better with us here, than those from the Sierras; the reason is plain. The figure in the Flore of Mons. Louis Van Houtte (Vol. XIX.) represents the Santa Rosa Island form as truthfully as a representation can be made. In the notes on Lilies and their culture by Dr. Wallace (1st portion), I find this species wrongly enumerated as one of the

[*] This is the description of *Washingtonianum Purpureum*, which has a coast range, not of the true *Washingtonianum* which comes from the Yosemite Valley.

[†] This form is the one known as *Bloomerianum Ocellatum*.

Canadense Lilies. Its root is ovoid, not rhizomatous; nor does it ascend as high as Devil's Gate. What Roezl found there was one of the Canadense* varieties, and not *L. Humboldtii.*

Bulbs, Rhizomatous, with short fleshy scales.

3. *L. Canadense* (Linn.)—(a), var. *L. Parviflorum* (Hook.); (b), var. *L. Pardalinum* (Kellogg), var. *L. Puberulum* (Torr.); (c), var. *L. Californicum* (Hort.), var. *L. Walkeri* (Wood), var. *L. Hartwegii* (Baker). The above enumerated varieties of this species demonstrate the influence of the soil, location, and climate, more forcibly than any other species of our Lilies, because it is more generally distributed, and has a wider range throughout the entire state. It is therefore not to be wondered at, that so many excellent botanists describe different forms of this variable species under so many different names.

(a). The form of *L. Canadense* var. *Parviflorum* (Hook.), occurring largely in boggy soil, west of the great Redwood belt, and on the immediate coast, presents, even there, differences in size and form, well calculated to lead astray. There, wherever exposed to the daily continuous westerly winds, it attains hardly 2 feet in height, bearing often but a single small flower, of a deep red colour, with the sepals but slightly recurved towards the tip, but, wherever sheltered, either by trees or shrubbery, it attains a height of from 3 to 5 feet, bearing numerous flowers of a less reddish tint, and arranging its leaves, at least a part of them, in whorls, while those of the exposed plant are all scattered, and few in number. This form extends along the immediate coast from Vancouver's Island to Oregon and California. This long linear extension and range is common to many plants of the immediate western coast.

(b). Proceeding, however, eastward along a stream into the interior, to a point where the coast climate changes gradually into that of the inland coast valleys, and where an abundance of sunshine and shelter is added to that of moisture, we find the beautiful and charming form described by Dr. Kellogg under the name of *L. Pardalinum.* Here in deep recesses, on the banks of streams, in such favourable localities the plant attains a height of from 6 to 9 feet, here its rhizomatous bulb ramifies and multiplies rapidly, forming clusters several feet in diameter; stems shoot up side by side from every terminating point of the ramifying and radiating bulb, giving the plant a gregarious appearance. Perhaps, nowhere, in this state, is this gregarious character so well and plainly exhibited, as in the Bear Valley on the Sierras, at an altitude of 4,000 feet, where acres of a wet meadow are densely covered by this magnificent variety. The whorls are here usually broken up, and the large leaves are indefinitely scattered all over the huge stems, which are variously branched, bearing numerous flowers, with strongly curved perianths of a bright yellowish red colour, copiously spotted with purple spots on the face. But if we proceed from the inland coast valleys farther eastward,

---

* Probably *L. Puberulum*, as we received from him a number of fine bulbs of this kind along with those of *Humboldtii* and *Washingtonianum.*

and enter the large valleys of the interior, where the climate is hot and the air dry, we soon lose sight of this plant, even on the banks of streams. Crossing these, and ascending the foot hills of the Sierras, to an altitude of from 2,500 to 4,000 feet, we meet it again in all its glory in wet localities, growing in wet boggy soil, mostly subject to overflowing at some time during the year, its bulbs are imbedded but a few inches beneath the surface of the soil. At San Francisco it blooms readily in cool-houses.

(c). The next marked form, L. *Californicum* (Hort.), L. *Walkerii* (Wood), L. *Hartwegii* (Baker), L. *Puberulum* (Torr.), differs very strikingly from the preceding variety, in the form and arrangement of its leaves, and in habitat. The leaves are usually arranged in dense and numerous whorls, only the uppermost are scattered, linear lanceolate, acuminate, and of a dull green colour, while those of the preceding form are mostly spathulate or oblanceolate, and of a bright green colour. This form we find on moist slopes of the lower foot-hills of the Sierras, as as well as those of the coast ranges where the climate approaches, more or less in character, that of the interior valleys. In these thus characterised localities, the plant is neither copiously supplied with moisture by heavy dews, or dense fogs, nor by an abundance from below.

4. L. *Parvum* (Kellogg).—"The specific name of this species refers solely to the small size of the flower, for in every other respect, this plant attains as large a size as any of our Lilies, if not larger. It begins at an elevation in the Sierras, where to my knowledge L. *Pardalinum* ceases to grow, namely at an altitude of 4,000 feet, and extends upwards to 8,000. It is found growing exclusively on the banks of mountain streams, or in shady swampy places, through which a constant stream of cold water runs. The leaves are mostly scattered over the entire stem, spathulate or oblanceolate, and somewhat glaucous. The ramifications of the branches, and the number of flowers, depend upon the size to which the plant developes. The perianth is of an orange yellow, spotted with purple, and but slightly recurved at the tip. Its cultivation seems to offer more difficulties than any other of our species. Botanists either collecting or studying Californian plants, cannot bestow too much care upon their habitats, and can never possess of one and the same species, too large a quantity of specimens collected at different localities. In a country like this, where there are in fact but two seasons, the wet and dry, passing abruptly from one into the other, the proximity to, or the distance from, the foggy coast, the general physical and mechanical properties of the different soils, the elevation (whether west and north or east and south), and the distance from the rainless belt bordering this State in the south, or from the rainy belt approaching it in the north, must be carefully taken into consideration. Omitting for the present any remarks on those parts of California situated south of latitude 35°, and those north of latitude 40°, there are distinguishable in middle California the following ten well marked botanical regions or belts from west to east :—1. *The immediate sea coast belt.* 2. *The Redwood belt.* 3. *The hilly or mountainous park and chapparal belt.* 4. *The Sacramento and San Joaquin valleys.* 5. *The lower-foot hills of the Sierra Nevada to 2,000 feet altitude.* 6. *The middle*

Sierra belt, between 2,000 *to* 4,000 *feet.*   7. *The higher Sierra belt.*   8. *The Alpine region.*   9. *The Eastern slope, and* 10 *the Eastern basin.*"—*Garden,* vol. 5, *p.* 1, 1874.

Let us, in the first place, says Dr. Kellogg, "consider the Lilies, how they grow." In a climate like that of California, distinguished by a wet and long dry season, we find these bulbs located say about 6 to 10 inches deep, and the fibres or roots shooting downwards 10 inches to a foot below that point, in search of food and moisture. Is it not evident, then, that such bulbs require a flower-pot at least 18 inches deep? Hence, ordinary pots must be utterly useless, or worse—cramping or inadequate to meet even primary natural conditions. Let anyone take an improvised 5-gallon tin can, or the like, which is good enough, not to say the best; paint it rudely inside and out to preserve it; punch, say at least, three large holes in the bottom of it; plant, as in nature, in any good compost, and set your can, keg, or crock, as the case may be, in a shallow pan of water. You will soon have the pleasure of seeing a stout stem, of the thickness of your thumb, rising up and flowering gorgeously. If a plant spends its vital force in vain, searching for food or moisture, little or nothing else can be accomplished. *Abronia Arenaria*, as the specific name indicates, grows in sand. If found on deep sand-drifts of the bay shore of San Francisco, or inland, it shoots down a stout fusiform root of indefinite length, but often poor and puny is the top that creeps not far from the crown, with perhaps few flowers and a little fruit. But mulch a moist, brackish, cracky soil, with only 6 or 8 inches of sand, and it will go down to, or a little into it, spread abroad its forked subdivisions and fibres, almost or quite horizontally; the crown-sprouts now run riotously, mantling the sand with vines, full of pink flowers in fruitful umbels unnumbered. Cultivators are apt to complain that many of their bulbs, ere they bloom, lose one essential beauty of plants, viz., their radicle leaves, which, they say, "dry up, and leave the stems looking naked and bare." Bulbs are frequently found upon exposed hills and slopes, rocks, &c., descending down dry and very hot valleys into débris and alluvial bottoms, where sand or loam with underground moisture abounds. *The very same plants are seen to rejoice best where they find some shade and shelter,* otherwise they bespeak a struggle for existence, *i.e.*, their leaves prematurely or naturally dry up early to save exhaustion. In half shade, along high banks and slopes, contiguous to creeks, with adequate subsoil moisture, we see *Cyclobothra Alba*, with long and beautiful glaucous leaves, say an inch and a half wide, 18 inches to 2 feet in length, accompanying the flowers, ten to twenty in number; the golden *C. Pulchella* and most others tolerate more sun and drought, with their companions the *Manzanita* (*Arctostaphylos Glauca*) Oaks, &c., near whose shades it is wont to linger; but its best forms love rich, rocky, half shady drains, leaf and flower being companions to the close. Witness *Seubertia Laxa*, 2 to 4 feet high, and the *Dichelostemas* and *Brodiæas*, with from ten to fifty flowers, and green leaves with similar grace, completeness, and beauty. The list might be extended; but what we desire to say and impress on our readers is, that the same plants exposed are barely one-quarter as large as these, and have no green leaves at all, or at best a poor apology for them; and so of numberless others.

What lesson do such facts teach? Surely that the cultivator should imitate nature in her best aspects, and it is by no means difficult to exceed even her highest standard. Bulbous plants form no exception. It would, indeed, be folly to fold one's hands at the very first failure; for with what delight do we behold one joyously filling up the full measure of its glory! In the loose soils in which we usually place our bulbs are they as well situated as in their native matrix? The soil then must needs be packed firmly* and uniformly. It is the life-struggles with difficulties that bring out the best qualities of the man—the fruits and flowers, roots and bulbs—born of the great mother. Resistance above reacts below, gives spread, depth, and vigour in the direction of least resistance. The root—the strong foundation—is of the first consideration in all structural building, and should be well laid, cherished, and preserved. We do not say it should be founded upon some suitable rock, but we sometimes think so; radiated heat and graduated temperature, sweetness of drainage, and (it would seem reasonable) that in due time some resistance from below, also, are all requisites of high culture. May not the cultivator, in his undue solicitude, be also to blame, and by some shortcoming fail, or from excess undo by overdoing? Suppose he flood too continuously between loose scales, adding excessive heat withal, ought he not to expect just the result urged? Now, we seldom see in nature bulbs which are sheltered by shrubs, rocks, logs, bark, leaves, &c., or those in very compact soils, rotten at the tips of the scales, and hence a lure to maggots and grubs; nor often in such sandy and gravelly soils as readily absorb, drain, and disperse any excess of top moisture. We appeal to the observations of careful collectors. Let us, then, copy the best conditions, and we feel assured the result will confirm our rather hasty hints.

"In conclusion, we dare not presume that even a tithe of what we ought to say has been noted, in short, we have confined ourselves only to what may be considered peculiar to climatic conditions. Erudite and complex recipes relative to proper mixtures of soils, and common management may well be left to the knowledge and judgment of those who believe in them. With such a wealth of sunlight and heat above as falls to the lot of California, *and no lack of the necessary medium moisture below*, I see no reason why we may not allow nature, under human hands, to grow her magnificent white *Lady Washington* Lily 6 or 7 feet high, with ten to thirty or more flowers, just as we see it wild. *L. Humboldtii*, too, is a perfect giant among Lilies, when at its best making a right super-royal display. Even our little orange *L. Parvum*† I found at the Sierra summit over 5 feet high, and bearing fifty flowers, carefully counted, but the plant was sheltered and shaded by an old emigrant water tank stilted up, now dry, and long ago abandoned, but its roots found a fair supply of water from beneath."—*The Garden, Jan.* 4, 1873.

---

* We are not advocates for packing soil closely round a bulb, we believe that this is very prejudicial.

† We have seen this most graceful Lily both at Kew and in our own garden with stems 5 ft. high.

"I have bloomed all the known American Lilies this season except *L. Catesbæi*, and give you briefly the result.

"Of Eastern Lilies *Superbum* and *Canadense* have many varieties very similar, and growing out of difference in soil, climate, &c. *Carolinianum* (*Michauxii*) is a variety of *Superbum*, rare, and quite distinct from the specific form.

"*Philadelphicum* varies in colour in different localities, and has but one noted variety, *Wansharaicum*, which differs from the specific form in larger size and brighter colours, probably owing to richer soil. *Catesbæi*, found in the sandy lands of S. Carolina and Georgia, is a very distinct Lily, dies down in August, and should be transplanted immediately, as it has a growth in the fall like *L. Candidum*.

"Of the Western Coast species but four are yet known, although a great many varieties are announced by European florists.

"*Humboldtii* and *Bloomerianum Ocellatum* vary but little in bloom, but the first has very large and the latter small bulbs.

"*Roezlii** is a synonym of the last.

"*Washingtonianum* and *W. Purpureum* (Eel River sp.) vary somewhat in colour, depending on differences in soil and climate.

"*Pardalinum Puberulum* and *Californicum* are the same species sent out under different names. *Columbianum†* and *Parvum* are very similar, the first from Oregon and the latter from California.

"The best botanists on the Pacific Coast acknowledge no other Lilies than those mentioned. A great many of my western Lilies, although planted a year since, have not yet made their appearance; on examination this fall the bulbs are all right."—*J. C. Atkinson, Kentucky, U. S., Nov.* 19, 1877.

"Two or three years more will be required before the Californian Lilies can be well cleared up; if then, the work shall have been done by a bold hand, we may see them all brought under the three species : *Humboldtii, Washingtonianum,* and *Pardalinum. Columbianum* certainly, as I have flowered it, is a dwarf *Humboltii* from the northern part of the Pacific coast. I am told that all these three species, as we go north, from their southern limit towards Columbia, or from the vicinity of the coast towards the Alpine regions of the Sierras, grow less in stature and assume other variations more or less striking. I much doubt whether the new *L. Van. Houttii* is anything more than *Washingtonianum*, with a deep coloured and long tubed flower. The variety of *L. Superbum* which grows in the swamps near the coast of Georgia and Florida, called *L. Carolinianum* or *L. Michauxii*, is chiefly distinguished from the type by broader (even oval) leaves which are fewer and more scattered, and (in the plants which I grow) by darker, almost mahogany coloured flowers. It is as distinct from the typical *Superbum* as that is from *Canadense*, but these two species doubtless run together, and run into *Pardalinum*, their western form.

* The *Roezlii*, described by Baker in his Synopsis has a rhizomatous bulb, and is more nearly allied to *Canadense* than to the *Humboldtii* form, all whose bulbs are ovoid and globose.

† The bulb of *L. Columbianum* is globose, a small *Humboldtii;* that of *L. Parvum* is rhizomatous.

"For *Hansoni*, Mr. Baker's description in monograph will answer with these alterations: Bulb pyriform, and, I am sure, annual; leaves of *L. Martagon*, usually three 10—15 leaved verticils, with a few scattering ones chiefly above them 8—18 lines wide, colour scarcely as dark as orange. The description of *Avenaceum* is badly mixed up. This is my plant—Bulbus parvus, ovoideus perennis, squamis pluribus lineariis, medio constrictis. Caulis glaber teres 1½—2 pedalis, foliis sœpissime 3—6 in verticillum unicum ad medium caulis aggregatis, reliquis sparsis, lanceolatis 2—3 poll longis glabris 5—7 nervatis. Flores 1—3 bracteis ovato-lanceolatis, pedicellis apici cernuis 1½—2 poll longis, Perianthium leviter odorum, segmentis splendide coccinnis, concoloribus, oblanceolatis 15—18 lin longis, 3—4 lin latis valde revolutis, filamenta 9—12 lin longa, anthuris 3—4 lin longis. Ovarium 4—5 lin longum, stylo declinato 12 lin longo. *L. Canadense* grows in low meadows near brooklets, the bulbs two or three inches under the soil in low banks safe above the overflow of winter and spring. *L. Superbum* chooses similar situations in the States further south. *L. Philadelphicum* only grows in dry soil, as in rocky hills or sandy plains in the partial shade of species of Pinus and Quercus. *L. Catesbœi* is found in low pine barrens, in the States, south of Virginia. *L. Washingtonianum*, my correspondent tells me, grows six inches deep in well drained soil high up on the north side of the mountains of California. *L. Humboldtii* chooses the vicinity of streams in mountain meadows, growing among shrubs and grass, and *L. Pardalinum* in similar situations. I succeed well with all these in my garden by giving some a dry situation, others a cool or slightly moist one. In America we have lost so many of our important bulbs of *Auratum* the first or second year, from their shedding their leaves and decaying throughout in midsummer, that the practise has prevailed of planting in dry soil, as though it was wet that rots the bulb. *Auratum* will endure better in dry soil than will *Speciosum*. As I have read of the surprising growth of the former species in peaty and moist soils reported in English horticultural journals, I have thought a good deal on this matter, and have proposed giving some *Auratum* this treatment. I have a bed of them in strong clay loam, rather heavy and moist, such soil as I give to *Speciosum*, and they thrive as well as those anywhere else. I have been convinced that the loss of *Auratums* should rather be attributed to the extreme heat of our climate than to wet; in a heated soil the decay among the scales which must perish each year, seems to be communicated to those scales which should remain sound, and to the whole plant. So I have come to cover all my Lily beds with a large layer of leaves from the woods; I put this on in the fall to exclude the severe frosts of our winter (the soil is usually frozen to the depth of two or three feet), and assisting the young shoots to come through it. I let it remain through the summer to keep the soil in a cool and humid state; of course with this treatment I join the most thorough drainage. I have been wont to shade partially by means of lath screens above or on the south side of the plants, and I still think this advisable for rare and choice species, because the intense heat of the sun in this country is very trying to the foliage of Lilies, but in ordinary cultivation the shading of the soil will suffice very well. It is to this shading of the soil that I attribute chiefly my success in growing every genus of Lilies, which, in this country, is thought to be quite remarkable. I lose few important bulbs, and from my beds no larger proportion drop out, than do in dry summers of *Canadense* in its native haunts.

"It is too soon to speak of the results of my hybridisation among Lilies. This one fact I will communicate however, for several years I have bloomed seedlings of *Canadense*, produced only, I am sure, by pollen of various other species, but always unaltered from the type. Such has been the experience of Mr. Parkman, and Mr. Hanson has given up this species as incorrigible."—(*From an old and valued Correspondent in North America*).

LILIUM SUPERBUM AT HOME.

"The most gorgeous of all our meadow flowers is the Turk's-cap Lily (*L. Superbum*). It generally grows in wet places, often in or near a ditch, and attains a great height, I have seen it in a neighbour's garden on dry ground scarcely less luxuriant—5 feet high, with a great number of gorgeous reflexed flowers on every plant. The blossoms continue a long time in the garden, but in the meadows usually meet an untimely end at the hands of the mower, who seldom cares enough for botany or beauty to preserve or transplant them." *Albany Cultivator, Garden, vol. 8, p. 55.*

LILIUM SUPERBUM IN OHIO.

"In moist localities, through the woods here just now, this fine Lily is in perfection, its flower spikes rising up to a height of 6 feet or more, producing 12 or 15 flowers on a single spike. The buds, before they open, are very pretty, being bright orange scarlet, the inside spotted with dark purple. Lifted in autumn, and planted in a well enriched flower bed, they do remarkably well, and form a very attractive addition to the flower garden. A bed in the flower garden here, just now planted with it, is the prettiest one we have." *M. Milton, Cleveland, Ohio, in Country Gentleman.*

"For more than thirty years I have grown all the principal sorts of Lilies that could be obtained in European collections, and without mentioning the regular autumn trade sorts, have had all that were really hardy in our climate; but my real pets have been the Japan sorts of the *Speciosum* type, introduced by Dr. Siebold. These have been erroneously known under the name of *Lancifolium*, and its different varieties, as *Rubrum*, *Album*, *Roseum*, and *Punctatum*. The first was crimson spotted, the second fine white, the third rose spotted, and the last blush or pink spotted. I have ever been curious to know in what manner the *Punctatum* originated, as it has a habit which none of the others have. It always comes up in the bed several days before the others, keeps ahead, and flowers fully a fortnight sooner than they do. So much in advance, indeed, is it, that I have had

·the shoots badly nipped by late frosts, when the others, just coming out of the ground, were not in the least injured. My first object was to hybridise; but, as I had then only the *Album* (*Punctatum* having done blooming), *Speciosum* was fertilised with *Album*, and *vice versa*. The result was that every individual blossom produced a pod of fine plump seed, and in three or four years we had many thousand seedling bulbs, fully grown and in bloom. Seeing how readily fertilisation was effected, I thought I would try still farther to ensure hardiness, and next season I planted bulbs of *Tigrinum*, *Canadense*, *Superbum*, *Longiflorum*, and *Candidum*, so as to have them in bloom at the same period as *Speciosum*. All succeeded, and I had no fewer than twelve packets of seed, the result of fertilisation, from which I raised the finest of all the Lilies of the type yet produced, including the variety known as *Melpomene*, each petal of which is completely covered ·with blood-red, excepting a clear white border on every petal, and the papillæ, which are of a black-crimson. In some of the hybrids the form was completely ruined, such as *Candidum* and *Longiflorum*; but the old *Speciosum Album*, fertilised with *Tigrinum*, yielded very beautiful deep-coloured flowers. For upwards of fifteen years I continued to grow these ·Lilies from seed, and produced many fine kinds; but none to excel *Melpomene*.

"From 1850 to 1865 I cultivated four beds of Japan Lilies, numbering ·several thousand bulbs; an awning was erected over the beds, and from August 20th to October 1st they were in fine perfection. *L. Brownii* (Van Hontte) is another grand Lily. Is it different from *L. Japonicum*? *L. Longiflorum* is a fine Lily, but it is not so hardy as *Candidum* or *Speciosum*. A bed of it, 50 feet long, loaded with its great trumpet-shaped ·fine white flowers, is a glorious sight. *L. Eximium* is too much like *L. Longiflorum*, *i.e.*, if I had the true sort from Van Houtte. *L. Takesima* ·is a great improvement on *Longiflorum*; it produces more flowers, and the ·outside of the petals have a slight brownish tinge. *L. Testaceum* is a desirable Lily, but its lanky stem and meagre foliage detract from its otherwise good qualities, particularly the very distinct colour of the flowers. Our American Lilies are very showy and beautiful, but their treatment is often misunderstood, as the bulbs of our eastern sorts are all annuals, flowering but once. Our botanical works say nothing of this, and a great many years ago, I failed to bloom them, as I set out the old bulbs. I soon, however, discovered my error when digging them from their native woods; and, again, they are fastidious as to soil. They never do well in loam, and only flourish in a very loose peaty earth, in which American plants are generally grown. *L. Canadense* and *L. Superbum* will succeed in any wet place; but *L. Philadelphicum* will only thrive in a comparatively dry situation. In July, 1873, I dug up bulbs of the latter in their native habitats, by the sides of the roads and in peaty pastures, in full bloom. These were laid in a box of sandy peat until October, when they were planted for convenience in boxes a foot square, and 6 inches deep, and last July they all flowered beautifully, and produced a quantity of seeds. Its deep orange crimson flowers spotted with black-purple, erect habit, and tiny foliage, make it very attractive; bulbs of it not much larger than a pea, often produce one flower. *L. Canadense* is indigenous in my grounds (where before they were cleared and planted I have dug up quantities), and even now, where a spot is neglected for two or three years, plants of it spring up, showing their nodding yellow-spotted flowers, probably from scales, dormant bulbs, or seeds lying in the soil. *L. Superbum*, our grand Lily, might well be taken for an improved variety of *Canadense*, as the only material variation is the size of the flowers, their deeper colour, and its more reflexed petals. The bulbs are not globose, nor perennial. In fact, this Lily is precisely the same as *Canadense*; the bulb flowers but once, and emits a runner to take its place. I have been through swamps in which it grew 7 feet high, with from ten to twenty flowers. I have dug up hundreds of its bulbs, and had a bed 80 feet long and 5 feet wide of *Superbum* and *Canadense* for nearly ten years. You will nearly always see the old dry stalk standing about 4 inches from the new shoot, and anyone knowing the habits of this Lily, can dig it any time after flowering, before frost, from the old dry flower-stems. They grow most abundantly among thickly matted roots in peaty swamps, where it is almost impossible to dig them, except with a sharp hatchet and very strong spade." *C. M. Hovey, Garden, vol. 7, p.* 420.

These descriptions of Lilies in their native haunts, of their climatic and other surroundings, are especially valuable; the more so, as coming not only from skilful and accurate observers, but from horticulturists who have had considerable experience in Lily culture. To them, therefore, we desire here to express our thanks for their communications; and we trust our readers will not fail to profit by the many valuable suggestions therein contained.

CHAPTER IV.

GENERAL REMARKS ON CULTURE.

We now include several letters and articles on Lily culture from the most distinguished growers, that have appeared at various times in our Horticultural Journals.

" *Lilium Auratum* is without doubt the most popular of the Lily tribe, and bids fair to become the most popular of plants, now that its price has placed it within the reach of the humblest. Numerous distinct and beautiful varieties are in cultivation, and a fair field is open to the hybridist, as a most distinct and lovely variety, *L. Parkmanni*, a cross between *L. Auratum* and *Speciosum*, was exhibited at South Kensington lately. As to the varieties of *Auratum*, their distinctiveness consists not only in the size, colour, and shape of the flowers, but also in the number of flowers borne on a spike. Some of the varieties have from three to six flowers on a spike, others from thirty to forty. I obtained a number of bulbs of *Auratum* of nearly equal size, imported from Japan, in February, 1867. No notes were made of their growth or flowering in that year, but in the following three seasons the subjoined notes were made. The produce of each bulb was each year repotted in a pot by itself.

No. 1.—1868	had	1 spike	16 flowers		No. 3.—1868	had	3 spikes	9 flowers
1869	had	4 ,,	32 ,,		1869	had	3 ,,	10 ,,
1870	had	6 ,,	134 ,,		1870	had 14 ,,	33 ,,
No. 2.—1868	had	1 ,,	25 ,,		No. 4.—1868	had	2 ,,	13 ,,
1869	had	1 ,,	24 ,,		1869	had	4 ,,	25 ,,
1870	had	2 ,,	39 ,,		1870	had	9 ,,	75 ,,
No. 5.—1866	....		had 2 spikes 7 flowers
1869	....		had 2 ,, 9 ,,
1870	....		had 2 ,, 7 ,,

The remaining roots did not succeed well; bulbs were not increased to a large extent, and not more than one or two flowers were borne on a spike. No. 1 had flower-spikes 10 feet in height, and the largest number of flowers on a spike was thirty-five. Some of the varieties do not grow more than from 2 to 3 feet in height, and have the finest individual flowers.

"Nearly all the Lily tribe are of easy culture, and *Auratum* is no exception to this rule. October is a good month to repot the bulbs; it is not advisable to dry them off, as is done with Hyacinths, Tulips, and other bulbs. Water ought to be administered sparingly previous to potting, and as soon as the leaves assume a yellow tinge the stalks may be cut over and the bulbs potted. In potting, some cultivators disturb the bulbs as little as possible, merely scratching away the loose soil with a pointed stick, and repotting in a pot a size larger; I consider it best to shake the soil entirely from the roots, separating each bulb, and saving the fresh roots as much as possible. As many as a dozen bulbs are planted in a 13-inch pot, three of the larger bulbs are placed in the centre, and the remainder round the inside of the rim. I find they succeed well in a compost of three parts of turfy loam and one part of leaf mould and rotted manure, with a portion of silver sand to keep the material open.

"If the compost in which the bulbs are potted is somewhat moist, no watering will be required. The pots ought to be plunged in a cold frame, and I do not know of anything better for this purpose than cocoa-nut fibre refuse; and if the pots are completely buried in it, so that there is at least 4 inches of the fibre over the surface of the soil, there will be no danger of the bulbs being injured by frost. The lights ought to be kept off the frame, except during severe frost and drenching rains. The bulbs will continue to make roots all the winter. The cocoa-nut fibre refuse ought to be removed from the surface of the pots in March, and if the bulbs are doing well roots will be found pushing upwards into it. The plants ought to remain in the cold frame until May, when they can be placed on a hard bottom in a sheltered position out-of-doors until the flowers begin to open, when they must be removed to the greenhouse or sitting room. Manure water may be occasionally administered to them, but they will do well without it; of course if they are wanted for exhibition or any other special purpose, extra care must be bestowed upon them. If they have to be removed any distance when in flower, the anthers ought to be wrapped round with tissue paper,* in order that the dark

* Thin silky Japanese paper, or a filmy web of cotton-wool, will answer the purpose equally well.

D

brown dust may be prevented from shaking off on to the petals, as it sadly disfigures the flowers. I have seen them brought to an exhibition when this precaution has been neglected, and the flowers were entirely spoiled."
—*J. Douglas, Hort. Jour.*, Oct. 20, 1870.

" There are few who have not seen and admired the gorgeous beauties of one or other of the many varieties of Lilies now in cultivation, or who have not been charmed by the stately purity of *L. Candidum* and its sweet odour. It was, however, reserved to *L. Auratum* to take us by storm, and bring the merits of this beautiful genus of plants prominently before the public. Never before, probably, has there been anything like the demand for a particular flower that has now existed for years for bulbs of this Lily. Hundreds of thousands have been sent over from Japan, and it is to be hoped as many more will follow, so that every one who has a garden may feast his eyes on one of the most magnificent flowers it is possible to see. Some of the varieties of Lilies, such as *Martagon*, *Tigrinum*, *Candidum*, *Chalcedonicum*, and a few others, will do in almost any kind of soil, and succeed admirably in such as is of a stiff loamy nature. The choice kinds, however, are more particular, and require either peat or plenty of sharp grit, but in the latter case it must be where they can drive their roots down in a cool, moist bottom. The margins of Rhododendron beds, where gaps occur among the plants, is just the place to grow them to perfection, and in no position do they show up so effectively as when backed by the rich glossy deep green leaves of this favourite shrub. Failing a situation of this kind, the next best place is the shrubbery border, as it is essential they should have partial shade and shelter of some kind.

" The heads of flowers require this on account of their enormous size and consequent liability to be blown about and damaged by the wind, while the roots will only succeed really well where they are so situated as to be screened from the sun, which causes the ground to become too much heated and robs it of its moisture. This dryness of the soil is one of the most frequent causes of failure in Lily culture, as it generally occurs at or about the time the plants are developing their flowers, when they require more assistance than they do at any other time, owing to the demand that is made on the roots, and if these cannot respond in a proper manner the bulbs as a natural consequence become so weak and exhausted that they dwindle away and eventually die altogether. To grow them in the style in which they ought be had, one of the principal and most important things is to keep the foliage fresh and healthy up to the latest period possible, so as to prevent any premature ripening, which must of necessity take place at the expense of the bulb ; and this can only be done by affording them an abundant supply of water and mulching the soil immediately surrounding them. Although the price of most of the best kinds of Lilies is somewhat against them, they are of such a permanent character compared with most other plants, that their first cost ought not to be a matter of consideration, as they are really cheap in the end, and there is nothing that can at all compare with them in the grand display they make and the small amount of labour entailed in their cultivation.

" Unfortunately of late the best and most valuable of our hardy plants have been sadly neglected, and almost elbowed out of existence to make room for others, the merits of many of which consist merely in the bigness of their leaves, or whose beauty at the best is only of such short duration, that it in no way compensates for the room they take up under glass, and the constant recurring expense there is in raising them and getting them fit to plant out. In the cultivation of Lilies there is nothing of this, for if a proper position be chosen, and suitable preparation made, they become more vigorous each succeeding year, and increase at such a rate as to form grand masses if left undisturbed. For shrubbery borders, where they can be kept clear of the roots of trees or other surface-feeding plants, there is nothing more suitable to grow, than Lilies, and there are few gardens but have an appendage of this kind, which would be greatly improved by the introduction of a few clumps of the different varieties of these stately plants.

" If it is intended to grow them in borders at the front of shrubs, the proper course will be to dig large holes from 2 to 3 feet across, and as much deep, and to fill these in with properly prepared soil, such as a mixture of leaf-mould and the turfy trimmings from the road-side, or any old pasture that has a sharp gritty soil. This should be chopped up small, and the whole well mixed up together, but on no account ought manure to be added in any form, or it will be likely to cause the bulbs to rot away before they are in a sufficiently forward state to make use of it. If applied at all, it should be towards the bottom of the hole, where it can only be reached when the plant is in an advanced stage of growth ; at which time the roots are actively at work, and can turn it to proper account.

" Having filled in the holes with the parings from the sides of paths or roads, or any good turfy loam and peat, which should be rendered tolerably firm by gentle treading, the next thing is to plant the bulbs, either singly, or in groups of three where bold masses are required. Excepting for such as *Giganteum*, with its massive leaves and gigantic stem towering aloft, most of the others look best placed in clumps triangularly at from 6 to 9 inches apart, and the front plant so arranged as to face the border or walk, in which case they are seen to great advantage. In placing the bulbs in position, it is of the greatest importance that they should have a good handful of sharp clean sand under their base, and a shovelful of the same scattered over and around them, which will keep them in a clean healthy state, and prevent them from rotting—a thing they are very liable to do, if the soil is allowed to come in immediate contact with them. The proper depth at which to plant is about 6 inches, and when all is covered in securely with the same kind of mixture that the holes have been previously filled in with, the surface should be mulched over with some half-rotten leaves, cocoa-nut fibre, or any material of that kind, to keep out frost ; for, although Lily bulbs are perfectly hardy when they become established, they are readily injured after being fresh planted, especially if at the time they are forming young growth, or emitting their large fleshy rootlets.

" The principal attention required through their growing season is to keep them securely staked and tied as they advance; the best and neatest supports for which purpose are bamboo rods of suitable length, as in colour and structure they so closely resemble the Lily stems that they are scarcely observed, whilst they are far stronger than any other stick of double their size. It is the practice of many cultivators of Lilies to take up their bulbs after they have done blooming, and to winter them out of the ground; but this tends to weaken them very considerably, as the large fleshy roots that would live in the ground if left undisturbed, are completely destroyed; and not only is this the case, but the bulbs shrivel a good deal, thereby losing much of their weight and vital force, which prevents them starting away so strong or flowering with anything like the vigour and freedom they do when not interfered with. This being so, the stems should be simply cut away close to the ground when thoroughly ripe, which they generally are by the end of October; and in order to keep them snug for the winter it is as well to repeat the mulching. Treated in this way they soon become strong and throw up immense stems, that carry from ten to twenty or more of their magnificent flowers, many of which are so strongly perfumed as to scent a moderate-sized garden.

" For pot culture *Auratum* is most valuable, as are also the several kinds of *Speciosum* which come in later in the autumn. These give a richness and character in the greenhouse or conservatory at that season quite unattainable by any other plant, and a few pots of each should therefore be grown wherever there is such a structure to be furnished. Single bulbs of *Auratum* may be grown in deep 6 or 8 inch pots to great perfection, and are even more suitable to stand among other plants than when numbers are grown together. The best soil for them is a mixture of good fat fibrous loam and peat, in the proportion of two-thirds of the former to one of the latter, with just sufficient sand to keep it open and porous, that water, of which they can scarce have too much when growing freely and flowering, may pass through readily. In potting, the bulbs should be placed low down in the pot, and simply covered, so as to leave sufficient room to pack rough pieces of turfy loam around the young stems as growth proceeds, in which they will root freely and grow considerably stronger than they otherwise would. In the case of all dormant bulbs, and especially the Lily, any soil used for potting should be in a nice healthy state as to moisture, which will obviate the necessity of having to water till they have started well into growth and are able to take it up before any injury results from its lodging about their base and among the scales of the bulbs, which is a frequent cause of so many coming up weak and afterwards dwindling away altogether. The best place to stand them till they appear above the soil, is under the greenhouse stage away from drip, or in any cold pit having a damp firm bottom impenetrable to worms, as there the soil can be kept in much the same state with regard to moisture as at the time of potting, and the longer it remains in that condition without having to water, the stronger and better will the growth be.

" After the pots have become well filled with roots and the plants are moving on freely, weak liquid manure applied occasionally will be of the greatest assistance to them till just after the flowers are fully expanded, when its use should be discontinued, and less water given as the ripening off proceeds—a process that in no case should be hurried on, as is.

frequently done by laying them down on their sides. It is quite time enough for this when they begin to show the sere and yellow leaf, and to die off, a time when heavy rains or any excess of wet would prove injurious. At no season, however, will Lilies bear the amount of drying-off that most other bulbs can endure, and the pots containing them should, therefore, be placed to winter where they will not be subjected to currents of air, or in such a position as that the soil would lose too much of its moisture. The great mistake many make who grow Lilies in pots, is in not attending to them sufficiently early as regards shifting and dividing, for if this operation is too long deferred, it is impossible to perform it without injuring or destroying a large portion of the thick fleshy roots, which all Lily bulbs have in such abundance when in a state of good health; and, therefore, the necessary re-potting, &c., should be done as soon after the tops die away as they can be taken in hand. This ought in all cases to be carried out with as little disturbance as possible to the old ball where there are any live roots in possession, by carefully picking out, with a sharp-pointed stick, the soil which it may be requisite to remove.

"In the raising of new Lilies from seed there is a fine field open for the hybridist, and there is no lack of choice varieties to work from. *Auratum*, when grown out in the open, seeds freely in favourable seasons, and so also does *Giganteum*, both of which are, on that account, and from their general superiority over most others, capital sorts to breed from, although there is no reason why efforts to obtain new varieties of great worth and distinctness should be confined to any particular kind. As the flowers do not require any delicate manipulation, such as is needed by most others, any amateur can work at it with an equal chance of success, as those more skilled in the art. The principal thing is, when the blooms expand, to remove the anthers from all those to be fertilised, which may be done by clipping them off with a pair of sharp-pointed scissors. This must be accomplished before any of the pollen becomes ripe, otherwise some of it is sure to fall and adhere to the pistil, which nature has so abundantly provided with viscid matter, to insure that at least some portion of the pollen grains, may fall on it and adhere, and thus carry out their allotted functions. Plants, as a rule, will always become fecundated with their own pollen much more readily than they will with that from other species, hence the necessity for removing their anthers while they are in an unripe state. Both these and the pistil are so conspicuous in the Lily, and the important part both serve is so generally understood, that any attempt here at an explanation would be superfluous. To those unacquainted with either, a mere cursory glance will show their several positions, and the purposes they are intended to serve, and how readily they may be turned to account in increasing our floral treasures, and adding to our pleasures and happiness. It should be borne in mind that bees may frustrate the work, even after the removal of the authers; and in order to guard against this, the flowers to be operated on should be protected by placing very fine gauze or hexagon net over them, keeping the net from chafing them by using a few twiggy sticks stuck in the ground on which to support it.

"When the stigmas are in a fit state, as may be seen by the coating of glutinous matter they will have on them, the ripe pollen from any other Lily may be readily introduced, either by using a camel's hair brush, or by nipping off the anthers, and holding them between a pair of tweezers, in which way they can be carried, and the stigma slightly touched till thoroughly coated with the snuff-like pollen. One plant will bear sufficient of this, if judiciously and carefully used, to fertilise a great many, and each separate flower on the same plant may be crossed with as many varieties, and if each is numbered to correspond with a memorandum kept of the kinds employed, the result can be seen afterwards, and the work will thus be rendered more interesting. Having operated on the flowers as above, they should again be protected with the gauze or net, which should be allowed to remain on till the seeds are fit to gather, as birds are fond of them ; for I unfortunately lost the whole of mine last year from their depredations, while I considered them safe.

"Anyone who commences such an interesting branch of gardening as this, is sure not to rest satisfied with trying his hand on Lilies, but will seek fresh honours with other flowers equally deserving of attention ; and if those who make a blade of grass grow where one never before grew, deserve well of their country, how much more must the originator of any new and beautiful flower do so, the sight and possession of which is destined to be a new source of delight to so many ? It is only those who have once tried the occupation of raising plants from seed, the result of artificial fertilisation, that can realise what pleasure there is to be derived from the work, and how absorbingly interesting it is to watch the seedlings from day to day, noting each change in leaf or bud, and hanging with fond hope on the ultimate result, to be revealed only when the bloom—so slow in unfolding for one's impatience—shall open ; and yet perhaps then, if disappointing as a whole, the success is sufficient to give fresh zest, and spur one on to renewed effort."—*T. Sheppard, Gardeners' Chronicle, March 24th,* 1877.

"Will you allow me to say a word or two ? I have been misunderstood in being supposed to have recommended growing Lilies in pots, to the exclusion of the open ground. For some years past I have urged growing all the Lily tribe among dwarf shrubs, recommending especially Rhododendrons in peat, and long ago I exhibited a collection of blooms from a bed in an old garden at Wandsworth, to show how well Lilies bloom and stand bad weather in sheltered situations, and have quoted the garden of a friend in the not very genial climate near Rochdale to show that *Speciosum* can be bloomed well in unfavourable situations. I have also been misunderstood in being supposed to produce fine growth by means of stimulants. I have been constantly told at South Kensington that the fine growth of the Lilies I exhibited was due to high manuring, and found it almost hopeless to correct this impression, so perhaps you will allow me to say that (perhaps with the exception of *Tigrinum,* the *Fortunei* variety of which Mr. Standish informs me he grew best well manured) Lilies are grown best without manure—that the Lilies of finest growth exhibited by me, and among them was *Speciosum Splendidum*, standing 7 feet 9 inches in its pot, and 2 feet 6 inches over the base of the flowering part of the stem—had neither solid nor liquid manure. We have one large clump of *Auratum*, protected from north and east winds by large shrubs, but with no dwarf ones among them; last year these Lilies had shoots more than a foot high when the late frost bent their heads to the ground; they afterwards stood up again, but neither growth nor bloom was as good as usual. *Szovitzianum* was proved by Mr. Berkeley to succeed admirably, planted out in his stiff soil. I do not believe that in any but exceptional seasons *Longiflorum* can be perfectly grown except in pots, or at least under cover; stems between 3 and 4 feet high, with four and five blooms 8 inches long, can be thus grown, but I never but once got anything like this out-of-doors—one plant reached the full growth in a dwarf Rhododendron bed in peat, but the blooms were not perfect. I believe there will be similar experience with all the early growing Lilies—those which are well above ground before danger from frost is over (*Longiflorum* is well up with us out-of-doors now, in a warm corner); but that the other Lilies may be grown perfectly out-of-doors in suitable situations, and some of the *Superbum* type, especially deep-rooting ones, probably better than in pots. We had special pots, made much deeper than the ordinary ones; these gave good results, but not yet very markedly so. As to soil, I believe the beautiful old *Candidum*, and a few others, like stiff soil, but nine out of ten Lilies grow best in peat, or peat two-thirds to one-third loam, which seems best for pots; the loam, if stiff, mixed with sharp sand. The effect of difference of soil with some Lilies in pots is less than might be supposed. In November, 1871, we tried two experiments in this direction. No 1 was planted with eight bulbs of *Speciosum Album*, in a large pot in soil composed of two parts loam, one part river sand, and half a part old dung; and a corresponding pot with the same number of similar sized bulbs, in two parts peat, one part loam, and one part river sand. Experiment No. 2: six large bulbs of *Speciosum Rubrum*, in two parts loam, one part old dung, and six of exactly the same size in two parts peat, one part old dung. In these two experiments the pots with the peat showed rather the best results, but there was no great difference, but in none of the three were the results as good as in our usual compost."— *G. F. Wilson, Heatherbank, Weybridge. Gard. Chronicle.*

"I send one or two notes of experience lately gained when planting Lilies. For many years past I have urged friends who grew Lilies to allow plenty of room for the roots, especially for pot Lilies. We had pots specially made, deep in proportion to their diameter; and some two years ago, wishing to plant Lilies at the side of lawn-beds where there were many trees, which, while they gave shade and shelter, would pull from their soil, I copied the pots used by my neighbour and friend, Dr. Bennett, to plunge his palm-trees in summer round his lawn, and sunk some of these in which had been planted bulbs of *L. Auratum*, *Krameri*, and *Canadense*. A few days back I took them up, and found the roots much longer than even I expected, one not very large *Auratum* bulb, when measured by a rod, showed exactly 4 feet from the top of the bulb to the end of the roots. This, I think, shows well that a great depth of soil is required to give Lily bulbs really fair play. If we could examine some of my friend, Mr. MacIntosh's giants, I suspect we should find some roots 6 feet long. Lilies are sometimes reproached, especially *Auratum*, with dying, and not coming up; and it is said that, notwithstanding the vast numbers yearly imported from Japan, the number of bulbs in this country does not increase, if they do often die, they at least afford ample means for the race being perpetuated. In 1871 I sowed in two not very large boxes, *Auratum* seed which we had saved, and placed them in the garden, where they had no attention beyond an occasional watering in dry weather, and a mat screen in very hot weather. I lately broke up these boxes in which some of the bulbs had this year flowered, and took out 200 fair-sized bulbs to plant, besides a lot of small ones. Again, in 1874, I sowed seed of *L. Californicum*, a great favourite of mine, the most richly painted of all the North American Lilies, in two large seed-pans, and have just potted, or rather boxed, about 200 bulbs from them, some of them very good ones. When potting Lilies, it is curious to notice how, without any apparent cause, some bulbs of the same species, planted at the same time in the same soil, and subjected to the same treatment, are found much more thriving than others. Last year, owing to so much of my time having been taken up with other and much less pleasant horticultural work, I had to leave many of my Lilies unpotted. I now find the above differences much exaggerated, owing to the longer time any mischief has had the power to act. In some pots all the bulbs are in perfect health, in others about half, in others most of them are dead. It is, course, most unreasonable to expect, as some seem to do, that great Lily bulbs will go on flowering in perpetuity. After a certain time, under the most perfect conditions of health, they come to their natural end, in many cases leaving only offsets; such require some years' growth before they can take their parents' full place."—*George F. Wilson, in Gard. Chron., p.* 660, 1877.

"Though my experience in Lily growing, dates back to a time when cultivators in general had not been awakened to the charms of this most beautiful family, I must begin by confessing that we have still many things to learn, and perhaps some to unlearn. In some seasons, notably when cold and wet follow after drought, even practised cultivators, except in most favoured situations, find that 'blight and spot' greatly injure the growth and flowering of some species, even though the bulbs may be unhurt. The best situation for planting Lilies—at least in the southern counties—is a cool sheltered one, a very safe place is near the edge of a Rhododendron bed, soils that will grow Rhododendrons will also answer for most soils of Lilies. I can give two examples where Lilies succeeded when left almost to themselves: one was in an old fashioned garden, with a small lawn inside the main lawn, and sheltered, and partly shaded by shrubs and trees. In the centre bed, among some dwarf Rhododendrons, I planted many sorts of Lilies, all of which succeeded perfectly. Blooms of *Auratum*, gathered after a week of unusually stormy weather, were taken up to the Royal Horticultural Society, to show how little they had suffered. In the same garden *Auratum* and *Longiflorum* bloomed well in a peat Rhododendron bed, sheltered by the house, in a full southern exposure; but in this case watering was almost essential. The other situation is in the garden of a friend near here; his *Auratums* are planted near the edges of large Rhododendron beds, and are partially sheltered by a high bank, and by belts of trees at some little distance; his Rhododendron soil suits admirably, and there appears to be moisture in the soil some little way down, which the roots can reach. The result is, that season after season, in the most unfavourable ones, hardly a Lily is injured, and their flowers, on stems from 6 to 10 feet in height, surpass any I have seen elsewhere. In Lancashire, not far from Rochdale, a friend has long grown *L. Speciosum*, blooming it well in an exposed border without taking up the bulbs. Most gardens have a north border where there are spaces between small shrubs; if a little peat and sandy loam is dug in, and the bulbs planted 5 or 6 inches deep, Lilies are almost sure to thrive. Some Lilies, however, such as *Candidum*, *Martagon*, *Szovitzianum*, and *Chalcedonicum*, require a stronger soil, and like loam. All the Tiger Lilies grow well in ordinary soil; the old *Tigrinum Sinense* is well known in gardens, but *Tigrinum splendens*, which richly deserves its name, is but little known. Very many bulbs of *Tigrinum Fortunei*, which has a very woolly stem, are sent out in mistake for *Tigrinum Splendens*, the original error having been widely extended by means of stem bulbs. *Tigrinum Splendens*, has more the character of the old *Tigrinum Sinense*, only magnified in height, size of flowers, and especially in size of spots. It shows beautifully in Rhododendron beds, in the centre of other beds, indeed, in any situation for which its height—7 or 8 feet, or with large bulbs, probably 9 feet or more—does not disqualify it. *Tigrinum Flore Pleno* is a showy Lily, which lasts long in flower. I think *Tigrinum Erectum* a desirable variety, but with this opinion the floral committee of the Royal Horticultural Society does not agree. *L. Longiflorum*, with its varieties *Eximium*, *Takesima*, &c., sometimes bloom very well in borders, but care should be taken that they are not injured by spring frosts. This Lily is such an early one that, unless protected by the leaves of Rhododendrons, or otherwise, its growth is apt to be checked. This season, *Longiflorum* in a very cool sheltered situation here grew high and bloomed well. The comparatively recently introduced North American Lilies, such as *Humboldtii*, *Washingtonianum*, *Puberulum*, *Pardalinum*, *Robinsoni*, *Californicum*, &c., no doubt will soon be grown perfectly in borders; but here, at least, though some thrive well, others, in places where they ought to succeed perfectly, have not always done so, the foliage of *Humboldtii*, especially, not keeping its healthy colour. Cultivators must not be discouraged when newly imported bulbs do not show up the first season. I have just been examining two small beds, in each of which twelve fine bulbs of *Humboldtii* were planted. The soil of one bed consists of two parts of peat, and one of loam, the other of loam with a little sharp sand mixed; in neither bed the bulbs made upward growth, but on examination, seem healthy, and have made roots. In adjoining beds, with the same two soils, a dozen *Szovitzianum* in the peat and loam made miserable growth, while the dozen in the loam bed have many of them flowered well and seeded. In the other two beds the six *Auratum* all came up fairly, but the six in the loam and sand bed were rather the strongest ; all the bulbs were newly imported ones. The above, I think, shows that imported bulbs of different Lilies have different times of establishing themselves, and that with cold and wet in the early part of the season the soil which suits Lilies best in normal seasons may not then give the best results. Many of the varieties of *L. Superbum* are very beautiful, they like shade, and rather moist soil. Some years back, I do not know whether it still exists, there was a grand undisturbed bed of *Superbum* at Messrs. Waterer's, at Woking ; this Lily was at home in the moist peat, its great tall stems, with richly coloured flowers, had a very fine effect. *L. Canadense*, in all its varieties, grows easily, and is very beautiful. It is usually said, find the native habitat of a plant, and reproduce it as nearly as you can ; if a Lily be found in shady places, grow it in shade ; but a distinguished Dutch chemist—botanist, who has himself done great things as regards introduction of different plants, especially into Java, once showed me that this was not a universal law, or rather that what appears to be the reproduction of the habitat, is really not so ; and that one unattainable condition sometimes changes the whole circumstances so completely, that he had known plants which, in their own country, flourished in shade, when transported, to thrive best in sun. The moral is, I think— where possible, try experiments for yourself, plant a few bulbs in very different situations—the first year will tell you in which direction to steer. I must end with a few words on pot cultivation. We have some thousands of bulbs, both little and big, planted in the open, but I think there are some species which cannot be brought to their full beauty except under a roof. Perhaps the simplest way is to mention how our Lilies are treated : which species succeed well here, and which do not. Till lately the Lily-house was an orchard-house, 60 feet by 20. In this, Lilies answered very well, except in very hot weather, and then some of them, when in bloom, were moved to a rough shed, open at the front, and facing north. Last year a house was put up, giving as much air as possible, in our shadiest corner ; it gets only the east sun. The Lilies succeed very well, and the blossoms last longer than in the orchard-house. Had we the situation, a house should be placed in complete shade, for I feel sure that some Lilies would thrive best there. The soil we use for most Lilies consists of two parts fibrous peat, one part loam, and, if the last is at all stiff, some sharp sand is added. In this *Speciosum, Longiflorum, Canadense, Californicum, Pardalinum, Parvum, Puberulum, Thunbergianum, Coridion, Hansoni, Tigrinum, Giganteum*, and some others, flourish and increase ; *Auratum, Krameri, Superbum*, and *Leichtlinii*, only in some seasons. The last, from its distinctness, is a favourite here ; we are trying it with more loam. *Chalcedonicum, Tenuifolium, Buschianum, White Martagon*, &c., bloom for a time, but the bulbs waste, and we lose them. *Brownii* occasionally succeeds splendidly, but is uncertain. We continue trying different soils, and earlier removal to the cooler house."—*G. F. Wilson, Garden, vol. 8, p. 277.*

"I have never found any difficulty in growing *L. Japonicum (Brownii)*, which thrives with me on peat and leaf-mould. I winter the pot of this and other Lilies, plunged, like Hyacinths and such things, in sawdust, anywhere out of the reach of actual frost. I think the first, or slow growing period, should be prolonged as much as possible, after which the warmer berth of greenhouse or conservatory encourages development to a high degree. A free circulation of air is, however, indispensable, and the contrary most prejudicial—to wit, anything of continued close and moist treatment.

"Much as I object to peat for general cultivation, Lilies undoubtedly like it. They will, however, do well and healthily in loam with leaf-mould or very old hot-bed manure. This is all that is necessary for the *Martagons* and other hardy sorts, still I find myself giving a 'bit of peat' to a favourite. *Longiflorum* will flourish planted under a wall for years; and I have had beds of it in great beauty under peat treatment, in a genial situation. It is apt, as my friend Mr. Wilson says, to suffer from early frosts. In this case gangrenous spots appear on the leaves, and the plants are checked and injured. Even the common white Lily sometimes suffers in the same way here. *Japonicum (Brownii)* sometimes lies dormant for a year, which I believe is induced by too dry a season of rest. *Wallichianum* I never could induce to start at all. *Tenuifolium* came up freely from seed, and throve in absolutely pure sandy loam, under a glass frame in front of my stove. *Testaceum* luxuriates with me out-of-doors in strong loam, heavily manured. Lilies seldom grow or flower strongly the first season out-of-doors, after transplanting. They sometimes, too, resent division in-doors. When a mass is broken up for stock, rather small pots should be used, and the plants brought on slowly.

"By the way, *Longiflorum* forces very fairly, becoming after that operation almost a perpetual, jumping up and flowering at all sorts of odd times, something '*In tempore quod verum omnium est primum*'—say just in time for your Christmas ball. *Candidum* forces well."—*R. T. Clarke, in Hort. Journal.*

The following are the particulars of the specimen of *L. Auratum,* illustrated in the *Gardeners' Chronicle,* Feb. 15th, 1873, page 215 :—

"A single bulb, measuring 2 inches in diameter, was obtained early in 1865. It was potted in a 7-inch pot and placed in a cool greenhouse, where it produced three flowers on one stem. In 1866 it was repotted in a 9-inch pot and received similar treatment : the plant threw up two stems, producing altogether seventeen flowers. In 1867 it was repotted in an 11-inch pot and treated as before : the plant threw three strong flowering stems, and three smaller ones, producing altogether fifty-three flowers. In 1868 the plant was shifted into a 16-inch pot, and placed, in the month of February, in a temperature of 45° to 50°, where it remained until it flowered : the plant threw up five strong stems, and seven smaller ones, producing altogether a hundred flowers. In 1869 it was turned out of the pot and a small portion of the old soil taken away from the ball ; it was then put into a 17-inch pot and treated as before up to the flowering period, when it was taken to a cool conservatory : the plant threw up thirty-nine flowering stems, ranging from 2 to 9 feet in height, from the top of the pot, and producing altogether 193 flowers, many of which measured from 11 to 12 inches in diameter. In 1870 the bulbs were left in the same pot undisturbed : they threw up forty-three stems, producing altogether 208 flowers. In the autumn of 1870 I carefully separated the bulbs, about seventy in number, not breaking a root more than I could possibly avoid. Having ready a pot 24 inches in diameter, I commenced with the largest bulb, which measured 7 inches in circumference, placing it in the centre of the pot, and seven other bulbs each about 6 inches in circumference, around it, twenty others, averaging from 4 to 5½ inches, around these, and outside seventeen more, gradually diminishing in size to 1 inch in circumference, filling up with soil at the same time ; twenty-five other bulbs (making in all seventy bulbs, the produce of one original bulb in five years), were scarcely formed, and were put elsewhere. The bulbs were on the whole more solid and compact than I have usually seen. This done, the pot was placed in a cold pit, protected from frost, until the month of March. It was then taken to a cool greenhouse, where it remained until it flowered. The plant threw up about seventy stems, measuring from 18 inches to 9 feet 6 inches from the top of the pot, producing on the whole 225 flowers, averaging 10 inches in diameter, and was photographed on the 16th August, 1871, a copy of which was presented to the Royal Horticultural Society, South Kensington. In 1872 the plant was left undisturbed and wintered in a cold pit as before, where it remained until the stems were about 18 inches in length, but as it got too large for the place, and as I had no accommodation for it under glass at the time, I was compelled to leave it out under the shelter of a south wall during May and June ; the weather being very wet and cold, the plant suffered very much ; the foliage was much smaller, also the stems, and many of the flowers. There were about eighty stems on the plant, producing altogether 240 flowers, a few of which did not properly expand, which I attribute to the fact of the plant having had a severe check in the months of May and June.

"The plant still remains in the same pot, and has been kept in a cool house during the past winter. It has lately had a surfacing of about an inch of the same material that I use for potting, viz., good turfy loam, two parts ; peat, one ditto ; cow manure, one ditto ; with a little coarse leaf mould and silver sand well incorporated.

"At the present time there are seventy stems showing, about the half of which seem strong enough to bear flowers.

"I do not find any advantage in using liquid manure of any kind until roots are emitted from the base of the stems, which generally takes place in a healthy plant when the stems are from 6 to 18 inches in length. At that period I invariably add about an inch of the above-named compost, to encourage and strengthen the flowering stems and flowers. After the stem roots are fairly established in the soil, I apply liquid manure once or twice a week up to the time the blooms expand, and I invariably find the blooms to expand during the night, and their average duration to be about nine days.

" The blooming season past, the pots are placed in an open situation, exposed to the sun, to ripen the bulbs, care being taken not to let them get saturated with water, or become too dry at any time, as I believe there are more bulbs lost through these two extremes than by any other cause."—*J. Smith, Quarry Bank Gardens, Allerton, Wavertree, Liverpool. March*, 1873.

" We have frequently recommended that Lilies should be planted in Rhododendron beds, the soil, and slight shelter and shade of the shrubs assisting them perfectly. We had, however, no idea of the splendid results to be this way obtained till we saw Mr. MacIntosh's garden, at Duneevan, Oatlands, Weybridge. Here *L. Auratum*, planted near the margin of masses of Rhododendron, attains au astonishing degree of vigour, and sends up such noble pillars of its huge blooms as we have never seen equalled by any other plant, whether grown under glass or in the open air. Each noble tuft of Lilies, well defined, tells as well iu the picturesque garden landscape of the place as well-grown and well-placed trees of the variegated Maple do. The smallest and most recently planted specimens are from 5 to 6 feet high, while the old-established plants range from 9 to 11 feet high, so that one has to look up at the colossal bouquet of flowers borne by each plant of this noble Lily. From 110 to 140 full-sized blooms are borne by each tuft (originally one bulb). Some few of the plants have now (Aug. 7) passed out of flower, others are yet to open, while the majority are in the full glory of blossom ; the varieties show such a variation as to the time of flowering, that their season here lasts nearly three months. The beds are on a steep bank ; they are for the most part of sandy peat, with wet sand within 2 feet of the surface, and the garden is perfectly sheltered from all strong winds. No examples of Lilies in pots, as seen at our best shows, give the faintest idea of the specimens in this garden, or of their extraordinary effect in the garden landscape. With such effects from one single Lily, we may well expect great aid from them in the embellishments of the gardens of the future."—*Garden, vol.* 8, *p.* 99.

" We have here a large quantity of *L. Candidum* in very big clumps ; but, from some cause, these have never succeeded as they ought to have done, only every fourth or fifth maturing a flower-stem. As soon as they had done flowering, when the stems were beginning to get dry at the eud of August, I took up all these clumps and separated the bulbs. I found then that the greater quantity of bulbs had no roots at all ; in fact, wretched* little slugs had eaten them off close to the bulb as fast as they grew. After separating and cleaning each bulb, I put them into a tub of soot and water for two days, to kill any embryo slugs that might have escaped my notice. I then planted the whole in a row, 5 inches apart each way, and 4 inches deep. Half the row was strongly dressed with soot and half with lime. Another row had no lime or soot except what

* My friend means the reverse ; "happy little slugs."

they retained from the tubbing. I took up some of the last row the other
day, and found my friends, the slugs, calmly browsing on the newly-
formed roots, as calmly as if soot was not an *infallible preventive* (?) against
their ravages. On lifting those dressed with lime, I found the bulbs firm,
and growing fast with long fleshy roots. It is certainly marvellous how
quickly these Lilies reproduce themselves; each scale which has been
injured in separating the bulbs has now at its base a small offset the size
of a cob-nut. Some bulbs of *L. Chalcedonicum* that were left in the
potting shed have produced from twenty to thirty offsets wherever they
were bruised. I think that there can be no doubt that the time to transplant all Lilies is directly the stems begin to wither, before a single new
root has formed. People make a great mistake in repotting their Lilies
in spring, when the soil is full of new roots, instead of in the autumn,
when there is nothing but old roots in the pot. I have over 500 bulbs of
Candidum, and the effect of 500 flower-spikes in a long row is something
splendid; my long border last summer seemed like a white stream of
foam flowing down the garden. Mr. Ruskin is coming to Bingham next
spring, and I shall get him to time his visit for the flowering of these
white Lilies. I fancy the transplanting will make them at least a week
later; and this is just what is wanted in order to escape the early frosts,
when the flower-stem is only a few inches high.

"Of the rarer kinds, I have perhaps done best with the *White Martagon*,
which is quite a Lily for the open border. Two years ago I purchased a
small bulb of this, about as big as a small walnut. It forgot to flower last
year, but did so twice this year, producing two good spikes. The flowers
are creamy-white, and more fleshy than the common *Purple Martagon*.
I am going to grow all border Lilies, such as *Tigrinum*, *Martagon*,
Chalcedonicum, *Monadelphum*, and others, in soil from earth-closets, which
is, I think, the very thing for such as can stand a strong soil. Mine is a
very strong loam. In wet weather it is little better than clay, and in dry
weather it is worse than baked brick. So I have to make an artificial
soil for all my rarer herbaceous plants in the open border. I have done
well with *Speciosum* out of doors, but I prefer a sandier soil. For the
varieties of *Speciosum* I have hitherto used soil from the interior of willow
trees, which is an excellent substitute for peat. I never saw the varieties
of *Speciosum* so grand as at Chester, the soil there appeared extremely
light, almost too sandy for *Auratum*, but *Excelsum* was fully 7 feet high,
and the bulbs enormous. This Lily, otherwise called *Testaceum*, or
Isabellinum, ought to be more commonly grown, for, in shape and
colour, it is exquisite. After carefully looking at it, no one can doubt its
being a hybrid between *Chalcedonicum* or *Pyrenaicum*, and *Candidum*. It
has the same shaped buds as *Candidum*, but hanging down like *Chalcedonicum*. The flowers are in form like the latter, but have the mid-rib of
the former. The colour is something between the two—cream, flushed
with red, and slightly marked with the marks of *Chalcedonicum*. Can
any one tell us whether this Lily is now grown in China or Japan?
Tradition says it was imported from Japan,* but how can it be a hybrid

---

* Amongst the numerous paintings which we have received from time to time from
Japan, were a series executed by one of the best artists in Yeddo (Tokio), representing all

if neither of its parents are grown in Japan ? The chances of a hybrid seed being perpetuated, unless under a gardener's care, are so small, that one can only believe this Lily is a hybrid of English origin. It seems to me an extraordinary thing that so little should be known about the origin of this; but it gives hopes to us hybridisers, when we consider that neither of the supposed parents are more than 3 feet high, and yet the offspring grows fully 7 feet. If from Pelargonium Inquinans and P. Zonale have been raised the magnificent florists' flowers now common in every garden, what ought we to expect when we begin to hybridise with such Lilies as *Giganteum*, *Auratum*, or *Tigrinum Splendens!* The difficulty about raising hybrid Lilies is, that too many seeds are apt to form in the pod, so that none of them properly ripen. This has given me a good deal of trouble ; and I should be thankful to any one for advice on the subject, and also for a list of such Lilies as make plump seeds which will germinate freely. Has the common *Candidum* been known to seed in England ? I suppose that if one wants to increase the size of bulb in any Lily, the best way would be to break off the flowering stem as soon as buds are forming.* I have observed this to be the case with *Pyrenaicum*, in which variety, if anything injures the flowering stems, the bulbs becomes enormous. Probably we should not hear of nine-tenths of imported *Auratum* bulbs completely disappearing in three years if they were prevented from flowering the first year by breaking or heading down the stems. I have lately been planting *Auratum* bulbs, 6 inches deep, in sandy leaf soil, with a good drainage placed 2 feet deeper. These clumps of three bulbs each, are about 4 feet apart, and in the middle of a border, the whole length of which I have laid with 3-inch piping, loose-jointed, 3 inches under the surface. I can turn a tank of water down this piping, and so water all the Lilies at once without watering the top of the ground. Close to this tank is a pump from a land-spring well, to fill it with. I have made a small tank in the border, about 8 feet long, 18 inches deep, and 4 feet wide, with cemented sides. This tank is filled with leaf-soil, and will always be kept in a swampy state from the droppings of the pump. There is no indication as you pass the border of there being a tank underneath ; but I nevertheless hope to grow all the American Swamp Lilies, such as *Superbum* or *Humboldtii*, as well as they grow in their native habitats.

"Since writing the above, I have searched in the grass for any scales of the White Lily that were lost when we pulled them to pieces. I found a good many scattered about, and nearly all had on them bulblets of the size of a large pea, entirely formed since the end of August, and that, too, when merely protected by long grass. I have this afternoon been digging up in a neighbouring nursery about three dozen bulbs of *Auratum*. Many of the bulbs were planted late, and flowered indifferently ; but, on taking

the known Lilies of Japan. In these most beautifully executed paintings (some of which are now in the possession of Mr. G. F. Wilson, of Heatherbrook, *see Garden*, Sept. 9th, 1876, p. 254), the birds and insects are most faithfully represented. We must, therefore, conclude that the Lilies, though amongst them are some very curious forms, are equally correctly delineated ; amongst these *Testaceum* is depicted.

* We have observed this to be the case with many sorts, the foliage becomes larger and darker.

them up, we found some of them had as many as twenty tiny offsets. The thirty-six have given me more than 400 offsets, some the size of a cob-nut, and some about half as big as a pea. Will any authority on Lilies kindly tell me how long such offsets take to become flowering bulbs.[*] I never shall forget seeing, for the first time, *Krameri* in bloom last July, when the rain was falling in torrents. Among a lot of other Lilies in the open border was a bloom of *Krameri*, and I was fairly surprised by the depth of colouring. The bloom was a very indifferent one, but reminded me in its shape more of *Longiflorum* than of *Auratum*. I expected to find a washed-out purple tinge, like that wretched fraud, the rose-coloured *Lily of the Valley*; but here was a veritable blush Lily, as deep, it seemed to me, as the old Provence Rose. Besides the commoner kinds, I have *Krameri*, *Brownii*, *Eximium*, *Washingtonianum*, *Tigrinum*, *Splendens*, *Giganteum*, *Auratum*, vars. *Diadem*, *Virginale*, *Macranthum*, and *Pictum*, *Martagon Album*, *Dalmaticum*, and the true *Catesbæi*, all of which I mean to use for the purposes of hybridisation.

"There are three Lilies that should be common in our borders, viz.— *Martagon Album, Dalmaticum (Catani)*. and *Monadelphum*."—*Frank Miles, Bingham, Notts, Nov.,* 1875, *Garden, vol.* 8, *p.* 456.

From the same correspondent.

" My White Lilies (*Candidum*) have been good, certainly better than I expected, the lime mixed with the soil in which they were planted I consider a perfect success, but not the soot, though it did no harm. I put some (*Candidums*) absolutely in lime, and digging them up the other day I found them quite unharmed, after a year, but not many roots. However, they were quite sound and plump, and I think we may consider lime quite harmless, and as it kills and sickens the small slugs it must be a good thing.

"No doubt these Lilies will be grand another year, but this terrific spring was enough to choke the ardour of any gardener. When I came home at the end of April I vowed I would never plant another Lily; nothing seemed moving, the soil was ice cold, and never got warm all the season. Where the soil was light the *Auratums* did splendidly, but the particular batches, with the pipe underground, are planted deep in wet silt, and I don't think we can tell till another year how the thing answers, my impression is that it will be a great success. I planted three clumps 8 inches deep, with a cubic yard of silt from a clay watershed, three Lilies to each. They were planted late in April, 1876, and made fair growth and a few good flowers. This year, of one clump in the least sunny position there is no growth; of another clump, only one stem, but that splendid, a grand truss of flowers; the third clump threw up four healthy stems and a few flowers.

" I dug down to the first clump when I found it was making no show, and found the bulbs in a first-rate condition, evidently they were lying dormant and fattening, and I fully expect good growth and flowers next year, if they escape the villainous frosts of April and May. A great number of my Lilies lay dormant this year, but I think it is better in the end, and in a measure owing to the cold soil, which never got properly

---

[*] Under favourable circumstances two more years—that is, in their third year.

warm. Amongst those which made no growth, but whose bulbs are much increased thereby, I mention *Brownii, Pulchellum* or *Concolor, Monadelphum, Callosum, Maximowiczii, Dalmaticum Superbum* (one bulb in tank), and a few others. I do not think I used the earth closet soil properly. I ought to have put it below for the Lilies to root into when they were in full growth instead of immediately round the bulb. One bulb of *Szovitzianum* had a quantity put some distance beneath it, and its growth was splendid, more than 3 feet high from the bulb to the top of the flowers, and that in spite of its being stripped three parts of the way of its leaves by the frost in May.

"This example showed me that earth closet soil may be a capital thing for Lilies if properly applied, as when I came down in April I really thought the growth was done for, it looked so wretched : after that, the Lily rooted into this soil, started afresh, and bloomed splendidly.

"You also ask about swamp American Lilies in the tank. *Humboldtii* (I believe it wants more warmth) did not appear, nor did one *Superbum,* but another did first-rate, and seems well suited. I expect these will do well in future, but the American kinds need thorough establishing."—*Frank Miles, Bingham, Notts., Nov.* 1877.

"I am fond of Lilies, but unfortunately for me, my only plant of *Wallichianum* is going to bloom at my home at Bingham, in Nottinghamshire, while I am in Cardigan ; therefore, I fear I shall not see it. Dr. Moore, of Glasnevin, told me that he was the first to grow this Lily, but, somehow, he has never succeeded since ; doubtless, it requires greenhouse treatment, and does not begin to grow till many months after other Lilies. My bulb showed no signs of growth till the middle of July, and I began to think it never would, but it then began to grow vigorously, and was in first-rate condition when I last saw it. My plants of *Auratum* have been very fine this year, and I will give my experience of imported bulbs. Last January I bought fifty *Auratum,* and planted them in a bed of loam, sand, and leaf-mould, on the north side of a Yew fence, so that the sun did not scorch the soil in hot weather ; they soon began to develope, and all made strong growth during the spring, but, being small bulbs, I did not expect them to make much progress the first year. Some grew 3 feet high, some 4 feet or more, and bore from four to seven flowers, of which I removed all but two, in order to prevent the bulb from being weakened, by carrying too many flowers the first season. Nearly every Lily was different, some being striped with magenta, some with hardly any spots, and some with many spots ; one of them was a very fine variety, with a deep magenta stripe running almost into the centre of the flower ; this magenta, however, turned brown after the first day ; but I have never seen, and never expect to see, an *Auratum* Lily banded with pure scarlet, as described in nurserymens' catalogues[*]. The so-called *L. Rubro-Vittatum,* sold at Messrs. Stevens', were not particularly highly-marked varieties of *Auratum.* I have had one *Auratum* stem about 9 feet high,

* We have, for several years in succession, flowered the true *Auratun Rubro-Vittatum,* here alluded to by Mr. Miles, for description of which, refer to Baker's Synopsis, later on.

E

and one with seventeen flowers on it, and I have had one gigantic flower
10½ inches across the bloom, and measuring across the fully expanded
petals, from tip to tip, 16 inches. With me, the general height of
Auratum this year, varied from 6 to 9 feet and upwards. As to the
number of flowers on a single stem, we have had some this year (1877) with
thirty seven ; last year, one with a fasciated stem bore seventy eight. I do
not consider this year that they have progressed so well with me as when the
sun has been less powerful. I have just succeeded in flowering *Neilgherrense* out of doors, the first, I believe, that has flowered in this county ;
it has now gone off after being out about a week ; the stem was 4 foot 7
inches high, and the flower measured about 7 inches across. Cultivators
sometimes tell me, that they plant Lilies from 18 inches to 22 inches
deep, but in this cold county the sun's influence is not strong enough, at
that depth, to bring up the young growths in spring. I believe 8 inches
is the proper depth for the finest bulbs, and then only with light soil
above ; I know that the bulbs are not injured by frost, and I do not think
they are by wet, because I have a small bulb about 10 inches deep in
ground that was quite boggy, which yielded seventeen fine flowers this
summer, and was much earlier in its growth (though not in its flowering)
than any of the Lilies planted in drier soils. I always put sand round the
bulb ; it prevents the snails and slugs working into the scales. Since
writing the above at Cardigan, I have returned to my garden. I have
lately been lifting my plants of *Auratum*, and planting them in the
open border ; they turned out fine healthy bulbs, and are growing well ;
*some had flowered without making a single root below the bulb, the
flowers and stalks being entirely supported by the roots from the stems
above the bulb.* The roots that are now forming under the bulb are
manifestly increasing and feeding it, and then the bulb throws up a stem,
which is in turn, in a great measure, supported by its roots above the
bulb. This is a good argument for tolerably deep planting. *Speciosum* and *Auratum* should never be grown in pots with no soil above
the bulb. Some Lilies seem to make no root-growth above the bulb ;
Croceum does not, nor do the *Martagon* Lilies ; such, should evidently
not be planted deeper than from 3 inches to 4 inches. Everybody who
loves hardy flowers, should have the white *Martagon*, on account of its
loveliness in form and colour ; next to it I should place *Martagon Dalmaticum* var. *Catanii*, a blackish purple Lily, to my mind a royal colour.
My white *Martagon* grows freely in turfy loam, and seeds freely, and I
have no doubt that all the *Martagons* will do well in that soil. *Colchicum*, otherwise known as *Szovitzianum*, is a grand Lily for the
herbaceous border, delicate in scent, and very distinct in every way ; it
grows about 4 feet high, and has large citron-coloured flowers spotted
with black. There is also a perfectly pure yellow variety without spots,
Monadelphum. *L. Chalcedonicum* (The Turk's Cap), is known to all,
but few people have seen the large variety known as *Chalcedonicum
Majus*. Lilies of the *Chalcedonicum* variety grow superbly in the sandy
soil of Glasnevin, and you could find many stems with a corona of six or
seven flowers, but this form of *Majus* eclipses them all ; there was
only one flower on a strong stem, but that flower was almost as

big as a bloom of *Szovitzianum*, very much marked and ribbed with deeper red : this will be a grand form for our gardens. I was well pleased with my journey to Ireland, for there I saw the true *Longiflorum Eximium* in Dr. Moore's nursery in the Botanic Gardens. This Lily is as completely distinct from *Longiflorum*, as *Auratum* is from *Speciosum*, though I do not suppose the plant I saw had attained its full proportions. I think the tube must have been some 9½ inches in length, and creamy white in colour. It was quite different from the Lily I received last year, from the New Plant and Bulb Company, as *Eximium*, and whether it was quite the same as Mr. Wilson's variety, which is completely distinct from *Longiflorum*, I cannot determine until I see them side by side. Mr. Wilson's variety, judging by a photograph, is very much longer in its tube than the normal form, much more reflexed, and larger in all its parts. The one at Glasnevin* seemed to me longer still than *Longiflorum Wilsonii*. While on the subject of white Lilies, I have this year bloomed *Auratum* var. *Virginale*, a pure white, with no spots, but of a pale lemon colour, very distinct ; but the whitest of all Lilies, and whiter even than the white Ramanas Rose (*Rosa Rugosa alba*), is the flower of the variegated *L. Candidum*. This variety and *Candidum Speciosum* bloom with me at least a week later than the normal type, though the botanical authorities declare *Speciosum* to be the earlier form of *Candidum*, it blooms later with me. I believe we may set down *Candidum* var., *with golden foliage*, as the whitest of all hardy plants ; the foliage, also, is very ornamental in winter and spring. A grand variety for the open border is *Brownii* ; it is a very large form of *Longiflorum*, with rich chocolate exterior, and such stamens ; the petals are reflexed to such an extent, that one might imagine the flower had been invented by some idealist. It will succeed perfectly in the open border, planted in turfy loam. I have not yet seen *Longiflorum* succeed untouched in a cold climate ; it always comes up too soon, and gets caught by March winds, but, I firmly believe, *Brownii* does not suffer from the diseases common to *Longiflorum*. I have never succeeded well with *Speciosum* and its varieties, though I have bought, from time to time, most of the highly described varieties ; with me, they were in no way different from the ordinary forms. I have still a liking for the variety known as *Purpuratum*, but I have never seen such magnificently coloured plants of *Speciosum*, as those grown by the famous Abyssinian traveller, Mr. Mansfield Parkyns, at Woodborough, in this cold county of Notts. .His soil is good, rich, unctuous, clayey loam, rather red in colour. (How is it that the bulbs grown in Holland are so much finer than those grown in England ?) *L. Concolor* flowered well in the open border, and I believe it will become a great favourite where the smaller and more delicate herbaceous plants are appreciated. Whoever grows *Omphalodes Luciliæ* ought to grow *L. Concolor*. The latter has stems 18 inches high, and exquisite little red flowers spotted with deeper red, opening like falling stars, and afterwards becoming reflexed.

* Very probably the form known under the name of *Madame von Siebold*, which possesses a larger tube than any other at present known variety, is the one grown at Glasnevin.

Tigrinum Splendens is of course the future *Tiger* Lily of our gardens. I saw a splendid specimen at Woodborough, and expect to learn much from that garden in the future. The double *Tiger* Lily is a grand plant when properly grown, and I think well of the form called *Tigrinum Erectum*; the flowers being set at right angles with the stem, appear very showy. I was much gratified by the sight of a glorious plant of *Giganteum*, with fan-tail stem, growing in Mr. Morgan's garden at Cardigan. This plant is in strong loam, and is always left to itself, young bulbs taking the place of the exhausted growths. It was growing in the full sun, in front of a greenhouse; and the *Belladonna* Lilies later in the year were a perfect picture; but mine are quite a failure; I believe our climate at Bingham, is too cold for these *Amaryllids* and for *Giganteum*, though I mean to give both a fair trial. I have planted some bulbs of *Auratum* in silt brought down by a neighbouring stream, to see how that will suit them. For these bulbs I removed nearly a ton of soil from my garden, and in its place introduced an equal quantity of this silt. I believe the *Californian* Lilies would grow vigorously in this soil, and I mean to try the *Washington* Lilies in it. I saw some fine spikes of these Lilies at Glasnevin, but the bloom was past its best. Again, let me advise all cultivators to grow in turfy loam, *L. Excelsum*, for the backs of herbaceous borders, and not to be content till they are 7 feet high. Other Lilies for the herbaceous border are *Auratum, Tigrinum, Splendens, Candidum, Umbellatum, Incomparable,* and *Brownii.*"—*Frank Miles, The Garden,* February 3rd, 1877.

"I live upon solid chalk rag, with a 3 feet deep super-soil of sticky grey clay, which is like putty in winter, and baked as hard as a brick in summer. I am perpetually being burnt or frozen up; and yet the white Lily (*L. Candidum*) makes a gorgeous show, unless we have some late spring frosts; *L. Testaceum, Martagon, White Martagon,* and *Tigrinum* flourish; *Croceum, Bulbiferum,* and *Pyrenaicum* do fairly well; I have succeeded in getting *Chalcedonicum, Pomponium, Pardalinum, Superbum, Auratum, Dalmaticum,* and *Thunbergianum* to flower; and *Humboldtii* comes up healthy and strong but goes off when about a foot high. I have just been taking out the soil of a narrow bed, nearly 3 feet deep, and filling it with a mixture of peat, leaf-mould, cocoa-refuse, silver sand, and yellow loam, the top spit consisting of old pasture and the ant hills thrown up on the only boggy field we have in the parish, and in this I mean to plant all the rarer kinds I can procure, together with *Amaryllis Formosissima, Vallota Sanguinea, Hedychium, Gardnerianum,* &c., covering all the more delicate sorts with cocoa-refuse during the winter months."—*Rev. Harpur Crewe, Drayton Beauchamp, Tring, Garden, vol.* 8., *p.* 530.

The soil at Colchester, on the hills on which the town stands, is light and very dry—a well in my garden, 40 feet deep, never holds any water. In the valleys the soil is cool and loamy, a river meandering round one half of the town. The rainfall average is among the lowest in England. Consequently, in dry summers, such as in that of 1874, in which no rain fell at Colchester for sixteen weeks, we lose a great many bulbs. In 1871—a rainy season—our bulbs, on the other hand, did remarkably well, flowering very freely and turning up in the autumn fine large roots, the stems studded with numerous smaller offsets. This season again (1875), owing to the copious rains of July, our Lilies have grown well, but the drought that followed in August and September did mischief to the varieties of *Auratum* planted in light dry soils; but those planted in the valleys in cool loam, especially where sheltered by Mulberry trees, and favoured by the heavy dews arising from the low-lying meadows, have flowered remarkably well, and the bulbs have turned up to our complete satisfaction. I may further add, that we have not the great natural advantage which Mr. Wilson possesses, of an abundant supply of peat close at hand; our Lilies are in this respect somewhat at a disadvantage. We grow out-of-doors nearly all the kinds in cultivation, both recently-imported and home-grown bulbs, and having watched their behaviour during dry and wet, hot and cold, summers, my observations may perhaps be thought worthy of record. I may further add, that in our light soil on the hills of Colchester, we have no fear of spring frosts hurting *L. Longiflorum, Auratum,* or *Speciosum,* the air being too dry; but in the valleys it is another matter altogether. The more I see of this beautiful tribe the more I am convinced that Lilies require, so far as their roots are concerned, a cool bottom, abundant moisture, and, for most kinds, a free drainage; for instance, the slope of a hill facing south-east or south-west, with water from above percolating through the sub-soil, so as always to afford a supply, yet without stagnation, would be an admirable site. The formation of the tall erect Lily stem, having its flower buds concealed at the top, suggests the idea that it is naturally destined to find its way upwards among low-growing herbage and shrubs into the full light of day, to mature in sunshine its flowers and seed pods. Such, at any rate, is the account given us by our Indian correspondent of the beautiful and stately *L. Wallichianum,* whose noble large white flowers may be noticed miles away from the opposite bank of a deep Himalayan valley, growing some 10 or 12 feet in height, yet only just peering out above the surrounding brushwood and jungle."

I have noticed, more especially in the *Martagon* section, and among the North American forms, but in a less degree in many other Lilies, that fresh roots are found very soon after the flowering time; there is a brief period of rest coincident with the drying up of the foliage, and the growth recommences with the autumnal rains. If in October, a bulb of *Puberulum* or *Speciosum* is lifted, fresh healthy roots are found actively at work, if one may judge from their enlarged bulbous extremities, thickly fringed with mycelioid processes; further, if a few roots be dried, and then exposed

to moisture, young roots will be soon emitted. Now, what does this point out? The bulb is not at rest, as we might suppose, but, in autumn and winter, growth is going on, and preparation is being actively made for next year's flowering. I draw from this a conclusion of some importance to Lily cultivators, viz., that Lilies, to ensure good growth, should be planted out in their places as soon after flowering as possible, so that none of the young roots may be disturbed, and fair time may be given them to prepare for next year. In purchasing Lilies I should like to give my orders very early in the season, and I should request that none of the roots be cut off the bulbs, but that they should be sent to me freshly taken up and packed in some moist material. Indeed, some of the Dutch growers recognise this, for, though they expose their roots intended for sale to the action of the sun and air, to dry the bulbs and give them a colour (according to the custom of the trade), yet *they require that the bulbs they purchase shall be supplied to them quite fresh, and with the roots uncut*; of course with imported bulbs this cannot be; but it is manifest that a bulb planted (say in October), rooting and drawing its supplies of nourishment, must be in a far better condition to support active growth in early spring, and develope a fine head of flowers, than one planted in January or February, kept dry all the winter, having hardly time given to it to emit a few roots before the stem shoots up and development progresses at a rapid rate. All Lilies ought to be in their places, where they are to remain, by the end of October. Another question arises out of these remarks. Do Lily bulbs make fresh growth every year, the old growth decaying more or less, as does that of the Crocus? I believe they do, for the following reasons :—
1. When the stems shoot up from the centre of a bulb, it opens up and widely separates the old scales, and much enlarges the size of the bulb. I have been surprised to find bulbs, under such circumstances, of the size of a medium orange when in flower, though when planted they were only as large as a five-shilling piece. 2. Fresh growth, recognised by its white, fresh, firm appearance (light not yet having coloured it), takes place inside the bulb, pushing out the old discolored scales. In kinds such as *Longiflorum, Speciosum, Auratum,* and *Martagon,* where the color of scales is well marked, I have seen many bulbs, freshly dug up, entirely composed of new growth, a few only of the old scales remaining. 3. When Lilies degenerate, as they often do in pot culture, they get smaller and smaller every year : the tints of their flowers also degenerate. Now, in this case, is it not because the new growth under unfavourable circumstances become smaller and smaller each year, till, at length, it ceases altogether, and the bulb dies? The same thing oftens happens to many bulbs grown out of doors in unfavourable conditions; they get weaker and weaker every year till they die, unless moved to a more suitable spot. I should much like to watch some Lily bulbs grown in a glass pot,

planted against the side, so that all the processes of growth might be watched. 4. Amongst the North American forms with rhizomatous bulbs, such as *Superbum, Puberulum,* &c., fresh growths are emitted every year, in the form of bulbs or stolons; from these the flower stem shoots upwards in the following year, so that each year there is a succession of new growth. From these considerations, it follows that well chosen bulbs, planted early, must be in the most favourable condition to flower freely, and make good growth the succeeding year, producing a fine display of highly-coloured blooms. Hence the following rules:—1. Plant deeply, say 6 to 8 inches, so that the roots may easily get into a moist sub-soil, and be sheltered from the scorching, drying influence of the sun's rays. 2. Plant early in the autumn, so that the roots may be at work all the winter. 3. Choose fresh undried bulbs, with, if possible, new white central growth, whose roots have not been cut off nor dried. 4. Plant in a cool shady border not exhausted by roots of trees, where the roots may always obtain moisture, and yet not be saturated; where the surface of the ground is shaded from the sun's rays, and yet where the buds and leaves may enjoy sunshine to perfect the flowers; such, for instance, as a sloping bank, with water percolating its subsoil, with a south-eastern or south-western aspect in our southern counties, and with a more southern aspect as we go farther north. Carpet the soil with low-growing foliage or flowering plants, such as Rhododendrons, Saxifrages, Sedums, Golden-leaved Chickweed, Dwarf Pennyroyal, Veronica repens, &c.: "Sedum glaucum (grey), S. Lydium (green), S. acre elegans (pale yellow), Saxifraga Rosularis, (silvery white), S. hirta (green), Antennaria tomentosum (white), Herniaria glabra (green)," are all given in *Garden, vol.* 15, *p.* 48, as "surface rooters, looking equally well in winter and in summer, in order of merit as named, for carpeting bulb beds" or, in the absence of anything better, use Mignonette or Chickweed rather than allow full exposure to the sun's scorching influence. 5. During the growing season, *i.e.*, from the time that the stem pushes above ground to the time when the flowers begin to open, let an abundant supply of moisture be provided. In India, they have their rainy season, during which *L. Wallichianum* shoots up aloft; in Japan, they have abundant rains during May and June for six to eight weeks; this, coinciding with my own experience, makes me confident that, drainage being provided, we can hardly give too much water at that season. 6. Where Lilies are grown in pots, it will be found advantageous to protect the upper roots by placing masses of fibrous peat and loam on the surface of the pot. 7. If pots are used, and they can hardly be avoided for some kinds (and that Lilies can be well grown in pots, the practice of Mr. Wilson amply proves), then large pots must be used to provide abundant room for root action—pots with straight sides and broad bases are, for this reason, better than those with narrow bases—

and abundant moisture must be provided daily during the period of growth. 8. The Japanese plant their bulbs sideways, to prevent the wet lodging between the scales and rotting the bulbs. They use also a top dressing of night soil during the winter months; but from what I learn, they do not produce such fine blooms as we do in Europe. 9. If from circumstances, bulbs have to be planted after Christmas: then to avoid sunscorching, and to afford the best chance for making new growth, plant in a moist place, where the foliage will be shaded during the greater part of the day, and do not let the plants flower—or at most, bear only one flower-bud—this will give the best chance for healthy growth, and bloom in the year succeeding. *Alexander Wallace, Colchester.*

"The advice given by Dr. Wallace as to the use of large pots requires some qualification. For example, if a small bulb be placed in the mass of soil contained in a large pot, the chances are that much of the soil will become sour before its rootlets reach the sides or bottom of the pot, and then the decay of the root-fibres is the result. Mr. G. F. Wilson suggests that after having well drained the pot, it should be filled with peat and fibrous loam in layers, since the Lily roots feed on the Loam greedily, which in its turn is kept sweet and fresh by the antiseptic property of the intervening layers of peat. Other growers use half-bushel pots, about one-third of their depth being filled with an inverted pot and abundance of crocks, and eight or ten good bulbs of *Humboldtii, Neilgherrense,* or other Lilies are then planted in a fresh, porous compost of fibrous loam, leaf-mould, peat, and sand, the result being that the body of soil, although large, is soon filled by healthy roots, and is prevented from becoming soddened by the ample drainage provided. The cool bottom, so essential to the well-being of all Lilies, is provided by placing the pots on moist soil mulched with cocoa-nut fibre or spent tan. A more copious supply of water is requisite in the case of pots drained as above described, but it is far more easy to give plants water or liquid manure than to remedy any injurious influence exerted by stagnant or soddened compost. It may be safely said that no Lily bulb blooms twice from the same centre, and although most of the Japan Lilies seem to produce flower-stems from the same bulb (on closer examination we find that the flower-stalks spring from new buds formed within the old bulb every season), they are, in fact, new bulbs formed within the parent one, *but remain attached to the same base,* drawing in part sustenance from the surrounding scales, which are only undeveloped leaves. The common American Lilies, such as *Superbum, Canadense,* and *Philadelphicum,* found growing in low meadows, are perpetuated in quite a different manner. The bulbs are produced on large subterranean stems growing a few inches below the soil. This stem lengthens and produces one or more new bulbs every year, those formed the previous year blooming but once, then commencing to decay, their substance being attracted by the younger growth. In digging up one of these Lilies we sometimes find a string of bulbs of various ages all attached to the creeping stem, but only the last-formed or youngest will bloom after transplanting. Other species of bulbs and tubers increase in a different manner, each having peculiarities or individual characters of its own, although all obedient to a general and similar law. If we, therefore, only study that portion of the vegetable kingdom which is seen aboveground, one-half is overlooked, for it is not unfrequently the case that the most interesting part is hidden in the earth."—*F. W. Burbidge. Garden, vol.* 9, *p.* 115.

CHAPTER V.

SPECIAL EXAMPLES OF CULTURE.

We now give a few instances of special cultivation of particular Lilies, thinking that they will be interesting to our readers.

LILIUM LONGIFLORUM IN SCOTLAND.

"I planted bulbs of this Lily in a mixed border about the middle of last March, and on the 12th of the present month (August) they produced their first flowers, all of which are now beautifully expanded, each measuring fully 6 inches long. They are trumpet-shaped, very pure white, and are deliciously fragrant. This, I think, is a wonderful production, and when it can grow here to such perfection it may, I think, with safety be grown in any garden in Scotland."—*W. Laurie, Alva. Garden, vol.* 8, *p.* 188.

"We observe specimens of *L. Longiflorum* still (Oct. 16, 1875) in flower in Covent Garden. It is important to know that it is possible to secure this handsome and useful plant so long in perfection."—*Garden, vol.* 8, *p.* 320.

"The bulbs of *L. Longiflorum* come up with me in a cool house. As soon as the flower buds show, early in spring, I cut the stems down to the surface of the earth ; four or five shoots will then come up and bloom with far finer flowers in September and October than would otherwise be the case, and continue in perfection very much longer. I find in turning them out of the pot in December as many bulbs as shoots, all of the same size. I suspect this is the case with *Humboldtii*, but that the large bulb annually decays, I know from personal observation, is not the case."—*Amateur, Garden, vol.* 13, *p.* 160.

L. Wallichianum.—"This rare and handsome Indian Lily flowered in the garden of the Rev. A. Rawson, of Bromley Common. Its flowers, which are long-tubed, measure nearly 8 inches across, the petals being of a creamy yellow colour, and curiously revolute. The leaves measure from 8 to 10 inches in length, and about half an inch in breadth. This species bears some resemblance to *L. Philippinense* in its habit of growth and narrow foliage, but is quite distinct from all other Lilies" (*see* p. 21).—*Garden, vol.* 8, *p.* 320.

L. Auratum—"I do not know if it is anything now, but I get some of my best bulbs from cuttings. The small shoots which frequently come up round the bulb, if cut off a little below the surface of the earth, readily strike and form a bulb, and as more shoots come up I continue the operation during the summer. I have got some of these to bloom the following year."—*Amateur. Garden, vol.* 13, *p.* 160.

" As an instance of finely flowered *L. Auratum* there was, in the autumn of 1875, in the garden of Mr. G. A. Partridge, of Westgate-Street, Bury St. Edmunds, a plant of this Lily which bore no fewer than fifty spikes, and was considered to be the finest specimen of this plant that had been produced in that part of the country."—*Garden, vol.* 8, *p.* 220.

Lilium Giganteum.—" The soil of my garden, like that of the Rise of East Sheen, continued into Richmond Park, is a gravel of a good binding sort, excellent for the walks. It rests upon London clay. The depth of the gravel with me is from 10 to 16 feet, and affords good drainage to the beds ; but, for any special growth, loam and bog earth must be added. The gravel was removed in 1860 to a depth of 8 or 10 feet, and many loads of bog earth, with some loam and a little lime, were put in to receive the Rhododendrons and Azaleas, in the round Rhododendron bed on the lawn. In May, 1872, I planted three bulbs of *L. Giganteum* in three of the interspaces of the Rhododendron bushes, which spaces had the best aspect in regard to sunshine.

" Silver sand, as usual, was put about each bulb, set at the depth of 6 inches, in the above soil, with the addition of old leaf-mould, which had been rotted with occasional drenchings of diluted liquid manure. There was a feeble sign of growth in the autumn of 1872,[*] and the bulbs were protected through the winter of 1872 and 1873 by a slight covering of dried Fern. In May, 1873, three of the leaves began to rise, and diverge from each bulb. They were carefully protected from occasional frosts, but no flower stem was developed this summer. After similar winter and spring treatment (as against frosty nights in May), a grander spread of the fine broad, bright, glossy, leaves appeared, and in June, 1874, I occasionally gave the Lilies diluted liquid manure ; from one only of the three did the magnificent columnar flower stem, 2 inches thick, spring up to the height of 6½ feet, which became crowned with nine flower buds, the first of which opened on the 2nd of July, lasting to the 9th, and the others in succession, with a like period of bloom. A broad band of violet contrasted with the enamelled whiteness of each gracefully recurved petal ; and as one sauntered over the lawn in the vicinity of the large clustered flowers, their delicate perfume, diffused through the summer air added to the pleasure. They formed seed pods 3 inches long by 1½ in diameter."—*Professor Owen, Garden, vol.* 7, *p.* 191.

L. Giganteum.—" My experience of the hardiness of this stately Lily for out-door cultivation quite confirms that of Professor Owen. I purchased a small root of it four years ago and kept it for two years in a cold frame, where it produced small healthy foliage for two successive years, but showed no indication of flowering, nor did it increase much in size. In the autumn of 1872, I planted it out in a bed devoted to American

---

[*] This was the result of planting in May, and a whole year was lost ; if the bulbs had been planted in October the growth would have been as described in 1873.

plants, in which the soil consisted mostly of peat, with a slight admixture of loam and leaf-mould. In the summer it made a vigorous growth of foliage, which was nearly all cut down in the succeeding winter. Last spring a rich display of foliage was produced from three or four crowns, one of which threw up a strong flowering stem, nearly 3 inches in diameter at the base, 7 feet high, and bearing thirteen flowers all of which ripened seed.

" During the last year it seems to have quite doubled in size, and now forms a mass of seven or eight crowns, which are commencing to throw up foliage. The plant seems perfectly hardy under a most trying winter. My garden is 600 feet above the sea level, and during the last four months we have had a continual alternation of severe frosts and sudden thaws. The clump of L. Giganteum has had no artificial protection save a thin sprinkling of cocoanut fibre, but the partial shelter afforded by the Andromedas, amongst which my Lilies have been planted, has, I doubt not, been effective in sheltering them from excessive summer heats and winter frosts. Under such circumstances I believe the whole of the Lilies would be perfectly hardy in the open-air, and an undergrowth of small ornamental evergreens (Kalmias, Andromedas, Sedums, Heaths, and small Rhododendrons) adds much to the effect of a bed of Lilies which would otherwise be unsightly except during a few weeks from June to August. In a mixture of rich peat and leaf-mould, strengthened with a little loam, nothing can exceed the vigour with which nearly all the known species of Lily thrive with me in the open-air, and the increase in the size of the bulbs is much more rapid than under pot culture. I flowered last year upwards of twenty species in the same bed as that containing *Giganteum*; *Pardalinum*, which was a single small bulb two and a half years ago, produced four stems between 7 and 8 feet high, which, collectively, bore eighty-seven blossoms ; and *Szovitzianum* twenty-eight flowers on a single stem. *Umbellatum*, and many other species were equally luxuriant, the only species that did not succeed with me in the open-air were *Auratum* and varieties of *Speciosum*, but this I think was due to bad condition of the bulbs."—*George Maw, Benthall Hall, Broseley, Garden, vol. 7, p. 218.*

"I have now in flower a specimen of L. *Giganteum*. The flower stem is 9 feet 1 inch in height, and 6 inches in circumference at 2 feet from the ground; it bears eleven flowers, nine of which are fully developed at the time I am writing, and the others just unfolding. Each flower is about 8 inches in length. The effect of this plant is extremely fine, and situate, as it is, in a bed of Rhododendrons, the flat heads of these rather add than otherwise to its stately and majestic appearance. After flowering, the bulbs die ; but perpetuate themselves by throwing up each one or more offsets. The one in flower here, is an offset from one which flowered in a greenhouse in 1872, and, in the autumn of that year, was planted out of doors in the situation it now occupies. In 1873, it increased considerably in size, and made two more offsets ; in 1874, three more were made, and the others much increased in size, so that, when growth commenced this season, there were six bulbs of different ages, the oldest of which (three years), is now in flower as above described. There will be, I hope, two bulbs sufficiently strong to flower next year, and of course, others following

for succeeding years. Do the bulbs ever flower in less than three years ?*"
—*J. Uphill, Moreton, Dorchester, Garden, vol.* 8, *p.* 20.

L. Giganteum.—"We have grown this Lily at Thursley, in Surrey, for several years, in ordinary garden soil, keeping it in a cold pit from the frost during the severe winter months, and have considered those that did not exceed 6 or 7 feet in height as failures. Our finest last year measured 9 feet 8 inches, from the top of the pot, and bore fifteen blooms all perfect. Our bulbs came originally from Dangstein, where I believe they grow most years, wholly in open ground. The plant I understand is a native of Nepaul."—*See Garden, vol.* 7, *p.* 256.

L. Giganteum, see Gard. Chron., March, 1877, *p.* 277.—"A friend lately brought me from his garden in Norfolk, a bulb of *L. Giganteum,* and told me how the Lily was grown there. As the treatment is rather different from what I have tried and heard of and seems to be thoroughly successful, I requested a note of it, this may, I think, be useful to some of your readers. The bulbs were planted by the side of a rich vine border, which had *a heavy dressing of horse and cow manure.* These have grown strongly, have flowered, and seeded, while other bulbs planted near, but not in such rank stuff, do not make large bulbs, and have not flowered."
—*G. F. Wilson, Heatherbank, Weybridge Heath.*

CHAPTER VI.

ON HYBRIDISATION OF LILIES.

As on this important point depends the introduction of new forms, we quote the published experience of some of the most successful hybridisers.

"Ten or twelve years ago I began a series of experiments in hybridising Lilies, and have continued them at intervals up to the present time with results, some of which are worthy of being recorded. My first attempt was to combine the two superb Japanese Lilies, *L. Speciosum* and *Auratum.* The former was used as the female parent. Four or five varieties of it, varying from pure white to deep red, were brought forward in pots under glass; this was necessary because *Speciosum* does not ripen its seed in the open air in the climate of New England (United States). When the flowers were on the point of opening, the anthers were carefully removed from the expanding buds by means of forceps. As the pollen was entirely unripe, and as pains were taken to leave not a single anther in any of the flowers, self-impregnation was impossible. The pollen of *Auratum* was then applied to the pistils, as soon as they were in a condition to receive it. Impregnation took place in most cases: The seed pods swelled, and promised an ample crop of seed, but the experiment was spoiled by the bad management of the man in charge of the greenhouse, in consequence of which the pods were attacked by

---

* Probably not, they sometimes require five years to perfect a flowering bulb.

mildew. In the next year I repeated the attempt, with the same precautions. This time the seed was successfully ripened. Being sown immediately a portion of it germinated in the following spring, and the rest a year later. In regard to this seed, two points were noticeable, first, it was scanty, the pods, though looking well, being in great part filled with abortive seed or mere chaff, and next, such good seed as there was, differed in appearance from the seed of the same Lily fertilised from the pollen of its own species. The latter is smooth, whereas the hybrid seed was rough and wrinkled. About fifty young seedlings resulted from it, and their appearance was very encouraging, because the stems of nearly all were mottled in a manner characteristic of *Auratum*. Here, then, was a plain indication of the influence of the male parent. The infant bulbs were pricked out into a cold frame, and left there for three or four years, when, having reached the size of a pigeon's egg, they were planted in a bed for blooming. This was in 1869. Towards midsummer one of the young hybrids showed a large flower-bunch, much like that of its male parent *Auratum.* The rest, about 50 in all, showed no buds until some time after, and when the bulbs at length appeared they were precisely like those of the female parent, *Speciosum.* The first bud opened on the 7th of August, and proved a magnificent flower, 9½ inches in diameter, resembling *Auratum* in fragrance and form, and the most brilliant varieties of *Speciosum* in colour. In the following year the flower measured nearly 12 inches from tip to tip of the extended petals, and in England it has since reached 14 inches. It has been exhibited under the name of *Parkmanni.* In this one instance the experiment has been a great success, but of the remaining 50 hybrids not one produced a flower in the least distinguishable from *Speciosum.* The influence of the alien pollen was shown, as before noticed, in the markings of the stem, and also in the diminished power of seed bearing, but this was all. Next year, wishing to see if the male parent would not make his influence appear more distinctly in the second generation, I fertilised several of these fifty hybrids with the pollen of *Auratum*, precisely as their female parent had been fertilised. The crop of seed was extremely scanty, but there was enough to produce eight or ten young bulbs. Of these, when they bloomed, one bore a flower combining the features of both parents, but, though large, it was far inferior to *Parkmanni* in form and colour. The remaining flowers were not distinguishable from those of the pure *Speciosum.* While making these experiments with *Speciosum* and *Auratum* I made similar attempts to produce hybrids of other Lilies. In the spring of 1867 I planted twenty or more strong bulbs of *Superbum* in a favourable spot, and, when they began to bloom, fertilised them with the pollen of *Speciosum, Auratum, Tigrinum, Chalcedonicum, Umbellatum, Thunbergianum, Longiflorum,* and *Tenuifolium.* All the anthers were previously removed before ripening, by slitting the sides of the still unopened bud, and extracting them with forceps. There were no other plants of *Superbum* in the garden or in the neighbourhood, so that in this case, as in the former, fertilisation by the pollen of their own species could not take place. Seed-pods, large and well shaped, were formed in abundance, but when they ripened in October some of them contained nothing but chaff, others had a few imperfect seed, while others gave a fair supply of seed as good as could be desired. It was sown in pans, germinated in due time, and produced several hundred young bulbs, but when these came into bloom not a single flower of them all was in the least distinguishable from the pure *Superbum*. Of eight different male parents not one had impressed his features on his hybrid offspring. Not only in their flowers, but in their leaves, stems, and bulbs, the young plants showed no variation from their maternal parent. In the following year I set some of them apart from the rest, and applied to them, as to their mothers before them, the pollen of several species of Lilies. This time the seeds were extremely scanty, a few, however, were produced, but the plants and flowers that resulted from them, were to all appearance *Superbum*, pure and simple.

"Another subject of experiment was *Umbellatum*, which I fertilised with the pollen of *Auratum*. Seed was produced in abundance, and the young plants began to bloom in the second year. Many of them were not to be distinguished from the pure *Umbellatum*, others showed unmistakeable marks of their hybrid origin in the defective condition of the organs of reproduction, the anthers being abortive or wholly wanting, as were also, in a few cases, even the pistils. In some instances the corolla was deformed, some of the petals being absent, and others small and ill shaped; but while the influence of the alien pollen was shown in these defects, no features of the male parent appeared, either in form, colour, scent, or manner of growth. No Lily seems to offer better prospects to the hybridiser than *Longiflorum*. The species itself is not a good seed bearer in our climate, but one of its varieties, known as *Longiflorum Takesima*, bears seed very freely. This variety is also distinguished by superior vigour of growth, and by the dark markings of its stem; the pure white of the large trumpet-shaped flowers seems peculiarly fitted to receive impressions of colour from an alien parent; I therefore fertilised it with the pollen of a deep variety of *Speciosum*. The operation was performed under glass, and with the greatest care. The seed was abundant, and being *sown immediately it all germinated in the following spring (see* page 12). When the flowers opened, two years after, they showed no sign whatever of the male parent, the pure white was without tint or spot, neither did the foliage and stem show the slightest trace of foreign influence; the plants were in pots. I removed a number of them to the greenhouse, and, having no pollen of *Speciosum* at hand, I fertilized them with that of *Auratum;* several refused to bear seed, while others produced it freely. The young plants resulting from this last experiment bloomed in the spring of 1874. Neither *Speciosum*, their grandfather, nor *Auratum*, their father, had produced any effect whatever on the pure white of their petals; they showed differences of habit among themselves, some being very tall and vigorous and others compact and bushy, with a tendency to bloom in clusters, but these may have been mere seedling variations with which the hybridisation had nothing to do. Yet distinct evidence could be seen of the action of the alien pollen: some of the anthers were small and abortive, and some of the pistils were imperfect, but what was more to the purpose, was the changed colour of many of the former, the white petals had completely resisted the foreign influence, but the yellow anthers had undergone a marked change, about half of them were turned to a chocolate colour, approaching that of the anthers of the male parent, though not so deep. I determined to try the effect of fertilisation in the third generation, and applied the pollen of both *Auratum* and *Speciosum* to ten or twelve of the young hybrids whose organs of reproduction appeared to remain perfect; not one of them would bear seed. In the present summer (1877) I repeated the experiment on a larger scale, and fertilised about fifty flowers, after removing the anthers before they ripened. Nine of these produced seed pods, all of which were small and deformed except two, these two contained, along with the chaff, a few seeds of promising appearance, the remaining seven were full of chaff alone. The reproductive power had been nearly destroyed by hybridisation repeated through three generations. What will result from the few seeds obtained remains to be seen. Some* Lilies refuse to be fertilised by the pollen of certain other Lilies. Thus, I have found that *Speciosum*, so readily fertilised by *Auratum*, will give no seed to the pollen of either *Brownii*, *Longiflorum*, *Canadense*, *Tenuifolium*, or *Umbellatum*, yet the converse does not always hold true for several of these last named species will bear seed when fertilised with the pollen of *Speciosum*.

"A great number of subtle influences may modify the results of experimental hybridisation, yet those described above were so various, and extended over so many years, that the general facts to which they point may, I think, be regarded as assured. An eminent botanist has suggested to me that the tenacity with which Lilies fertilised by Lilies of other species retain their characteristics unchanged may be explained by supposing that the offspring are really no hybrids at all but results of parthenogenesis, that curious phenomenon which sometimes occurs in the lower order of animals, and by which a single impregnation continues to take effect in several successive generations; in other words, that a Lily of which the flower was fertilised in any one year by its own pollen, may bear seed in the next year, without being fertilised again. There are two good reasons for believing that parthenogenesis had nothing to do with the examples in question. In the first place, the Lilies subjected to experiment were young plants that had never bloomed before; in the next place, every species fertilised by me with the pollen of another species showed, with the single exception of *Superbum*, evidence of hybridity which, though slight, was convincing. This evidence consisted in markings of the stem resembling those of the male parent, in a changed colour of anthers, also resembling that of the male parent, and in the frequent occurrence of abortion in both anthers and pistils, with consequent sterility. That the seedlings were really hybrids there can be no

* I should not expect to obtain a favourable result by intermarriage between such dissimilar forms as *Auratum* (*Archelirion*) and *Longiflorum* (*Eulirion*). Success, I think, will more probably be obtained by hybridisation between members of the same group, as, for instance, *Thunbergianum* and *Croceum*, *Candidum* and *Washingtonianum*, *Longiflorum* and *Brownii*. Among the *Martagon* family between *Chalcedonicum* and *Martagon Album* or *Szovitzianum*, between *Excelsum* and *Maximowiczii*, and between *Krameri* and *Speciosum* in the *Archelirion* group.

reasonable doubt, though nobody would have suspected it from casual observation. The conclusion is that Lilies, or at least the principal species of the genus, when hybridised, produce offspring which show the features of the male parent very slightly, or only in exceptional cases. These exceptional cases are, nevertheless, so remarkable at times, that the rarity of their occurrence ought not to discourage the hybridist."—*Francis Parkman, United States, Garden, Jan. 5, 1878.*

On Hybridisation of Lilies, by C. M. Hovey, late President of the Massachusetts Horticultural Society.

"With us Japanese Lilies begin to open their first flowers on the 20th of August, almost to a day, when our weather is warm and dry, and they continue in great beauty until destroyed or defaced by frost, about the 2nd or 3rd of October. We have noticed the bad effects of damp weather on the blooms, and, to prolong them in perfection, have put an awning of cotton cloth over the beds to protect them from heavy dews and the hot sun, which immediately affect the delicate texture and brilliant spotting of the petals.

"*Auratum* does not appear to be very successfully treated, and it is believed that, notwithstanding the tens of thousands of its bulbs that are annually imported overland, and sold in our markets in very fine order, not one in ten can be found alive the second year. There is no doubt it is much less hardy then *Speciosum*, requires a lighter and warmer soil, and a drier situation, and will not readily submit to the rough and ready cutting under which the latter will thrive, *Speciosum* being in fact, just as tough as *Tigrinum*. *Auratum* is difficult to raise from seed. It usually vegetates the first season, but the seedlings appear weak, and gradually disappear; at least, such has been my experience in regard to it. Three years ago, I had four very large plump seed pods on one plant, some of the flowers of which were fertilized with *Speciosum;* and, though only a small portion of the seed was fertile, what did vegetate gradually faded away under the same treatment as *Speciosum*. On the other hand, as I stated previously, *Speciosum*, fertilised with *Auratum*, seemed to furnish seedlings, which received renewed vigour from fertilisation. My first experiments of any extent were commenced in 1846, when I had some two dozen fine plants, in pots, grown for that purpose, many of them being 7 feet high. I then fertilised *Speciosum* with *Superbum, Candidum, Speciosum Album*, and *Chalcedonicum; Punctatum* with *Speciosum, Aurantiacum, Superbum*, and *Chalcedonicum; Album* with *Speciosum*, and some others. Three years is the usual time for the seedlings to bloom ; and as they rarely make their appearance until the second year, it was in 1850 that they produced flowers. By this time (three years) many of the labels, corresponding with the above crosses, had rotted off, and were unfortunately lost. However, suffice it to say, that to us, who watched them with a florist's eye, everyone appeared to differ. In some, the petals were much reflexed ; in others, they were narrow ; some were rosy, others very deeply covered, some of the spots or papillæ were small, others large; some of the spots crimson, others, almost black. The worst among them were better than the old *Speciosum ;* but I found my list too long, and the distinctions too fine, except to those who could—like the true

Tulip fancier—readily distinguish minute differences; and, after cultivating them for three or four years, I selected the best nine, and named them as follows :—Melpomene, Terpsichore, Erato, Urania, Polyhymnia, Clio, Thalia, Calliope, and Euterpe—names under which they were subsequently distributed throughout the United States. I soon ascertained that there was a vast difference in the character of the bulbs; some of them were increased with great difficulty, and when in later years I had hundreds of bulbs of Melpomene, I only had a dozen or so of Euterpe. They would not make offsets, either above or around the old root ; but, from want of time, I did not find the opportunity of ascertaining and recording which crosses were affected in this way. I continued my experiments in succeeding years, in the way of cross-breeding, but kept no record of them. I only know that some, crossed with *Longiflorum* and others, completely ruined the shape of many of the flowers. Among all my seedlings there is not a pure white, although *Album* was fertilised with *Speciosum*, and, as is generally supposed, the female parent has a prevailing influence on the progeny. There was not even a pink spotted one like *Punctatum*, as one would have supposed there would have been. Some years subsequently, I raised several whites, and one long, large, flower, quite distinct, but it accidentally got thrown out of the pot when in a dormant state. I also raised a very distinct variety, with flowers about half-way in size between those of *Chalcedonicum* and *Speciosum*, with stems more densely clothed with leaves, and the petals blush-white, with pale lilac-rose spots. This I named " Eva." It increased slowly, and is still rare in collections, but it is a beautiful variety. To show how enthusiastic I was about this Lily, I may mention, that in 1871, I had over a pint of seed, and after disposing of a good deal of it, I still have nearly half the quantity. It vegetates when three or four years old. Long ago the late Mr. Groom gave us some account of his seedlings, between *Bulbiferum* (*Elegans, Baker ?*) and *Atrosanguineum*, and when at his nurseries, in 1844, I bought the set, eighteen in number, some of the names of which were Voltaire, Talisman, Rubens, Vulcan, &c. ; at first I grew them in pots, fearing they might not be hardy ; but in this way I lost some of them, and as I gave so much attention to the Japan sorts, they were neglected, and I turned them out into a bed where they flourished well. They grew about a foot high, and produced an umbel, consisting of from three to six flowers, the colours being deep dull blood red, speckled and mottled with purplish crimson. They were, however, too much alike, only lasted in flower a short time, and did not increase rapidly. Are they still in cultivation in England ? As regards improvement, I do not expect much from the yellow and red kinds crossed with each other. If, however, a handsome lemon, or buff, or buff-spotted, could be produced, it would be an acquisition. The red and yellow are strong ; but it is only the clear and delicate white grounds that are desirable. All may be crossed with *Speciosum* and *Auratum*, by which process the size may be increased"—*Garden, vol. 8, p. 2.*

CHAPTER VII.

M. DUCHARTRE ON LILIES.

"The Present State of our Knowledge respecting the *Genus* ' Lily,' and the Geographical Distribution of its species."—*Comptes Rendus* for 1871.

"The Lily (Lilium) includes some of the most remarkable species in the whole vegetable kingdom—species distinguished alike by the nobility and elegance of their port, their beauty, and the size and diversity of colour in their flowers. Amongst them are a few of the oldest denizens of our gardens, whilst the recent efforts of botanical travellers have from time to time secured the introduction of new species, which have been regarded with good reason as possessing special interest. The beauty of their flowers has attracted the attention of horticulturists to these plants for a good many years, but by botanists they have been somewhat neglected. Their botanic nomenclature has gradually become more and more confused, as in the majority of cases, specific names have been conferred upon mere varieties, and these names have been entered in our catalogues, without the slightest notice of their distinctive characteristics, whilst very frequently the same plant has received different names at one and the same time. Lastly, the recognised names of well-defined species have occasionally and without reason been transferred to other species which had previously been themselves described and named.

"The difficulties thence arising can only be removed, by a careful and painstaking study of as large a collection as possible of living and, consequently, of domesticated plants. Our dried collections are for the most part badly supplied with specimens of the genus, and, moreover, dried specimens at the best can afford but very imperfect notions of the configuration and colour of the flowers.

"For some years past my efforts have been directed towards the formation of a collection of this sort, but, from various circumstances, the results attained were not as complete as I should have desired. Such as it was, my collection is now no more. Like others, it came to an end amidst the troubles of war. (Siege of Paris).

"This circumstance has induced me, not, indeed, to attempt a Monograph of the Genus, which would necessitate a greater expenditure of time and more ample materials than I have at command, but to put on record a clear and definite account of the knowledge thus acquired of this lovely and generic group. In the first place, it appears desirable to give a succinct idea of the present state of our knowledge respecting the genus, and of the additions which have been made to it from time to time. And here I must not omit to express my obligations to the excellent memoranda of M. M. Leichtlin, of Baden, who has long studied these beautiful plants with laudable assiduity, and has succeeded in forming a collection, which may be described without fear of contradiction as the finest in existence (1871).

"Within a few years of the close of the last century very little was known of the species peculiar to the south of Europe, the Levant, and the western part of North America. In 1774 Linnæus described nine species, five of which were indigenous to the old continent, viz., *Candidum*, *Bulbiferum*, *Pomponium*, *Chalcedonicum*, *Martagon*; and three were peculiar to North America, viz., *Superbum*, *Philadelphicum*, and *Canadense*; the ninth was common to the southern parts of both continents, *Kamschatkense*. About the same time Gouan named and described the Pyrenean Lily, *Pyrenaicum*. A few years later, in 1786, Chaix distinguished as a separate species the Orange Lily, *Croceum*, found in Dauphigny and on the Alps, which had previously been regarded as a variety of *Bulbiferum*; whilst in America, Walter made known the charming Catesby Lily, *Catesbœi*, found in the swamps of the United States. Towards the close of the eighteenth century a notable addition was made to our knowledge of these plants, by the publication of Thunberg's work upon the flora of Japan, previously treated of by Kæmpfer alone, but which for more than fifty years had supplied science and our European gardens with a goodly number of remarkable plants of all kinds. Thunberg made us acquainted in his memoir with five species, viz., *Cordifolium*, *Speciosum*, *Longiflorum*, *Lancifolium*, *Maculatum*;* the history of which he completed in another work, published in 1811, wherein he described two more new species, *Elegans*,† and *Japonicum*.‡ Two of these same Japanese species are the

---

* Another little known Japanese species, and one which, like the preceding, is not common in European gardens, is that which Thunberg ("Flora," p. 135) originally considered to be *L. Canadense*, but which he referred to his *Maculatum* in 1794. Later still he gave a figure of it in the "Mem. de l'Acad. Impér. des Sciences de St. Petersburgh," iii., p. 204, pl. 5, fig. 1. Judging by this figure and the description which accompanies it, the Spotted Lily is rather more than a foot high, its glabrous stem is rounded, striated or furrowed, unbranched as far as the inflorescence. It bears numerous leaves of moderate or small dimensions, lanceolate, tapering at the base, but still sessile, with several nerves prominent on the under surface. These leaves form a sort of false verticil at the base of the inflorescence. This latter consists of from four to six flowers of moderate size, bell-shaped, with the extremity of the segments slightly rolled back. The colour is indicated as blood-red, marked in the interior of the flower with points and spots of deep purple. Dr. Asa Gray ("Diagnostic Characters of New Spec. of Phænog. Plants, collected in Japan by Ch. Wright," "Mem. of the Amer. Acad.," vi., p. 434), cites this plant, with doubt, as a variety of *L. Superbum* (Linnæus), a determination open to criticism. This Lily is now referred by Mr. Baker (and we think correctly) to the form now known and described, in his Synopsis, as *L. Medeoloides*. The Lily exhibited at the Royal Horticultural Society, June 17, 1874, and figured in *Florist*, Sept., 1874, as *L. Maculatum*, is really *L. Hansoni*.

† The Japanese Lily, which Thunberg called *L. Elegans* ("Mem. de l'Acad. de St. Petersb.," iii., p. 203, pl. 3, fig. 2), and which he at first in his "Flora," p. 135, had called *L. Philadelphicum*, and afterwards, in his memoir of the plants of Japan ("Trans. Linn. Soc.," ii., p. 333), *L. Bulbiferum*, is described as about 18 inches high, with a smooth, simple, rounded stem ; its leaves of moderate size, alternate, and the stem terminated by a large, flesh-coloured, bell-shaped flower, the oblong segments of which are more or less turned back at the extremities. Thunberg compares this species to *L. Bulbiferum*, from which it is distinguished by its simple, smooth stem, neither striated or divided ; by its scattered leaves of a more ovate-oblong form ; and lastly, by the pieces of the perianth, which are oval, and not narrowed into a stalk at their base. The figure which he gives is very indifferent. It has now been made clear that this description and name applies to the subgenus now called *Thunbergianum*, after its introducer Thunberg.

‡ It is not easy to ascertain what is the plant which Thunberg designated in 1783 in

magnificent ornamental plants, *Speciosum* and *Longiflorum*, now often seen in our gardens.

"Thus, the number of species known during the first few years of the present century had almost doubled since Linnæus wrote his last general treatise. The impetus had been given, and from that moment the results became more and more apparent. From Japan, a land which may be regarded as specially favoured in respect of these plants, an English seaman, Captain Kirkpatrick, who touched there in 1804, brought two new species, one of them the beautiful Tiger Lily, *L. Tigrinum Gawl*, which by its hardihood and the brilliancy of its cinnabar-red blooms, spotted over with deep reddish brown, has become a common garden flower; the other, with large white flowers of an agreeable perfume, was subsequently named by M. Planchon, *Odoratum* (or *Odorum*).* But the chief importer of Japanese Lilies was Dr. F. von Siebold, of Wurzberg, who visited Japan between 1823 and 1830, in the capacity of physician to the Dutch embassy, and up to his death, which occurred in 1866, never ceased to collect and to encourage the collection of these plants for introduction into Europe. To him we owe the production, or at any rate the knowledge, of *Callosum*, Sieb., with pretty small red punctuated flowers; of Thunberg's Lily, *L. Thunbergianum*, Roem and Sch., a fine species, of many varieties, with large flowers, sometimes deep red, sometimes apricot-yellow, sometimes orange-red, always more or less spotted (to which I believe, have been assigned as varieties *Fulgens*, Ch. Morr., *Venustum*, Hort. ber.); and *Eximium*, Court., with very large white flowers, like those of *Longiflorum Takesima*, which last is also due to Von Siebold; likewise two elegant plants with single flowers of medium size, variegated yellow, orange, or brownish red, of which (one)—*Partheneion*, Sieb. and W. ("Lis des Vierges")—is only a variety of the other, *Coridion*, Sieb. and W., a poppy-coloured Lily; *Puniceum*, Sieb. and W., which is another form of *Unifolium*, Fisch.; and lastly a fine plant, still rare in Europe, *Alternans*, Sieb., with orange flowers spotted with yellow and streaked with brown.†

his "Flora Japonica," p. 133, under the name of *L. Japonicum*. In the catalogue of his collection, M. Leichtlin indicates by a ? that he is by no means certain of the specific identity of the Lily cultivated by him under this name; in truth the characters by which Thunberg distinguishes his species, are deficient in exactness, while the bad figure which he gives certainly does not dissipate the doubts engendered by his description. It is even in some respects in opposition to his text, for it represents the segments of the perianth as oblong-lanceolate, acutely pointed and acuminate, while in the text they are described as elliptic. On the whole, according to this botanist, *L. Japonicum* is a plant about 2 feet high, with a rounded glabrous stem, bearing a small number of alternate rarely opposite leaves, which are very shortly stalked, lanceolate acuminate, glabrous, pale on the lower surface, which is marked by five prominent nerves. The stem is terminated by a single, whitish, bell-shaped flower, about 3 inches long. This Lily is described as very beautiful by Thunberg, who adds, that *while spontaneous at Miaco and elsewhere*, it is often cultivated by the Japanese as an ornamental plant. From an inspection of Thunberg's dried specimens in the herbarian, at Upsala, Mr. Baker considers this name and description to apply to the plant introduced by me in 1870, under the name of *L. Krameri*.

* This, we believe, is the form re-introduced by us in 1870, as *L. Japonicum Colchesterii*.

† This form, we believe, to be better known as *Thunbergianum Alternans*, now not uncommon.

"Siebold also attempted to introduce into Europe the golden-banded Lily, *Auratum*, Lindley, which, however, was only really acquired in 1860, (by the side of which we may place its varieties *Rubro Vittatum*, *Virginale*, *Pictum*, *Rubro pictum*), and *L. Wittei*, Suring, quite recently received.

"Not long since have been described and figured Leichtlin's Lily, *Leichtlinii*, a large citron-yellow flower spotted with purple, by Dr. Hooker, and Maximowicz's Lily, *Maximowiczii*, by M. Regel, a fine orange-scarlet flower, spotted on the lower portion with purplish black.

"To complete this enumeration of Japanese species, we must mention a very imperfectly-known species named by Asa Grey, *Medeoloides*, from a single specimen in bloom;[*] another called by Dr. Lindley *L. Fortunei* after its importer, the specific identity of which is not very clearly established, (now *L. Tigrinum Fortunei*), lastly, Wilson's Lily, *L. Wilsoni*, Herb., with large orange-red flowers, dotted with dark purple and relieved with bands of gold colour. Perhaps we should add also the nankeen Lily *L. Testaceum*, Lindley, the identity of which is not very clearly established, but which many writers regard as a hybrid.

"The Asiatic continent has supplied numerous additions to the genus. China, which possesses several species common to Japan on the one side, and Corea on the other, has two species peculiar to itself, viz., *Concolor*, Salisb.,[†] with umbellate blooms of a uniform orange-red colour, which although introduced into England in 1806, is still very rare ; and the Chinese Lily, *L. Sinicum*, Lindley, a small species carrying two or three scarlet flowers of medium size, which was introduced into England in 1824.[‡] The noble Brown's Lily, *L. Brownii*, Br., whose vast blooms of

* We consider that *L. Medeoloides* and *Avenaceum* are closely allied forms, and Mons. Duchartre in his observations "Sur le Genre Lis," page 53, seems to agree with us.

† Salisbury gave the name *L. Concolor* to a species said to have been imported from China into England by Greville in 1806. It is still very rare in gardens, although it should be grown more extensively on account of its large flowers, which are about three inches across, and grouped in threes or fours in a terminal umbel. At the base of the inflorescence is a verticil of three or four floral leaves, which are erect, not revolute, and coloured of a fine minium-red colour. The plant is about 18 inches in height, its slender rounded stem is glabrous. In a fine cultivated specimen which I have in my herbarium, the stem bears 10 alternate leaves uniformly distributed throughout its length. These leaves are of an oblong-lanceolate acute form, narrowed at the base, 5 to 7 centimètres long (2—2¼ inches), glabrous, slightly ciliated, paler beneath ; the upper leaves rather wider than the lower ones. The pistil is shorter than the stamens, and the style is of the same length as the ovary. There is a variety with a solitary flower, which Link ("Enum." i. 321) considered as the type of the species. *(Baker).*
We are inclined to consider *Partheneion*, *Concolor*, and *Sinicum*, as merely climatic varieties of the same form.

‡ In 1824 a charming little Lily was introduced from China to the garden of the Horticultural Society of London. The stem of this plant did not exceed 25 to 30 centimètres (8—10 inches) in height, and was terminated by two or three flowers of medium size of a fine scarlet colour. Lindley called this plant *L. Sinicum*, and gave a woodcut of it ("Flow. Gard." ii., 1851-1852 ; "Misc.," p. 115, c. ic., xylog. 193). The plant flowered the same year it was introduced, but it seems to have been soon lost, and it is to Mr. Fortune that we owe its re-introduction. It has, nevertheless, remained very rare in gardens up to this time. The stem of this Lily is downy, almost cottony : its leaves are alternate linear-oblong, covered with a slight down, and the three upper ones are gathered together in a whorl at the base of the inflorescence. The segments of the perianth are revolute, smooth on the inner surface, and slightly downy along their

purest white are tinged with purple on the exterior, is also generally regarded as a Chinese species. Lastly M. E. A. Carriére, who was sent to China by the Jardin des Plantes at Paris, has given us the "Lis faux-tigre," *L. Pseudo Tigrinum*, Carr., which was described and figured by him in 1867.[*]

Our knowledge of the East Indian species does not carry us back beyond the last fifty years. In 1820 Wallich discovered in the Himalayas the beautiful *Giganteum*, Wallich, which, by the size and shape of its huge stem and long petiolated leaves, has a peculiar port, which is reproduced only in the Japanese *Cordifolium*, Thunberg. The same botanist in 1826 discovered another Indian species, with a great number of white blossoms, tinged on the outside with green, which he supposed to be the "Lis à longe fleur" of Japan, but which was named by Roemer and Schultes, in 1829, Wallich's Lily, *L. Wallichianum*. With this species we range *Tubiflora*, R. Wright, another Indian species, with very large flowers of purest white, figured and briefly described by Mr. R. Wight, in the year 1853, in the 5th vol. of *Icones Plantarum Indiæ Orientalis*. To this species I am inclined to refer as varieties *Neilgherrense* and the *Wallichianum* of the last-named botanist. It was not until 1825 that the Nepaul Lily, *L. Nepalense*, D. Don, was described by David Don, although it had been discovered in 1802 or 1803 by Francis Hamilton or by Buchanan, a large flower of greenish yellow, the throat and tube of bright purple. In 1839 Dr. Royle, in his work on the plants of the Himalayas, added two more species of Lily to those already known in

median furrow. As in the preceding species, the stamens are shorter than the perianth, and longer than the pistil. The obovate ovary is at most as long as the style. In 1857 a description and coloured plate of the same Lily were given in the "Flore des Serres" (second series, vol. ii., p. 19, pl. 1206), but as M. Planchon, the author of the description just cited, remarks, there were some slight differences between the specimen there figured and the type characterised by Lindley. (*Duchartre*).

[*] *L. Pseudo-Tigrinum* is stated by M. Carrière to have been sent from China to the Jardin des Plantes, Paris ("Rev. Hort.," Nov. 1, 1867, 410—412). Mr. Max Leichtlin, however, in a letter, stated that it was a native of the Liu-Kiu-Islands, which are to the south of Japan, between 24° and 28° of north latitude. *Pseudo-Tigrinum* attains a height of more than 3 feet. It resembles in general aspect, and in many of its characters, *Tigrinum*, a fine species common in Japan, and of which I shall have to speak further on. This species has since been determined to be identical with Maximowicz's Lily.

Pseudo-Tigrinum differs from *Tigrinum* in several particulars ; its rounded stem is clothed, especially in the young state, with white appressed hairs ; the leaves are numerous, alternate, crowded, linear, 10 to 12 centimètres (4 inches) long, 6 milli-mètres to 12 [†]centimètres (½ inch to over [†]4 inches) wide, narrowed to a point almost immediately above the base, channelled on the upper surface, which is glossy, and with the mid-rib very prominent on the glabrous lower surface. Its flowers, at first obliquely ascending, become afterwards horizontal, somewhat distant one from the other ; they are of a fine red colour, marked internally with deep brown points and spots, and in the centre are provided with rather prominent tubercles. The segments of the perianth are widely spreading and revolute. The style is red, and greatly exceeds the stamens in length, and is terminated by a thick stigma with three unequal lobes. M. Carriére says this species may be easily distinguished from the nearly allied *Tigrinum* by its rounded stem, which is not brown but green, and slightly mottled. It produces no bulbils in the axils of its leaves, and these latter have only a single rib, while each leaf of the Tiger Lily has from five to seven. The plant is very hardy ; it has only recently been well known. (*Baker*).

    † Surely these are misprints for 12 millimètres and 1 inch.

India : one a pretty plant with rose-coloured flowers, treated by him as a Fritillary, under the name of "Thomson's Fritillary," has since been named by Dr. Lindley (in 1845) as Thomson's Lily, *L. Thomsonianum* ;* the other, distinguished by its linear-lanceolate leaves, is *L. Polyphyllum*, Royle, which bears two or three white flowers of medium size.

To Klotysch we are indebted for descriptions of two Indian species of Lily, discovered in the Himalayas by D. Hofmeister, during the visit of Prince Waldemar of Prussia to that part of India. These are the Triple-headed Lily, *L. Triceps*, Klo.,† a name indicating the separation of the stalk into three short thick branches, with a single white pendulous flower ; and the dwarf Lily, *L. Nanum*, Klo., a low plant, also with white pendulous flowers of small size.

More recent additions to the Indian species of Lily are not wanting in the Neilgherry Lily, *L. Neilgherricum*, Ch. Lem., which would seem to have been discovered by the collector Thomas Lobb, but described and figured by M. Chas. Lemaire, in 1863, in *L'Illustration Horticole*.

"To this list I would add *L. Punctatum*,‡ Jacquem, some dried specimens of which are in the *hortus siccus* of the Jardin des Plantes at Paris, probably having been procured by Jacquement from the Himalayas. They are accompanied by a note stating that the flowers of this undescribed species are of a livid yellow, dotted with vinous purple, and possess an agreeable odour.

"The western and central parts of Asia have been explored by Russian botanists, who have brought from thence several fine species. The first-named region has supplied three species with punctuated yellow blooms in the form of those of the white *L. Monadelphicum*,§ Marsh and Bieb., the specific name of which indicates its distinctive character, and to which M. Koch adds, as a simple advanced form of the species, *L. Loddigesianum*, Roem. and Sch., which reappears with a recurvated perianth in Szovit's Lily, *L. Szovitzianum*, Fisch., known in our gardens under the name of *Colchicum*, with a perianth greenish at first, and afterwards of an ochreous colour, small and strongly reflexed, as in *L. Ponticum*, Koch. The central and more northerly parts of Asia supply a charming group of species with small blooms of a lively poppy red—the Slender-leaved Lily, *L. Tenuifolium*, Fisch., a species found all over Southern Siberia ; the Graceful Lily, *L. Pulchellum*, Fisch., with a short stalk and single red punctuated flower ; the "Lis Mignon," *L. Pumilum*,|| Roed., of Daouria, closely resembling the slender-leaved species, but with larger and more rigid leaves, without the nectariferous dust ; lastly, Busch's Lily, *L. Buschianum*,¶ Lodd., upright punctuated flowers. To this list must be

---

* Since then another similar form *L. Hookeri*, has been introduced.

† *L. Triceps* is now referred by Mr. Baker to *L. Oxypetalum*, and *L. Nanum* is considered by him to be Fritillaria Gardneriana.

‡ This Lily is evidently closely allied to *Polyphyllum*, and is referred by Mr. Baker accordingly. *See* Synopsis.

§ There seems confusion here. *Szovitzianum* or *Colchicum* is the very beautiful and graceful canary coloured richly punctuated Lily, *Monadelphum* is the unspotted form of the same Lily.

|| Referred now to *Tenuifolium*.

¶ *Buschianum* must now be considered a form only of *Pulchellum*.

appended *L. Spectabile,** Fisch., found in South Siberia, and common as a garden flower, which in a cultivated state produces magnificent clusters of flowers of a fine minium red, intermingled with orange; also, " Lis Avenacé," *L. Avenaceum,†* Fisch., found in Kamschatka, Mantchouria, the Kurile Islands, and Japan, with single blooms of medium size, of a poppy red or orange, lightly reflexed and but little spotted.   Europe herself has furnished several new species to the list in the course of the present century.   Sixty years ago, Bernhardi made known the Carniolian Lily, *L. Carniolicum,* found in Carniolia and Istria, and a close neighbour of *Pomponium,* with pendulous red and tawny-coloured flowers, with prominent lineations of a reddish brown.   In 1842 Ebel found the "Lis grêle," *L. Gracile,‡* Eb., in Montenegro, but saw it in fruit only; lastly, in 1844, M. Grisebach discovered the Albanian Lily, *L. Albanicum* (the name of which indicates the habitat), which is closely connected with the Pyrenean Lily, with a single recurved, pendulous yellow flower; and more recently, through M. Max Leichtlin, the blood red *Martagon Dalmaticum* has been added to our list.

Regarding the species hitherto discovered from a geograpical point of view, we may divide North America into two vast regions separated by the chain of the Rocky Mountains, in other words, into the Atlantic and Pacific regions.   In the former, the four species already named— *Superbum, Canadense, Philadelphicum,* and *Catesbœi*—are the only ones as yet described, those more recently discovered must be regarded as mere varieties (?). §   Of these the most remarkable are the variety of *L. Phila- delphicum,* known as *Wansharaicum,* or *Wansharicum,* from its having been found in Wanshara County, Wisconsin.   It is a remarkably fine and well coloured variety of *Philadelphicum* in respect of its flowers, but has alternate leaves, not verticillated like the last.   On the other hand, the Pacific species, which appear to be more numerous, were, previous to their introduction by M. Leichtlin a short time since, wholly unknown. Three of these species were described in 1863, by Dr. Kellogg, in a scarce work, the "Proceedings of the Natural History Society of St. Francisco."   These are the Californian Leopard Lily, *L. Pardalinum,* Kellogg, with pendulous flowers, orange, with large brown spots, as to the upper half, and a fine red colour on the lower half, without the least fusion or intermixture ;of colours (and its allied forms *Puberulum* and *Californicum*); the Miniature Lily of the Sierra Nevada, *L. Parvum,* Kellogg, a plant of low stature (?), with five to nine upright blooms of an orange yellow colour, with deep purple red at the tips, and dotted in the central portions; the magnificent Lady of Washington Lily, *L. Washing- tonianum,* Kellogg, a splendid plant of the Sierra Nevada, with verticillated leaves and white flowers, of a delicious perfume, which latter assume a purplish-lilac hue.   A very fine species, Humboldt's Lily, *L. Humboldti,* Roezl and Leichtlin, has been recently discovered in the Sierra Nevada by

---

* Now known as *Davuricum.*

† We consider this form and *Medeoloides* to be closely allied, the former bears a yellow, the latter a red flower.

‡ This is still a doubtful undetermined form, not yet in the hands of cultivators.

§ Add, also, the very pretty *L. Carolinianum* (Michauxii), introduced to notice by M. André Michaux in 1803, and others mentioned further on.

M. Roezl, and introduced by him into Europe through M. Leichtlin. The flowers are large and numerous, inodorous, orange-coloured, and spotted with deep brown.

"In a few catalogues we have seen a Californian Lily, *L. Californicum*, Hort., and a Columbian Lily, *L. Columbianum*, Hort., the names indicating the habitats of the species. These plants have neither been figured nor described, and are wholly unknown to me. The preceding enumeration, which has no pretension to completeness, shows that Linnæus, in 1874, was acquainted with 9 species; Persoon, in 1805, knew of 17; Kunth, in 1842, enumerated 40, which number should properly have been 37; lastly, Spae, in a memoir bearing the date of 1847, the most recently-published monograph of these lovely monocotyledons, reckoned 44 distinct species, which number should have been reduced to 39, or at most 40 species. I have myself been able to bring the number up to 68, in spite of the suppression of certain members proposed to me as distinct species, but which I hold to be simple varieties.

"The genus Lily has thus in the course of twenty-three years received an addition of fifty per cent. to the number of its known species; an enormous increase, testifying to the interest which these beautiful plants have excited amongst scientific travellers.

"The foregoing details also point to a very remarkable arrangement of the known species in respect of the geographical distribution.

"They belong exclusively to the southern portion of the continents of Europe, Asia, and America, their presence on the latter being limited to the southern half of North America.

"Of these three regions, Asia has the greatest number of species; Europe the next; America, if we take into consideration its vast extent of surface in reference to the number of species hitherto described, ranks last.

"In Asia, the eastern portion is richest in species, the southern next, then the west, lastly, Siberia and the north.

"The genus is wholly unrepresented in the Southern Hemisphere. It does not extend to the tropic of Cancer, or, if a few of its species reach thus far south, as in India, it is only upon high mountain chains.

"One consequence of this peculiar geographical distribution is that Lilies, in our climate, are not hot-house plants. One and all of these species may be grown in the open air, with due care to protect the more delicate from frost. Their culture, therefore, is very simple.

Since the foregoing remarks were written by Duchartre in 1870, the following new forms have been added to our lists, and all are fully described in the Synopsis further on.

From Japan.—(1). L. LONGIFLORUM VAR. FOLIIS ALBO MARGINATIS, possessing a foliage more pubescent than the ordinary type, bluish green, and margined broadly with silvery white; first obtained by me in 1870.

(2). Another variety of the same Lily, MADAME VON SIEBOLD, distinguished by a very long and widely expanded tubular flower, stated to attain the length of 7 inches.

(3). LILIUM BATEMANNIÆ (*Talsta Zuri*), a fine autumn-flowering Lily, first obtained by me in 1875, with umbels of 6—12 medium-sized flowers, of a deep apricot tint, unspotted, stem 4 feet high, with narrow lanceolate light green foliage; in habit and growth resembling very much *L. Leichtlinii.*

(4). LILIUM WALLACEI, a grand form; very distinct. It is, in the opinion of Professor Baker, a garden hybrid, and probably a cross between *Maximowiczii* and *Concolor*; it is cæspitose in habit, each bulb throwing up from 4 to 6 flowering stems; first obtained in 1876.

(5). LILIUM KRAMERI. This beautiful and remarkable Lily is well figured in Van Houtte's "*Flore des Serres,*" v. 20, *p.* 2061, also in "*The Garden.*" Was introduced by me in 1870.

Several varieties of the *Thunbergianum* group. Amongst which may be especially noticed, (6), SPLENDENS, a very early flowering form, with large expanded cup-shaped perianth, nearly allied to *Wilsoni,* (7), MARMORATUM, and (8), MARMORATUM AUREUM, both early forms, with broad-petalled flat perianths, (9), VAN HOUTTEI, (10), HORS-MANNI, both later flowering, broad-petalled forms of rich deep colour, (11), ALICE WILSON, a most beautiful and novel form, of a rich citron tint, (12), MAWII, and several other as yet unnamed varieties.

Also several very fine varieties of *Auratum*, viz., (13), PICTUM, (14), VIRGINALE, without spots, (15), RUBRO VITTATUM, with a broad crimson streak instead of a yellow central band, and (16), RUBRO PICTUM, a variety intermediate between the last named and *Pictum.*

Several varieties of L. SPECIOSUM, viz., (17), KRAETZERI and others. From N. America we have (18), BLOOMERIANUM OCELLATUM, resembling much in growth and perianth, *Humboldtii,* but differing in the shape and size of the bulb, and also in the peculiarity that each spot in the flower encloses a dark eye.

(19). WASHINGTONIANUM PURPUREUM or Eel River species, a very distinct form; the flowers, after being open for 2 or 3 days, assuming a beautiful purple tint; and (20), PARRYI, allied to *Washingtonia-num,* and named after its discoverer, Dr. Parry, from Lower California.

Several varieties of the *Canadense* and *Superbum* group more especially, (21), ROEZLII, *see* Synopsis, and two new forms, described in the "*Gardeners' Chronicle,*" v. 10, *p.* 622, as (22), MARITIMUM (Kellogg), and (23), LUCIDUM (Kellogg), both allied to *Canadense.*

From Japan, the very beautiful early *Martagon*, (24), HANSONI.

Perhaps one of the most interesting addition is (25), PHILIPPI-NENSE, one of the *Longiflorum* group, brought over from the Island of Luzon by Mr. Wallis.

(26). DAVIDI (Duchartre), a new form, somewhat resembling *Coridion*; introduced to our notice by dried flowers brought over from Central Asia by the Abbé David.

From the Himalayas, (27), Hookeri, a form nearly related to *Roseum*, but now referred by Mr. Baker to Fritillarias.

Even in Europe.—Chaiixii (28), a new form of *Croceum*, with but few spots, and Pomponium Verum (29), the handsome scarlet early *Martagon*, are discoveries of Mr. George Maw; (30), Croceum Tenuifolium, allied to *Spectabile*, (31), Croceum Grandiflorum, an improved garden form, (32), Carniolicum Unicolor, a form without spots, (33), a double form of Candidum, and (34), another variety of the same Lily with flowers splashed with purple, and (35), a very beautiful form of the same Lily, with foliage deeply margined with golden yellow, a great ornament to our winter gardens.

(36). Several improved forms of Davuricum Umbellatum.

Lastly we must not forget to add the very beautiful seedling forms raised by hybridisation mentioned by Mr. Hovey, page 65, notably, Melpomene and Parkmanni.

By the exertions of our Plant Collectors and Plant Merchants, all the above named forms, with very few exceptions, have been introduced in such numbers, as to be within reach of all Lily growers. The same may also be said of many of the kinds mentioned by Duchartre as rare and scarce, more especially we may specify *Thunbergianum Aurantiacum Vernum*, the original form described by Thunberg, and figured in Paxton's Mag., v. 6, p. 127, *Thunbergianum Alternans. T. Wilsoni, Hansoni, Medeoloides, Catesbæi, Buschianum, Polyphyllum, Wallichianum, Neilgherricum, Nepalense, Wansharaicum, Cordifolium, Japonicum, Colchesterii (Odoratum), Carolinianum, Columbianum, Humboldtii, Parvum*, and many others. All of which may be procured by collectors and cultivators at very reasonable prices.

CHAPTER VIII.

ON

LILY BULBS.

(From F. W. Burbridge's Paper in Garden, vol. 11, p. 111).

Revised by Dr. Wallace.

Their Form, Colour, and Uses.

The form of Lily bulbs, even of the same variety, is liable to vary according to different phases of their growth; thus young bulbs, before flowering, have plump, closely imbricated scales, but when the flower-stem pushes up, the scales become thinner and wider apart. Imported bulbs are sometimes loose and open, especially if they have been kept in a dry atmosphere, just as the scales of Pine cones open under similar conditions. It is, perhaps, impossible to discover why the flat-scaled American Lilies such as *Washingtonianum*, *Purpureum*, and one or two others, have assumed the sub-rhizomate or oblique-creeping habit so characteristic of the thick short-scaled bulbs of *Pardalinum*, *Canadense*, *Parvum*, and others. I have seen over a thousand *Washingtonianum* bulbs, and considerable quantities of *Humboldtii*, and *Bloomerianum Ocellatum*, all showing this oblique sub-rhizomatous habit; and those of *Washingtonianum*, in particular, looked as though they had grown among flat rocks or shale found in some Californian districts, embedded under 8 in. or 10 in. of the soil in upland localities. Whatever the object of this bulb extension may be, however, matters but little, the result of it being that the hungry young roots are enabled to push their way into fresh soil every year. Different conditions of nutriment again, as supplied by more or less suitable soils, affect both the size, shape, and colour of all Lily bulbs, although not so much as to remove the almost indescribable characters by which the practised eye distinguishes them. The color of Lily bulbs in different soils is very variable, this variation depending in a great measure on the oxidization due to atmospheric exposure, this exposure being regulated by the density of the soil, or its permeability to light and air.* That there is some other inherent cause for this colour development, however, is shown, since, in precisely the same soil, bulbs of *Brownii* turn purple on exposure, while bulbs of the *Martagon* and European *Turk's-cap* Lilies as invariably become yellow under the same treatment. The whole question of local colour predominating in any part of the plant, as shown in some Lilies, is very interesting, and often is an aid to garden nomenclature, when the colors of the flowers alone fail us. Thus, Mr. Barr informs us, he was long in arriving at any tangible characters by which to distinguish the different varieties of the extremely variable *Speciosum*, until he observed the local colour of the flower-stems, leaves, and anthers of the flower, which simplified the whole matter. The Dutch growers expose most of their bulbs so as to give them a good colour, but, apart from mere appearance, the practice is not a desirable one ; indeed, the purchaser has to pay for the colour in the shape of lessened vigour, due to the evaporation consequent on exposure. Of course this drying and colouring process is essential where bulbs have to be stored for months, so as to be ready for transit or sale, but all cultivators are now tolerably well agreed that the sooner Lily bulbs are re-planted after they are moved from the soil the better. Colour alone cannot be taken as a character in determining Lily bulbs, since in *Speciosum* we find yellow, orange, and brown, reddish-purple, and

* Slight chemical differences in the fluid composition of the bulbs of the different sorts would cause this, but each kind preserves its peculiar tint unchanged under exposure.

even dull crimson bulbs, all yielding precisely the same coloured flowers: or perchance we find that a light coloured bulb produces dark rosy-crimson spotted flowers, while the white-flowered *Speciosum Album* often has bulbs of deep purplish-crimson colour. The yellowish-white bulbs of some of the orange Lilies, as in the forms of *Elegans*, become bright purplish-crimson if fully exposed to the sun and air for a few weeks, and the same is observable in imported bulbs of *Wallichianum*, the bulbs of which, are yellowish-white when removed from the soil. Perhaps the forms of *Martagon* are most constant in colour, their bulbs being of a bright yellow, as are also those of *Albanicum*, *Pyrenaicum*, and other European *Turk's-cap* Lilies. *Brownii* frequently has an oblate purplish bulb dotted with dark markings; some, however, are yellowish-white, and while *Washingtonianum* and *Humboldtii* generally (and I have seen them in heaps of several hundreds together) have pale greyish or yellowish-white bulbs, *Bloomerianum Ocellatum* (a variety of *Humboldtii*) has purple-dotted bulbs very similar to those of *Brownii* in color, and dotted in the same manner. The most delicate color I have seen in any Lily bulb is observable in the fresh young bulb growth of *Superbum*, where the white scales are suffused with soft rose colour; *Canadense* and *Pardalinum* have yellowish scales; while *Canadense Parvum* has scales as white as dogs' teeth, and not unlike them in shape, only much jointed. The curious and sharp-pointed scales of the bulbs of *Avenaceum* (true), are clear yellow in colour, and being jointed in the middle the jointed part is readily broken in potting or digging up the roots, and then one could readily imagine that the husked fruit of Avena or Oats had become mixed with the soil. The white flowered Lilies of the *Longifolium* type, such as *Neilgherrense*, *Wallichianum*, *Philippinense*, the European *Candidum*, and the Japanese varieties of *Longiflorum* itself are somewhat alike in the shape and color of their freshly dug bulbs, the form being the ordinary ovoid type, with white or pale yellow scales.

" As to the uses of Lily bulbs, apart from their flower-yielding properties, but little needs to be recorded. The bulbs of *Callosum* and those of *Tigrinum* are eaten by the Japanese, who boil, roast, and preserve them in various ways. The bulbs of some of the American Lilies are, or have been, also frequently eaten by the Indians.

STRUCTURE OF LILY BULBS.

I cannot do better than quote Mr. Baker's summary of bulb structure from his " Revision of the Genera and species of Tulipæ," p. 219, where the main points of interest are thus set down :—

" Firstly, throughout the tribe of the petaloid monocotyledons, viz., Lilium, Fritillaria, Erythronium, Tulipa, Calochortus, and Lloydia, the

bulbs are strictly determinate and monocarpic, the main axis elongating
into a flower-bearing stem, and the bulb, *the cycle of existence of which
is from one to three years, either dying or remaining, but in either case
developing a new bulb in the axil of one of its scales.** All the plants
of this tribe are able, in a state of nature or under cultivation, to
hold their ground and increase more or less by means of bulb reproduction, independently of being multiplied by means of seed.

In the structure of these bulbs we may define four leading types :—
1. The Squamose Perennial Bulb, as exemplified in the Old World
   species of Lilium.
2. The Tunicated Bulb, as in the Old World species of Fritillaria.
3. The Annual Laminated Tunicated Bulb as in the Tulipa, Calochortus,
   and Lloydia.
4. The Tunicated Corm as in Gagea, &c.

" In what is called a Perennial Squamose Bulb the old scales remain,
and a new bulb is developed into a flower-stem *in their centre ;* in the
third and fourth types the old scale or scales die, and the new
floriferous stem is developed outside them. Secondly, we get in the
tribe, side by side with a general uniformity of flower structure, every
range of transition, from a typical squamose bulb (Lily) through a
typical tunicated bulb (Tulip), to a tunicated corm (Erythronium),
the difference between them depending upon the breadth and thickness of the enlarged bases of the leaves, their duration, their
uniformity or difference in texture, whether they all, or some only,
grow out to produce leaves aboveground, and whether some only, or
all, are dilated below the surface into reservoirs of nutriment.
Bulblets or Bulbillæ quite similar in structure to those produced in
the axils of the underground leaves, are regularly present in the axils of
some of the leaves of the stem in *Lilium Bulbiferum* and *L. Tigrinum,*
in Fritillaria Macrophylla, and in the Mexican species of Calochortus,
and are occasionally developed in some other Lilies *if the inflorescence
be injured.*" The nearest allies of the Lilies are the Fritillarias, in
most of which we get *a well marked type of structure,* for which I am
not aware that any distinctive name has been proposed. Take the
bulb of Fritillaria Meleagris at the flowering season and we find as
follows :—in the centre, the flower producing stems, bearing from its
base, but not above the bulb as in Lilium, a tuft of slender radicular
fibres. Tightly pressed against the base of the flower stem are a
couple of hemispherical scales, not thin and flat as in Lilium, but half
as thick as broad (say half an inch broad and a quarter of an inch
thick), rounded on the outside, flat on the inside, where they are
pressed against one another and the base of the flower stem. These
are the bases of single leaves, homogenous, not at all laminated in
structure. From the summit of each, before the development of the
flower stem, arises an oblanceolate leaf, which dies down before the

* Or at the point of insertion of the stem with the rootstock.

flower is produced. In the autumn these two scales produce in their axils buds in the same way as in Lilium, one of which produces the flower stem of the following year; and on the outside they are wrapped in two or three membranous tunics, which have never produced leaves or fulfilled any nutritive function. This type of structure is scarcely varied through about half the genus Fritillaria, and it is this type that is distinguished in the synopsis of the genus *as the tunicated bulb* (2).

"But in the American Fritillaria there are no outside tunics, and the scales are numerous, not large and flattened as in Lilium, but small granules as thick as wide.

"Upon this difference, Dr. Kellogg has proposed to separate the American Fritillarias, as a genus, under the name of Liliorhiza, but there is no difference in flower structure between the Old World and New World species, while the bulb of the New World Pudica is sometimes barely distinguishable from those of the Meleagris group; and we get the Liliorhiza group represented in Asia in Kamtschatkensis and in the Old World F. Imperialis and Persica, which were classed as Lilies by the pre-Linnean authors, we get a large, perennial, squamose bulb, without any tunic, not materially different in any way from that of Lilium, with the scales as thin, but not so regularly formed,

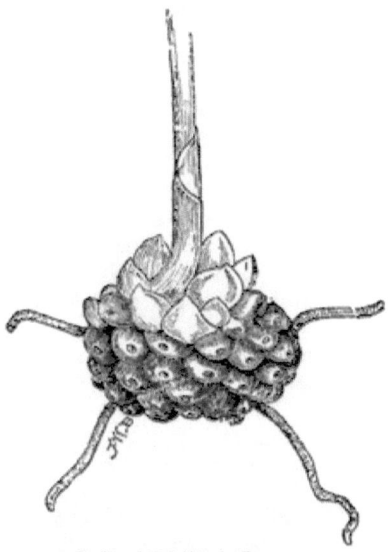

Bulb of Fritillaria Recurva.

and broader at the base; so that it will be seen that Fritillaria, which has been little studied from this point of view, presents great variety and much interest in its bulb structure, and runs over the line of transition which separates the squamose (or scaly) from the tunicated (or coated) type.

(3). "The third type of structure, *an annual laminated tunicated bulb*, runs with much modification, as regards the number and thickness of the laminæ and the texture and persistence of the tunics, through Tulipa, Calochortus, and Lloydia In all these, radicular fibres are developed from the stem on the underside of the bulb only, and at the end of the flowering season the old stem may be traced down to its base quite slender and cylindrical, with all the nutriment absorbed from the leaf bases that have nourished it; and outside of it, within the same external tunic, stands the bulb, well developed, which is to bear the flower stem of the following year. In Tulipa, the outer tunics are brown and leathery, the inner tunics several in number, and so thick that the bulb is broad ovoid in shape; and by the side of the old stick-like stem and well developed bulb that is to flower next year may be traced the nascent bulb of the year following, *so that the bulbs are in the third year when they reach the flowering stage.* The subordinate bulbs thrown out from the base of the old ones are often lengthened out upon rhizomes, and it is this that is meant in the Synopsis, when the bulbs are said to be stoloniferous, and it is upon the difference whether these accessory bulbs are sessile or stalked, that the distinction between Reboul and Parlatore's " Tulipæ Gregariæ " and " Tulipæ Erraticæ " depends.

" In Calochortus the structure is similar to that of Tulipa, but the inner tunics are fewer, and the outer thinner. In the Mexican species of Calochortus the outer dry coats form a dense mass of reticulated fibres, mixed with little cellular tissue, like those of Crocus Vernus and C. Reticulatus. In Lloydia Serotina the outer coats are thin, grey, and membranous, and the inner coats so little thickened that the bulbous dilatation at the base of the stem is very slight, and we thus get an oblique rhizome-like bulb, similar to those of Allium and Rhiziridium. But the essential structure is identical with that of Tulipa, and it is said that, owing to the thinness and dryness of the tunics, and the high Alpine stations in which the plant grows, by careful dissection its history may be traced out for eight or ten years. Here it has been clearly shown that the accessory basal bulbs are sometimes sessile and sometimes stalked in one and the same species, according to circumstances.

(4). " In the section Gageopsis of Lloydia we have a fourth modification of structure, a *tunicated corm.* Here, as in Gagea, the floriferous stem is nursed and nourished by the modified base of a single leaf, which leaf is fresh and green at the time that the floriferous stem is developed, springing, of course, from the tip of the corm, whilst the stem arises close to it from a little on one side the corm. In some species of Gagea the nascent corm of the year following may be seen protruded from the side of the old corm at the flowering time, already bearing a well developed leaf. This is the case in the two-leaved species, like G. Arvensis.

" In some other species it may be seen at the flowering time, but does not grow out into a leaf, and in some others, as in our English G. Lutea, it is invisible at the flowering time, and these have always a solitary leaf. In Erythronium, also, the flower stem is nursed by the much thickened base of a single leaf. In a newly discovered American species a very remarkable kind of rhizome has lately been figured and described by Dr. Asa Gray.* The corms are nearly half a foot deep, and a lateral offset springs from the base of the stem

* American Naturalist, July, 1871.

near the surface of the soil, about midway between the corm and apparent basis of the solitary opposite pair of leaves. The offset works downwards, sometimes remaining short, sometimes lengthening out, and its apex dilates into a new corm.

"The *squamose perennial bulb*, as exemplified in all the Old World species of Lilium, consists, in its mature form, of a large number of thin, flat, lanceolate or oblong-lanceolate scales tightly pressed against one another, face to back, and spirally arranged around a central axis, which is not produced, either vertically or horizontally. From the under side of the central axis proceeds downwards a dense tuft of fleshy fibres, and from the upper side is produced the flower-stem of the year, its lower part, between the summit of the bulb and the surface of the soil, giving off copious radicular fibres, which assist greatly in procuring the nourishment and strengthening the hold upon the ground of the developed flower-bearing stem. This underground root-bearing portion of the stem above the bulb is often vertical, but in some species, as for instance *Leichtlinii*, will creep for a length of 6 inches, so that, if grown in a pot and the bulb planted in its centre, the stem will spring up from the side of the pot.* All these numerous flattened scales of the bulb possess potentially the power of developing new bulbs in their axils, and will do this, in some species at any rate, under cultivation, if a bulb be broken up and properly treated; so that what with bulb-reproduction and what with seed-reproduction, a skilful operator may in three or four years multiply fifty-fold his stock of a desirable species or variety. But in a state of Nature there is only one new flower-bearing stem developed each season from the centre of the bulb, and a few from the axils of the decaying outer scales. A new bulb, whether grown from seed or from bulblets developed in the axils of the aboveground leaves of the floriferous stem, or produced in the axil of one of the bulb-scales, takes not less than three years, under the most favourable circumstances, before it developes a flower-bearing stem. The first season we get an ovoid mass, perhaps a quarter of an inch in thickness, composed of half-a-dozen tightly imbricated scales, which sends out three or four slender radicular fibres from its base. At the end of the next summer we have a bulb as large as a Hazelnut, with a copious development of strong radicular fibres from its under side, and the half-dozen scales prolonged above the soil into a rosette of oblanceolate leaves. Next year, if circumstances be favourable, the flower-bearing stem is developed; and then, if nothing untoward happen, the bulb goes on living for an indefinite period, sending out each year a flower-stem from its centre and shredding off old scales with buds in their axils—more copiously in some kinds, less copiously in others—from the circumference all round. In two

---

* It has been seen to come up 2 feet from the bulb, thrusting itself through a gravel walk.

G

of the Californian Lilies (*Washingtonianum* and *Humboldtii*) this type of structure is modified by the central axis of the bulb being prolonged horizontally, so that the scales are thrown out of a regular spiral, and the mature bulb is irregular in shape and more or less flattened laterally. Here, then, we get a squamose bulb taking the first step to pass off in the direction of a true rhizome; but the fleshy scales are quite similar to those of the typical form. The direction of the rhizome is vertically oblique, the new scales being formed at the deepest end.*

"A second modification of this type of structure I cannot do better than describe in the words of Duchartre (*Observations sur le genre Lis*, p. 28) :—'To give an idea of this development, allow me to report what I have seen in *Canadense*, as examined at the commencement of the month of March, and, in consequence, at a time when only the first indications of the vegetation of the year were observable. At the base of the stem, which had flowered the preceding year, and of which there remained only a small portion hidden in the ground, was found the bulb from which that stem had issued forth, a bulb formed of short scales, still fleshy and fresh for the most part, pointed and laxly imbricated, which, taken as a whole, was about twice as broad as deep. Immediately above this bulb was the remainder of the old stem, bearing a ring of root-fibres now dead and dried up. Finally, the extreme base of this same old stem was prolonged below the bulb with a diameter nearly double that which it had above; and after half an inch or more it ended by a broad truncation. It is from this old stem which has flowered in the preceding year, immediately below the old bulb, and very likely from the axil of a scale that has fallen, that the horizontal branch is originated, which at its extremity bears the new bulb from which the conical summit of the shoot, which will soon develope into the flower-stem of the year, is already seen to arise. This rhizome does not reach a length of more than 1 inch or 1½ inch. From its points of origin it descends a little into the soil, then raises itself to become horizontal, and finally rises at its extremity to form the axis of the new bulb, and to be finally continued as the new flower-stem. In its underground progress it bears small spiral scales, thick and fleshy, of which the first are slightly spaced, but those at the end of this subterranean branch grow closer and larger, forming thus the new bulb. From the anterior portion of this rhizome, especially from the part that bears the lower part of the young bulb, arise numerous thickish rootlets, on the healthy action of which the vitality of the new vegetation evidently depends. Later on in the year the old bulb disappears, the horizontal rhizome thus becoming free. Then

---

* It may be observed that *Washingtonianum* loses its elongated or sub-rhizomatous character of bulb growth when cultivated in our gardens, the bulbs assuming a more regular or typical ovoid habit.

the rhizome dies in the part which does not produce rootlets, and at the same time a new rhizome arises from the base of the bulb of the year, to form in its turn at its extremity another bulb to yield the flower-stem of the year following. There are produced, then, in these Lilies a succession of subterranean bulb-bearing branches, or a series of successive generations, each of which has an annual bulb for its fundamental basis.

"In parting finally from this squamose type of structure I wish to point out that there are three different kinds of 'rhizome' in different species developed in connection with it, all of which are spoken of in books under the general term 'rhizome,' but which are not homologous, viz. :—First, the produced oblique central axis of the Californian Lilies ; second, the lower part of the horizontal branch originating from a bud developed in the axis of a leaf-scale, which branch at its extremity bears a new bulb, as in *Canadense*; third, the lowest part of the flower-bearing stem above the bulb when it creeps below the surface of the soil, as in *Leichtlinii.*"*

One thing which has puzzled me a good deal in my studies among Lily bulbs has been the not unfrequent occurrence of jointed scales. This is constant enough to become quite characteristic in the case of *Canadense, Parvum, Philadelphicum, Avenaceum* (not *Hansoni*, often until quite recently miscalled *Avenaceum*), and one or two others of the American kinds. This peculiarity is, however, not solely confined to the American species, since the broad-jointed scales are found in one form of the extremely puzzling *Davuricum*. I was much perplexed after having sketched a bulb of the proliferous entire-scaled form of this species in one collection (which the possessor guaranteed true to name, having bloomed it), to find a totally distinct-looking bulb at another collector's, with jointed scales, of the identity of which its owner was equally confident. When Mr. Elwes called to see my original sketches of Lily bulbs, however, he relieved my anxiety by informing me that the proliferous form has long been grown in Dutch gardens for exportation to this country, and that formerly it was sent here as a substitute, and under the name of *Catesbæi*. The other form, with jointed scales, appears to be the native condition of the plant, and blooms more freely than the proliferous form, otherwise

* *L. Wilsoni,* which is generally considered a member of the *Thunbergianum* group, has a mode of development unlike that which is met with in any other known cultivated species. This plant emits from the outer scales of the matured bulbs a kind of underground runner, which terminates in a flower stem ; but its chief peculiarity is, that it bears at intervals of 2 or 3 inches, as it progresses, young equal-sized bulbs, which afford excellent means for the rapid increase of the plant. The bulbs of the original plant propagated themselves in this way, and seedlings of it which have reached the flower stage, and which may consequently be safely identified, possess in a full degree this remarkable habit, which, as we learn from Mr. Wilson, is not found in any other species, the horizontal portion of the flowering stem of *Leichtlinii* not being (at least normally) bulbiferous, and, moreover, proceeding from the crown of the mature bulb.—*Florist and Pomologist, Dec.* 1874, *p.* 269.

flowers, foliage, and habit, excepting bulbs, are precisely similar. It is possible that a long course of culture by the Dutch florists may have induced this free production of offsets or bulblets at the partial expense of flowers, which are rarely produced, but on this point more information is desirable. The form of the scales of Lily bulbs varies from the ovate or bluntly lance-shaped scales of *Candidum*, *Auratum*, *Speciosum*, and *Longiflorum*, all representatives of what may be called the typical or ordinary ovoid Lily bulb, so often figured in botanical books, through a series of bulbs, having more or less fiddle-shaped or constricted scales, as is the case in *Leichtlinii*, *Croceum* and its variety *Croceum Aurantiacum*, *Concolor* and its varieties, *Callosum*, *Tenuifolium*, and also in *Brownii*. Bulbs having broad panduriform scales slide into the thick, narrow-scaled bulbs of the American Lilies, with distinctly jointed scales, through the jointed form of the European *Davuricum*, to which we have already directed attention. The bulbs of most of the American Lilies of the *Superbum* type are but one-jointed, and this led me to think that, instead of the leaf having been shed from the thickened petiole, as is so evident in *Catesbœi*, leaving a scar, the diminished leaf itself had become bulboid in like manner with the petiole. This view, however, does not seem to hold good, since in *Davuricum* it is nothing uncommon to find some scales with two joints, and in the little American *Parvum* three or even four joints are not uncommon. I am particular in pointing out this jointing because I can find so little written on this point, which is one of much interest to the teretologist and structural botanist. The first reference I can find respecting the articulated scales of Lily bulbs is in the " Proceedings of the Academy of Natural Sciences of Philadelphia," for 1876, p. 412, where it is recorded that " Mr. Thomas Meehan remarked that some bulbs of *L. Pardalinum*, received last spring from Dr. W. P. Gibbons, had the scales articulated in the middle. The upper portion of the jointed scale fell off easily at the slightest touch, giving the blunt ends of the remaining portion the appearance of grains of Indian corn as they were arranged along the rhizome. Dr. H. N. Bolander has since informed him that it is a common characteristic of the species. It does not, however, appear to have been noticed by monographers of this genus. He had since found that the eastern *Superbum* had the same character, it was, however, by no means regular. Some bulbs would have a large number of reticulated scales, while others had but a few here and there, and they were as likely to be found among the inner as the outer scales. The scales of Lily bulbs were but the dilated and thickened bases of ordinary leaves. There were no articulations in the normal leaves, and it was difficult to trace any morphological relationship in these scale joints.

GROWTH.

The growth of Lily bulbs is a matter of great importance to the cultivator, and it is now fairly settled that out-door culture—the bulbs being planted in the open border—is best for the majority of Lilies, the only exceptions being, perhaps, *Philippinense* and its late-flowering Indian ally, *Wallichianum*. A deep, rich, sandy loam, on a gravelly bottom, seems to suit all the strong-growing European Lilies, and also the more robust of the Japanese kinds. *Auratum*, *Speciosum*, *Testaceum*, and even the creamy-tinted, wax-like, *Neil-gherrense* grow well, perhaps best, in the cool, deep, peaty soil of Rhododendron beds in positions sheltered from rough winds, where they receive copious supplies of water during hot summer weather. Mr. McIntosh adopted this last system of culture some years ago, and every one who has stood beneath his 11 feet high clumps of *Auratum* will agree with me that for *Auratum* no other system of culture is as good. A third group of Lilies, such as *Canadense*, *Pardalinum*, *Superbum*, and their varieties, may be designated "bog Lilies," since they like a rather wet peaty compost, or, perhaps, I should say, the comparatively dry banks of a stream, where their roots can descend to the moisture when in full growth. *Neilgherrense*, *Wallichianum*, *Philippinense*, and one or two others, although doubtless quite hardy in sheltered positions on warm, dry soils, can scarcely be looked upon as likely to make a perennial growth in the open air generally, and had perhaps best be treated as pot Lilies, or, better still, they may be planted out in the light, rich border of a conservatory from which frost is excluded.

As a rule, of course all additions to the weight of bulbs are due to the action of the foliage, but, as we shall see presently in the case of *Neilgherrense*, a bulb may grow and form young bulbs out of its own substance, long before the end of the stolon or under-ground stem has appeared above the ground, and, when the old scales of Lily bulbs are used for propagating purposes, this growth, or rather change of form and substance, takes place to a considerable extent before any foliage makes its appearance, the inherent growth power of these bulb-scales being closely analogous to that of seeds. It will be seen that the growth of a flowering bulb of a Lily is more complicated than that of a non-flowering bulb, since in the latter all the root-power of the plant is expended in taking up nourishment for the enlargement and fattening, or plumping out of the bulb; but in the case of a flowering bulb, there is a struggle continually going on between the flower-buds, flowers, and seed-pods, and the bulbs, which shall obtain most of the nutriment collected and elaborated by the roots and leaves. Thus, it is possible for the bulb to be itself absorbed by the act of flowering, and this is nearly always the case when flowering bulbs are planted in small pots of poor compost, or in any medium which cripples root action. Lily bulbs should never be

dried off like Hyacinths and Tulips; their scales should never be
allowed to become dry, since any part of their weight or substance
lost by evaporation weakens the bulb in inverse proportion. If Lily
bulbs be planted in deep moist, well-enriched, porous soils, their
bulbs increase in number and bulk, and this will be found to be
especially the case in those of the *Bulbiferum* and *Thunbergianum*
types. Apart from increase of bulk by division, it has been observed
(*see* page 14) that a yearly increment of growth occurs in the centre
of the bulb; the outer and old scales are pushed farther apart by new
growth, and the bulb increases in size more or less, according to
its nature and health. In choosing bulbs, therefore, in addition
to preferring a hard, weighty bulb, choose also one that has
a light coloured plump interior or "heart," showing good recent
growth for next season's flowering. We were particularly led to
these observations by noting some bulbs of *Brownii* which had grown
well last year but did not flower; the bulbs were half as large again
as when planted, the interior was filled up with light-coloured new
scales, outside of which were a few discoloured scales evidently of
former growth. Therefore, when we hear it said that a Lily bulb
takes a year to recover itself after importation or transplantation*—
—this really means one of two things—namely, either during that time
an offset has been developed (from the bulb planted) to the flowering
stage, or an increase of heart-growth has taken place in the interior or
"heart" of the bulb planted, from which the flowering stem rises the
second year after planting; and one or other of these processes is what
generally takes place when bulbs have suffered in transplantation;
but imported bulbs, if of good size, generally bloom the first year,
unless they are kept out of the ground too long and become
shrivelled—a sure indication that much of their substance has been
lost by evaporation, and so weakening is drought on Lily bulbs that
a plump, fleshy bulb the size of a Walnut will produce a much
stronger flower-stem than a large bulb, the scales of which have
become shrivelled and flabby. One season the late frosts destroyed
the young growth of some bulbs of *Testaceum*, and they were thought
to be dead. The bed where planted was used as a barrow path, and
in the ensuing autumn, when the path was dug up, the bulbs were
found quite fresh and plump, being, in point of fact, much finer than
others which had not had their growth injured. This leads us to the
question whether we might not with advantage grow two sets of all
our fine Lilies, allowing each set to flower alternately. At any rate,
all the evidence we have on this phase of Lily growth goes to prove
that we might advantageously strengthen our imported Lily bulbs,
by topping the flower-stems so as to prevent the production of flowers,
even if we did not, spring-frost-like, destroy the growth altogether

---

* Which, however, but rarely occurs in the case of *Auratum* and *Speciosum*, although
Pardalinum and *Humboldtii* frequently fail to bloom the first season after importation.

for a season. In the autumn of 1876, some bulbs of *Davuricum* produced secondary stems, bearing flowers and buds (blanched and misshapen, of course) underground, concerning which, the grower gave me the following particulars:—" I have succeeded in finding a specimen of the Lily this morning; a few weeks ago I could have found a more perfect one, having the flowers and leaves more fully developed. Last autumn I removed my two-year-old beds of *Davuricum*, and in the majority of cases I found specimens similar to the one sent ; some, through the ground being hard and dry, could not attain a perpendicular position, but grew round the bulbs, grasping them so tightly that you could not move them without breaking. The beds in question had been planted two years,

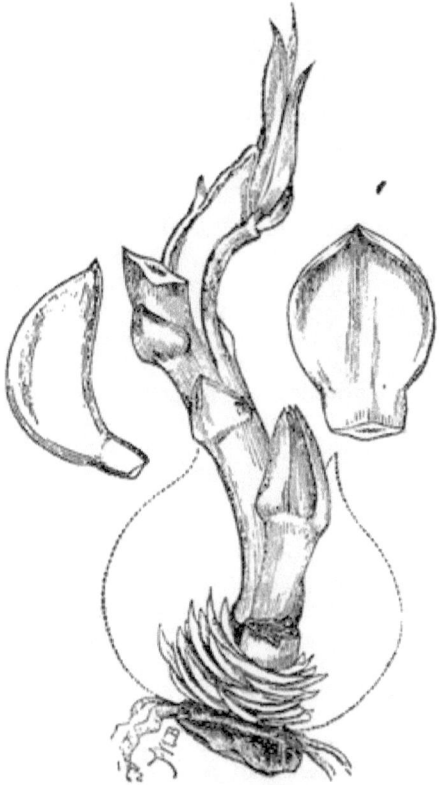

Anomalous growth in Lilium Davuricum.

and were fine bulbs to begin with, and they all flowered the first season, and then divided, forming one and two bulbs. The second season they flowered well, and some of the commoner sorts were selected to supply cut flowers. It is to this fact that I attribute this peculiar freak: I observed that after cutting off the entire head of flowers with some 6 in. of stem, that the remaining portion of the stem soon died, just in proportion to the length of the stem cut. If the head of flowers and an inch or so of the stem only were cut, the remainder lasted much longer, and in some cases died off naturally, *i.e.*, at the same time as those stems which had not been cut; I find if the flowers are nipped off individually, one may get very fine bulbs, but I believe in all cases where the flowers are ruthlessly cut, we get emaciated bulbs, or, as in this case, start the maiden bulbs into growth prematurely. This second growth may have been accelerated by the hot weather followed by showers just about the time the bulbs were dying down. In all cases that came under my observation the

second growth was made by maiden bulbs which were attached to
bulbs which had flowered. I dare say I found 200 or 300 bulbs
similar to the one sent; in nearly all cases I broke the stem clean
out; they are now forming a new shoot from the base of the old one,
but I do not expect they will flower."

INCREASE.

Bulbous plants possess an advantage over many others, inasmuch
as they are able to reproduce themselves or even increase themselves
without the aid of seeds, nothwithstanding which fact, however, the
latter organs are in most cases very freely produced, and this is
especially the case with Lilies. Apart, however, from the natural
processes of division and seminal reproduction the cultivator enhances
the multiplication of these charming flowers by layering the flower-
stems (after having removed the flower-buds) in light, moist compost,
thus facilitating the production of the axillary bulbs, which in
the case of *Bulbiferum* and *Tigrinum* are plentifully produced without
any artificial assistance whatever. It is now well known that by
removing the flower-buds of Lilies as soon as they appear a much
larger bulb-growth is obtained; but it does not appear to be so
generally known that this removal of the flowers tends greatly to
promote the development of axillary or stem bulbs, and especially is
this the case if the flower-stems be layered in leaf-mould, or any
other light moist compost calculated to foster the growth of the
little bulblets after they appear. One Lily at least (*Neilgherrense*)
naturally adopts this method of reproducing itself, as will hereafter
be illustrated, and there is no artificial method of Lily propagation
more deserving of notice than this by amateurs, especially as it is,
after seeds (and raising seedling Lilies is a long process, as one must
wait from three to ten years ere they bloom), the only method of
propagation, which can be carried out without materially weakening
the flowering bulbs. Another excellent plan of propagation, and
one long practised by the Dutch bulb growers, is to strip the scales
off old bulbs and plant them in light rich soil, after which they are
treated much in the same way as bulbs raised from seed, but they
come into bloom at least a year sooner.* Another plan followed, is
to overhaul in autumn the stock of bulbs, and after taking out the best
ones for planting, to throw the defective ones remaining into a large

* " Every Lily scale if removed with a sharp knife, so as to have a small portion of the
base adhering to it, will produce the first year a bulb about the size of a pea, on the side
of the small portion of base left, and in some cases two or three bulbs. By allowing
these to remain in the seed pan, if not inserted too thickly at first, they form a large bulb
on the side of the small one. (??) They are then shaken out, and some five or six put in
a 6-inch pot, when some of them would bloom, but I never allow them in their third
season to do that. In the autumn they are fair-sized bulbs, when they may be planted
out singly, or if of the *Speciosum* section, four or five may be put in an 8 or 10-inch pot."
—*Edina, in Garden, vol.* 15, *p.* 82.

basket with a little Cocoa-nut fibre, place in a shed, and leave until March without disturbing, by which time they are one mass of young bulblets, thousands having been produced by the old, partially-decayed scales, each little bulblet bearing one or two green leaf blades.

If we could make ourselves perfectly certain as to which of the cultivated Lilies are wild species or types, and which have been produced by seminal variation and hybridism by the Japanese and Dutch cultivators, we should find the bulb structure of Lilies far more characteristic and tangible than at present, although even now the bulbs of Lilies are quite as well suited as aids to classification, or arrangement of species, as are the corms of Crocuses or Fritillarias. Speaking of Japanese Lily cultivators, it may not be generally known that Lilies and other typical plants (as Iris and Pæonias) have been cultivated and improved by particular families in Japan, just as are Lilies, Hyacinths, Narcissi, and Tulips at present in Holland, only that this culture has been going on in Japan, generation after generation—one might almost add ages; its origin is lost in legends and mythical obscurity. If one could get at translations of Japanese and Chinese gardening and botanical literature, what a world of discovery in plant improvement would be opened up to us, and how much would some of the botanists, even of our own day, have to regret, that they did not give the "inner Celestial" trade-growers more credit for their skill in originating and fixing sports and seminal varieties, if not sexual and vegetative hybrids! In referring to the characters of Lily bulbs, it must be owned that in some cases a great difference is observable between the bulbs of two apparently distinct types, or species, but it is impossible to define the difference in words; and this brings me to a point on which I lay great stress, namely, that in figuring any plant the root-growth should in all cases be included in the drawing, as worthy of equal consideration with the aboveground development of stem and leaves, especially as it is the foundation, whence they spring into life and loveliness; and I feel sure if this practice were adopted in botanical works, many of the now common doubts and misunderstandings as to figures would be prevented. Individual bulbs of any species of Lily, like individual Apples or Pears, are very variable, and those who have many Lily bulbs through their hands, are apt to form their ideal of the bulb of any given species from the bulk, taking note of the maximum and minimum variations in a manner of which their ideal bulb is a mean or average. There is, however, a right and wrong method even in this apparently faultless style of estimating variable characters, for it is possible to imagine correctly what the bulb of any species should be from extreme specimens, and to draw or write about it as though one had actually seen such a specimen. In the illustrations to follow, this source of error has been carefully guarded against, and although it is not to be expected, that we have been fortunate enough to hit everybody's ideal of the bulb-growth of the species figured, still every figure has been carefully made from an actual bulb. Nor did I altogether trust to my own experience in the matter, since the selection of the type specimens in nearly all cases, was made for me by Mr. G. F. Wilson, Dr. Wallace, Mr. Horsman, Mr. Bull, Mr. Barr, and other well-known Lily importers and cultivators. Not a scale has been added or sacrificed for artistic purposes, and in most cases the original sketches are reproduced of the natural size.

SUB-GENUS I.
CARDIOCRINUM.

Lilium Cordiflorum.—The stately *Cordiflorum* and *Giganteum* (the latter now pretty generally grown in our gardens) are readily distinguished from all other Lilies by their broadly heart-shaped, Funkia-like leaves, the large thickened bases of which become some-

what indurated and permanent, forming what may be called a bulb, but one essentially different in texture and general appearance from the bulbs of all other Lily species. *Giganteum* is so similar to the Japanese *Cordifolium*, both in foliage and flower, that I follow Mr. Baker in considering them merely forms of the same plant,* a little varied, perhaps, by different climate, soil, and other conditions mainly dependent on geographical distribution. If all other characters fail, however, the plants are readily distinguished by their bulbs, which differ in several particulars, but like those of many other Lilies, more in general appearance than in describable characters. Mr. Baker describes the bulb of *Cordifolium* as being " in every respect like that of *Giganteum*, but smaller, and with thicker, more wrinkled, and less regular scales." I also find the bulbs smaller, and the scales thicker and more succulent, smooth, even

L. Cordifolium (Japan and China); half natural size ; from cultivated bulb ; colour, green and brown.

glossy when freshly dug. I have not seen dry bulbs, but as a rule the more fleshy and succulent bulbs are when fresh, the more wrinkled they become when dried. Both are deciduous in November, and the bulbs of *Cordifolium* are then plump and glossy, the size of a

* I can hardly agree with this, I consider these two very different both as to growth, flower, and bulb, see my remarks on these differences, in " Synopsis," next chapter.

duck's egg or larger, and formed of five or six (in very large bulbs more) thick, rounded, whitish scales, which become green, suffused with brown, if exposed to the light and air. These scales are semi-circular or lunate in section, the cut part or interior being formed of rich green cellular tissue, among which are embedded numerous longitudinal fibres, which terminate suddenly at the articulation between the petioles of the decayed leaves and the apex of the bulb scales, leaving a clean scar, as shown in the engraving.

L. *Giganteum* has larger and more elongated scales of a rough leathery texture, and often fibrous externally, and the articulation between the petiole and the top of the scale is not a clean one, as in *Cordifolium*, but each scale is terminated by an irregular tuft of fibres, as shown in the figure. The bulbs of both these plants have a cæspitose (?)* or clustered habit of growth, as in many other species, but their extremely thick scales, formed of green cellular tissues and longitudinal fibres enclosed in an indurated or leathery, glossy or fibrous coat, serve to distinguish them at a glance from their allies.

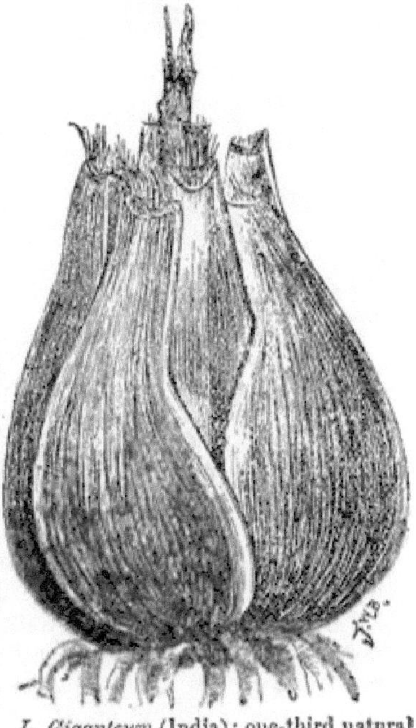

SUB-GENUS II.

EULIRION.

L. *Longiflorum.*—This is a highly variable plant in aboveground growth and flower, but the bulb structure is remarkably constant in form and colour, the main points of difference being the relative size and thickness of the scales and bulbs. The bulb structure of this plant closely resembles that of the common white *Candidum*, being of the typical ovoid type, with lance-shaped imbricated scales of a white colour changing to pale yellow on exposure. The illustration,† on page 92, shows the contour of these better than any description could possibly

L. *Giganteum* (India); one-third natural size; from a cultivated bulb; colour, brownish.

do. The old flowering bulb of July, 1875, which yet bears the remains of the flower-stem, has, as will be seen, been succeeded by a

---

* Hardly the correct term, the fact being that after flowering, the old bulb is absorbed, leaving five or more offsets at its base, and these, if left alone, grow up in a clump.

† The contour of *Candidum* is much more like the figure given, page 94, of *Wallichianum* than that of *Longiflorum*, being longer vertically, with scales more closely appressed and overlapping.

new bulb, and this, at the time the sketch was made in November, 1876, had already commenced to throw up its growth or flower stem. This is the earliest of all Lilies in making its growth; if we except *Candidum*, in which the young scale leaves of autumn succeed the foliage of spring so quickly, that practically it may be considered an evergreen species.

L. Neilgherrense.—The Lily now grown in gardens under this name — like others, a very variable one—is by Mr. Baker held to be a form of *Longiflorum*, and will be so considered here, although differing in its late-blooming habits and curious method of self-increase, apart altogether from its larger flowers, different geographical distribution, and occasional change of colour. Its bulb-growth is very similar to that of *Longiflorum*, but the scales are fewer and thicker or more fleshy, and the entire bulb is generally more pointed, the scales being tinged with purple, as in its ally *Wallichianum*, and not uniformly yellow, as in the forms of *Longiflorum* proper. It has been pointed out that the bulbs of "this species have the merit of increasing rapidly in size, and multiplying both by offsets and by the long horizontal subterranean stems, which are so remarkable in some specimens. I have seen them come up more than 1 foot from the bulb, and even descend to the bottom of the pot and come out through the drain hole." Mr. Barr kindly allowed me to turn out and examine several of his large pots of this species, in each of which ten or twelve bulbs had been placed, and about half of these bulbs had thrown up flower stems, and had also increased in size. Some of the bulbs, however, and, as it seemed to me, the weaker ones, had produced underground stems which had coiled themselves around the sides of the pots, and bore small bulbs at intervals, as shown in the

L. Longiflorum (Japan); one-half natural size; cultivated bulbs; colour, yellow.
N.B.—The bulb* of this has often the flattened top and restricted base of *Brownii*, but is always white or clear yellow, never purple-stained.

* The bulb figured here is, I believe, that of a small *Eximium*; the true *Longiflorum* has, as described, a flattened top and restricted base like the figure of *Brownii*, on page 96.

sketch ; some of these subterranean stolons were fully 2 feet in length, each having from five to six bulblets, according to the length or number

L. Neilgherrense (India, Neilgherry Hills) ; one-half natural size ; (*a*) cultivated flowering bulb ; (*b*) cultivated subterranean stem-producing bulb, the stem bearing bulbils at the nodes ; (*c*) section of scale ; colour, yellow or yellowish white, sometimes tinged with purple or brown.

of the nodes, and here and there a few root-fibres. These fibres, however, were not so strong as the whorl of roots near the base of the flowering stems, and the bulbs which produced these bulblet-bearing stolons, had not increased in size, by the increment of new growth ; indeed, in some cases where the stoloniferous bulbs were larger than usual, they seemed to have, as a rule, exhausted the parent bulb. Mr. James McIntosh, of Oatlands, Weybridge, planted a bulb of this plant in his garden, in May, 1876, which produced a flower stem 4 feet 7 inches in height, bearing a solitary flower fully 7 inches across the funnel-shaped mouth. The beautiful *Philippinense* (*see* Bot. Mag., t. 6260), a slender, grassy-leaved species, introduced from the Philippines a year or two ago by Messrs. Veitch & Son, has the bulb structure of *Longiflorum*, which it also resembles in flower; indeed, botanically it is interesting, as showing the extreme development of the peculiarities that mark the Eulirion group.

L. Wallichianum.—The bulbs of this plant are in form like those of *Neilgherrense*, the main difference being in the remarkably thin margins to the scales, and in the dried and exposed bulbs acquiring a deep purplish red colour, quite distinct from anything I have seen in any of the *Longiflorum* type, the scales having thin, scarious margins. This exhibition of colour in the bulb would seem to imply that *Wallichianum* is more closely allied to *Japonicum* or *Brownii* than to its ally *Neilgherrense*, although some forms of the latter part are said to show pink or rose colour in the flower; and that this tint is present even in plants of the white and buff-coloured varieties, is shown by the purplish-brown stem, since this is the result of red colouring matter having blended with the green colour; but, as we have before stated, vagaries of colour in the bulb are so unaccountable and perplexing, that no reliance can be placed on them specifically, and even in the case of individuals, there is apparently no relation between the colour of the bulb and that of the flower. The flowering bulb from which our engraving was made was a large and developed one of a deep purplish red or port-wine colour, but the most peculiar characteristic seemed to be the scarious, membranous margins to the closely imbricated scales. The individual bulb kindly sent to us by Mr. Horsman, of the Colchester New Plant and Bulb Company, is interesting as having supplied the stately inflorescence from which Mr. W. H. Fitch prepared his beautiful water-colour sketch. Our illustration is exactly natural size, literally scale for scale, but, as a rule, the bulbs of this species do not attain so large a

L. Wallichianum (Central Himalayas); natural size; from cultivated bulb; colour, dull crimson, with membranous scale margins.

size, except when grown under the best cultural conditions. *Wallichianum*, although introduced to Glasnevin many years ago by Major Madden, never seems to have attained anything like its native vigour in our gardens, and its extremely late-flowering habit is against its ever taking a place among the hardy species, although it may by a suitable course of culture be made to bloom earlier. The success already attained by Mr. James McIntosh in growing its ally *Neilgherrense*, in his Rhododendron beds at Oatlands, Weybridge, seems to show that the above conditions are suitable to both plants. A correspondent, writing from Mussooree, thus describes the climatic conditions under which *Wallichianum* is sometimes found in its Indian habitats:—"Flowers in August, but more usually in September. It is a hardy plant, and here defies both heat and cold. I find it growing at an elevation of 5500 feet on the open grassy hills, with a slope sometimes of 45°, not under forest shelter but in open tracts, the soil full of bits of lime-stone pebbles, and the matrix composed of lime, clay, and vegetable mould. From the great slope of the hill it is thoroughly free from surplus water, the temperature of the summer sun being from 120° to 130°. From June to the end of September it grows in a perfect deluge, and often is enshrouded in mist for days together, that being our rainy season. From September to December it gradually dies down in a fine warm temperature by day, with hoar-frost at night in November. Little rain falls during these months. Sometimes there is but little snow in winter, say 3 inch to 4 inch with hard frost; at other times the snow lies over them 2 feet in depth, but this is unusual. The bulbs lie at a depth of 6 inches to 9 inches, and are uninjured. The plant seldom or never produces seed, but is propagated by suckers or by bulblets from some part of a long root [? underground stem, as in its ally, *Neilgherrense*], so that the flowering plants are surrounded by numerous young ones of various ages." Another correspondent thus writes:—"this *Wallichianum* is a magnificent Lily; I have seen it in the Himalayas 8 feet high."

L. Japonicum.—This is another variable plant, represented in gardens by *Japonicum*, *Brownii*, *Krameri*, and their forms, all of which are, however, too nearly allied to be separated otherwise than under the above specific heading. *Krameri* has rather a small bulb, say the size of a large Walnut, and such bulbs generally throw flowers; indeed, plump bulbs but little larger than a Cobnut frequently produce a solitary bloom. The bulb structure and growth of *Krameri* is almost identical with that of *Longiflorum*,* and this seems

* I cannot agree with this statement: the bulb of *Krameri* being very like that of a small *Auratum*, but the scales are thinner, narrower, softer whiter and more numerous, and there is almost always a keeled mid-rib to the lower scale. The growth also of *Krameri* is very like that of a small *Auratum*, but the lower part of the stem is denuded of leaves, it bears a few alternate leaves commencing half way up the stem. See description, in Synopsis.

the best argument against this plant being a hybrid* between *Speciosum* and *Japonicum*, since there are none of the characters of *Speciosum* in it at all, and it had best be considered as a well-formed, delicately coloured *Japonicum ;* or if a hybrid, then *Longiflorum* and

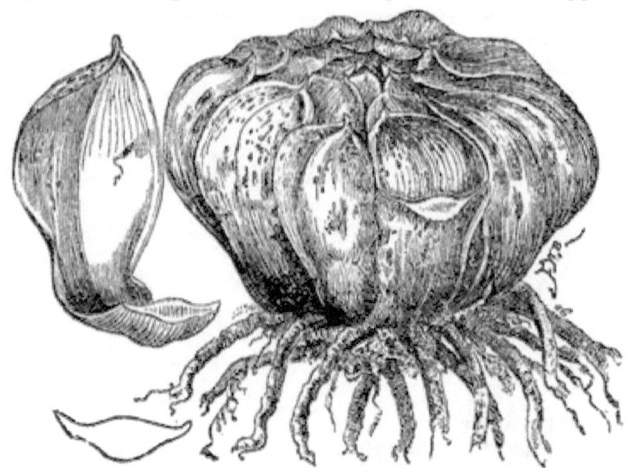

L. Brownii ; half the natural size ; colour, yellowish white, much tinged and dotted with purple.

NOTE.—*L. Longiflorum* often has bulbs exactly this size and form, but either pure white or clear yellow, never, or very rarely, suffused or dotted with purple.

Brownii must have been the parents. The colour of the *Longiflorum*-like bulb is white, shaded with yellow, and sometimes suffused with brown. The bulbs of the robust-growing *Brownii* are peculiar in shape, being somewhat like a Tangerine Orange, oblate in form, the base being curiously constricted, as shown in our sketch, made from a fine bulb kindly sent by Dr. Wallace. The colour of the scales in the specimen sent was white, much suffused and dotted with purple, but in some soils the bulbs are yellowish-white, and do not turn purple on exposure, although the yellow deepens in tone considerably. Dr. Wallace has pointed out that the bulbs of this noble Lily are peculiarly liable to decay at the base, and after carefully examining the bulbs of this plant, I believe that this is due to their singular structure, the scales being very much hollowed out at the base, and as these become closely imbricated cup-fashion, the moisture, which find an entrance at the flat apex of the bulbs where the scales

---

* I cannot understand, why everyone should look upon *Krameri* as a garden raised hybrid ; it was sent to me in 1870, as growing freely and indigenously 3,000 to 4,000 feet above sea level, and from the quantities imported (from 5,000 to 10,000 yearly) it certainly can be no garden hybrid. In shape of bulb, stem, foliage, and contour of flower, it most resembles a small *Auratum*, and if I were to choose another parent, I should name *Concolor* or *Pulchellum* as most likely ; but I should as soon call *Auratum* a hybrid as *Krameri*. Compare also Thunberg's remarks, p. 68, in foot note, "that this Lily grows spontaneously (indigenously) at Miaco, and elsewhere in Japan" (1783).

are pointed and looser, is prevented from effecting its escape below, and so rots the bulb. As this particular kind is so liable to suffer, it would be well to adopt the Japanese method of planting the bulbs sideways to prevent the lodgment of superfluous moisture. A glance at our figure of the bulbs of *Longiflorum* shows the bulb of that plant, slightly different in shape to that of the *Brownii* form, but the two types slide into each other almost imperceptibly.*

L. Candidum.—This is doubtless the best known of all Lilies, forming clumps of bright yellow bulbs, which differ from those of *Longiflorum* mainly in having some of their broader scales terminated by leaves. It is the only evergreen Lily we have, and its golden-margined and striped-foliaged varieties are mainly valuable for winter decoration on this account. In good, rich, well-drained soils this

Lily increases rapidly by offsets and scale-bulbs, but it very rarely bears fertile seed. It is one of the parents of *Testaceum*, the bright scarlet Turk's-cap (*Chalcedonicum*) being the other, and seeing that it is so robust and floriferous, one can only hope that Mr. Frank Miles and others who have taken up the cross-breeding of Lilies, will be successful in improving or varying the forms and colours of some of these free-growing old kinds. Our engraving shows reduced views of the bulbs and scales in different positions. It is very rare, however, to find a solitary bulb of this species, as, indeed, of any other perfectly hardy and vigorous-growing Lily, as these, if planted in rich, deep soils, form large

L. Candidum (Southern Europe); one-third natural size; cultivated bulb; scales of ditto natural size; section of ditto and reduced figure of bulb and winter foliage; colour, yellowish white.

clumps, some of the old flowering bulbs breaking up into four or five

---

* Bulbs of *Brownii* on exposure to light assume a red or reddish brown tint, the scales are broad and all pass up, overlapping, and terminate together at the apex of the bulb, thus giving it the peculiar oblate shape so well given in the figure.

The bulb of *Japonicum* (*Colchesterii*) is large, ovoid or round, not constricted at the base, not flattened at the top; white or yellowish-white, not tinted with purple, never red or brown. The scales, which are somewhat narrow and acute at tip, differ in length, the outer ones terminating at about two-thirds of the height of the inner scales.

H

bulbs, but all fused together on the old root-stock. I have seen clumps of the common white and orange Lilies dug up fully 2 feet in diameter, these being formed of flowering bulbs, old clustered masses of scales, and offsets of all sizes.

L. Washingtonianum.—This beautiful Lily is found on the Sierra Nevada, at an altitude of 5000 to 6000 feet, and during the winter months its bulbs are frequently covered with 15 to 20 feet of snow. Mr. Baker describes its bulbs as being " oblique, white, sub-rhizomatous, with small, lance-shaped scales," and judging from about 1200 imported bulbs of this plant in splendid condition which I saw in November last, that description is accurate. The oblique and elongated habit of growth was well shown in those bulbs, two forms

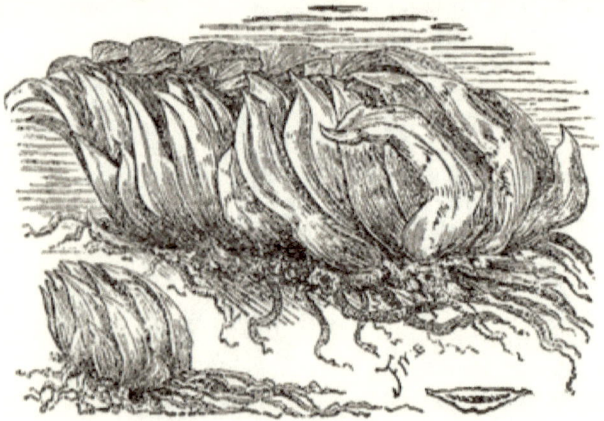

L. Washingtonianum (America, Sierra Nevada), rather more than one-third natural size ; imported bulbs. The smaller figure one-fifth natural size.

of which are represented in the engravings, one of a full-sized old bulb, these being 6 to 8 inches in length. Even the plump, short, young, imported bulbs have an oblique appearance, as in the smaller figure, but this habit of growth becomes changed under our garden culture, where the bulbs assume the ordinary ovoid type of growth.

L. Washingtonianum Purpureum.—The Lily now grown in gardens as *Purpureum** has a rounder, plumper bulb of a yellowish-white colour, shaded with brown, and its habitat is different to that of *Washingtonianum* proper, since it is found at a lower altitude in the Yosemite valley, "in a climate of perpetual spring." It is by some called *Washingtonianum*, "Eel River variety," since it is tolerably abundant in the moist valley of that stream ; its umbellate style of flowering may serve to distinguish it from the type. The bulb-growth, although very

* The bulb of *Purpureum* is only very slightly oblique and elongated, it might be termed ovoid, slightly oblique. Its scales are few compared with those of *Washingtonianum*, of a coarser texture, dirtier in colour, thicker, broader, and with a distinct keel on the lowest scale near its insertion ; the whole bulb is much smaller.

distinct in imported specimens, cannot be trusted as a distinguishing character, since cultivated bulbs of *Washingtonianum* proper are nearly identical with those of *Purpureum*, and even the points of difference between the native bulbs of both plants are not more than can readily be accounted for as being due to difference of soil and climate.* *Humboldtii*, although very different to *Washingtonianum* in its flower, has an ovoid, oblique bulb, somewhat similar in shape to the smaller figure, but occasionally it approaches the rhizomatous habit of *Washingtonianum*, as seen in the larger figure.

SUB-GENUS III.

ARCHELIRION.

L. Tigrinum.—The bulbs of this variable plant are, according to Mr. Baker, " perennial, globose, with oblong, lance-shaped, acute scales."

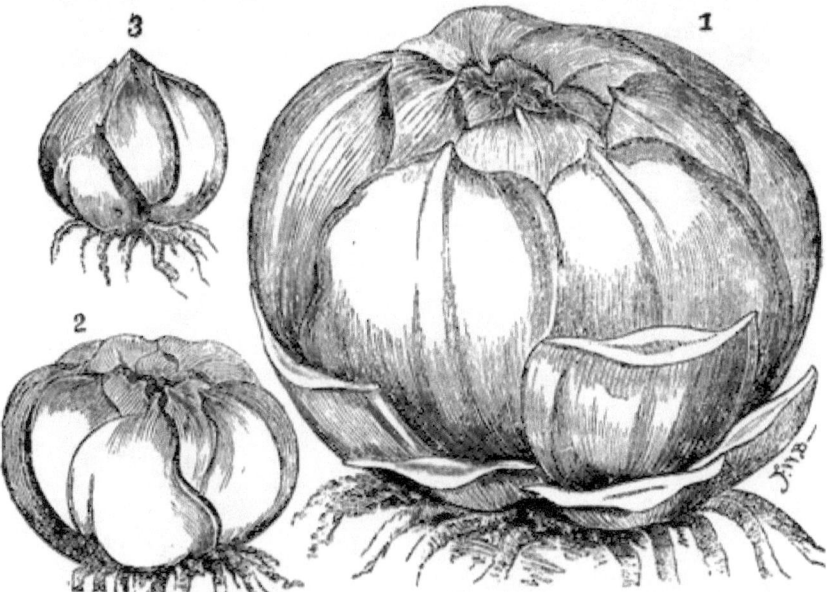

(1.) *L. Tigrinum Sinense* (China and Japan), natural size ; large cultivated bulb. (2.) *L. Leichtlinii*, two-thirds natural size. (3.) Small bulb of the same ; colour, yellowish white.†

The specimen selected for me by the Colchester Bulb Company was, as shown in the engraving, as large as an Orange, and of a similar

---

* I can scarcely agree to this.

† The large figure of *Leichtlinii* is true, but fig. No. 3 is not so correct, the tip, or young growth, is in reality very slender, like a small spike, in the figure it is triangular, with a broad base ; the scales ought to be fewer, broader, and the bulb flatter at the apex. The figure given reminds me more of *Concolor.*

oblate contour, the scales being very few in comparison with those
of such bulbs as *Bulbiferum* (*Thunbergianum*), and very much broader.
We have a small group of so-called species with this type of
bulb-growth, such as *Leichtlinii, Maximowiczii : Tigrinum Fortunei*,
is, so far as I have seen, the largest and most vigorous in bulb-
growth, after which we descend to the smaller but similarly shaped
bulbs of *Maximowiczii* (syn. *Tigrinum Jucundum*), and the still
smaller ones of *Leichtlinii*, which vary from the size of a Filbert to
that of a large Walnut, all being whitish in colour* and having an
oblate contour with broad scales. The plants we have enumerated
above, together with *T. flore pleno* and *T. Splendens*, are clearly
shown to be related by their bulb structure; and Mr. Baker, in
describing *Leichtlinii* as a species, on the authority of Dr. Hooker,
remarks that it flowers in July in gardens at the same time as
Tigrinum. It seems to me most probable that this plant is a yellow
seedling variety, raised in Japanese gardens; nor is this change of
colour remarkable, since we have one or two varieties of the crimson
scarlet Chinese or Mongolian *Concolor*, distinguished by their yellow
flowers.

   L. Leichtlinii.—The bulbs of this plant are described by Mr. Baker
as being "small, perennial, globose; scales few, broad, acute, thick,
closely imbricated." *Leichtlinii Majus* is said by Mr. Baker to be a
large and deeply-coloured form of † *Maximowiczii*, of which the
Colchester New Plant and Bulb Company sent me a well-developed

L. Maximowiczii, cultivated bulb, natural size ; colour, soft yellow, like an Ash-leaf
Kidney Potato.

* Reddened by exposure to light, *Leichtlinii* is always yellow after exposure.
† I cannot endorse this statement. *Leichtlinii Majus* of Mr. Wilson is a larger, more
robust form of *Leichtlinii*, colour yellow. *Maximowiczii* has the Tiger red colour.

bulb, from which it appears to me, together with what I gather from Baker's description that the whole group will have to be placed under *Tigrinum*.

L. Maximowiczii has a sub-globose or oblate bulb the size of an Orange, and is composed of about thirty broad, closely-imbricated scales of yellow tint; indeed, the texture of the outer scales is just that of a smooth Kidney Potato. Our figure is an exact representation of a well-developed bulb.

L. Speciosum.—This plant has a bulb the size of a large St. Michael Orange, globose, brown or brownish-red as a rule, sometimes white or yellowish* the scales being thick, fleshy, broad, lance-shaped, and

L. Speciosum (Japan); natural size; imported flowering bulb, with a reduced figure of freshly-dug specimen; colour, white-yellow, orange-brown, or reddish-purple.†

closely imbricated in newly dug bulbs, but with loose or open scales in dried imported specimens. Our figure shows a full-sized flowering

* The bulbs of *Speciosum Rubrum*, *S. Roseum*, and *S. Album* are all red, rosy, or purple, sometimes yellow. Those of *S. Punctatum*, and *Japonicum Album* are always yellow.

† These figures do not please me, the smaller figure is too much flattened at the apex, the central scales generally push up to a point as in the figure of *Neilgherrense*, p. 93, in the larger figure, the scales are too lax and wide apart, the figure reminds me of an old bulb decaying—there is no young close growth depicted; vertically the figure is too short. Bulbs of *Speciosum* are very compact, very solid, and very tall, the scales all curl up to a point like those in the figure of *Davuricum*, p. 104, and as compared with those of *Auratum*, are longer, broader, thinner, blunter at the tip, fewer in number, and of a softer texture.

bulb with open scales, and a reduced sketch of a freshly dug specimen, in which the curved fleshy scales are closely imbricate. The
bulbs of this plant are extremely variable in colour, varying from
white to deep purplish-crimson, especially in light porous soils. This
plant has been largely propagated from seeds by the Dutch growers,
and formerly by Mr. Groom, Messrs. Henderson & Son, and other
bulb cultivators in this country; hence we find numerous minor
differences in growth and colour of the flowers.

L. Auratum.—The bulbs of this variable species are as large* as,
and similar in colour, shape, and structure to, those of the last-named
plant, a fact which goes some way to prove their near alliance,
especially when we find this more fully proved by the fact of these
two species having hybridised together, the beautiful *Parkmanni* being
the offspring of these two species, as also was an earlier hybrid called
Purity, certificated some years ago by the Royal Horticultural Society
at South Kensington.

L. Philadelphicum (Canada and N. United States);
natural size; from an imported bulb; colour,
white or yellowish.

SUB-GENUS IV.
ISOLIRION.

L. Philadelphicum.—Mr.
Baker describes the bulbs
of this plant as " small,
annual, stoloniferous; scales
fragile, thick, nearly club-
shaped," and I have else-
where found them described
as being produced in a rhizomatous manner in their
Canadian and Carolinian
habitats; my figure was
made from a specimen
selected from a small importation of fifty or one hundred
roots, and represents a full-
sized bulb; I saw no traces
of rhizomatous growth, but
it is possible that they had
been broken up before transit, previous to their having
been counted and invoiced.

* Bulbs of *Auratum* vary much in size and shape, generally they are of a whitish or
yellow colour, on exposure to air getting a pink or reddish brown tint, as compared with
the preceding species, the scales are more numerous, of a much closer texture, more
compact, more acute at the tip, and shorter as to length; they overlap in several
tiers before reaching the summit of the bulb, which is flattened. In *Auratum* the
tendency is to extend its growth laterally, in *Speciosum* vertically.

The bulbs vary in size from that of a Cobnut to a large Walnut; but large and small alike bore traces of the old flowering stems. I found the scales thick and club-shaped, as described by Mr. Baker, while the fragility to which he alludes is due to most of the scales being jointed about the middle, so that the upper half is apt to be snapped off if the bulbs be not carefully handled. As shown in our sketch, the scales in the new-growing point of the bulbs bear a few slender, flexuose leaflets, but this is not always the case. The bulbs of this Lily are very much like those of the Californian Fritillaria Recurva, which also has jointed or articulate scales, but a much thicker root-stock or depressed stem than our present plant. Some American authors have described this plant as having stoloniferous or rhizomatous bulbs, but I have seen no evidence of this being the case; it is, however, a point on which we require fuller evidence from those who have collected the plants in its native habitats.

L. Catesbæi.—"The bulb of *Catesbæi* is very peculiar and unmistakable. It is figured, though not very well, in the Botanical Magazine, t. 259, and may be easily recognised by its small-sized, thin, pointed, white scales, some of which are in weak bulbs prolonged into a narrow leaf. I believe the plant grown as *Catesbæi* in some nurseries is the one figured in the Botanical Magazine, t. 872, as *Pennsylvanicum*, but which is really a Siberian Lily, and, I think, differs from the true *Davuricum* in the form of the bulb, which is very remarkable in both these species" (Elwes, in *Garden*). Mr. Baker says, "Bulb exactly like that of *Philadelphicum*," but I hold that fresh bulbs are very distinct. I saw a small parcel of thirty or forty bulbs one morning, and the very fact that these two species were so distinct in bulb structure while their aboveground growth is in some points very similar, led to the preparation of this series of sketches and notes on Lily bulbs. *Oxypetalum* is the only Lily I know which

L. Catesbæi (United States); from imported bulbs; colour, white.

has similar bulbs, but the scales of that plant are pointed, whereas nearly all the smooth white scales of *Catesbæi* bear a scar at the apex where a leaf has fallen away, nearly all the young scales being terminated by slender, sinuate leaves, as shown in our illustration.*

L. Bulbiferum.—An extremely variable plant, the bulbs of the different forms varying in size from that of a small Walnut, as in *Thunbergianum Alutaceum* (a dwarf, apricot-coloured species, which bears its erect flowers on stems 2 or 4 inches in height) to large, plump bulbs the size of a large Orange, and having very closely imbricated scales, as in *Thunbergianum Splendens* and in *Umbellatum Maculatum* of gardens. Mr. Baker describes the bulbs as "ovoid-perennial, scales few, broad, and acute." Our illustrations give some idea of the variability of bulb-growth observable in the varieties or forms of this species. The bulb of *Umbellatum Maculatum* sent us from Colchester was fully 4 inches in diameter, the numerous fleshy, broadly lance-shaped, purplish scales, being closely appressed so as to give a remarkably solid appearance to the whole bulb. Mr. Baker describes this as a "luxuriant garden form of *Davuricum*." With it came the smaller bulb of *Croceum*, with broader and fewer pinky-white scales, and these are more constricted than in *Umbellatum*. *Thunbergianum Splendens* has bulbs similar to those of *Umbellatum*, but smaller, with purple-tinted, closely-appressed scales, and the bulbs are apt to assume the flat-topped contour so characteristic of *Brownii* and *Longiflorum*.† *Davuricum* proper is rather peculiar in its bulb-growth, and we figure two of the most distinct of its forms. One type has ovoid bulbs composed of narrow, lance-shaped, fleshy scales, these last being extremely brittle at the base, indeed, the old flowering bulbs are apt

L. Davuricum (Europe, Dahuria); natural size; cultivated bulb; colour, whitish.

to fall to pieces unless handled very gently. This form, as

---

* The illustrations of *Philadelphicum* and *Catesbæi* are both perfectly correct.
† Bulbs of all the *Umbellatum* family are more or less flattened at the top.

shown in our sketch, is very proliferous, numerous little bulblets being formed at the base of the bulbs, and among the wig-like mass of roots at the base of the bulb. It has long been grown

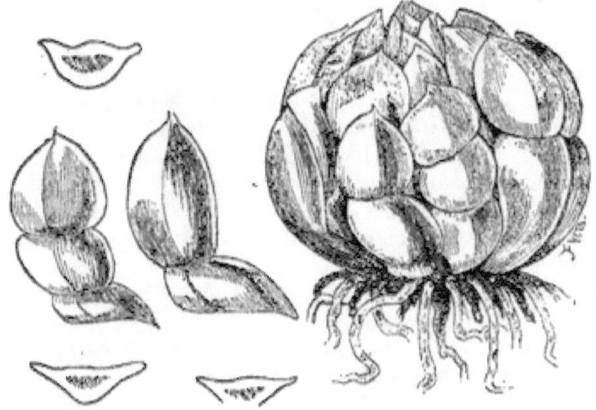

L. Davuricum (Europe, Dahuria) ; natural size ; from a large imported bulb ; colour white.

by the Dutch florists, by whom this proliferous habit of scale propagation has doubtless been fostered. Another form I saw, which, although identical with the last in aboveground growth, has a more

L. Thunbergianum Wilsoni, well-grown flowering bulbs ; colour, yellowish white, suffused purple or brown.

globular bulb composed of shorter, blunter, and more fleshy scales, many of the latter being once, and some even twice, jointed as shown in the sketch. Mr. Elwes tells me he received similar bulbs from Maximowicz, and that he is instituting further inquiries respecting them. Another distinct Lily placed under the heading of *Bulbiferum* by Mr. Baker is *Wilsoni* (of Leichtlin), for a bulb of which I am indebted to Mr. G. F. Wilson himself. The largest bulb which could be found at the time is here figured, and resembles that of *Bulbiferum* in size and contour, being composed of thick, closely appressed, pinkish scales. Herr Max Leichtlin, who is the authority for this species, suggests that it may possibly be a hybrid between *Elegans (Thunbergianum)* and *Speciosum*. *Bulbiferum* has long been grown in European gardens, and, like many other species, has become differentiated by seminal reproduction.

L. Concolor may be taken as the type of a group of Siberian, Chinese, and Japanese Lilies, having very distinct bulbs; and Mr. Baker's description of the bulbs of *Concolor* will almost include all of them. These are small yellow or scarlet-flowered species of slender habit, the most distinct being *Callosum, Tenuifolium,* and *Concolor* with its distinct forms (viz., *Sinicum,* with solitary, broad scaled-bulbs, *Partheneion,* with cæspitose or clustered bulbs, *Coridion,* also with cæspitose bulbs, but distinguished by its yellow flowers); *Pulchellum,* bulb ovoid, scarcely 1 inch long (bearing red, black-dotted flowers), and a yellow-flowered variety, cultivated in Japan, being found wild on

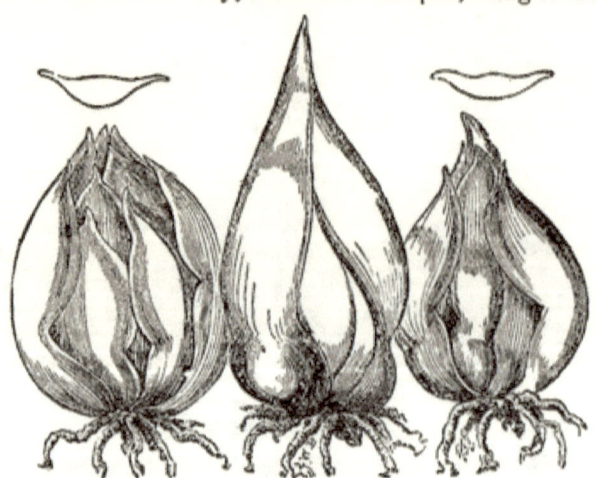

L. Concolor (China and Japan), half natural size, from a well-grown cultivated bulb; colour white, rosy tipped.* | *L. Tenuifolium* (Siberia), from a cultivated bulb, half natural size; colour, waxy white, and rosy tinted. | *L. Pulchellum* (Siberia), from an imported bulb, half natural size; colour, white.

* We believe this drawing to represent *Pulchellum*; it is not *Concolor*.

stony hills in Chinese Mongolia. All the bulbs of this section have few, but thick wax-like scales, which are not only as a rule closely imbricate, but folded round each other in a more or less convolute manner. The only Lily which has bulbs anything like these three types is the Indian *Polyphyllum*, except that Mr. Elwes remarks, that he has seen somewhat similar bulbs (presumably those of a species of Lily) from California. *Concolor** has ovoid bulbs, composed of eight or ten fleshy-white constricted or fiddle-shaped scales as shown in the sketch. *Callosum* has similar bulbs, but inclined to be oblate in form—that is, not so much pointed; and there are in the bulbs of this plant more scales, these being constricted, as in the last-named type. *Tenuifolium* has extremely variable bulbs, some being ovoid, the size of a large Walnut, and composed of eight or ten scales; others being quite slender, formed of two or three narrow elongated scales. A yellow variety of *Concolor* (var. *luteum*) is figured at t. 885 of the "*Gartenflora*" for December, 1876, and may possibly be identical with the yellow variety of *Pulchellum*, alluded to as being wild in Mongolia.

L. Tenuifolium—The bulbs of this plant are very strong and variable, and when full-grown, perhaps more nearly resemble those of the Indian *Polyphyllum* than any other species. They vary in shape from being almost cylindrical and very narrow (scarcely thicker than a pencil) to more swollen, fusiform bulbs, 1 inch in thickness, and over 2 inches in length. The few waxy-white scales are not only imbricated closely, but firmly clasp each other, just like the infolded central leaves of the American Agaves. The fusiform bulbs of this plant slide into the ovoid form, as seen in the bulbs of *Concolor* and its varieties, these being intermediate in shape between the elongated bulbs of *Tenuifolium* on the one hand, and the more globose-shaped bulbs of *Callosum* on the other.

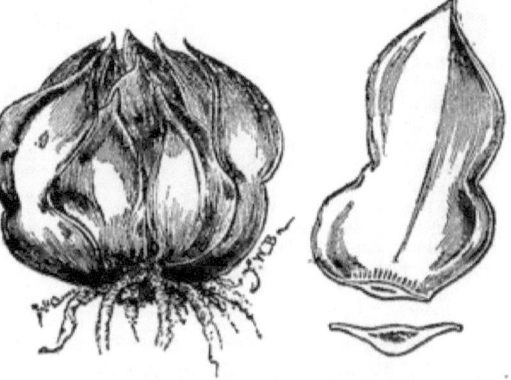

L. *Callosum* (Japan), from an imported bulb, two-thirds natural size.

* *Pulchellum* and *Buschianum* are the same : *Concolor* differs in growth, and somewhat in form of bulb, being smaller, and more compact, with scales closely imbricated, like those of *Tenuifolium* ; the bulbs are rarely found single, but generally in clusters, and exhibit a great tendency to break up and form a group. The figure (No. 3) of *Leichtlinii*, page 99, has more the shape of *Concolor*, but it should not show more than two scales, overlapping one another, and the top should be more pointed.

L. Callosum.—A distinct little scarlet-flowered Japanese Lily, recently introduced to our gardens, and evidently, by its growth and bulb structure, nearly allied to *Concolor* and *Tenuifolium*. The bulbs are rarely larger than a Walnut, formed of a few—say ten or twelve fleshy-white, somewhat fiddle-shaped scales. Our sketch, page 107, was made from a large but typical specimen, but some of the smaller bulbs are more ovoid, and have the closely imbricated, clasping scales, so characteristic of *Tenuifolium*.

SUB-GENUS V.
Martagon.

L. Medeoloïdes (A. Gray).—This Japanese plant is said to be intermediate between *Avenaceum* and *Martagon*, " but is distinguished by its erect flowers, falcate (not revolute) segments, and short stamens and pistil."

L. Avenaceum (Japan); from a fine imported bulb; natural size.

Bulbs, as generally imported, are about a quarter the size figured.

Bulbs of these species, with drawings of the plants, have been sent over to us by our Japanese correspondents for years; but, owing to the thinness of the scales, they have generally perished on the journey. We have, however, succeeded in establishing and flowering this year, for the first time, a few plants. We see no difference between the bulbs sent over to us under the name of *Medeoloides*, and those here figured as *Avenaceum*.

The bulbs of *L. Avenaceum* a Japanese, Kamschatkian, Manchurian, and Kurilean plant, are pale yellow or straw coloured,* globose varying in size from that of a Hazelnut to that of a medium-sized Walnut, the narrow scales being lanceolate, slightly triquetrous, sharply pointed, many of them being distinctly articulated about the middle, and readily broken if roughly handled. The name *Avenaceum* or Oat-scaled, is peculiarly applicable to the bulbs of the true plant, since the upper halves of the scales when broken off closely resemble Oats in form and colour.

L. Maculatum (Hansoni).—There has been some little misunderstanding about this plant; there can be but little doubt, however, that the *Maculatum* of the "Botanical Magazine," t. 6,126 is really *Hansoni*: the *Maculatum* of Thunberg being acknowledged by Mr. Baker to be *Medeoloides*. *Hansoni* is figured in the "Florist" as *Avenaceum*, but it is a distinct Lily, and was shown at a meeting of the Royal Horticultural Society, in 1874, by Mr. G. F. Wilson, of Weybridge, who kindly supplied the bulb from which the drawing was made.

* Assuming a pinkish tint on exposure to the light.

Mr. Baker long regarded this plant as synonymous with *Maculatum*, and the same opinion was expressed at the meeting at which the plant was shown by Dr. Hooker. Herr Leichtlin, however, who is an authority on all that concerns the genus to which this plant belongs, considers the name of *Maculatum* as being synonymous with *Medeoloides*, a figure of Thunberg's published in the "Memoirs of the Academy of St. Petersburgh," being the authority for this opinion; this figure is looked on by Mr. Baker as in some degree supporting Herr Leichtlin's opinion, without, however, fully proving it. In his "Notes on Lilies," published in the Linnean Society's "Journal," Mr. Baker has adopted for the present plant the name *Hansoni*.

L. Hansoni (Japan); from a well-grown cultivated bulb; half natural size; colour, yellowish white, suffused with purple.—1 and 2, scales, in different positions; 3, section of scale, natural size.

This figure well illustrates the autumnal bulb, on the left is seen the young growth, which will flower next season; in the centre the old flower stem; to the right old last years scales.

Thunberg's description of a bell-shaped perianth by no means agrees with the present species. The plant is about 4 to 6 feet high, with distinct whorls of leaves 1 inch wide on the lower part of the stem, near the top of which the leaves became alternate, a rather loose umbel of five flowers crowning the whole. The flowers are very distinct in form, having scarcely any tube, so that the blossoms are fully 3 inches across; they are of a deep tawny orange colour, with a thickish cluster of black spots towards the base. The flowers are somewhat nodding, but the style makes an angle with the top of the ovary so as to assume an upward direction. The ovary itself is very deeply six-winged. This Lily flowers in June, and is perfectly hardy.*

* This description does not do justice to the plant and should be compared with that given by us in the Synopsis in the next chapter.

L. Canadense.—A variable plant, long known in cultivation, having been figured and described by Parkinson as long ago as 1629. Mr. Baker describes the bulbs as " emitting runners 5 to 6 inches long; scales thick, obtuse, scarcely ½ inch long." The bulbs are borne an inch or two apart, on a stout rhizome, and are about 1½ inch in

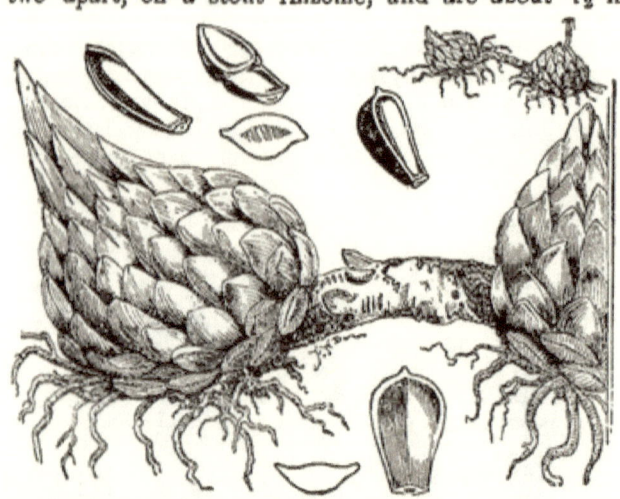

L. Canadense (Canada, United States, California) ; imported bulb ; natural size ; small figures show rhizomatous habit of growth and jointed or entire scaled bulbs ; colour, white, yellow if exposed, rarely suffused with pink.

diameter. The yellow scales are very variable in shape and size, some being short and rounded, others lengthened and lance-shaped, some few of them being jointed. *Canadense Parviflorum* has its bulbs clustered more closely together, something in the way of those of *Superbum.*

The pretty little *L. Parvum* has a very distinct bulb, formed of a rhizome 2 or 3 inches in length, covered with clustered, white, jointed scales, as shown in our illustration. I have seen a whole importation of such bulbs on

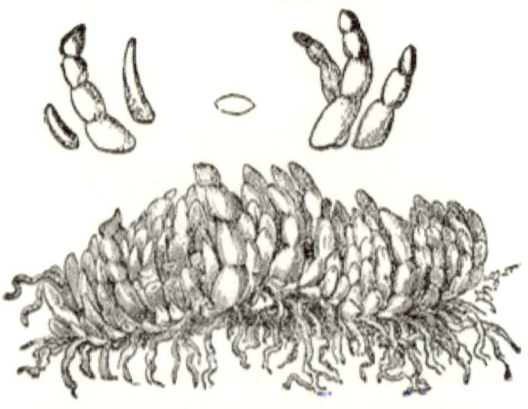

L. Parvum (= *L. Canadense Parvum*) ; imported bulb ; natural size ; colour, ivory white, yellowish if exposed.

arrival, and although they were very variable in size, I noted none in which there was a tendency to have the scales arranged bulb-fashion around a vertical root-stock; indeed, the bulbs are elongated just as in *Washingtonianum*, only narrow, fleshy, ivory-white, jointed scales are here substituted for thin, lance-shaped ones.

L. Superbum.—A stately bog Lily, likely to become a permanent inmate of our garden. Mr. Baker describes the bulb as being "large, cæspitose, globose perennial; scales numerous, acute, closely

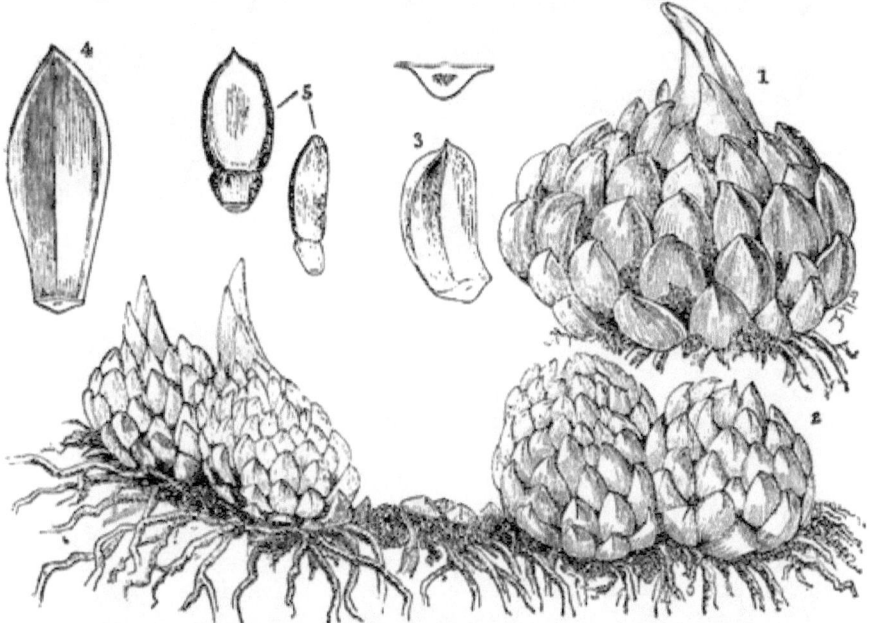

L. Superbum (America—Eastern United States); from a cultivated specimen. 1. Bulb, natural size. 2. Rhizome-bearing bulbs, about one-half natural size. 3 and 4. Variable entire scales. 5. Ditto, jointed scales, section, &c. Colour, white, delicately suffused with salmon pink.

imbricated, tinged with red."* *Carolinianum* has bulbs somewhat similar, but with more numerous, thinner, more acute scales, which become richly pink on exposure to light.

L. Pardalinum has bulbs quite distinct, yet rhizomatous, zigzagged, forming little mat-like masses of roundish oblate bulbs, and thick, scaly rhizomes. The bulb scales of this Lily are in some specimens almost all jointed near the base, and can easily be rubbed off.

* This description might lead to the inference that the bulb of *Superbum* was not rhizomatous, whereas it is so exactly like that of *Canadense* that it would probably be impossible to separate the species, were a lot of bulbs of each kind mixed together. The scales in *Superbum* are perhaps a little stouter and blunter, and embrace the rhizome more fully, whereas in *Canadense* they are rather superimposed.

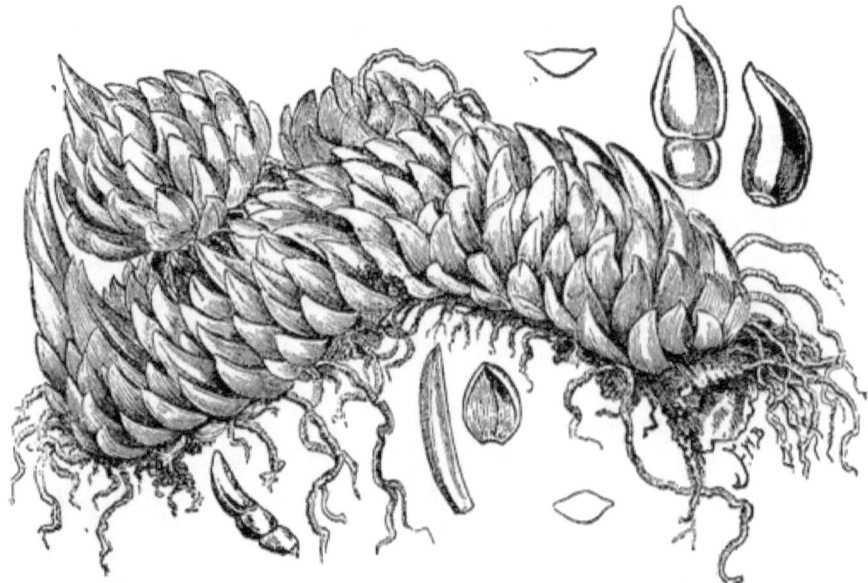

L. Pardalinum (California), from a good-sized cultivated specimen; the small figures show entire and jointed scales and sections of the variably-shaped scales, &c. ; colour, white or yellowish, rarely suffused with pink.

L. Columbianum.—Mr. Baker describes the bulb as "ovoid, perennial, small, white, acute, with lance-shaped scales," and also adds that the plant "scarcely differs from *Canadense*, var. *Parviflorum*, except in the bulb not being rhizomatous." I have seen this pretty little variety in flower, and consider it a dwarf, small-flowered variety of *Humboldtii*, analogous to, and, so far as above ground development goes, not unlike the small-flowered forms of *Canadense*, *Canadense Parviflorum*, and *Parvum*,* but, as Mr. Baker so well points out, easily recognizable by examining the bulb-growth.

L. Humboldtii.—A very stately Lily, attaining a height of 8 to 10 feet even when grown in pots. Mr. Baker describes the bulbs as being "large, 2 to 4 inches in diameter,† oblique, perennial, not rhizomatous; scales ovate, lanceolate, acute, 2 to 3 inches long." I have seen an importation of several hundreds of fine bulbs of this plant, all singularly alike in form, being ovoid, globose, the pointed scales all curving and facing one way, while the thick roots pointed in the opposite direction. The typical *Humboldtii* generally has white scaled bulbs, but specimens sent by the New Plant and Bulb Company from Colchester were yellowish, tinged with pink or purple. Examples of

* Quite unlike these Lilies when in flower, but in growth not unlike *Superbum* and *Canadense.*

† We have imported bulbs 6 or 7 inches in diameter, and 4 or 5 inches vertically, weighing 1 lb. each.

Bloomerianum Ocellatum were small, plump, and purplish, profusely dotted with purple, as in *Brownii.* In one importation of *Bloomerianum Ocellatum* there were about half the bulbs with white scales and half with purple ones, from which it was at the time inferred that there were two varieties, but, on flowering, both sets gave flowers precisely similar in colour. If the figure of the bulb of *Columbianum* were enlarged four or five times it would stand very well for that of *Humboldtii.**

L. Martagon.—Another extremely variable plant, bearing white, red, purple, nearly black, and yellowish flowers on conical spikes, the bulbs of all the forms being of a bright yellow colour. Mr. Baker describes the bulb of this species as being "ovoid, 1½ to 2 inches long, yellowish, perennial, with very numerous narrow scales." Our figure of *L. Carniolicum Albanicum* shows the general contour and size of the bulbs of *Martagon.*

L. Columbianum (America), cultivated bulb,   *L. Carniolicum Albanicum* (Europe) ; natural
natural size ; colour, yellowish white.   size ; cultivated bulb.

L. Carniolicum.—The bulb of this plant is of the size of a duck's egg, globose, or slightly pointed, the scales being broad, lance-shaped, and ½ to ¾ inches in breadth. Sometimes, however, we find enormous

* Occasionally we find bulbs of *Humboldtii* elongated, and in shape resembling the larger figure given, on page 98, of *Washingtonianum.*

I

bulbs of this species 5 to 7 inches in diameter, formed of several centres, each of which throws up a stem. The colour of the scales is generally white or yellowish, the more exposed slightly tinged with purple. The bulbs of the *Albanicum* variety are more ovoid in shape, tapering to a point above, and the scales are twice as numerous and as long (say about 2½ to 3½ inches), but only half as broad, many of the scales being only ¼ to ½ inch in breadth, and of a bright yellow colour, as in *Martagon*.

L. Szovitzianum.—This plant has a large, ovoid, pointed, perennial bulb, the scales of which are narrow, lance-shaped, closely imbricate, and pointed, most of the inner scales being white, but the outer ones yellow, often tinged with pink or purple where exposed. Our figure of the bulb of *Carniolicum*, var. *Albanicum*, very nearly resembles that of *Szovitzianum*, except that the yellow scales of the last-named are rather broader; the general contour and appearance, however, are identical, and the bulbs grow to twice the size given in the figure.

L. Polyphyllum.—This is by no means a well-known Lily, although I learnt from the late Mr. M'Nab that it had been growing in the open ground in the Botanic Garden at Edinburgh for several years, and had flowered pretty regularly. Seedlings from the first flowering specimen have also since bloomed, no difference having been observed in

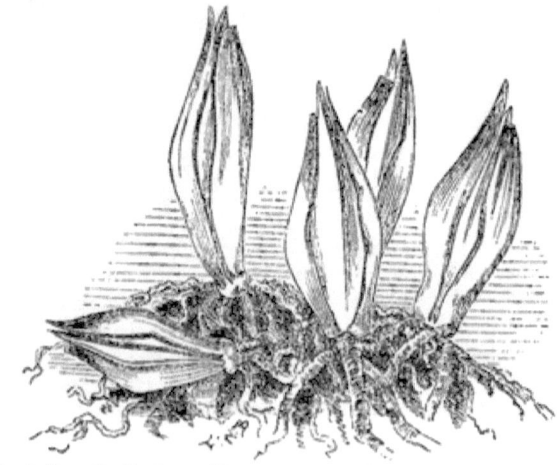

L. Polyphyllum (Indian) ; seedling bulbs, about four years old ; colour, white.

their growth or flower, although other species were flowering near the parent plant at the time it was in blossom. It has been grown in other gardens, and was described by Royle as *Fritillaria Polyphylla*, under which name it was received at Edinburgh; and this may have prevented many Lily growers from obtaining the plant,

L. (*Fritillaria*) *Polyphyllum* (India) ; full-sized cultivated bulb from Colchester.

thinking it belonged to a not over beautiful and allied family, but that it is essentially a Lily in bulb and flower there can be no doubt.

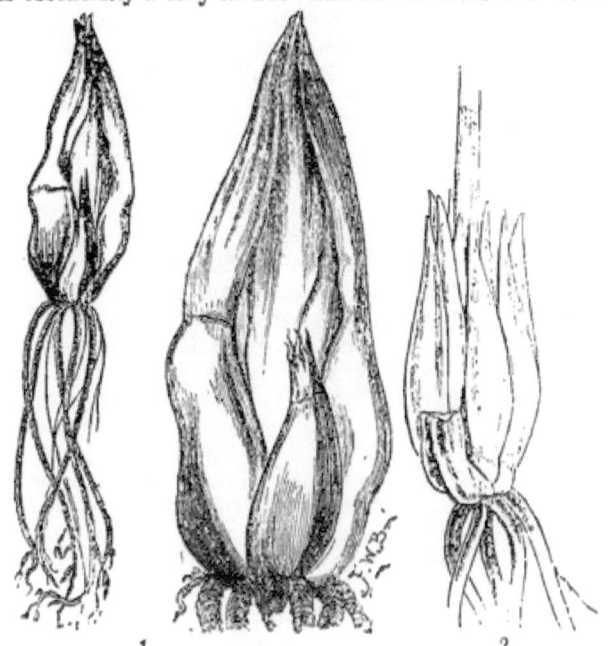

1. 2.

(Fig. 1.) *L.* (*Fritillaria*) *Polyphyllum* (India) ; cultivated bulb from Edinburgh Botanic Garden. (Fig. 2.) *L.* (*Fritillaria*) *Oxypetalum* (India) ; flowering bulb, from *Bot. Mag.* vol. 79, t. 4731 ; colour, white.

My sketch of the singular narrow seedling bulbs was made in
January, 1877. I sent a copy of it to Mr. M'Nab, who succeeded so well in the open-air culture and seed propagation of
this plant; he in reply remarked, "The bulbs are certainly very
distinct, quite of the shape you figure, but somewhat larger."
Another gentleman writes, "It is one of the most unmistakeable
bulbs I know, except, perhaps, that of *Oxypetalon*. The bulb of
Polyphyllum attains 3 or 4 inches in length, when fully grown,
and it may be distinguished at the age of one year from seed with cer-
tainty." *Polyphyllum* is said by a correspondent to belong to the Turk's-
cap* group; grows in good, tolerably moist vegetable mould on a slope in
a thick shrubbery, and flowers there in June at an elevation of 6500 feet
Quite recently bulbs of this species have been imported by the Colchester New Plant and Bulb Company, so that it will doubtless soon
become better known in our gardens if not coddled to death, as happens
to so many plants and bulbs from elevated and consequently comparatively cool habitats within the tropics. Mr. Horsman tells me that
the imported bulbs of this plant acquire a large size in the open air
at Colchester. Our illustrations represent seedling bulbs of this
plant when about four years old, a well developed flowering bulb as
grown at Edinburgh, and also another grown at Colchester.

L. *Chalcedonicum*.—A well-known and beautiful plant, the most
vivid in its scarlet colour of all the Lilies. There are now several
varieties, the plant having been grown from seeds by some of the
Dutch bulb-growers. Considering the size of the plant and comparatively small area of leafage, the bulb is enormous, being as large
or larger than a duck's egg, ovoid in form and pointed, the scales
lance-shaped and closely imbricated, some of the outer ones being
slightly constricted about the centre. Many of the bulbs are 3 to 4
inches in length, and fully 3 inches in diameter, the colour of the
inner scales being whitish, and the outer ones yellow, some are
suffused also with purplish-pink or orange.

L. *Pyrenaicum*.—This is sometimes considered as being only a
robust, broad-leaved, large-flowered form of *Pomponium*, with which
plant it agrees very closely in bulb structure, the bulbs being 2 or 3
inches in diameter, ovoid, formed of numerous yellow or brown-
stained scales.

L. *Pomponium*.—A pretty yellow, orange, or red-flowered Lily,
similar in habit to *Chalcedonicum*, but with narrower leaves. The
bulbs are ovoid, formed of closely-imbricated, yellow scales, which
vary from 2 to 3 inches in length, the whole bulb being 2 to 3 inches
in diameter.

L. *Testaceum*.—This distinct plant has a globose bulb, when fully
grown, the size of a large Orange (much like the figure, page 104,

---

* The petals are reflexed, like those of *Szovitzianum*, but the perianth is more tubular
than any other in this group, approaching more closely in that respect to *Longiflorum*.

of *Davuricum*, only larger), the broadly lance-shaped, fleshy scales being 2 to 3 inches in length, and closely imbricated in freshly-dug bulbs, more open and loose in the old flowering specimens, and whitish in their colour, some of the outer scales becoming light rosy-purple on exposure. Large bulbs after flowering give rise to three or four centres, a not uncommon occurrence, however, in other vigorous-habited Lilies. The plant is unknown in a wild state, and is thought to be a hybrid between the common white *Candidum* and scarlet *Chalcedonicum* or scarlet *Turk's-cap* Lily.

Duchartre has pointed out the great difference observable in the periods occupied by the germination of different kinds of Lily seeds, inasmuch as while those of *Tenuifolium* germinate in a few weeks, and form little bulbs bearing several leaves within the first year, the seeds of *Auratum* and of other kinds lie in the ground at least a year before they show any signs of leaf growth. A proportionate difference is observable in the time which elapses between the germination of the seed, and the blooming period of the resulting seedling plants; and seeing that these differences exist, it is not surprising to find that there is an individuality about some Lily bulbs, notably in the case of *Polyphyllum*, *Auratum*, and *Tenuifolium*, by which they may be identified the first or second year from seed, or, at least in most cases, long before they have attained their full dimensions and flowering stage. Neither botanists nor cultivators give plants sufficient credit for their indescribable characters, which are often, as in the case of Lilies, observable almost from the appearance of the first young seed growth. These characters in the case of many nearly related varieties of other cultivated plants, as in Heaths, Rhododendrons, and Grape Vines, are amply sufficient to enable cultivators to distinguish plants of any variety with unerring accuracy, notwithstanding the fact that any attempt to describe their minor differences in words would be useless for purposes of discrimination and selection. Hence it is no uncommon occurrence to find cultivators who can recognize unmistakably almost all varieties of Heaths or Grape Vines by their woody growth or foliage alone. And if ever we are to know anything more of plant life in its highest bearings, we must put in practice De Candolle's advice to Mrs. Somerville, and live with, and observe the cycle of plant growth in all its stages from the germination of the seed to the full development of the fruits. Although our sketches and descriptions herewith concluded show a remarkable diversity in the form and growth of Lily bulbs, it must not be supposed that the underground stem development of Lilies, Crocuses, Fritillarias, and other allied bulbous plants is alone worthy of consideration, since the true root growth of many trees, shrubs, and herbaceous plants is in many cases even more distinct and constant in character than are the aboveground stems, leaves, flowers, or fruits.

In concluding these remarks on Lily bulbs, it may be as well to give a short summary of the whole. Lily bulbs vary in form and colour, according as the soil in which they are grown is dense or porous; but fresh bulbs of all the distinct types or species are easily recognizable, and that even from the earliest stages after propagation by means of seed. The practice of drying off Lily bulbs, however convenient or necessary it may be for trade purposes, is a bad practice, and should never be adopted by cultivators, inasmuch as no well-planted Lily bulb is injured by the rainfall and cold of our climate, although it may be necessary to protect its young growth occasionally. The typical forms of Lily bulbs are ovoid, with closely-imbricated and lance-shaped scales; globose or orange-shaped, with broad, oblong, pointed scales; rhizomatous, having the scales either distributed regularly along the upper part of the rhizome, or gathered together in the form of bulbs at indefinite intervals. The typical scales of Lily bulbs are lance-shaped, or oblong and pointed, some of the Japanese, one European, and several American kinds having much thickened, articulated, or jointed scales. Well-nourished flowering bulbs increase in size by the increment or extension of new buds or growth; if starved, however, the bulbs become absorbed in flowering, and of course die. The propagation of Lilies is effected by seeds, bulb-division, planting old bulb scales, or by layering the flowering-stems after having removed the young flower-buds. The Dutch, English, and Japanese have for many years been engaged in producing seminal varieties; hence some of the natural lines of demarcation which formerly existed between the species have become indistinct.

CHAPTER IX.

MR. BAKER'S SYNOPSIS OF ALL THE KNOWN LILIES.

From the *Gardeners' Chronicle*, 1875, and the *Garden*, vol. 7., p. 297 (by permission),

WITH EXTRACTS FROM HIS MONOGRAPH ON THE REVISION OF THE GENERA AND SPECIES OF TULIPEÆ. *Linn. Soc. Journal Botany, vol.* 14.

As I have read from week to week the interesting papers on Lilies, new and old, that have appeared, I have been reminded of the great want which there is, of a systematic revision of the genus, and of some document in which all the species and leading varieties now known, should be arranged in a systematic order, and so defined that, by its means, miscellaneous garden and dried specimens coming to hand from time to time might be readily named, and their place in relation to other forms understood. I have often wondered that the systematic literature of a set of plants that have been such deserved favourites with flower lovers from time immemorial, should be so very scanty. Amidst the enormous mass of our own horticultural literature, there is nothing of the kind which I mean; and now, Spae's monograph is more than 20 years old, and difficult or impossible to procure. As I have a few ideas of my own about the best arrangement of Lilies, I will, if you will allow me, attempt to work out a Synopsis fit for every-day working purposes, upon the same plan that I followed for Narcissus. At present, for want of such a Synopsis, any one trying to name a Lily has usually to lose a great deal of time in hunting about in different books and journals, and from the botanical point of view we particularly need a careful comparison of the numerous Lilies which have been described and figured since Spae's time in the various horticultural periodicals with the older-known types, and many of these older-known types with one another, in order to understand which of them are really worth taking into account as well marked species; and, far more than is the case in Narcissus, a great deal still remains to be done in working out and explaining which are the characters that are most safely to be relied upon to distinguish the well-marked species from one another. I want to try in this paper to place the acknowledged species of Lilium upon the same footing as regards comprehensiveness as those which are adopted in our approved handbooks for ordinary use for wild plants, such as Hooker's "Students' Flora," or Syme's "English Botany." I am convinced that it is only by doing this that a Synopsis fit for working purposes can be constructed, and that by following this plan, the natural relationship of the forms can be most fully and clearly shown; and if in attempting to do this I overlook or misunderstand any characters which are valuable for distinctive purposes, I hope that your horticultural readers will not fail to correct what I have mistaken, or to add what I have omitted. This is a genus in which there is an especial need, in order to put it upon a sound botanical footing, for botanists and horticulturists to work together.

Generic Characters.

Plants of the temperate zone of both the New and the Old World, with scaly bulbs, numerous leaves, either scattered or in whorls, and with handsome summer-blooming flowers produced in racemes or solitary. Perianth, corolla-like, deciduous, in six divisions, funnel-shaped, with equal ob-lanceolate segments, which are more or less falcate in the expanded flower, smooth, or on the upper surface marked with flat prominences, white, or of a splendid yellow or red colour, never tessellated, the claws furnished with a distinct nectari-ferous groove, which, however, is sometimes wanting; stamens, six in number, equal in length, faintly perigynous, included; filaments, elongated, thread-like, or slightly flattened, more or less curved;

anthers, versatile, attached on the inside by the middle of the back, dehiscing outwardly along the entire margins; ovary, sessile, cylindrical, three-celled; ovules, numerous, horizontally arranged in each cell; style, club-shaped, more or less curved, most frequently longer than the ovary; stigma, rounded, three-lobed; capsule, coriaceous, obovoid, six-angled, with a three-valved loculicidal dehiscence; seeds numerous, discoid, margined, and with a brown membranous skin.

First, I will give a few notes on the characters in which the species differ from one another.

Bulbs.—The bulbs in the great body of the Lilies furnish no important modification in structure. So far as I am aware, they all present the type of fleshy imbricated lanceolate scales which we see so often drawn in botanical handbooks.

Stem.—There is nothing about this that needs to be mentioned now.

Petiole.—True Petioles, sometimes as long as the leaves, are present in *Cordifolium* and *Giganteum*, and short but distinct ones in *Speciosum* and *Auratum*; but in the majority of species the leaves are quite sessile.

Leaves vary greatly in number, shape, texture, veining, direction, and arrangement. The presence of bulblets in the axils is not, I think, invariably of specific value. The large rotundate-cordate leaves of *Cordifolium* and *Giganteum* are very different to the lanceolate or linear leaves of all the others. One of the best characters for distinguishing species is furnished by the arrangement of the leaves of several of them in regular whorls; but this character, useful though it be, is not entirely trustworthy. I believe that all the verticillate species are liable to have the whorls broken down, sometimes partially, occasionally entirely, in exceptional cases—a variation that is very puzzling when a specimen of this kind comes to hand by itself, without any warning of its exceptional character.

Inflorescence.—I believe that although several of the species are always single-flowered in the wild state, they all may be made to produce more than one flower under cultivation, and still more readily may the species that commonly yield three or four flowers when wild be made to show from twelve to twenty in gardens. There is always a tendency, too, in what are typically thyrsoid racemes, to become congested into umbels under cultivation, and of what are properly scattered bracts to fall into whorls.

Perianth.—Good characters may be had from the position of the individual flowers, whether erect, drooping, or intermediate in direction; very good characters also from the shape of the flower, whether permanently funnel-shaped, with the divisions spreading falcately towards the lip only when fully expanded; or bell-shaped, with the divisions more or less spreading, or often decidedly recurved. The shape of the segments of the perianth furnishes also excellent characters. Here we may trace at least four distinct types, with intermediate gradations :—1, oblanceolate, broadest above the middle, narrowed gradually to the base, as in *Longiflorum, Candidum,* and *Japonicum;* 2, obovate-spathulate, broadest about the middle, narrowed suddenly into a distinct claw, as in *Bulbiferum, Catesbæi,* and *Philadelphicum;* 3, ovate-lanceolate, decidedly broadest below the middle, without a claw, and narrowed gradually in the upper half, as in *Speciosum* and *Auratum;* 4, lanceolate, narrowed gradually from about the middle to both ends, as in *Martagon, Chalcedonicum,* and *Pomponium.* In the colour of the flower we have two principal series :—1, unspotted white, liable to be tinged with yellow, green, or purple; 2, bright shades of red and yellow, very liable to interchange or mix with one another, spotted usually with dark purple. Only about four of the species will not rank readily in one of these two series. The character of the keel and surface of the inner face of the segments in their lower thirds should be noted carefully in the living plant. Here we have three principal types :—1, the face not at all papillose and keel not distinctly hollowed out, as in *Candidum* and its allies; 2, the face more or less distinctly papillose, but the groove indistinct and glabrous, as in *Speciosum, Pomponium,* and *Martagon;* and 3, the face papillose, and the groove a distinct hollow, bordered by raised hairy lines, as in *Bulbiferum* and *Tigrinum.*

Stamens.—The filaments generally place the anther on a level with the stigma, and fall not far short of the mouth of the flower. Both style and filaments are decidedly shorter than the perianth in the erect-flowered *Concolor,* and in several of the drooping-flowered species of the *Martagon* group; and the stamens are decidedly shorter than the style in *Candidum.* In the direction of the filaments, and shape of the fully expanded flower, there is a uniform correlation. In the funnel-flowered Lilies all the filaments run parallel with one another and the style towards the mouth of the flower, resting against its lowest divisions, and curving a little upwards towards their points. In the bell-flowered Lilies the style is distinctly curved, and the filaments diverge on all sides from the centre.

Pistil.—In all the species there is a more or less distinctly clavate ovary. In all, there is a moderately short style, clubbed at the end by a stout, bluntly three-lobed stigma.

Capsule.—The Capsules, as far as I have seen them, of all the Lilies are quite uniform in general structure. To the question of how far there are differences in shape that may be used for specific characters, I have paid too little attention to living plants to speak with confidence on this subject.

The following is an outline of what I believe to be the most natural primary division of the genus. I believe that no one who will take the trouble to master the characters of these five groups, and once

understand them by the aid of living specimens, will find any difficulty
in referring any flowering specimen to its proper position.

SUB-GENUS I. CARDIOCRINUM.

Perianth, funnel-shaped, with oblanceolate segments, falcate only at the
apex.

Leaves, stalked, heart-shaped, ovate—

> 1, *Cordifolium* ; 2, *Giganteum*.

SUB-GENUS II. EULIRION.

Perianth, funnel-shaped, with oblanceolate segments, which are falcate only
at the apex ; leaves, linear or lanceolate, sessile, or nearly so.

Tube scarcely widened from the base to the middle—

> 3, *Philippense;* 4, *Wallichianum*; 5, *Longiflorum* ;
> 6, *Neilgherrense*.

Tube gradually narrowing from the base to the neck—

> Leaves, scattered—

>> 7, *Odorum;* 8, *Brownii;* 9, *Krameri ;*
>> 10, *Nepalense;* 11, *Candidum* ; 12, *Belladonna*.

> Leaves in whorls—

>> 13, *Washingtonianum* ; 14, *Washingtonianum-*
>> *Purpureum ;* 15, *Parryi*.

SUB-GENUS III. ARCHELIRION.

Perianth, open, funnel-shaped, with deeply spreading segments, which are
broadest below the middle ; stamens, diverging from the curved style.

Leaves, sessile—

> 16, *Tigrinum* ; 17, *Oxypetalum*.

Leaves, shortly-stalked—

> 18, *Speciosum ;* 19, *Auratum*.

SUB-GENUS IV. ISOLIRION.

Perianth, erect, with segments, which are falcate in the expanded flower,
but not revolute ; stamens diverging on all sides from the straight style.

Leaves in whorls—

> 20, *Philadelphicum* ; 21, *Medeoloides*.

Leaves scattered.—Style shorter than ovary—

> 22, *Concolor*.

> Style longer than ovary—

>> 23, *Bulbiferum ;* 24, *Croceum ;* 25, *Davuricum ;*
>> 26, *Elegans ;* 27, *Catesbœi*.

Sub-genus V. MARTAGON.

Perianth, cernuous, with the segments very revolute; stamens diverging on all sides from the curved style.

Leaves in whorls.

American species; bulbs, annual, bearing rhizomes—

28, *Canadense;* 29, *Pardalinum;* 30, *Superbum;* 31, *Lucidum;* 32, *Roezlii;* 33, *Columbianum;* 34, *Humboldtii.*

Old-world species—

35, *Martagon;* 36, *Avenaceum;* 37, *Hansoni.*

Leaves, scattered.

Leaves lanceolate—many norved—

Perianth, falcate above the middle—
38, *Monadelphum.*

Perianth, revolute to below the middle—
39, *Polyphyllum;* 40, *Ponticum;* 41, *Carniolicum.*

Leaves, narrowly linear—with one or few nerves—

Segments of the perianth, from six to twelve lines broad in the middle—
42, *Testaceum;* 43, *Leichtlinii;* 44, *Batemanii;* 45, *Pseudo-tigrinum;* 46, *Wallacei.*

Segments of the perianth, from three to six lines broad in the middle—
47, *Pomponium;* 48, *Chalcedonicum;* 49, *Callosum;* 50, *Tenuifolium.*

NOTE.—The *Notholirion* group (Himalayan Lilies), with tunicated bulbs, stigma cleft into three subulate hooked divisions, are now referred by Mr. Baker to the *Fritillarias.* *See* end of this Chapter.

SUB-GENUS I.

CARDIOCRINUM (Endl.) (HEART-SHAPED FOLIAGE LILY).

Perianth, funnel-shaped, with oblanceolate long-clawed segments, which, in the expanded flower, are falcate only at the apex, and are not papillose on the inner surface, and have a shallow groove on the keel; stamens, slightly curved, and parallel with the style; leaves, heart-shaped-ovate, with a reticulated venation and long stalks. It is distinguished from the other sub-genera by its *Smilax*-like leaves.

This first genus is at the same time the finest and most distinct of all the true Lilies, being completely different from all the rest in possessing long petioles, and in the shape and nerving of its leaves. Thunberg, who was the first of the post-Linnæan botanists, to gather and describe the plant, placed it originally in *Hemerocallis*, but on better second thoughts changed his mind, and admitted it into *Lilium*. Salisbury, long ago, made for it a distinct genus, which he called *Sausserea,* but, by a genus Salisbury meant something quite different to what we usually understand by the name. Kunth and Endlicher place it in a section by itself, which they call *Cardiocrinum.* There are two geographical races, or sub-species of the plant, one of which inhabits Japan, and the other the Himalayas, and all recent authors, following Zuccarini in Siebold's "*Flora Japonica,*" speak of these as two distinct species.

1. *L. Cordifolium.*—Thunb. Linn. Trans. ii., 332; Schult. fil. Syst., vii., 420; Siebb. et Zucc. Flor. Jap. fasc., iii., 33, t. 13, fig. 2 and 14; Kunth, Enum., iv., 268; Miquel Ann. Mus. Lug. Bat., iii., 157; *Hemerocallis Cordata,* Thunb. Fl. Jap., 143; Gaertn. Fruct., ii., 484, t. 179, fig. 5.—The bulb (*see* page 90) of this plant is, in every respect, like that of *Giganteum,* but smaller, and with thicker, more wrinkled, and less regular scales; stem, 3 to 4 ft. high, naked

at the bottom, and with the leaves at first arranged in rosettes, the lowest ones stained with blood red, the stem-leaves ovate, deeply heart-shaped, and with long stalks; the raceme, in the specimens which I have seen, is not quite a foot long, contains from four to ten flowers, and, when fully expanded, is from 9 to 14 inches across, the foot-stalks of the flowers being patent, from 3 to 8 lines long, with ovate, acute, caducous bracts; perianth, narrowly funnel-shaped, from 4 to 6 inches long, with the tube gradually narrowed from 3 or 4 lines at the base; the segments, which in the upper part are from 6 to 9 lines long, being gradually narrowed

Heart-shaped leaved Lily
(*L. Cordifolium*).

in the lower two-thirds of their length; stamens, one-third of the length of the perianth; anthers, yellow, 4 to 6 lines long; capsule, like that of *Giganteum,* but more wrinkled. Japan* and the Kurile Islands, at an altitude of from 400 to 600 feet; Oldham, 866; Wilford, 1,000; *Maximowicz.* Blooms in our gardens in the beginning of August.

L. Glehnii (F. Schmidt), is a variety of the above.

Description of this Lily, flowered at Kew for the first time in 1877.

"The flowers are whitish on the exterior, marked with purple on the interior, especially towards the base of the two inner segments. These coloured spots evidently serve as sign posts to insects; which in visiting the flower for the honey, must necessarily pass between the spots in question

* Sometimes found 1 foot deep in the soil of the forests of Japan, generally in moist situations.

and the anthers, which are curved downwards, so that the insects would brush out the pollen therefrom. This is one of innumerable illustrations of adaptation and design offered to the intelligent plant lover. It was at one time supposed that the Japanese *Cordifolium* was the same as, or a variety of *Giganteum* of Nepaul. From our figure, however, it will be seen that the differences between this species and *Giganteum* are well marked. The leaves are more distinctly cordate than in *Giganteum*, the flowers less numerous and more crowded, the bracts much broader, the flower buds erect, not pendulous, the flowers of a different shape, more widely spreading at the limb, the segments of a different form, and the curvature and relative length of the stamens quite different.* We do not know if these are general characteristics, as we speak only from the specimen before us. It would seem that botanists have been misled by the examination of dried specimens only. Much allowance must be also made for individual variation. The entire height of the stem is 26 inches. The first fully developed leaf scar is exactly 12 inches from the base of the stem, and is about half an inch broad. Six inches below this is a small round scar about $\frac{1}{2}$ inch broad, which may have given origin to a very small leaf, which must soon have withered. In the 4 inches above the second well developed scar, are crowded the insertion of no less than six leaves. This exactly agrees with M. Max Leichtlin's statement that the stalk is not leafy but rises bare to the height of from 1 to 2 feet, and then 6 to 8 leaves appear in a sort of rosette. The following are exact measurements of the Kew specimen :—1st leaf 6 inches. 2nd leaf 12 inches. 3rd leaf 14 inches. 4th leaf 15 inches. 5th leaf $15\frac{3}{4}$ inches. 6th leaf $16\frac{1}{2}$ inches. 7th leaf $17\frac{1}{2}$ inches. 8th leaf 18 inches. 9th leaf 19 inches, 1st flower 20 inches, above the base of stem."—*W. T. Thiselton Dyer, Gardeners' Chronicle, vol. 8., p. 406.*

2. *L. Giganteum.*—Wallich, Tent. Fl. Nep. 21, t. 12-13 (excl. syn.) ; Kunth, Enum. iv., 268 ; Hook. Bot. Mag. t. 4,673 ; Flore des Serres, t. 771-2 ; Belg. Hort. iii., t. 21.—*L. Cordifolium*, D. Don, Prod. Nep. 52, non Thunb.—Bulb (*see* page 91), globose, cæspitose, perennial, 3 to 4 inches thick ; scales, ovate, somewhat spreading ; stems, 6 to 10 feet high, terete, smooth, green, $1\frac{1}{2}$ to 2 inches thick at the base ; radical leaves, green, not tinged with red ; stem-leaves, 12 to 20 in number, extending to the base of the stem, scattered, ovate-acute, deeply cordate at the base, of a deep green colour, reticulated-veined, the lower ones 12 to 18 inches in length and breadth ; leaf-stalks, erect-patent, channelled, 9 to 12 inches long, the upper ones gradually smaller, and on shorter foot-stalks ; raceme, of 10 to 12 flowers, and from 1 to 2 feet in length, attaining a foot in width when fully

* We have noticed also the following differences. 1. The bulb of *Cordifolium* is much smaller than that of *Giganteum*, being no bigger than one of the offsets found at the base of the dead flowering stalk of the latter species, and in shape much resembles a Filbert. 2. The bud at starting has the outer leaves more closely imbricate and of a pinkish character. 3. The leaf in *Giganteum* is more acutely cordate ; the length of the stalk greater, and the colour much lighter. 4. The foliage in *Cordifolium* is more or less pendulous ; in *Giganteum* more erect. A good figure of this Lily is given in *Gardeners' Chronicle, vol. 8, p. 305.*

Giant Lily *(L. Giganteum).*

expanded; bracts, boat-shaped, large, ovate, caducous; pedicels, 3 to 12 lines long, at first almost nodding, but ascending when bearing fruit; perianth, funnel-shaped, fragrant, 5 to 6 inches long, white, tinged with purple on the inside, and with green on the outside; tube, gradually widened from the base (where it is 6 or 7 lines in diameter) to the neck (where it is from 18 to 21 lines in diameter): segments, oblanceolate, 9 to 12 lines broad at the base of the upper quarter of their length, gradually narrowed towards the base, inner ones broader; stamens, two-thirds the length of the perianth; filaments, flattened downwards, nearly straight, 3 to 3½ inches long; anthers, yellow, 3 to 4 lines long; pollen, yellow; ovary, cylindrical, 1 inch long; style, scarcely curved, 1½, or nearly twice the length of the ovary; capsule, broadly oblong, 2 or 3 inches long, obtuse-angled, umbilicated at the apex; neck, large, top-shaped. Temperate region of the whole Himalayan chain, from Kumaon and Gurwhal to Khasia[*] and Sikkim, at an altitude of from 5,000 to 10,000 feet. "It flowers in the rainy reason, from May to the end of July."—Wallich.

NOTE—A peculiarity of this species (and, we believe, of *Cordifolium* also), is that seedling bulbs or offsets grow on increasing in size till in a period of from three to five years a large bulb is formed, in the case of *Giganteum*, from 5 to 7 inches in length, and 10 to 15 inches in diameter, hitherto the foliage has been broad and low growing; but when the bulb has attained the size mentioned, it throws up in the spring a much thicker bud, by many likened to a young cabbage, whence a stout stem arises, sometimes 6 inches in diameter, and from 5 to 10 feet high, studded with numerous flowers, resembling somewhat the flowering spike of an *Aloe*, forming a striking and beautiful object. In the meanwhile, the bulb exhausted by the process, decays and disappears, leaving from three to five small offsets at the base of the stem, which in due course, increase in size, and under favourable circumstances, repeat the performance.

[*] The native name in Assam is "Kalang Tatti."

SUB-GENUS II.

EULIRION (Endl.), FUNNEL-FLOWERED LILIES.

Perianth, funnel-shaped, with long-clawed oblanceolate segments, which are falcate only at the apex, not papillose on the inside, seldom dotted ; groove on the keel shallow ; stamens, slightly curved, parallel with the style ; leaves, linear or lance-shaped, sessile, or nearly so ; flowers, fragrant, often white, never brilliant red nor yellow.

KEY TO THE SPECIES.

Tube scarcely widened from the base to the middle......
- 3 *Philippinense.*
- 4 *Wallichianum.*
- 5 *Longiflorum.*
- 6 *Neilgherrense.*

Tube gradually narrowing from the base to the neck.
- 7 *Odorum.*
- 8 *Brownii.*

Leaves scattered ....
- 9 *Krameri.*
- 10 *Nepalense.*
- 11 *Candidum.*
- 12 *Belladonna.*

Leaves in whorls ....
- 13 *Washingtonianum.*
- 14   ,,   *Purpureum.*
- 15 *Parryi.*

3. *L. Philippense.*—Hort. Veitch ; Baker, Gard. Chron., 1873, with a plate, Bot. Mag., t. 6,250.—Bulb, ovoid, perennial ; stem, 1½ to 2 feet high, one-headed, very slender, terete, smooth, green, or spotted

Philippine Islands Lily
(L. Philippinense).

with purple ; leaves, thirty to forty in number, scattered, patent-falcate, narrowly linear, 3 or 4 inches long, 1½ to 2 lines broad, smooth, three-nerved, and of a shining green colour; perianth, horizontal, white, slightly tinged with green on the outside near the base, narrowly funnel-shaped, 7 or 8 inches long ; tube ½ inch in diameter near the middle ; segments, oblanceolate, falcate only at the apex, long-clawed, 15 to 18 lines broad at three-quarters their length from the base, smooth and undotted on the inside; keel, indistinct, green ; stamens, a little shorter than the perianth ; filaments, greenish, slightly curved, 5 to 5½ inches long ; anthers, 2½ to 3 lines long; pollen, yel-

The shape of the flower as given above is not quite correct, the tube is too broad, and the segments not sufficiently expanded and revolute. A fine figure is given in *Gardeners' Chronicle*, 1873, p. 1141, by G. Worthington Smith, but too large for this work.

L. Philippinense was collected by Gustave Wallis, in the district of Benquet, in the Island of Luzon, 7,000 feet above sea level, in July, 1871. It grew among the grass in poor soil, partially shaded, on steep banks, the flowers are sweetly perfumed, and are said to be 10 to 12 inches in length. Its chief characteristic is the long very slender foliage.

low; style, together with the ovary, ½ an inch shorter than the perianth; Philippine Islands, Wallis in hort. Veitch.

4. *L. Wallichianum.*—Schultes fil. Syst. vii., 1689; Kunth., Enum., iv., 267; Wall. Cat. 5,076; Hook. Bot. Mag., t. 4,561; Lindl. et Paxt. Flow. Gard., 1850, 120, with a plate; Lemaire, Jard. Fleur, t. 105, 106; Flore des Serres, t. 612.—*L. Batisua*, Hamilt. M.SS.—*L. Japonicum*, D. Don, Prod. Nep. 52, non. Thunb.—*L. Longiflorum*, Wallich, Tent. Fl. Nep. 40, t. 20, non Thunb.—Bulb (*see* p. 94), ovoid, 2 to 3 inches long; scales, thick, white, acute, closely imbricated; stem, 4 to 6 feet high, green, straight, terete, horizontal at the base; leaves, fifty to sixty in number, somewhat distinct from each other, scattered, ascending, sessile, acuminate, smooth, green, the lower ones 6 to 9 inches long, 3 to 6 lines broad in the middle, three-nerved, the upper ones shorter and broader, often five-nerved; flowers, often solitary, sometimes two or three in number, fragrant, horizontal from the top of the pedicel or slightly ascending; perianth, white, greenish on the outside

Wallich's Lily (*L. Wallichianum*). at the base, 5 or 6 lines in diameter, at
One-third natural size.   3 inches above the base; 7 to 9 inches long; tube, 3 or 4 lines in diameter at the base; segments with oblanceolate claws, acute, 1½ to 2 inches broad at three-fourth their length from the base; stamens, 2 inches shorter than the perianth; anthers, yellow, 12 to 14 lines long; ovary, ½ inch to 2 inches long; style, together with the ovary, as long as the stamens. The sub-temperate region of the Central Himalayas (Kumaon, Nepaul, &c.), at an altitude of from 3,000 to 4,000 feet. In Max Leichtlin's garden there is a smaller and more slender form, with about twenty-five leaves, which are distinct from each other, the lower ones smaller than the upper ones; anthers, 6 lines long; and another form, which has numerous leaves (200) much more closely set, and a stem 5 feet high.

Perhaps this might fairly be placed as a species of full rank.* Both for the height of the stem and size and fragrance of the flower it is the prince of the forms of the *Longiflorum* series. There is an excellent figure by Fitch, in the "Botanical Magazine," drawn from living specimens introduced by Major Madden, from Kumaon, 1850; and this plate was copied into the "Jardin Fleurist" and the "Flore des Serres." In all the descriptive books, from D. Don down to Spae, the synonomy is more or less confused with that of Chinese-Japanese forms. The history of the plant is as follows:—It was first sent, in the dried state, to Europe about 1802, by Dr. Hamilton,

* Compare the description in pages 15 and 18.

under the manuscript name of Lilium Batisua. There are specimens of this date in the herbaria both of Sir Joseph Banks (at the British Museum), and of Sir J. E. Smith (at the Linnean Society). *"Batisua"* is its vernacular Nepaulese name, but it was never published with a diagnosis. In his "Prodromus" of the Nepaul Flora, Prof. D. Don publishes it as "*Japonicum*," with a diagnosis that applies to the real *Japonicum*, but not to the Nepaulese plant. Wallich next, in his "Tentamen," gave an excellent figure and full description of it under the name of "*Longiflorum*," and upon the information which he furnished, the younger Schultes separated it as a distinct species under the name of "*Wallichianum*," which both Kunth and Spae adopt, though without understanding clearly the true state of the case—that this is the one sole Himalayan form of the *Longiflorum* series, and that it is restricted to the Himalayas, and that both *Japonicum* and *Longiflorum* proper belong exclusively to Japan and China.

Comparing together the *Longiflorum* forms it is very interesting, from a geographico-botanical point of view, to note that we have here, as in *Cordifolium*, an extremely distinct species, represented in Japan and Hindostan by barely distinguishable forms. In *Cordifolium* there are but two of these so-called sub-species, one Japanese and the other Himalayan. In *Longiflorum* the conditions of the case are more complicated. We have four sub-species, one with a much wider area in the extreme east, a second Himalayan, a third belonging to the mountains of the Indian peninsula, and a fourth insulated in the mountain heights of the Philippines. Another curious point to note is, that the Neilgherry sub-species comes appreciably nearer to the Chinese-Japanese one, than does the Himalayan form. I should like much to direct the attention of cultivators, more to this beautiful and easily obtainable Neilgherry Lily, and should much like to know if all the forms could clearly be separated when grown in European gardens from the already known forms of the Chinese-Japanese plant, four of which, as I have said already (*Longiflorum, Eximium, Jama-juri,** and *Takesima)* are now passing about in our gardens under specific names.†

5. *L. Longiflorum.*—Thunb. Linn. Trans., ii., 333; Bot. Reg., t. 560; Lodd. Bot. Cab., t. 985; Bury, Hexand., t. 8; Kunth, Enum., iv., 266; Flore des Serres, t. 270; Miquel, Ann. Mus. Lug. Bat., iii., 157. —Bulb *(see* p. 96) perennial, globose, yellowish, with lance-shaped scales; stem, 1 to 3 feet high, straight, smooth, green, 3 or 4 lines in diameter; leaves, 20 to 40 in number, scattered, ascending, tolerably closely set, of a shining green colour, *five-nerved,* those at the middle of the stem 3 to 4 inches long, and 4 to 6 lines broad in

---

* *Jama-juri* means in Japanese, hill or mountain Lily, and is applied to several forms, such as *Callosum* and *Auratum*, which are found in these localities.

† Decidedly, yes. With the exception of *Jama-juri*, which form we are unable to recognise as distinct; but which is considered by Duchartre as identical with *Takesima*.

K

the middle, the upper ones more distant from each other, shorter, and lance-shaped; flowers, usually solitary (sometimes two to six in number), nearly horizontal; perianth, white, fragrant, narrowly funnel-shaped, 5 to 7 inches long; tube, 2 to 3 inches long, scarcely widened above the base; segments, oblanceolate, obtuse in the expanded flower, falcate in the upper fourth of their length, 12 to 18 lines broad at two-thirds of their length from the base; inner ones broader; filaments, white, 4 or 5 inches long; anthers,

Long-tubed White Lily
(*L. Longiflorum*).

The handsome long-tubed White Lily
(*L. Eximium*).

yellow, narrow, 6 to 9 lines long; pollen, yellow; ovary, 1 to 1½ inches long, and, along with the slightly curved style, scarcely exceeding the stamens in length; stigma, 4 to 4½ lines in diameter; capsule, narrowly oblong, obtuse-angled, umbilicated at the apex. Temperate regions of Japan, Oldham, 734, Maximowicz, &c.; China, Fortune, 57, 66, Reeves; Hong Kong, Capt. Urquhart; Formosa, Wilford, 548; Swinhoe; Oldham, 565; Capt. Champion; Loo-choo Islands, Capt. Beechey, C. Wright, introduced into Europe in 1810.* Of the

---

* M. Duchartre's comparison of these varieties is as follows:—"These splendid flowers may be grouped, in the first instance, according to the angle formed by the union of the flower and the stem supporting them. The flower of *Eximium* is at right angles with the stem or flower-stalk; while in *Longiflorum* and in *Longiflorum Takesima*, the flower forms an obtuse angle with the stem, a little more obtuse in the case of the former than in *Takesima*. The violet tint of the outer side of the flower suffices to distinguish the last mentioned variety, though it should be remembered that this tint, which is very manifest in the young flower-bud, disappears in the expanded flower on exposure to the light. This violet hue extends throughout the whole length of the prominent midrib of each division of the flower. The flowers of *Longiflorum* and *Eximium* are uniformly white.

The general form of the flower affords distinctive characters; thus in *Longiflorum Takesima* the form of the flower is tubular, inversely conical (funnel-shaped), with a wide base, and its divisions are but slightly turned back. The upper portion of the tube

various forms of this plant, the finest of all is *L. Eximium*, Court. Spae Mon., 14; Flore des Serres, t. 283-4.—*L. Jama-juri*, Siebold et De Vriese, Tuinbow Flora, i., 319, t. 11.—*L. Eximium Wilsoni*, Hort. Angl., is of taller growth, and has broader leaves and larger flowers, 8 or 9 inches long.—*L. Takesima* and *L. Abchasicum*, Hort., are forms of *Longiflorum*.

is dilated at the spot where the lobes begin, and in consequence of this arrangement the flower is moderately open. The flower of *Longiflorum* enlarges gradually and regularly from below upwards. The flower is more open than in *Takesima*, and shorter, and its six divisions are more widely spreading, the three outer ones are even appreciably revolute. In *Eximium* the tube is more nearly cylindrical, throughout its length; the aperture of the flower is oblique, and its six divisions are longer, narrower, thinner, and completely revolute. The dimensions of the flowers also serve to characterise the varieties. The flower of *Longiflorum Takesima* is 165 millimètres (6½ inches, about) in length, while the tube of the flower from the base to the origin of the lobes measures 95 millimètres (nearly 4 inches). The flower of *Longiflorum* (var. *Grandiflorum*, and hence larger than in the type) measures 140 millimètres in length=about 5½ inches, of which the tube from the base to the origin of the lobe measures about half (2½ inches); nevertheless, the diameter of the flower from tip to tip of the lobes is appreciably wider than in *Longiflorum Takesima*. Lastly, the flower of *Eximium* has a total length of 180 millimètres (more than 7 inches), of which 100 (4½ inches, about) are taken up by the tube. M. Lemaire has remarked ("Flore des Serres," iii., pl. 282, 284) that the filaments of the stamens are of unequal length in *Eximium*, while they are equal in *Longiflorum*, as they are also, according to M. Duchartre's experience, in *Longiflorum Takesima*.

To sum up, *Eximium* is characterised by its horizontal flower, which is longest of the three; by its narrow tube, but slightly dilated above; its wide and oblique limb, its oblong revolute lobes, and its unequal filaments.

Longiflorum has its flowers placed obliquely on the stalk, and almost erect; its flower is the shortest and the most widely expanded of the three; its lobes are wide, the three outer ones appreciably revolute.

Longiflorum Takesima has the flower obliquely inserted on the stalk, but less so than in the case of the last mentioned, intermediate in absolute length between the two others, the least widely expanded of the three, manifestly dilated at the throat, more or less tinged with violet externally, and with wide spreading (not revolute) lobes. As to the stem and leaves of these plants, the differences are so slight that no useful characters can be obtained from them. Nevertheless, it may be remarked that the leaves of *Longiflorum are broader, shorter, and thicker, and more fleshy than those of the other two*; while those of *Takesima* are the longest and narrowest, and usually 3-nerved.

M. Duchartre was originally of opinion that *Eximium* was a distinct species, but he no longer holds that view with the same confidence, and, moreover, he considers the two other forms as varieties of one species. *Eximium* has a strong and agreeable perfume, like that of orange blossom, and according to M. Leichtlin it may be distinguished from all the varieties of *Longiflorum* by its more compact habit (?) its shorter, more nearly sessile leaves (?), and generally by the great size of its snow-white flowers (nearly 8 inches long).—*Baker*.

Having for some years past been familiar with all these varieties of the *Longiflorum* group, we differentiate them as follows.

(a). With Purple Tinted Stems.	*Philippinense*, with tall slender stem, foliage narrow, frequent and acutely pointed, perianth 8 inches long, externally green tinted, tube long, funnel-shaped; disc broad, widely expanded, highly revolute; habit slender, flower large. *Takesima* (*Jama-juri* of Siebold), dwarf habit, foliage broad, perianth chocolate tinted externally, 5—6 inches long, tube bell-shaped, disc expanded, slightly revolute.

6. *L. Neilgherrense.*—Wight, Ic., t. 2,031-2.—*L. Tubiflorum,* Wight, Ic., t. 2,033-4.—*L. Wallichianum,* Wight, Ic., t. 2,035, non Schultes, fil.—*L. Metzii,* Steud. in Hohen. Ind. Or. Exsic., No. 954.—*L. Neilgherricum,* Hort. Veitch. Lemaire; Ill. Hort., x., t. 353.—Bulb (*see* page 93), globose, 2 or 3 inches long; scales, thick, lance-shaped;

The Neilgherry Lily
(*L. Neilgherrense*).

stem, 2 or 3 feet high, straight, smooth, decumbent for some length at the base; leaves, thirty to forty in number, of a shining green colour, ascending, firm, closely set, scattered (*i.e.,* not in whorls), [distinctly three-nerved, the lower ones 3 or 4 inches long, and 12 or 13 lines broad in the middle; flowers, one to three in number, ascending, white, fragrant; perianth, narrowly funnel-shaped, 6 or 7 inches long; tube, 2 or 3 inches long, scarcely widened above the base; segments, oblanceolate-clawed, in the expanded flower falcate only at the apex, cuspidate, callous at the apex, downy, 15 to 18 lines broad at three-quarters of their length from the base; stamens, a little shorter than the perianth; anthers, narrow, yellow, 9 to 12 lines long; pollen, yellow; ovary, 12 to 14 lines long, and, along with the slender style (which is from 3 to 3½ inches long), equal in length to the stamens; capsule, oblong, obtuse-angled. Temperate region of the Pulnies

.(b).

Wallichianum, stem tall, 4—6 feet high, foliage 3—5-nerved, narrow, acutely pointed, perianth green tinted externally, 7—9 inches long, tube long, funnel-shaped, disc widely expanded, highly revolute.

Neilgherrense, stem 2—3 feet high, foliage 3-nerved, very broad; perianth of a cream colour, shading into buff internally, 6—8 inches long, tube long, funnel-shaped, disc star-shaped, with expanded segments, not revolute.

With Green Tinted Stems.

Longiflorum, dwarf habit, foliage 5-nerved, broad and short, perianth bell-shaped, gradually increasing all its length, 4—5 inches long, disc widely expanded, only slightly revolute, like *Takesima.*

Eximium (Wilsoni of others), stem 3—4 feet high, foliage 3-nerved, crowded, long, narrow, acuminate; perianth funnel-shaped, 6—7 inches long, disc widely expanded, highly revolute, like *Philippinense.*

Madame von Siebold, a form, as regards foliage, intermediate between the two preceding, habit dwarf, perianth 7—8 inches long, bell-shaped, disc perfect, widely expanded, but not revolute.

For a very good paper on these Lilies, with woodcuts, *see* "*Florist and Pomologist,*" 1674, p. 171.

N.B.—We do not agree with Duchartre, as to any differentiation of these forms being obtainable from the angle formed by the union of the flower and the stem supporting them.

and Neilgherry Mountains,* in the Indian Peninsula; Wight, Gardner, &c.—*L. Tubiflorum* and *Wallichianum* (Wight), are forms with narrower leaves (6 to 9 lines broad in the middle), and with narrower perianth-segments (12 to 15 lines broad).

7. *L. Odorum (Japonicum)*.—Bury. Hexand. t. 2., Bot. Mag., t. 1,591; Lodd. Bot. Cab., t. 438; Reich. Exot., t 88; Kunth, Enum. iv., 257; Miquel, Ann. Mus. Lug. Bat. iii., 157.—*L. Odorum*, Planch., *L. Japonicum Colchesterii*, Fl. des Serres, t. 2,193-4.—Bulb, globose, perennial; stem, 1 to 2 feet high, straight, smooth, spotted with purple; leaves, 12 to 20 in number, scattered, ascending, dark green, more slender than those of *Longiflorum*, smooth, lance-shaped, acute, 5 to 7 nerved, 8 to 12 lines broad in the middle, the lower ones 4 to 6 inches long; flowers, sweet-scented, usually solitary, white on the inside, and more or less tinged with purple on the outside; perianth, 5 or 6 inches long, broadly funnel-shaped, gradually widening from the base to the neck, where it is from 15 to 18 lines in diameter; segments, oblance-olate-clawed, obtuse, in the expanded flower, falcate in the upper third part of their length, 15 to 18 lines broad at two-thirds of their length from the base; filaments, whitish green, shorter than the perianth by one-third; anthers, thick, oblong, 5 or 6 lines long; pollen, red; ovary, 12 to 15 lines long (together with the style, a little longer than the stamens); stigma, 4 lines in diameter; capsule, obovoid, 2 inches long, deeply and obtusely six-angled. Temperate regions of Japan, Maximowicz; Islands of the Corea, Oldham, 869.

A native of Japan, introduced to this country with *L. Tigrinum* in 1804, by Captain Kirkpatrick, of the East India Company's Service. There is a specimen, dried, from Kew Gardens, probably not much later, in the British Museum. It was gathered by Oldham in the Korean Archipelago, and is said to be also Chinese. It is not Himalayan, the plant intended by D. Don and

The Fragrant Lily (*L. Odorum*).

others, who have reported it from Nepaul, being *Longiflorum* var. *Wallichianum*. From all the forms of *Longiflorum* it may be distinguished by—1, its broader, fewer, and more spreading leaves; 2, the shape of the entire flower, and broader claw of its divisions; and, 3, its

* Gathered in the neighbourhood of Ootacamund, at an elevation of about 8,000 ft. by Dr. Wight, Gardner, &c., and northward in the Mysore territory, on Snowdon, and Dodabetta Peaks, by T. Lobb. The range of form which it presents in the breadth of the leaves and size of the flower, may be seen by Dr. Wight's three figures. It is quite as variable as the Japan-Chinese sub-species. A valuable late flowering, and we believe, quite hardy Lily. *See* page 20.

shorter anthers, with pollen tinged with red.   Both this and *Longiflorum* are rather tender in England, and need protection in winter.*

  8. *L. Brownii.*—Mielli, Flore des Serres, t. 47, is a tall, large-
flowered form, with from 25 to 30 leaves, and with larger flowers
more deeply tinged with purple on the outside than the preceding
form.   For plate of Bulb, *see* p. 96.

A magnificent Lily, frequently found in gardens under the name of *L. Brownii*, the origin
of which is very obscure.   Its specific name
presents certain difficulties, for it is not easy to
determine who was the author of it.   Spae, in
his memoir on the Lilies presented to the
Academy of Sciences at Brussels (July 5, 1845),
attributes it to F. E. Brown, nurseryman, of
Slough, near Windsor, in whose catalogue it
was inserted about 1838 or 1839.   According
to Spae, the name was reproduced by Miellez
in the catalogue of the exhibition held by the
Horticultural Society of Lille, in June, 1841,
Brown's Lily (*L. Japonicum* and in the catalogue of the Royal Agricultural
var. *Brownii*). and Botanical Society of Ghent, in June, 1843.
The same author gave a description and a coloured figure of it in the
first volume of the " *Annales de la Soc. Roy. d'Agric. et de Botan. de
Gand.,*" (i., 1845, p. 437-438, pl. 41).   Priority then belongs to the
name *Brownii*, of Brown; although in the same year (1845) M. Charles
Lemaire also described this plant in the " *Flore des Serres,*" (i., 1845,
p. 110), and illustrated it by an unnumbered coloured plate.

  As to the native country of this fine species, M. Lemaire says in
his article, " origin and specific name doubtful," and Spae writes,
" country unknown."   Siebold thinks it a native of Nepaul, and also
of China and Japan.   M. Max Leichtlin wrote to me recently, stating
that the plant was of Chinese origin, and on his authority I have
admitted this Lily as a native of China—very probably also of Japan,
but not of India.   Whatever be its origin, *Brownii* is a magnificent
plant, which has often been considered to be the problematical
Japonicum, very badly characterised by Thunberg.   Siebold's
catalogue for 1870-1871, p. 51, mentions it under the name of
Japonicum, Thunb., var. *Brownii*; nevertheless, as I have had several
specimens derived from different sources, and which have all presented
the same characteristics, I am disposed to think that it should be
admitted as a distinct and well-marked species.   Its stem is between

---

  * Three bulbs of this form were originally sent over to us in 1871-72, by M. Carl
Kramer, from Japan, as a fine form of *Longiflorum*, the bulbs were large and distinct in
shape.   We carefully planted them out of doors ; one of the three plants flowered ; we took
the flower to Kew, and it was identified with the figure given by Mrs. Bury ; but the bulb
dwindled away in a rather too cold and damp locality : subsequently, we obtained
further supplies of this very beautiful form.

2 and 3 feet high, thick, rounded, and glabrous. It is brown at the base in consequence of the great number of small reddish brown lines scattered over its green surface, its upper portion is unspotted. The numerous leaves are alternate, and scattered equally over the stem, linear-lanceolate in outline, acute at the point, narrowed at the base, with five or seven nerves prominent on the lower surface, slightly channeled above ; they spread widely, and offer at their extreme base a transverse callosity. They are very small at the base of the stem, where they soon dry up, and gradually increase in size upwards ; the three or four uppermost form a kind of false verticil at the base of the flower-stalk : these attain a length of 20 centimètres (about 8 inches). The flower is solitary, and very large and beautiful. It is of pure white in the interior, and even on the exterior of the three petals, which have only their prominent median nerve coloured of a purplish brown colour. This same tint is spread over the outer face of the sepals, which are margined with white. I have always found an agreeable and rather strong perfume in the flower, though according to M. Lemaire it is completely scentless, and in the opinion of M. Planchon nearly so. The flower is tubular, bell-shaped, with a spreading revolute limb ; the petals are much wider than the sepals, the stamens are bent downwards and have greenish awl-shaped filaments, supporting large brown anthers filled with reddish brown pollen. The stamens are as long as the tube of the flower, and are greatly exceeded in length by the style, which is much bent downwards and terminated by a deeply 3-lobed orange yellow stigma.—*Duchartre.*

In order to clear up the difference between the two forms, *Odorum* and *Brownii*, we adduce the following observations.

Having grown twenty-five plants of *L. Odorum* side by side in 1878 with one hundred plants of *L. Brownii*, we have noted the following differences.

L. Japonicum.	*L. Brownii.*
Bulb white or whitish yellow, never red or brown, broad at base ; the scales which are somewhat narrow and acute at tip, differ in length, the outer ones terminating at about ¾ the height of the inner scales.	*Bulb* on exposure to light assumes a red or reddish brown tint, the scales are broad, and all pass up overlapping, and terminate together at the apex of the bulb, thus giving it the peculiar shape (figured on page 96) known as oblate in form, the base being curiously constricted, much narrower than the apex.

Bud when about 1 inch above ground.

Green ; leaves broad and blunt, edged with a thin brown line showing a darker tinted venation ; apex, round, flat, blunt, resembling that of *Longiflorum.*	At first reddish brown with no green ; apex acute ; at about the height of 1½ inch, a little green shows under the red bracts ; resembling that of *Auratum,*

When about 3—4 inches high.

L. Japonicum.	L. Brownii.
Stem green, thickly irrorated with brown—or green with brown rings just below the insertions of the leaves; leaves 1½ inch to 2 inches long, of a bluish green colour, edged with a thin brown line, having a lighter coloured midrib on upper surface, erect, bluntly obovate, wide spreading, unfolded to base of stem.	Stem and bracts dark brownish red, the upper 1½ inch of bud only showing a green tint, tipped at the point more or less with brown both on upper and under surface of leaf; bracts closely appressed to stem, no leaves unfolded, bud closed up.

When about 8—10 inches high.

Stem a blue green, more or less irrorated with brown, getting darker near the base where it leaves the soil, the insertion of the leaf is marked with a brown line or patch; leaves alternate, continued down the stem to a distance from the soil of 2 inches; semi-erect or horizontal, not arched, not curving downwards at tip; broadest in the middle where they are four times wider than at the insertion, diminishing gradually thence to apex and base; about 3½ inches long, soft to the touch; bracts have died off and fallen.	*Stem* rich dark brown, with brown bracts adherent and fresh, the lower 6 inches unfurnished with leaves, leaves about 4½ inches long, harsh to the touch, lanceolate, pointed green with broader brown edging, more or less erect, curving in an arc, with the tips invariably pointed downwards. At its broadest part which is nearer the apex than the base, it is only twice as broad as at the insertion.

Apex of bud at summit of stem when 8 inches high.

Formed of 4 leaves, open, divergent, with their tips directed outwards, as in *Longiflorum*.	Formed of 4 or 6 leaves tightly closed together, as in *Auratum*.

Prevailing tint of plant.

Bluish green.	Bronzed red relieved with green.

Flower bud.

Pale green, tinted on the upper surface with brown, considerably swollen about the middle; blunt at the tip, one of the petals generally shorter than the others, exposing a yellow surface.	Chocolate or reddish brown, tinted both above and below; the tip which is acute being of a darker colour than the middle of the bud; shape long and narrow, only slightly thickened at about two-thirds of its length.

Flower.

When first opened disclosing a golden yellow interior, which fades gradually to a rich cream colour; tube dilating from base to disc, but especially dilated about one-third down; disc somewhat revolute, anthers light brown, fragrance very great, resembling that of the Cape Jessamine.	When first open disclosing a white or light creamy white tint, soon fading to a pure white, contrasting very beautifully with the rich chocolate coloured exterior. Tube cylindrical, and but slightly dilated; disc large, rounded, very greatly revolute; anthers dark brown; fragrance moderate like that of *Longiflorum*.

Compare likewise the following statement of the celebrated Bulb grower, J. H. Krelage, of Haarlem.

"About 40 years ago, there was cultivated with success in my father's garden, under the name of *L. Japonicum*, a fine and rare Lily.

"I cannot say whence it was introduced, but it is possible that my father bought it at the sale of the stock of the famous nursery of Voorhelm Schreevogt, in 1837. Of this Lily, there were sold annually a few dozen bulbs, especially in Belgium, at a price of 10s. 6d. each. It was then considered to be the true *L. Japonicum* of Thunberg, and was a form allied to *L. Odorum* of Planchon, figured and described in the "*Fl. des Serres*," t. 876-77.

"I find *Japonicum* under that name in the nursery catalogues of our firm in 1850—55, the last year at a much higher price than before. It had not been offered for a couple of years, as the stock had diminished too much. In 1858, it is again quoted at the former price, with a remark as to its rarity, but, in the following year, it was omitted, being lost or sold out, and since that time I have never met with this form in any collection. Planchon speaks about this Lily as being figured in Loddige's "*Botanical Cabinet*," t. 438, and states that it is in some points different from his *Odorum*. This is quite true, and both Lilies must be considered as two, perhaps closely allied, but different forms. *Odorum* was introduced to our nursery in 1854, and in the catalogue of that and the following year, it was noted that it was a distinct form of the old *Japonicum*. Both these Lilies shewed, at least from a horticultural point of view, so great a difference from *Brownii*, that if not considered a distinct species, they at least must be accepted as strikingly different varieties. *Brownii* was once cultivated and considered by some to be identical with Thunberg's *Japonicum*. This erroneous impression was, if I remember rightly, first cleared up by Spae in his "*Memoire sur le Genre Lis*," in 1845. M. Const Ghildorf, Ghent, in his catalogue (1844—45), writes about the two Lilies in question, as follows—In *Brownii*, the exterior of the petals is white striped with dark crimson, nearly $\frac{1}{4}$ inch broad, sepals greenish white, dotted with crimson, and bordered with clear white. The Japan Lily introduced in 1804, has only the top petals tinged with crimson.

"As far as I can judge, there are four different forms which I should be inclined to unite in two groups. One, consisting of *Brownii*, the finest of all, the most popular, as well as the most hardy and most easily grown. The other group should comprise the old *Japonicum, Odorum* of Planchon, and *Japonicum Colchesterii*. Being delicate and difficult to manage, the two former are at present probably lost in Europe. Their three forms are very closely allied to each other, but differ much from *Brownii*, especially in the bulbs."—*J. H. Krelage, Garden, v.,* 13, *p.,* 541.

After this evidence, we think no one will in future, mix up under one name, these two very distinct horticultural, if not botanical, forms.

In the Abbe David's collection of Chinese plants, there are some specimens gathered at Kin-liang, which appear to hold a somewhat intermediate position between *Longiflorum* and *Brownii*, having a more open flower than the former, and being apparently tinted with purple outside ; we should refer this form to our *L. Odorum.*

9. *L. Krameri.—Japonicum*, Thunb. Fl. Jap. 133 ; Mem. Acad. Peters., iii, 205, tab. v. fig. 2 ; Flor. and Pom. No. 73, t. 13, c. icone. —Hort. Wallace, Hook. fil., Bot. Mag., t., 6,058.—Stem, 3 or 4 feet high, slender, terete, smooth, spotted with purple ; leaves, distinct from each other scattered, fifteen or sixteen in number, linear-lance

shaped, acuminate, very shortly stalked, firm, green, five-nerved, with minute papillæ on the margins, 6 to 9 inches long, and 6 to 9 lines broad; perianth fragrant, horizontal, solitary, broadly funnel-

shaped, whitish with a slight reddish tinge, 6 or 7 inches long, gradually narrowed from the base to the neck; segments, oblanceolate-oblong, in the expanded flower, falcate above the middle in the upper third part, the outer ones 15 to 16, and the inner ones 20 to 21 lines broad; filaments about half the length of the perianth; anthers, of a dull brown colour, 8 or 9 lines long; pollen, red; ovary, 15 to 18 lines long, half the length of the slightly curved style; stigma, 4 to 4½ lines in diameter. Japan; flowers in the beginning of July. Probably a hybrid be-

Kramer's Lily (*L. Krameri.*)

tween *Speciosum* and *Odorum* (?), having leaves like those of the former, and perianth and anthers like those of the latter (v. v. ex hort. Wilsoni).—Var. Barrianum, Baker.—A smaller and slenderer form, with more numerous and more crowded leaves, which are three-nerved and from 2½ to 3 lines broad; perianth, white, 4 inches long; outer segments, 9 to 10 lines broad in the middle, inner ones, 15 to 18 lines broad; ovary, an inch long; style, ½ inch long; anthers. ½ inch long (v. v. in hort. Barr).

This novel and most beautiful form was sent over to me, for introduction into Europe from Japan, by M. Carl Kramer, in the winter of 1871—72, with 3 drawings, one white, one pale purplish blush, the third, similar in colour, but much larger in flower, of the size and shape of *Auratum* This Lily was at first received with incredulity, the drawings were considered exaggerated, and it was expected to turn out only a poor form of *Auratum*. Subsequent experience has, however, fully vindicated its fair fame as one of the most delicate and beautiful species of the Lily tribe. It is stated to grow wild on the mountains of Senano, in the island of Nippon, and also on the hills near Kioto, at a level of 3,000—4,000 feet above sea level, and ought, therefore, to be perfectly hardy in this country. The bulb, being small, bears the long journey to Europe very badly, at first few importations arrived otherwise than rotten, but now they come over, having been packed in clay, at my suggestion, by the thousand, in fair condition.

The young growth somewhat resembles that of *Auratum*, but it is more slender both as to stem and foliage, the latter is scanty, narrow, and pointed, the lower part of the stem is devoid of leaves. Out of doors, with us, it flowers in July, the colour varies from white, or white suffused with a faint lilac blush, to a rich purple, some of the deeper tinted forms are very beautiful. When fully established, it ought to be as hardy with us, as in Japan, and to produce 6 to 8 blooms. A considerable difference of opinion has arisen, as to whether the plant is really a species, or only one of the many distinct bybrids or seedling varieties, which Japanese gardeners know so well how to originate and perpetuate. Professor Baker suggests that it is a hybrid between *Japonicum (Odorum)* and *Speciasum*, but neither flower nor habit show the least trace of the last named species. Mr. T. Moore suggests that it is a hybrid between *Auratum* and *Japonicum*, if, indeed, it be not a mere selection from *Auratum* itself. Three forms were described by M. Kramer originally, but he added "there are many more startling varieties of it." It is no doubt one of the most delicately beautiful of all Lilies, and well deserving of the most careful culture. We think the fact that it is gathered on the mountains of Japan, and exported annually in thousands, quite disposes of the idea that it is any thing else but an indigenous form ; it may be originally a wild hybrid between *Auratum* and some other form, but it certainly did not originate in Japanese cultivation.

Compare Thunberg's remarks in the footnote on page 68, that his *L. Japonicum* "was spontaneous (indigenous ?) at Miaco and elsewhere, and often cultivated by the Japanese as an ornamental plant." Mr. Baker considers from his inspection of Thunberg's original specimen now in the herbarium at Upsala, that *Krameri* is the plant there referred to by Thunberg, in 1873, and described as an indigenous Japanese species.

10. *L. Nepalense.*—D. Don, Wern. Trans. iii., 412 ; Prodr. Nep. 52 ; Wallich. Pl. Asiat. Rar. iii., 67, 291, Cat. 5,078 ; Kunth, Enum. iv., 267.—*L. Ochroleucum*, Wall. in hb. Lindley.—Bulb, not known to me ; stem, 2 to 3 feet high, straight, slender, smooth ; leaves, 30 to 50 in number, scattered, of a shining green colour, ascending, smooth, lance-shaped, acute or linear, the lower ones 3 or 4 inches long, 6 to 9 lines broad in the middle, distinctly five to seven-nerved, the upper ones shorter and distant from each other ; flowers, solitary, or few in an umbel, slightly fragrant (pedicels with bracts at the base in a whorl of reflexed leaves), or few in a loose raceme, the lower pedicles ascending, 2 or 3 inches long ; nodding at the top ; perianth, 4 or 5 inches long, broadly funnel-shaped, whitish-yellow, more or less tinged with purple on the inside, often marked with scattered dots ; segments, oblanceolate-clawed, bluntish, in the expanded

The Nepaul Lily (*L. Nepalense*).

flower, falcate in the upper third part, 6 to 12 lines broad at two-thirds of their length from the base ; stamens, shorter than the perianth by one-fourth ; anthers, narrow, 6 or 7 lines long, pollen, yellow, ovary, 9 to 12 lines long, together with the style, a little longer than the stamens ; capsule, ovate, 2 inches long, obtuse-angled. Temperate regions of the Western and Central Himalayas, at an elevation of 7,000 to 9,000 feet above sea level, from Gurwhal and Kumaon to Nepaul. Wallich, Thomson, Jacquemont, &c.

Introduced into England in 1855. Evidently a very beautiful form. Unfortunately it is not in cultivation in Europe at the present time.

11. *L. Candidum.*—L. Sp., 433 ; Bot. Mag., t. 278 ; Red. Lil., t. 199 ; Bury, Hexand., t. 38 ; Reich., Ic. Germ., t. 445 ; Kunth, Enum., iv., 266.—Bulb (*see* p. 97), ovoid, perennial, large, yellowish ; first leaves produced in winter, sessile, oblanceolate, 1½ to 2 inches broad ; stem, 3 to 4 feet high, straight, smooth, blackish-green ; leaves, 100 or more in number, scattered, ascending, green, acute, two to five-

nerved, with minute papillæ on the margin, those at the centre of
the stem linear, 3 to 6 inches long, the lowest ones oblanceolate
obtuse, the upper ones gradually smaller, the highest lance-shaped,
1 to 1½ inches long, and pressed close to the stem ; raceme, short,
deltoid, containing from 6 to 20 flowers, and, when fully expanded,
6 to 8 inches broad; lower flowers nodding; bracts, lance-shaped or
linear ; pedicels, ascending, the lowest ones 2 or 3 inches long, often
with small bracts ; perianth, white, fragrant, broadly funnel-shaped,
2 or 3 inches long, gradually widened from the base to the neck

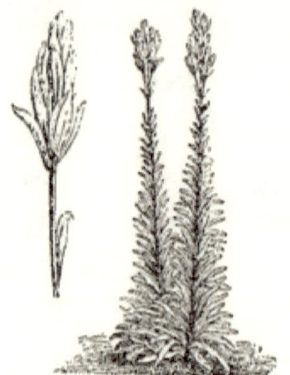

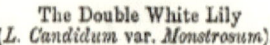

The Double White Lily
(*L. Candidum* var. *Monstrosum*).

The White Lily
(*L. Candidum*).

(where it is 1½ inches in diameter) ; segments, in the expanded
flower, falcate in the upper third part, obtuse, downy at the apex,
6 to 9 (or, rarely 12) lines broad above the middle ; stamens, shorter
than the perianth by one-third; anthers, yellow, 5 or 6 lines long ;
style, together with the ovary, much longer than the stamens, nearly
as long as the perianth.   Southern Europe, from Corsica to Northern
Persia and the Caucasus.

1. Var. *Foliis Aureo Marginatis* is a form, in which a broad golden
margin to the foliage prevails, especially valuable in a winter garden.
The flower is the same, but of a very pure white colour.

2. Var. *Striatum*, Flore des Serres, t. 735, is a form with flowers
streaked with purple on the outside.

3. Var. *Spicatum (Flore Pleno* or *Monstrosum)*, Hort., is an abnormal
form, the flowers being abortive, and the bracts dilated, white, and
petaloid.

4. Var. *Peregrinum*, Linn.—*Peregrinum*, Mill. Dict., No. 2 ; Hayne,
Arzne., viii., 27 ; Sweet, Brit. Flow. Gard., ser. ii., t. 367. A slenderer form, with a purple stem, narrower leaves, and segments of
perianth narrower, longer, more acute, and more spathulate. A
garden variety, long in cultivation, not yet found in a wild state.

This is one of the earliest, if not the earliest known Lily, held sacred to the Virgin ; and it may also be said, one of the most beautiful, most sweetly scented, and most useful for decorative purposes ; its petals soaked in brandy are a popular remedy for cut fingers and bruises.

12. *L. Belladonna* (Leichtlin).—Stem, a foot or more high, slender, smooth, terete, green; leaves, about twenty in number, lance-shaped, very shortly stalked, distant from each other, green, smooth, acuminate, patent, 1½ to 2 inches long, 3 or 4 lines broad in the middle; flowers, one to three in number, the terminal ones erect at first, the lateral ones horizontal when expanded; perianth, broadly funnel-shaped, 3 inches long, of a deep reddish colour on both sides, tinged with green at the base outside; tube, gradually widened from the base to the neck; segments, oblanceolate, not dotted, in the expanded flower falcate in the upper third part, 8 to 12 lines broad at two-thirds of their length from the base, the inner ones broader; stamens, shorter than the perianth by one-fourth; anthers, narrow, reddish, 3 or 4 lines long; style, slightly curved, and, together with the ovary, longer than the stamens; stigma, small. The plant has the habit of *Speciosum*, with a perianth like that of *Candidum*, only reddish. Described from Max Leichtlin's figure. It is, perhaps, a garden hybrid from *Speciosum* and *Longiflorum*.* It is believed to have come originally from Japan, having a great resemblance to the *Amaryllis*, from which it derives its name.

13. *L. Washingtonianum.*—Kellogg, Proc. Calif. Acad., ii., 13; Wood. Proc. Acad. Phil., 1868, 166; Baker, Gard. Chron., 1871, 709, t. 142; Regel, Gartenfl., t. 170; Flore des Serres, t. 1,975-6.— *L. Bartramii*, Nuttall, herb.—Bulb (*see* page 98), oblique, white, sub-rhizomatous, with small lance-shaped scales; stem, 3 to 5 feet high, terete, smooth, green, racemose at the top, bare below the raceme; leaves, in six to nine whorls, each containing from five to twelve leaves, or the upper ones scattered, oblanceolate, patent, sessile, smooth, 3 or 4 inches long, 8 to 12 lines broad above the middle, acute, green, gradually narrowed from the middle to the base; lateral veins, oblique and indistinct; raceme, from 6 inches to 1 foot long, containing from 12 to 20 flowers when expanded, 8 or 9 inches broad, pedicels ascending, the lower ones 2 to 4 inches long; bracts, small, oblanceolate or linear; perianth, fragrant, funnel-shaped, whitish, 2½ to 3 inches long, slightly tinged with reddish or purple on the inside; dots, few, small, lilac-coloured, scattered; segments, oblanceolate, 6 to 8 lines broad at two-thirds of their length from the base (from which point they are gradually narrowed to the base), falcate in the upper third or fourth part when the flower is fully expanded; stamens, shorter than the perianth by one-fourth; anthers, yellow, 5 or 6 lines long; ovary, 8 or 9 lines long, about

* Max Leichtlin informs me that he has not seen the plant, but only its picture, which was sent to him from America some years ago. Very little, therefore, is really known about this species (?) ; but, there is reason to believe that there are yet some unknown wonderful forms in Japan.

one-third the length of the curved style. California, in woods on the Sierra Nevada, &c.—Jeffray, 1,139; Bridges, 270; W. Lobb, 248.

The Washington Lily.
(*L. Washingtonianum*) (from a woodcut, kindly lent to us by Mr. Masters, of the *Gardeners' Chronicle*).

This noble Lily inhabits the western slope of the Californian Sierrá Nevada, and is found along the water-shed of the streams that run into the Sacramento. Professor Wood in the notice in the "Proceedings of the Academy of Philadelphia" above quoted, describes the plant as occurring in woods, here and there, from the Yosemite to the Columbia, and says further, "It is well-known to the miners, who recognise its superior qualities, and call it the *Washington* Lily." There are specimens in the Kew herbarium gathered by Jeffery in 1853, by W. Lobb in 1857, and also by Bridges. I am very glad to note that it has found its way at last into this country. It shows how Lilies have been neglected, when a plant like this has to wait 15 years for an orthodox botanical christening; and when growing in a country so much frequented and so easily accessible as California, it has to wait 17 years to reach the hands of our gardeners. Well, we have got it at last, and I hope we may not let it slip through our fingers, as we did in the case of *Nepalense*; and I only ask all those amongst your readers that can appreciate a fine Lily, to read the description I have just given, in order to realize what a treat is awaiting them.

14. *L. Washingtonianum Purpureum.*—A smaller and slenderer form; stem, 12 to 18 inches high; leaves, 1 to 1½ inches long; flowers, in umbels of four to eight; segments, more falcate, 5 or 6 lines broad, white when first expanded, but after a few days changing gradually to a deep vinous-purple colour, and with numerous small dots scattered over the entire inner surface; style, 9 to 12 inches long. California, on the coast ranges of the Sierras (*see* pages 22, 23).* Extensively cultivated in English gardens since 1873.

The Purple-tinted Washington Lily. (*L. Washingtonianum Purpureum*).

15. *L. Parryi.*—A new Californian Lily. Through the kindness of a correspondent, Mr. W. O. Gronen, I am enabled to furnish particulars of this new form, recently introduced into Europe, and placed by Mr. Watson in the Eurilion group. It has not yet, we believe, flowered in Europe.

"On one of my last botanical excursions in the vicinity of San Bernardino, Southern California, in the early part of July, 1876, I improved the opportunity to accept an often repeated invitation to visit the intelligent

* A very good description, with plates, of these two forms, is found in *Flor.* and *Pomol.*, 1874, p. 256.

brothers, J. G. and F. M. Ring at their mountain retreat near San Gorgonio Pass. Leaving the broad and picturesque basin of the Santa Anna Valley, near the emergence of this stream from the rugged mountain wall of the San Bernardino range, our route, after crossing Mill Creek, one of its largest eastern affluents, hugged close to the foot-hills bordering the upper Yucaipa Valley, thence by a more rapid ascent in a nearly direct easterly course, we reach an elevated bench, variously scattered with pine and oak groves, overlooking the broad sweep of San Gorgonio Pass, now traversed by the eastern extension of the Southern Pacific Railroad. In one of these mountain nooks the Messrs. Ring have located a Potato ranch, the elevation of over 4,000 feet above the sea level giving a sufficiently cool moist climate, while the adjoining mountain slopes afford an extensive summer cattle range long after the herbage of the lowlands has dried up.

"Owing to the lateness of the season, the early vegetation of this district had already given place to a more sparse mid-summer growth. In scattering groves of Pinus Coulteri, the ground was abundantly strewn with the massive cones of this peculiar species, its dense scales armed with formidable hooked spines; many of the largest cones were fully six inches in diameter, with a length of nine inches. At lower elevations throughout this district we find the large fruited Douglas Spruce quite common, this well marked variety in other particulars exhibiting the specific characters of this species in more northern and eastern localities. Among the rarities of this district we were able to secure a few specimens of Habenaria elegans (Bolander). The occasional perennial water courses here met with are mostly confined within deep and inaccessible ravines, but more frequently scant springs ooze out from beneath deep layers of porous strata, and spread out into boggy marshes generally choked up with rank willow and older growths, and occasionally expanding into small meadows of coarse grass and sedges. Near one of these largest expanses of moist, rich soil, is located the Potato ranch of Messrs. Ring, the special object of our visit. It is quite unusual, though none the less agreeable, to find in such secluded and unpretentious residences, indications of a refined taste exhibited in an excellent library, largely composed of scientific works, and books of exploration and travel, besides the necessary instruments for keeping up a meteorological record! No doubt from such resources the bachelor brothers find some relief from the tedium of their isolated location, and after the excitement and hardships of extensive travels on the north-west coast, seem reconciled to the independent solitude of a mountain ranch.

"Succeeding a cordial welcome, and the necessary care of our riding animals, the vegetation of this curious nook engaged our attention. On all the steep, gravelly slopes adjoining, there was the usual display of Californian evergreen shrubbery, including conspicuously the heath-like Adenostoma, which, under the common name of Chamisal, is largely used for fuel ; the holly-leaved cherry Prunus ilicifolia, exhaling a strong odour of bitter almonds; the Heteromeles arbutifolia, with glossy varnished leaves, and a prevalent form of "Californian lilac" (Ceanothus crassifolius), with thick leathery foliage; the dull, green hue which everywhere characterises the moorish growth is at this time of year partly relieved by brilliant scarlet festoons of Pentstemon cordifolius, trailing over adjoining bushes, or the less showy blossoms of Pentstemon ternatus. What, however, soon attracted more exclusive attention was a conspicuous yellow Lily, growing abundantly in the boggy ground adjoining the house, and sharing with the Potato patch the care and attention of the undisputed proprietors of the soil. Though not as showy as some other members of the Lily family in this region, there is a grace displayed in its large drooping flowers, surmounting a slender stem, beset with narrow scattered leaves, which occasionally are crowded at base into a distinct whorl; the plant varies in height from 3 to 5 feet, the number of flowers regularly unfolding from it is also variable, ranging from three to nine. The specimens then collected, together with later material, obligingly furnished by Mr. Ring, has supplied the necessary means for a complete description, and the whole having been placed at the disposal of Mr. Sereno Watson, who is now elaborating the endogenous flora of California, he has determined the same as an undescribed species, which he has complimented the discoverer by naming *L. Parryi*, Watson. At my request Mr. Watson has kindly furnished the following characteristic description :—

L. Parryi, Watson, Bot. Calif. ined.—"Bulb somewhat rhizomatous, of numerous crowded scales, fleshy and jointed, about an inch long, the upper joint broadly lanceolate; stem slender, glabrous, 2 to 6 feet high, 2-10 flowered; leaves usually scattered, occasionally the lower ones in a whorl; linear, oblanceolate, 4 to 6 inches long, and $\frac{1}{2}$ inch wide or less, mostly acuminate; flowers horizontal, pale yellow, sparingly and minutely dotted with purple; segments 3$\frac{1}{2}$ inches long, and 5 or 6 lines wide, with long, narrow claws, slightly spreading from the base; stamens and style $\frac{1}{2}$ inch shorter, equal; anthers, oblong, brownish, three lines long; capsules narrowly oblong, acutish, 2 inches long by $\frac{1}{2}$ inch in breadth.

"Of the section Eulirion, to which also belongs the Californian *L. Washingtonianum*. It is distinguished from the latter especially by its small bulbs, with jointed scales, its more scattered and narrower leaves, its small yellow flowers with less spreading segments, and its longer, narrower and acuter capsules." — *Dr. C. G. Parry, Proc., Davenport Academy of Nat. Science, vol. ii., p.* 188, where an excellent plate is given of this new form.

SUB-GENUS III.

ARCHELIRION (Baker), OPEN-FLOWERED LILIES.

Perianth, broadly funnel-shaped, or campanulate; segments, ovate, or oblong-lance-shaped, and deeply falcate in the expanded flower, dotted on the inner surface, and with papillæ on the lower part; groove on the keel very deep; stamens, diverging widely from the curved style.

KEY TO SPECIES.

Leaves, sessile; 16, *Tigrinum*, 17, *Oxypetalon*.
Leaves, shortly stalked; 18, *Speciosum*, 19, *Auratum*.

L

16. *L. Tigrinum.*—Gawl., Bot. Mag., t. 1,237; Red. Lil., t. 395 and 475; Kunth, Enum., iv., 259. — *L. Speciosum*, Andrews, Bot. Rep., t. 586, non Thunberg. — Bulb (*see* page 99.), perennial, globose, with oblong-lance-shaped, acute scales; stem, 2 to 4 feet high, blackish or brownish, with a white cobweb-like pubescence; leaves, deep green, scattered, smooth, ascending, firm, linear, 3 or 4 inches long, 3 to 6 lines broad in the middle, 5 to 7 nerved, the upper ones shorter, and bearing brownish red bulbils in the axils; raceme, consisting of 3 to 10 (rarely 20 to 25) flowers, broad, deltoid when expanded, sometimes 12 to 15 inches in length and breadth; bracts, small, ovate; pedicels divaricated, straight, nodding at the top, the lower ones 3 or 4 inches long, and often furnished with bracts; perianth, 3 or 4 inches long, and of a brilliant red colour, or tinged with orange; segments, broadly falcate, acuminate, callous at the apex, downy, 9 to 18 lines broad below the middle, the inner ones much broader, all with large dark-purple dots on the inner surface; claws, covered with numerous black-headed papillæ, groove on the keel very deep, and with pubescent edges; filaments, crimson, 2 to 2½ inches long; anthers, blackish, 6 to 8 lines long; pollen, crimson; ovary, green, 9 to 12 lines long; style, 1½ to 2 inches long, very much curved. I have not seen the capsule. Temperate regions of Japan and China. Flowers at the end of July and during the whole month of August. For the forms in cultivation, *see* T. Moore, Florist, 1873, 14.

T. Splendens.—Flore des Serres, t. 1,932; Wilson, Journal Hort., 1873, 251, with a figure; Floral Mag., t. 509 (Leopoldi), Hort., is a large-flowered, very late blooming form, with larger dots, broader leaves, and with black smooth stem.

The Double Tiger Lily
(*L. Tigrinum Flore Pleno*).

The Great Tiger Lily
(*L. Tigrinum Splendens*).

T. Fortunei is an early flowering form, having its stem densely covered with greyish fluffy pubescence.

*T. Lishmanni—.*Moore, Florist, 1873, 13, with a figure, is a form which has the dots confined to the central part of the segments, the upper part and the base being without dots.

T. Erectum has the pedicels less divaricated, and the flowers nearly erect. Introduced to our gardens in 1804 by Captain Kirkpatrick, but well known previously, though not named, by a figure published in 1791 by Sir Joseph Banks.*

17. *L. Oxypetalum*, Baker.—*Fritillaria oxypetala*, Royle.—Ill. Him., 388? Hook., Bot. Mag., t. 4,731 ; Lemaire, Fleur., t. 422.—*L. Triceps*, Klotsch, Reise, Wald., 33, t. 93.—Bulb, oblong ; scales, few, lance-shaped, acuminate, 1½ inches long : stem, slender, terete, green, one-headed, smooth, 1 to 1½ feet high ; leaves, 20 to 30 in number, at first densely rosulate, scattered, ascending, green, smooth, lance-shaped or linear, 2 to 3 inches long, and 3 to 6 lines broad in the middle ; perianth, horizontal, broadly funnel-shaped, 15 to 18 lines long ; segments, oblong, acute, broadly imbricated, 8 or 9 lines broad

Snake's-head Lily (*L. Oxypetalum*).

in the middle, purplish, tinged with green on the back, dotted with purple on the lower half of the inner surface, and with numerous papillæ crowded together at the base ; claw, short, deeply furrowed and bearded on the outside ; stamens, shorter than the perianth by one-third ; anthers, purplish, 3 or 4 lines long ; filaments, diverging ;

* To these we may add two more forms. *T. Fortunei Giganteum*, a pyramidal and fine form of *Fortunei*, and *T. Flore Pleno*, a remarkably handsome and vigorous variety, in which the perianth segments, instead of forming a single series as in the type, are multiplied into about six series, and are for the most part opposite, lying over each other in their recurved position, like the petals of the Hexangular Camellias.

This group may be considered one of the most popular and well known ; few objects, in autumn, stand out so conspicuously graceful as a group of tall well-grown *Tigers*, either the old *Sinensis*, or the grey hairy-stemmed *Fortunei Giganteum*, or the magnificent *Splendens*, especially if flanked on either side by a few blooms of *Auratum*.

It is also a most useful plant for harvest festival decoration, its time of bloom exactly coinciding. The old *Sinensis* is the first to appear, then, a fortnight later, *Fortunei* and *Flore Pleno*, and a fortnight later on, *Splendens*. So that for a period of about 6 to 8 weeks, *Tiger* Lilies together with *Speciosum* and *Auratum* are in full beauty.

The variety, *Lishmanni*, described and figured by Moore, does not, we incline to think, belong properly to this group, being not bulbiferous in the axils, but rather to be one of the forms of *Maximowiczii*, a recently introduced and very variable species, described later on. The great characteristic of the Tiger group, and one by which they are easily propagated, is the constant presence in the axils of each leaf of 1—3 bublets (*bulbillæ*), shiny and black, about the size of peas, which, in the autumn fall, or are gathered, and in 3 years time, will, if cultivated, produce flowering bulbs.

ovary, club-shaped, 5 or 6 lines long; style, straight, shorter than the ovary; capsule, obovoid-oblong, 9 to 12 lines long, obtuse-angled; valves, emarginate at the apex. Temperate regions of the Western Himalayas (Hoffmeister); Kumaon to Pindari, at an altitude of 8,000 to 12,500 feet (Strachey and Winterbottom).*

18. *L. Speciosum.*—Thunb., Linn. Trans., ii., 332; Bot. Reg., t. 2,000; Zuccarini, in Sieb. Fl. Jap., iii., 31, t. 12 and t. 13, fig. 1; Kunth, Enum., iv., 259; Bot. Mag., t. 3,785; Flore des Serres, t. 276.—*Lancifolium*, Mussche, Paxt. Mag., v., 267, with a figure, non Thunb. —Bulb (*see* page 101), perennial, globose, brown or brownish-red;

scales, lance-shaped, an inch long, somewhat loosely set; stem, 2 or 3 feet high, straight, terete, smooth, green, or spotted with red; leaves, 12 to 20 in number, scattered, distant from each other, very shortly stalked (the stalk pressed close to the stem), oblong-lance-shaped, acute or acuminate, of a shining green colour, firm, smooth, round at the base, the lower ones 5 to 6 inches long, 15 to 18 lines broad in the middle, and with five to seven distinct nerves distant from each other; raceme, deltoid, containing from three to ten flowers; pedicels, divaricated and furnished with bracts, the lowest 3 to 5 inches long, the central ones nearly erect, the lateral ones nodding at the top; perianth, 3 or 4 inches long; segments, ovate-lance-shaped, deeply falcate, 12 to 21 lines broad, the inner ones broader, white, usually more or less suffused with red, dotted with red on the inner surface, and with numerous papillæ; groove on keel deep and smooth; filaments, diverging widely, 2½ to 3 inches long; anthers, narrow, 9 to 12 lines long; pollen, saffron or red; ovary, 1 inch long; style, slender, very much curved, 1½ to 2½ inches long; capsule, obovoid-oblong, 2 inches long, obtuse-angled, umbilicated at the apex. Temperate region of Japan, flowers in the beginning of August.

The Red-spotted Japan Lily (*L. Speciosum* var. *Rubrum*).

For the forms in cultivation, *see* Dr. Masters, "Gard. Chron.," 1872, p. 1,522.

Punctatum, Lemaire (*Lancifolium*, Paxt. Mag., v. t. 267, *Albiflorum*, Hook., Bot. Mag., t. 3,785), is a form which has white flowers with red dots and papillæ.

---

* We have no knowledge of this form, it is evidently very closely allied to the *Fritillarias.*

It seems altogether out of place among the Lilies with its alternate short slender leaves, its few but elegant lilac tinted star-shaped flowers, scarlet anthers, and broad acutely pointed petals, much dotted towards the eye with black, and a bulb elongated like that of a *Fritillaria*, with but few acute scales.

Tametomo, Zucc., and Spae. (eximium, Hort. olim ; *Broussartii*, Morren, Mém. Acad. Roy. Brux., Feb., 1834, with figure ; *Vestale*, Masters, loc. cit.), is a variety which has white flowers without dots.

Teppo, *Krœtzeri*, Duchartre, has white very symmetrical flowers, the segments of which are marked with streaks of green on the outside, with green mid-ribs and green star shaped eye in centre of flower, and green stems.

A native of Japan, long known through Kæmpfer's drawing published by Sir Joseph Banks, but not introduced to Europe till 1832. As every one knows, it varies greatly in the size and colouring of the flower, but it is a most distinct plant, with no close affinity except to *Auratum*. Unfortunately it was first sent out into cultivation under a wrong name, *Lancifolium*,* and a name when once put into garden circulation, even when entirely erroneous, is very difficult to get changed. Let me beg of all my horticultural readers who have not done so already, to call this commonest and best known of the Japanese Lilies, in their catalogues and on their labels, by its correct name of " *Speciosum.*"

Confer the following extract from the *Gardeners' Chronicle* :—

Some time since Mr. Barr submitted to us a considerable number of specimens of *Speciosum*, with a view to getting their nomenclature definitely settled. This was no easy or satisfactory task, the degree of variation is considerable, the intermediate stages between one form and another numerous. To begin with, then, there are no absolute limits laid down by Nature herself, and any that may be made, are therefore arbitrary and liable to exception. Next, we have not sufficient evidence as to the constancy of particular forms. What security have we that the bulb, which this season produces flowers of any particular colour and form, will in the forthcoming season produce the same, especially if grown under different conditions. Again, there is the difficulty that with one or two exceptions, the varieties have not been authoritatively named. Neither Duchartre nor Baker have attempted to characterise the varieties of this species. What one grower calls *Roseum*, another calls *Rubrum*, and who shall decide which is correct ?

It may be well then to state the method adopted in the following attempt to come to some conclusion that may be serviceable to cultivators.

In the first place, we studied the specimens individually, one by one, so as to become acquainted with their prominent characteristics ; next, the several specimens were compared with each other, in order to see which marks were peculiar, which were general. This done, the next step was to look into the literature of the subject, and especially to compare the coloured figures that have been given, and to endeavour to ascertain whether any of the specimens before us conformed to the description or figure, and if so, to follow the botanist's rule of taking the oldest or first imposed name as the correct one, unless there be some special reason for deviating from the "law of priority."

All this demanded a considerable outlay of time and labour, and involved an amount of "detail" of which we do not think the cultivator would thank us to lay before him more than is absolutely essential for his purpose.

In brief, then, there is much variation in the colour of the stem, foliage, and particularly of the flower ; there is a good deal of variation in habit, and in the form of the leaf. There are also great differences in size and vigour, but these latter we may pass over as probably accidental. It may save time to put the results of our examination of Mr. Barr's specimens into a tabular form, thus :—

LILIUM SPECIOSUM, *Thun.* (var. HORTENSES).

A. Stems fasciated.

,,	brownish	...	...	...	...	...	FASCIATUM RUBRUM.
,,	green	...	...	...	...	...	FASCIATUM ALBUM.

* The true *Lancifolium* (Thunb.) is a miniature form of *Thunbergianum*.

B. Stems not fasciated.

  ,,   purplish brown.

flowers pink	RUBRUM.
,, white or nearly so ...	ALBUM.

  ,,   green.

flowers rose-coloured	ROSEUM.
flowers deep rose-coloured ...	SPECIOSUM. (proper).

flowers white or nearly so.

flowers white with rose-coloured spots	PUNCTATUM.
flowers quite white ...	VESTALE.

Concerning the fasciated varieties there is little need to speak. They differ in nothing from the other varieties, except in their fasciation. We have adopted the name *Fasciatum* to avoid confusion, though in some catalogues the name *Corymbiflorum* is used for the same varieties. Of the non-fasciated forms we have, first of all, a division into those which have green stems and those which have purplish-brown stems. We find in practice that this is a fairly good character; moreover, it is usually associated with the presence of a similar tint on the mid-rib of the segments of the flower, easily seen even when in bud. Of these purple-stemmed varieties there are two main forms, the one with pink, the other with white flowers. We propose that the name *Rubrum* should apply to the pink-flowered varieties with purplish stems. There is no figure, that we are aware of, of this variety. The white-flowered form of this section we propose to call *Album*, the *Albiflorum* of the "*Botanical Magazine*," belonging to another form.

Turning now to the green-stemmed forms, we have those with pale rose or blush-coloured flowers, in which the colour is not distinct; these we propose to refer to *Roseum*. The figure in *Paxton's Magazine*, vol. 5, plate 1, represents this form. Of the same colour, but much deeper, and with a defined white or whitish edge around the segments of the perianth, is the form we propose to call the true *Speciosum*. This is the plant well figured in the "*Botanical Register*," tab. 2000, by Lindley, under this name; also in the "*Flore des Serres*," t, 276-277. *Speciosum* var. *Kæmpferi* of "*Botanical Magazine*," tab., 3785, we take to be synonymous with this.

Of the white-flowered forms of this section we have one which is white with rose-coloured spots. For this the name *Punctatum*, given by Lemaire, "*Flore des Serres*," 276, seems most suitable, though if we were to follow botanical rules rigidly, it should be called by the Japanese name, *Tametono*. It is figured under the name *Albiflorum* in the "*Botanical Magazine*," t., 3785 and in "*Paxton's Magazine*," vol., 5, tab., 267, as *Lancifolium Roseum*. It has also been called *Broussartii* and *Eximium* in gardens, though the latter name applies to quite a different plant. So far as the bulbs of these varieties go, we have not personally had the opportunity of comparing any great number, but we are informed that the range of variation in the bulb is but slight. Lastly, for a variety with pure white unspotted flowers, we adopt the name *Vestale*.

Besides the typical form of *Rubrum* and *Roseum*, there are many intermediate (seedling) varieties, amongst these a few may be selected for special beauty.

1. *Speciosum Japonicum*, coming direct from Japan; with a broad crimson band, margined with white, introduced by us in 1869.

2. A form very similar to this, but, perhaps, rather broader in the petals; has gone under various names, as *Speciosum*, *Purpuratum* (Groom), *Schrymakersii*, &c.

3. A very richly coloured blood-red flower, with large petals, and of perfect shape; known as *Cruentum*.

4. *Macranthum*, a fine well-shaped form.

5. *Multiflorum*, a very free flowering form, with tall branching spike, &c., &c.

19. *L. Auratum.*—Lindl., Gard. Chron., 1862, 644b; Hook., Bot. Mag., t. 5,838; Flore des Serres, t. 1,528-1,531; Ill. Hort., ix., t. 338; Rev. Hort., 1867, t., 371; Miquel, Ann. Mus., iii., 156.—*Dexteri*, Hovey, Mag. Hort., Aug., 1862.—*Wittei*, Suringar in K. Koch, Wochens, 1867, 294.—*Speciosum*, imperiale, Hort., Siebold.—Bulb, somewhat like that of *Speciosum*; stem, 2 to 4 feet high, green, or

tinged with purple, slender, terete, smooth; leaves, 20 to 30 in number, scattered, distant from each other, very shortly stalked (stalk pressed close to the stem), lance-shape, acuminate, of a deep green colour, smooth, firm, five-nerved, the lower ones 6 to 9 inches long, and 9 to 15 lines broad; raceme, deltoid, containing from 3 to 10 flowers; pedicels, divaricated and furnished with bracts; perianth, 5 to 7 inches long; segments, broadly falcate, 1 to 2 inches broad in the middle (the inner ones broader), white, usually streaked with yellow in the middle, and with scattered purple dots and papillæ on the lower part of the inner surface; groove on the keel, distinct, and with smooth edges; filaments, 3 to 3½ inches long; anthers, narrow, 9 to 12 lines long; pollen, red; ovary, 12 to 14 lines; style, slender, very much curved, 2½ to 3½ inches long; capsule, 3 inches long, oblong, longer and narrower than that of *Speciosum*, emarginate at the apex.—Japan, Oldham,[*] 186, Maximowicz. There

The Golden-Banded Lily (*L. Auratum*).

are forms approaching *Speciosum*, with flowers streaked with red; some of these have from 25 to 30 broader leaves, and others from 40 to 50 narrower leaves.—*Wittei*, Suringar, is a variety with white undotted petals.

It was first introduced into Europe in 1862 by Messrs. Veitch.

Auratum is decidedly the grandest Lily known to cultivators; for description of its gorgeous magnificence and beautiful fragrance, *see* pp. 33, 43, 44.

It is a most variable form, hardly any two being alike, amongst the most prominent varieties we may mention.

(a). A fasciated form, with broad banded (not cylindrical) stem, containing from 30 to 100 flowers, generally small, crowded together in its summit.

(b). *Rubro-vittatum*, in which the yellow streak is replaced by a broad crimson band, the spots and blotches being large, and of a vivid crimson tint. In this variety there are only two colours, crimson and white; forming a most splendid contrast.

(c). *Cruentum*, a dwarf form, with flowers 11 inches in diameter, the streak is maroon, darkening to the centre, so as to produce the effect of a dark eye, the spots are purplish crimson.

* Uri is the Japanese word for Lily, and Yama for Hill : Yama Uri the Hill Lily, is the native name for *Auratum*.—Oldham wrote of it, "a splendid showy plant, growing chiefly in light rich soil amongst the shrubs and between the rocks."

(*d*). *Emperor*, in this, perhaps, the most beautiful form ; the eye is golden yellow, the whole is suffused, except at the margins of the petals, which are broad, by a rich blood red tint, as in *Speciosum* ; at the junction of white and red, the colours are streaky, and run into one another, there are the usual spots and blotches, but the narrow white margin does not exceed ¼ inch.

(*e*). *Rubro-pictum*, in this very beautiful variety the yellow band prevails on the lower half of the petal, where it is suffused, and gradually lost in a beautiful light crimson broad streak, continued to the apex of the petal ; the spots and blotches are also of the same crimson tint.

(*f*). *Pictum*, in this choice variety, the tip only or lower third of the petal is marked with a scarlet or blood red streak.

(*g*). *Virginale*, in this very beautiful form, there is no other colour but yellow and white, the spots, if any, and band being entirely of the former tint.

(*h*). *Wittei*, on this point we quote below M. Krelage's observations.—*Garden, vol.* 13, *p.* 180.

Lastly we must not omit to mention the splendid hybrids derived from *Speciosum* and *Auratum, Melpomene, see* p. 65, and *Parkmanni.* A coloured figure of the latter is given in the *Garden, vol.* 15, *p.* 456.

L. Wittei.—"As I have had both *L. Auratum,* var. *Virginale,* and *Wittei* in flower at the same time, I have been able to observe the decided difference between them. *Wittei* has not narrow, long petals, but rather broad and short ones. *Virginale* is papillose on all the divisions of the perianth, the outer as well as the inner, and these papillæ are very delicately tinged with light yellow. The divisions of the perianth of *Wittei* are totally glabrous. The last form I have never found among any lot of *Auratum.* *Virginale* I bought first in 1868 ; since that time I have found it sometimes among introduced lots of *Auratum,* and at present several of these plants are in flower in my nursery, which all have the papillose character on the perianth division, the petals being more or less narrow in the different plants. In consequence, I think I am right in considering *Wittei* and *Virginale* to be two different plants, leaving it to later examination to decide if *Wittei* must be considered as a separate species, or merely as a variety of *Auratum.*"—*F. H. Krelage, Haarlem.*

SUB-GENUS IV.

Isolirion, Erect-flowered Lilies.

Perianth, broadly funnel-shaped, standing erect for a considerable time, usually of a brilliant red or yellow colour ; segments, oblong, lance-shaped, spathulate, or clawed at the base with dots and papillose lamellæ on the inner surface, and with a deep groove on the keel ; stamens, diverging on every side from the erect style.

KEY TO THE SPECIES.

Leaves in whorls.—   20, *Philadelphicum*, 21, *Medeoloides.*
Leaves scattered : style shorter than ovary.—22, *Concolor.*
            style longer than ovary.—23, *Bulbiferum*, 24, *Croceum*,
            25, *Davuricum*, 26, *Elegans*, 27, *Catesbæi.*

20. *L. Philadelphicum.*—L. Sp., 435 ; Miller, Ic., t. 165, fig. 1 ; Bot. Mag., t. 519 ; Red. Lil., t. 104 ; Lodd. Bot. Cab., t. 976 ; Herb. Amat., t. 92 ; Bot. Reg., t. 594 ; Kunth, Enum., iv., 263.—Bulb, (*see* page 102), small, annual, stoloniferous ; scales, fragile, thick,

nearly club-shaped; stem, 1 to 3 feet high, green, slender, terete, smooth; leaves, twenty to thirty in number, lance-shaped, or linear, patent, slender, smooth, finely-nerved, sessile, the lower ones 3 or 5 inches long, 3 to 6 lines broad in the middle, arranged in whorls of four to six, or six to eight leaves, or few or many scattered; flower, solitary, terminal, erect, or a few in an umbel; pedicels, 2 or 3 inches long, ascending, with a whorl of large leafy bracts at the base; perianth, 2 or 3 inches long, of a brilliant yellowish red colour; segments, oblong-lance-shaped, 6 to 10 lines broad in the middle, with a distinct claw 6 to 8 lines long at the base, marked with large scattered purple dots on the lower half of the inner surface; groove, smooth, deep, margined on the edges by the revolute claws; sta-mens, shorter than the perianth by one-

The Canadian Whorl-leaved Lily (*L. Philadelphicum*).

third; anthers, 5 or 6 lines long; pollen, red; ovary, 9 or 10 lines long, about half the length of the style; capsule, narrowly-obovoid, obtuse-angled. North America, from Canada to Carolina.—Var. *Andinum*, Nuttall, Gen., i., 221.—*Umbellatum*, Pursh, Flora., i., 229.

Var.* *Wansharaicum*, Hort. Leichl.; Duchartre, Obs., 88.—Leaves, linear, all scattered. Rocky Mountains, Douglas, Bourgeau, &c.

L. Philadelphicum is common in open copses through Canada and the Northern United States, stretching westward to the Rocky Mountains, and southward along the Alleghanies to North Carolina, and of couse quite hardy in English gardens. It was sent by Bartram, in 1754, to Philip Miller, who figured it at t. 165 of his "Illustrations." The *Umbellatum* of Pursh, and *Andinum* of Nuttall, are simply luxuriant conditions of this plant, figured in the "Botanical Register." It stretches north-westward to the Red River and Sashatchewan territory, and occurs sparingly on the west side of the Rocky Mountains; but all the western specimens I have seen, though even when single-flowered retaining the whorl of bracts, have all the leaves indiscriminately scattered along the stem, as in *Bulbiferum*, and the leaves also are narrower (linear not oblanceolate) and firmer in texture than in the whorled typical Canadian and New England form. Geographically, *Philadelphicum* quite represents *Bulbiferum* in the New World, and when the whorls of the leaves are thus broken up, they come very near to one another, though distinct enough in the extreme states. But *Philadelphicum* has always a more

* This well-marked variety has a more richly coloured and larger flower than the ordinary type. Both kinds are early flowering, pretty, bright coloured, dwarf Lilies, and do best in dry warm soils.

distinct claw than any variety of *Bulbiferum*, and wants the cottony pubescence that occurs upon the stem and outside of the perianth of all forms of the latter.

21. *L. Medeoloides.*—A. Gray, Mem. Amer. Acad., vi., 6, 415 ; Miquel, Ann. Mus. Lug. Bat., iii., 156.—*Maculatum*, Thunb., Linn. Trans., ii., 334 ; Mem. Acad. Petrop., iii., 204, t. 5, fig. 1 ?— *Canadense*, Thunb., Fl. Jap., 204 ? (a figure of the bulb is given, page 108). Stem, 1 to 2 feet high, slender, smooth, terete, flexuose ; leaves, mostly arranged in a single whorl of seven to fourteen ; leaves, above the middle of the stem, oblanceolate, patent, tender, smooth, green, 4 to 6 inches long, 9 to 15 lines broad above the middle, acute, with two to four distinct lateral veins ; there are some- times a few scattered leaves above the whorl ; flowers, solitary, or two to three in an umbel ; pedicels, short, erect at the top ; perianth, 12 to 15 lines long, erect, of an open funnel-shape, and brilliant orange- red colour, marked on the inside with a few claret-coloured dots ; segments, lance-shaped, slightly falcate from the base, callous at the tip, channelled, downy, 3 to 4 lines broad in the middle, slightly spathulate at the base ; groove, on the keel indistinct, smooth ; filaments, half the length of the perianth ; anthers, 4 to 5 lines long ; ovary, club-shaped, 4 lines long ; style, erect, a little shorter.— Japan, near Hakodadi, C. Wright. The Corean Island, Herschel, in inundated woods, where it flowers in June. Oldham, 873 ; it approaches most closely to *Martagon* and *Avenaceum* ; but is easily distinguished by its erect flowers, falcate (not revolute) segments, and short stamens and pistil.*

22. *L. Concolor.*—Salisb. Parad., t. 47 ; Kunth, Enum. iv., 259 and 673 ; Fisch and Mey. Ind. Sem., 1839, 55.—*Sinicum*, Lindl. in Paxt. Flow. Gard., vol. ii., Misc. 115, t. 193 ; Lemaire, Ill. Hort., t. 100 ; Van Houtte, Flore des Serres, t. 1,206.—Bulb (see page 108), ovoid, perennial, small ; scales, few, whitish, oblong, acute ; stem, slender, about a foot high, slightly pubescent, suffused with purple ; leaves, 20 to 30 in number, ascending, scattered, lance-shaped, of a deep green colour, acute, 2½ to 3 inches long, 4 to 6 lines broad in the middle, indistinctly seven-nerved, fringed with papillæ on the edges ;

* An exceedingly distinct species, discovered near Hakodadi, Japan, in the United States North Pacific Exploring Expedition under Captains Ringold and Rogers, in 1853—56, and since gathered by Oldham in Herschel Island, one of the members of the Korean group. In general habit and foliage it is most like *Martagon*, but in the shape of the flower and its divisions, it resembles *Concolor* and *Pulchellum*.

Owing to the extreme smallness and thinness of its scales, this Lily is an extremely difficult one to introduce from Japan. Many hundred bulbs sent to us have dried up on the voyage.

So far as our experience goes, the bulbs of *Avenaceum* and *Medeoloides* are alike in form and shape, see page 108, but *Medeoloides* is said to have an erect purple spotted flower, with a broad *Martagon*-whorled foliage, its Japanese name, *Kuruma Juri*, may be translated 2 wheeled or 2 whorled Lily ; it would be as well to suspend judgment on the diversity of these forms till they are better known, at present but few specimens have flowered in Europe.

flowers, one to three in number; pedicels, somewhat downy, purple, ascending, 1½ to 2 inches long; sometimes bracteolated; perianth, 15 to 18 lines long, of a dark crimson colour, without spots on the inside, paler on the outside; segments, broadly falcate, lance-shaped, 4 to 9 lines broad in the middle, callous at the tip, somewhat downy, slightly papillose at the base; groove on the keel, deep, with smooth edges; filaments, half the length of the perianth; anthers, 3 or 4 lines long; pollen, red; ovary, club-shaped, 5 or 6 lines long, deeply furrowed, club-shaped, 3 or 4 lines long, shorter than in any other species; capsule, 1 inch long, obovoid-oblong, obtuse-angled. China; flowers in the end of June.—*Concolor*, Bot. Mag., 1,165, is a form in which the segments have a few dark spots on the inside, near the base.

Crimson Erect-flowered Lily
(*L. Concolor* var. *Pulchellum*).

Var. *Buschianum*, Lodd. Bot. Cab., t. 1,628.—*Pulchellum*, Rev. Hort., 1862, 131, with a figure.—*Concolor* var. *Sinicum*, Bot. Mag., t. 6,005. This variety sometimes grows taller, and has a larger and solitary bulb (the scales of which are few and broad), narrower dark green leaves, flowers sometimes four to six in number, segments of the perianth a little broader and of a brilliant crimson on the inner surface, the lower half of which is covered with numerous scattered small blackish dots; capsule, narrowly obovoid, ½ inch long, umbilicated at the apex. Southern Siberia.

Var. *L. Partheneion*, Sieb. and De Vriese, Tuinbow Flora, ii., 341, with a figure, scarcely differs from *Buschianum*, except in its slenderer habit, shining leaves, and cæspitose bulbs. Japan.—*Coridion*, Sieb. and De Vriese, loc. cit., Duchartre, Obs. 42, is the same plant with yellow flowers.

Var. *L. Pulchellum*, Fisch. and Mey., Ind. Sem. Petr., 1839, 56; Kunth, Enum, iv., 266, 676; Regel, Gartenfl., 1860, 81, t. 284, fig. 2.—Bulb, ovoid, scarcely an inch long; stem, very slender, about a foot high; leaves, 12 to 20 in number, narrowly linear, ascending; 2 to 2½ inches long, and 1½ to 2 lines broad; perianth, often solitary, red, 12 to 15 lines long; segments, oblanceolate, obtuse, 3 to 5 lines broad in the middle, covered on the lower half with numerous minute blackish dots; filaments, 5 or 6 lines long; ovary, 3 or 4 lines long, longer than the style. Eastern Siberia. A yellow-flowered variety is cultivated in Japan, Maximowicz; on stony hills in Chinese Mongolia, Meyer and Turczaninow, in herb. DC.

Under this head are included several very distinct forms, horticulturally speaking, viz. :—

1. *Concolor*, from Japan. This kind has cæspitose bulbs, mostly small, *i.e.*, the bulbs have a great tendency to break up and form a cluster, and are said to thrive best when left alone, and not torn asunder and re-planted as single bulbs ; it is rather a difficult Lily to grow, but in very wet summers, and on light soil, it has done well with us. It has a dwarf habit, scarcely a foot high, with erect light-green foliage, narrow, acute, 1 to 1½ lines broad, 1½ inch long, 3-nerved, very numerous, crowded ; late flowering, with two or three erect crimson star-shaped spotted flowers ; the native name is *Shemi-Juri*.

2. *Coridion*, in bulb, growth, and habit, similar to the preceding, but the flower is somewhat larger, of a rich yellow, flaked here and there with brown ; the handsomest by far of the group ; its Japanese name is *Ki-Fime-Juri*.

3. *Sinicum*, but little known in this country ; the Chinese form, growing 2 to 3 feet high from a solitary larger bulb, bearing a spike of 4—6 flowers, larger and more heavily spotted than those of the preceding forms ; brought over from China, in 1806, by the Hon. C. Greville, and again by Fortune in 1850 ; figured and described by Salisbury.

4. *Pulchellum*, also known as *Buschianum*, from Siberia ; a much earlier flowering form, growing 1½ to 2 feet high, with a star-shaped crimson flower, very similar to that of *Concolor*, but with narrower and smaller petals, possessing a solitary bulb, figured at page 106, with sparse arching foliage, 5-nerved, 1½ to 2½ lines broad, 1½ inch to 2 inches long, and of a deep green colour. The figure and foliage in the woodcut given (page 155) are those of *Pulchellum*, not of *Concolor*.

5. *Fartheneion*, a form closely allied, if not identical with, *Concolor* ; not sufficiently known to me to be acknowledged as a thoroughly distinct form.

Closely allied to these must be the form of *Davidi* (Duchartre M.S.), collected in the Manze country of Thibet, 9,000 feet above sea level, in June, 1869. Described as having an orange-coloured star-shaped flower with purple spots, a stem 2½ feet high, and foliage like that of *Tenuifolium*, but more sparse.

All these forms are exceedingly graceful for button-hole decoration.

23. *L. Bulbiferum* (Parkinson, Parad., 37, t. 2).—*Speciosum*, 433, ex parte ; Jacq., Fl. Austr., t. 226 ; Bot. Mag., t. 1,018 ; Fisch. and Mey., Ind. Sem., 1839, 54 ; Kunth, Enum., iv., 264, 674 ; Regel. Gartenfl., 1872, 231, with a figure of the bulb.—Bulb (compare p. 109), ovoid, perennial ; scales, few, broad, acute ; first shoots, broad, obtuse, tinged with red ; stem, 2 to 4 feet high, straight, furrowed, spotted with purple, covered with white cobweb-like down on the upper part ; leaves, fewer and more ascending than in *Croceum*, the lower ones about 3 inches long and 3 to 6 lines broad in the middle (the upper ones drawn back), and bearing bulbils in the axils ; flowers, in wild

The Umbellate Lily
(*L. Umbellatum*).

specimens, one to three in number, in cultivated plants often more numerous, and arranged in an umbel or deltoid raceme ; pedicels, thick, short, spotted with purple ; and covered with a white cobweb-like down ; perianth, 2 to 2½ inches long, erect, scentless, of a brilliant red colour, often tinged with orange at the bottom ; segments, oblong-spathulate, 9 to 15 lines broad in the middle, the inner ones less clawed than in *Croceum*, all with black dots, and numerous lamellæ and papillæ on the inner surface ; groove, ½ inch long, very deep, with pilose edges ;

filaments, 18 to 21 lines long; anthers, 3 or 4 lines long; pollen red; ovary, 7 or 8 lines long, half the length of the style; capsule, 1½ inches long, obovoid, obtusely six-angled, umbilicated at the top. Central Europe, and South-eastern Scandinavia, flowering in our gardens amongst the earliest, blooming in June, before *Croceum* and *Davuricum.—Latifolium*, Link, Enum., i., 321, is a large-growing garden form with broad leaves.—*Humile*, Miller, Dict. No. 4, is a small form, with narrow leaves.—*Pubescens*, Bernh., Kunth, Enum., iv., 265, is probably a garden form with peduncles thickly covered with cobweb-like down. For its various forms, *see* Parkins, Parad., 38.

Under the head *Bulbiferum* (rather than under the head of *Davuricum*, as Mr. Baker, does) we are inclined to class the numerous garden varieties, mostly raised from seed, some of which are very beautiful, generally called *Umbellatum*; they are all early flowering. The true type we hold to be a tall growing form, 3—4 feet high, with crowded large dark green lanceolate foliage, bearing bulblets in the axils (like the Tiger group), and having an umbel of large broad petalled cup-shaped flowers, of a rich dark cherry red colour, having an orange blotch, and a few black dots in the centre.

The seedling forms, classed as *Umbellatum*, do not as a rule carry bulblets in the axils, but should their flower heads be cut off early in the season, bulblets are often formed at the scar and in the axils of the then terminal leaves.

Some of the best seedling forms are *Punctatum* and *Immaculatum* (without spots), also known as *Rubens* and *Vulcan* by some growers, these are tall, strong-growing forms, very nearly approaching the type, with large, well-formed, cup-shaped, richly coloured flowers.

Erectum and *Bicolor*, dwarfer forms, with few or no spots, yellow centre, and rich cherry-coloured tips, very vivid.

Sappho, a dwarf, broad-petalled, symmetrical flower, heavily spotted and richly coloured.

Atrosanguineum and *Incomparable*, the very dark tinted, dwarf forms, remarkable for the intensity of their colouring; generally much admired.

24. *L. Croceum* (Fuchs.)—Chaix. in Vill. Delph., i., 322; Kunth, Enum., iv., 265 and 675; Fisch. and Mey., Ind. Sem., vi., 56; Gran. Flor. France, iii., 182.—*Bulbiferum*, DC., Fl. France, iii., 202; Bot. Mag., t. 36 (the figure much above the natural size).—*Aureum*, Parkinson, Paradisus, 37, t. 3.—Bulb, globose, perennial; scales, large, ovate-lance-shaped, not narrowed at the middle; first shoots, broad, obtuse, tinged with red; stem, 3 to 6 feet high, stout, furrowed, green, spotted with purple on the upper part, more or less covered with cobweb-like down; leaves, 50 to 100 in number, scattered, very close, patent, or the lower ones slightly squarrose, linear, the lower ones 3 or 4 inches long, 3 or 4 lines broad, three to five nerved, sessile, smooth, firm, never bearing bulbils in the axils; flowers, in

The Orange Lily (*L. Croceum*).

wild specimens, often solitary, in cultivated plants often 10 to 20 in number, arranged in a deltoid raceme or umbel; pedicels, ascending, 2 or 3 inches long, covered with white cobweb-like down; perianth,

erect, broadly funnel-shaped, 2 to 2½ inches long when fully expanded,
3 inches broad, at first covered with white cobweb-like down on the
outside; outer segments, oblong-lance-shaped, 8 or 9 lines long,
broad below the middle, spathulate at the base; inner ones, ovate-
lance-shaped, 12 to 14 lines broad below the middle, distinctly clawed
at the base, all of a brilliant orange colour, scarcely tinged with
crimson, cuspidate at the apex, somewhat downy, imbricated in the
expanded flower, marked with numerous dots and lamellate papillæ;
groove ½ inch long, very deep, with pilose edges; filaments, 15 to 18
lines long; anthers, 4 lines long; pollen, red; ovary, 8 or 9 lines
long; style, 12 to 14 lines long; capsule, obovoid, 1½ inch long,
somewhat acutely angled.   Switzerland, France, Northern Italy;
long grown in gardens under many forms.   Flowers in the beginning
of July, after *Bulbiferum.**

25. *L. Davuricum.*—Gawl., Bot. Mag., sub. t. 1,210; Kunth, Enum.,
iv., 264; Regel, Gartenflora, t. 740, and 1872, 295.—*Pennsylvanicum*,
Gawl., Bot. Mag., t. 872.—*Spectabile*, Link, Enum., i., 321; Reich.,
Ic. Exot., t. 30; Fish. and Mey., Ind. Sem., vi., 58; Kunth, Enum.,
iv., 676; Regel, Gartenfl., t. 349, 1872, 231, with a figure of the
bulb.—Bulb,† globose, perennial; scales, small, fiddle-shaped, acute,
white, brittle, contracted in the middle: first shoots, narrow, acute,
tinged with brown; stem, 2 or 3 feet high, slender, green, slightly
covered with white cobweb-like down in the upper part; leaves, 20
to 50 in number, ascending, sessile, linear, three-nerved, the lower
ones 4 or 5 inches long, 3 or 4 lines broad in the middle, never
bearing bulbils in the axils; flowers in wild specimens, often solitary,
in cultivated plants, few, in umbels or short racemes; pedicels, naked
or slightly covered with cobweb-like down; perianth of a brilliant
red colour, 2 to 2½ inches long when fully expanded, 3 to 4½ inches
broad; segments, oblong-lance-shaped, 9 to 12 lines broad below the
middle, scarcely imbricated in the expanded flower, less dotted and
lamellated than in *Croceum* and *Bulbiferum*, spathulate at the base;
groove, very deep, 3 or 9 lines long, with pilose edges; filaments,
red, 18 to 21 lines long; anthers, 5 or 6 lines long; pollen, red;
style, twice the length of the ovary; capsule, 1½ to 2 inches long,
obtuse-angled.   Central and Eastern Siberia, from the Altai
Mountains to Kamtschatka, where the bulb is eaten by the natives.

* The var. *Chaixii*, collected by Mr. Geo. Maw, comes up later, and flowers earlier than
Croceum, the flower-buds are visible from the very earliest stages of its growth.   In the
wild state it has never more than from 1 to 2 (rarely 3) flowers, while *Croceum* has 10 to
15, and its spike is twice as high as that of *Chaixii*, which averages 15 inches.   It
flowered with Rev. Harper Crewe, who pronounced it to be "very pretty and distinct,
and sure to become a favourite."—*Garden*, vol. 10., p. 37.
    The var. *Tenuifolium* is very frequently sent out as *Catesbæi*, but is closely allied
to *Davuricum*, and evidently a very tender and delicate Lily in this country; the
bulbs resemble those of a small *Croceum*, but easily break to pieces, the foliage is narrow,
acute, crowded; the flower much resembles that of *Croceum*: it is not easily cultivated.
    † For figures of these curious bulbs, *see* pages 104, 105.

It flowers in our gardens in July along with *Croceum*, and after *Bulbiferum*.* *Umbellatum*, of most gardens, is a luxuriant garden form of *Davuricum*. For its varieties, *see* Regel, Gartenfl., 1872, 295.

26. *L. Elegans.*—Thunb., Mem. Acad. Petr., iii., 203, t. 3, fig. 2.— *Bulbiferum*, Thunb., Linn. Trans., ii., 333.—*Philadelphicum*, Thunb., Fl. Jap., 135.—*Thunbergianum*, Schultes fil., Syst. Veg., vii., 415; Lindl. Bot. Reg., 1839, t. 38; Maund. Bot., t. 158; Regel., Gartenfl. 1872, 296.—*Aurantiacum*, Paxt. Mag., vii., 127, with a figure.— Bulb† like those of *Bulbiferum* and *Croceum;* stem, about a foot high, smooth, or slightly covered with cobweb-like down, or pilose, stout, furrowed; leaves, 20 to 30 in number, ascending, scattered, firm, deep green, smooth, distinctly five to seven nerved, the lower ones 3 to 4 inches long, the upper ones shorter, 6 to 12 lines broad in the middle, not bearing bulbils in the axils; perianth, usually solitary, 3 to 3½ inches long, when fully expanded, 5 or 6 inches broad, of an orange-red colour; segments oblong, spathulate, obtuse, scarcely dotted, much less lamellated and papillose than those of *Davuricum*, outer ones 12 to 13 lines, and inner ones 15 to 18 lines broad in the middle; groove, distincly excavated, 8 or 9 lines long, with pilose edges; filaments, 1¼ to 2 inches long *;* anthers, 4 or 5 lines long; ovary, 1 inch long, half the length of the style; capsule, obovoid, 2 inches long, sub-acutely six-angled, one half longer than its breadth. Japan; it flowers in our gardens in the beginning of July, under very many forms, of which the following are the most notable:—

Var. 1, *Brevifolium*, Baker and Dyer, "Gard. Chron.," 1872, 1,356.—*Alternans*, hort.; leaves, broader and shorter, the lower ones 2 to 2½ inches, the upper ones 1 to 1½ inches long, all 7 to 9 lines broad, and of a deep green colour; perianth, less open, of a pale red colour throughout, with a few black dots at the bottom: filaments and style a little longer.

Var. 2, *Bicolor*, Moore, "Floral Mag.," t. 104.—*Pictum*, hort. Siebold.—*Aurantiacum*, hort. Krelage; stem, scarcely a foot high; leaves, about 40 in number, narrower, the lower ones 4 to 6 lines broad; perianth, 3 to 3½ inches long; segments, broader than in any other variety (the inner ones 18 to 21 lines broad), with yellow centre, red sides, and a few dots near the base.

---

* It was originally figured in the Botanical Magazine, under the name of *Pennsylvanicum*, under the supposition that it came from America; but the mistake was corrected in the volume for 1809, and the plant re-named *Davuricum*, after the region of Siberia in which it is most abundant. This name, *Davuricum*, has priority over *Spectabile*, which only dates from 1821.

† We have been unable to obtain a satisfactory woodcut of bulbs of the true *Thunbergianum* type; they are in shape and size much like those of *Philadelphicum* on page 102, but the numerous scales are thinner, flatter, broader at the base, and more acute at the tip than are those of *Philadelphicum*. The bulb of *Thunbergianum Splendens*, page 105, approaches in form and size those of the *Umbellatum* group, and is altogether a coarser bulb than that of the true *Thunbergianum* type.

Var. 3, *Pardinum*, Moore, "Florist," 1861, 121, with a figure. This scarcely differs from var. 2, except in having a taller stem (2 to 3 feet), and the flowers few and in an umbel.

Var. 4, *Alutaceum*, Baker and Dyer, "Gard Chron.," loc. cit.— *Thunbergianum Aureum Nigro-maculatum*, Flores des Serres, t. 1,627: stem, dwarf; leaves about 30 in number; flowers, solitary; perianth of a pale apricot colour; inner segments, 12 to 13 lines broad, with numerous purplish dots on the lower half.

Var. 5, *Armeniacum*, Baker and Dyer, loc. cit. Stem, about a foot high: leaves, 30 to 40 in number, the lower ones linear; flowers one or two in number, orange, not dotted, and without lamellæ or papillæ; segments 9 to 12 lines broad.

Var. 6, *Citrinum*, hort., Wilson, scarcely differs from *Armeniacum*, except in having the stem 2 to 2½ feet in height, the leaves lance-shaped, and flowers two to three in number.

Var. 7, *Sanguineum*, Lindl., "Bot. Reg.," 32., t. 50. Stem, 1 to 1½ feet high; leaves, about 40 in number, lance-shaped; flowers, one to two in number; segments, broad; blood-red, slightly tinged with orange, and with a few small dots near the base; papillæ and lamellæ nearly obsolete.

Var. 8, *Atrosanguineum*, Baker and Dyer, loc. cit.—*Coruscans*, hort. Stem, 1 to 1½ feet high; leaves, lance-shaped; flowers, usually solitary; segments, broad, deep red, with numerous dots on the lower half; papillæ and lamellæ, numerous and only slightly raised.— *Hæmatochroum*, Lemaire, Ill. Hort., t. 503, is a similar form, with darker livid red flowers.

Var. 9, *Fulgens*, Morren, in Spac Mem., 29; Lemaire, Ill. Hort., t. 657, approaches *Davuricum*. Stem, 1 to 1½ feet high; leaves, about 40 in number, linear; flowers, often four to six in number, of a deep red colour; dots, lamellæ, and papillæ, almost obsolete.— *Venustum*, Kunth, Flore des Serres, t. 652, is a similar form with a more brilliant flower, more tinged with orange.—*Wilsoni*, hort., according to Max Leichtlin, is probably a hybrid between *Elegans* and *Speciosum*.

In early and mid-growth, apart from their flowers, just as the *Tiger* group may be recognised by a straight tall habit, more or less woolly stem, and crowded long pointed foliage; *Speciosum* by the broad alternate shiny leaves; *Martagons* by their tall habit, whorled or much broken up foliage; *Umbellatum* by the elongated, crowded, light green, rough, pubescent foliage, flattened at the top into an umbel as if crushed; so by its dwarf habit, smooth, rather broad and short shiny foliage, *Thunbergianum* may be easily differentiated from all other forms.

We have grown for years many varieties of the *Thunbergianum* group, and consider them to have been raised from one type by the horticultural skill of the Japanese, extending over a number of years, who, in dealing with this type, have produced strains of far greater excellence, in form, and in variety of colour, than has been effected by Europeans in dealing with the sister group, *Davuricum* or *Umbellatum*. It seems curious, that while no form of the *Thunbergianum* group has been found outside Japan, no form of *Umbellatum* has been as yet, *to our knowledge*, sent over to us as indigenous to those islands.

We are accustomed to divide this very variable group into three divisions, based upon the perianth or flower.

(*a*). With long narrow widely open petals and sepals, such as—

Armeniacum (Venustum), Fulgens, Atrosanguineum, Sanguineum, Alutaceum, Alternans, Flore Pleno, Prince of Orange.

These are mostly deep self-coloured flowers, with few spots, chiefly black.

(*b*). With broad symmetrical widely open petals and sepals, such as—

Bicolor, Marmoratum, Marmoratum Aureum, Van Houttei, Aurantiacum Verum, Alice Wilson, &c.

These are mostly in two or three colours, in improved tints, and shew a considerable advance in cultivation, &c.

(*c*). Cup-shaped, with broad petals and sepals, such as—

Brevifolium, Splendens, Wilsoni, &c.

These, in their erect cup-shaped form, large size, richness of spotting, and shot colour of tint, manifest a crossing with some other group, possibly *Auratum.*

Group (*a*). *Armeniacum (Venustum),* one of the latest flowering, a rich vermilion orange-coloured form, without spots, known at once by its peculiar twisted foliage, grows about 1 foot high.

Fulgens, also about 1 foot high, with spotted reddish flower.

Fulgens Flore Pleno, the double form of the above variety, remarkable more for its curiosity than for its beauty.

Fulgens Atrosanguineum, this is really a fine variety, being more robust in habit than *Fulgens,* and of a deeper rich blood-red tint.

Fulgens Alternans, a light tinted form of *Fulgens,* suffused and flaked with lighter tints.

Sanguineum (Biligulatum), an early form, inclined somewhat to be cup-shaped in flower, but with narrow petals ; reddish brown flower, with a few black spots.

Alutaceum, known under a great number of names by the Dutch growers ; a very distinct dwarf form, scarcely 6 inches high, with rich apricot-coloured flowers, symmetrically spotted ; suitable for edging. A larger form of this is known under the name *Grandiflorum,* with more robust habit, and larger richer coloured flowers.

But the most beautiful variety is that known as *Prince of Orange,* a spotted form, of a soft pleasing light buff tint, also dwarf.

Group (*b*). *Bicolor (Pictum),* one of the handsomest of the forms, but, alas ! the petals are flimsy, and its beauties are soon over ; a stout-growing form, from 1 foot to 2 feet high, bearing several large, broad-petalled, slightly cup-shaped flowers, yellow tinted, but tipped and splashed with crimson tints, and when quite fresh, with a lilac sheen, but few spots.

Aurantiacum Verum, figured in Paxton, vol. 6, p. 127 ; without spots, but with large open flowers, of a rich salmon yellow colour, a very fine form.

Marmoratum, a very early form, broad-petalled, of a rich deep crimson colour, flaked and tipped with orange, spotted.

Marmoratum Aureum, also very early ; more heavily spotted than the preceding form ; here, yellow predominates, margined with red.

Alice Wilson, a beautiful, broad-petalled, lemon-coloured, spotted form, one of the handsomest and rarest of the group.

Mawii, very large flower, orange crimson, and heavily and distinctly spotted, richly coloured.

Van Houttei, a very richly tinted deep scarlet form, with a yellow blotch in centre, and sometimes at the tip, broad-petalled ; a very beautiful and grand Lily.

Horsmanni, a deep blood red broad-petalled form, spotted ; one of the handsomest and most richly tinted forms.

Group (*c*). *Brevifolium,* distinguished by its very short, acute-pointed, broad, thick leaves, only 1½ to 2½ inches long, very early flowering, bears a cup-shaped flower of light reddish tint, shot with a purplish gloss, spotted, and having the tips flaked with yellow.

Splendens, one of the largest and most vigorous forms of this group, grows 2½ feet high, with stout stem, and *Umbellatum*-like foliage, very light green, 3 inches long, has an umbel of deeply cupped flowers, very large, of a rich apricot-yellow, with purple spots ; it is the earliest flowering form in the group.

Wilsoni (Pardinum) (Moore), this, on the contrary, is the latest to bloom in the whole section ; the stem is stout, about 2 feet high, slightly pubescent, bronzed below, green above, the leaves very short, glossy, of a very deep green, and curled downwards, the flowers very large, deeply cupped, apricot tinted, with a broad yellow band down the centre of the petal, purple spotted.

Both these two last varieties have a lilac sheen when fresh, and the bulbs are large and coarse, resembling much those of the *Umbellatum* section.

27. *L. Catesbœi.*—Walt., Fl. Carol., 123; Bot. Mag., t. 259; Lodd., Bot. Cab., t. 807; Sweet, Brit. Flow. Gard., ser. ii., t. 185; Kunth, Enum., iv., 263.—*Spectabile*, Salsb., Stirp. Kar., t. 5, non Link.—*Carolinianum*, Catesby, Car., ii., t. 58, non Michx.—Bulb (*see* page 103), like that of *Philadelphicum* (?); stem, 1 to 2 feet high, slender, terete, smooth, green; leaves, 20 to 30 in number, scattered, ascending, smooth, green, lance-shaped, or linear, the lower ones 2 or 3 inches long, 4 to 6 lines broad, the upper ones gradually smaller; perianth, solitary, erect, broadly funnel-shaped, 3 or 4 inches long, of a brilliant orange-red; segments, oblong-lance-shaped, 6 to 12 lines broad in the middle, distinctly cuspidate for some length, and with purple spots scattered over the inner surface; claw, chan-

Catesby's Orange Lily (*L. Catesbœi*).

nelled at the base, 9 to 15 lines, with revolute margins; filaments, 2½ to 3 inches long; anthers, narrow, 4 to 6 lines long; pollen, red; ovary, 9 to 12 lines long; style, slender, twice the length of the ovary. North America, from Georgia and Carolina to Florida.

This Lily received by us from the swampy regions of S. Carolina, is somewhat tender; the bulb has scales longer and more acut than those of *Philadelphicum*, and at the upper part, the outer claw-like scales exhibit a blunt scar, where the leaf has broken off: so that, in fact, the scales of this Lily, which are few in number, are the extended bases of the leaves, which are long, very slender, grass-like, and crowded at the base. The bulb is tender, and growing on during the winter must be kept under glass. We have flowered it, but we are not aware that anyone else has done so.

SUB-GENUS V.

MARTAGON (Endl.), TURK'S-CAP LILIES.

Flowers, in racemes, nodding, dotted, usually of a brilliant red or orange colour; perianth, broadly campanulate; segments, lance-shaped, deeply falcate; grooves, deep; stamens, diverging on all sides from the curved style.

KEY TO THE SPECIES.

Leaves verticillate, in whorls—

(1).—American Species (a), bulbs annual, rhizomatous—

28, *Canadense*, 29, *Pardalinum*, 30, *Superbum*, 31, *Lucidum*, 32, *Roezlii*.

(b), bulbs perennial, not rhizomatous—

33, *Columbianum*, 34, *Humboldtii*.

Leaves verticillate, in whorls—

(2).—Old world Species (c)—35, *Martagon*, 36, *Avenaceum*, 37, *Hansoni*.

Leaves scattered—

(c), leaves, lanceolate, many-nerved—
   perianth, falcate above the middle—
      38, *Szovitzianum*.

(d), perianth, revolute to behind the middle—
      39, *Polyphyllum*, 40, *Ponticum*, 41, *Carniolicum*.

(e), leaves, narrowly linear, with one or a few nerves—
   segments of the perianth from 6 to 12 lines broad in the middle—
      42, *Testaceum*, 43, *Leichtlinii*, 44, *Batemannii*, 45, *Pseudo Tigrinum*, 46, *Wallacei*.

(f), segments of the perianth from 3 to 6 lines, broad in the middle—
      47, *Pomponium*, 48, *Chalcedonicum*, 49, *Callosum*, 50, *Tenuifolium*.

In this Sub-Genus we have many superb forms, among which, we may place first the very beautiful, early-flowering, canary-coloured *Szovitzanum*, with its 20 or 30 bell-shaped, broad petalled flowers, beautifully spotted. *Excelsum* with its tall, peculiarly graceful, nankeen-coloured flowers, so exquisitely scented. *Tenuifolium*, elegant for its slender foliage, handsomest among dwarf Lilies with its spike of scarlet bells. *Humboldtii* and *Pardalinum* remarkable for their tall floriferous spikes of light orange flowers, variously spotted and tipped with carmine or scarlet. *Parvum*, one of the most beautiful and floriferous, small as to its individual flower, but excessively graceful, and very tall growing. *Columbianum*, remarkable for its golden bells. *Polyphyllum*, for its symmetrically purple spotted, bell-shaped, white flowers. The blood-red *Dalmaticum*, 6 to 8 feet high, bearing from 30 to 40 flowers. *Hansoni*, a very early stout-growing kind, likely, when better known, to be an universal favourite; and last, but not least, *Leichtlinii*, long acknowledged to be, with its delicately yellow tinted, purple spotted flowers, one of the most graceful Lilies in existence.

28. *L. Canadense.*—Linn. Sp., 435; Bot. Mag., t. 800 and 858; Kunth, Enum., iv., 258; Bury, Hexand., t. 12; Flore des Serres, t. 1, 174.—*Penduliflorum*, DC. in Red Lil., t. 105.—*Pendulum*, Spae, Mem., 28.—*Martagon* sive *Canadense Maculatum*, Parkins, Parad , 32, t. 2. —Bulb (see p. 110), annual, emitting runners 5 or 6 inches long; scales, thick, obtuse, scarcely ½ inch long; stem, 1½ to 2 feet high, slender, smooth, terete, green; leaves often arranged in four or five regular distant whorls of four to eight leaves (the whorls being, however, sometimes more or less broken up), oblanceolate, acute, 3 or 4 inches long, 6 to 9 lines broad above the middle, green, slender, five to seven nerved, the veins sometimes ciliated; flowers, solitary, or a few in an umbel or corymb; pedicels, 2 to 6 inches

The Canadian Bell-flowered Lily (*L. Canadense*).

long, nodding very much at the top, sometimes bracteolated; perianth, 2 to 2½ inches long, broadly funnel-shaped, a brilliant orange-red, segments, oblanceolate, 6 or 7 lines broad, falcate above the middle, with numerous claret-coloured spots on the inner surface, lamellated in the upper part; groove, distinctly sunk, with smooth edges; filaments, shorter than the perianth by one-third; anthers, 4 to 6 lines long; ovary, 8 or 9 lines long, a little shorter than the almost straight style; capsule, turbinate, obtuse-angled, 1½ inch long, not umbilicated at the apex; septa, delicate. North Eastern America, from Canada to Georgia. It recedes (along with *Monadelphum*) from the *Martagon* section towards *Eulirion*, the funnel-shaped perianth, in the expanded flower, being revolute only above the middle.—Var. *Penduliflorum*, hort., Leicht., is a form with segments revolute to or below the middle.

Var. 1, *L. Parvum.*—Kellogg, Proc. Calif. Acad., ii., t. 52; Regel, Gartenflora, t. 725; Duchartre, Obs., 98.—Bulb (*see* page 110) and perianth, like those of the type, but in our gardens the plant has a smaller and slenderer habit; stem, green, 1 to 1½ feet high; upper leaves, usually scattered; flowers, much less nodding, sometimes nearly erect; perianth, 15 to 18 lines long, brilliant orange-red, with numerous dots; segments, acute, 3 to 5 lines broad, falcate above the middle; anthers, oblong, 2 or 3 lines long; ovary, 3 or 4 lines long, half the length of the almost straight style. California, on the Sierra Nevada chain, at an altitude of 6,000 feet. Jeffray, 1,283. According to Kellogg, it attains a height of 5 feet, and bears as many as fifty flowers.

Var. 2, *L. Walkeri.*—Wood, Proc. Amer. Acad., 1868, 166.— Stem, 3 feet high, or more; leaves, tender, narrower, arranged in regular whorls of seven or eight leaves, the whorls being very distant from each other; lower leaves, 4 or 5 inches long, 4 or 5 lines broad, the veins very slender in comparison with the mid-rib; flowers, more numerous, arranged in an elongated raceme; perianth, funnel-shaped, 10 to 15 lines long; segments, 2½ to 3 lines broad, falcate only at the apex; stamens, a little shorter than the perianth; anthers, oblong, 1½ lines long; ovary, 4 lines long, half the length of the straight style; stigma, very small. California, Walker, Bridges, 268.

Var. 3, *L. Parviflorum.*—Hook., Flor. Bor. Am., ii., 281; *Sayii*, Nuttall, MSS.; *Canadense* var. *minus*, Wood, Proc. Acad. Phil., 1868, 166.—Stem, 2 or 3 feet high; leaves, in whorls, or most of them scattered; oblanceolate, tender, the lower ones 6 to 12 lines broad; flowers, solitary, or few in an umbel, nodding; perianth, 18 to 21 lines long, segments, oblanceolate, bluntish, deeply reflexed from the middle, where they are 3 or 4 lines broad; stamens, shorter than the perianth by one-third; anthers, 3 lines long; ovary, 6 lines long, as long as the style. British Columbia and Oregon. Nuttall, Douglas, Lyall, &c. Bulb, like that of *Canadense*; perianth, more revolute, but smaller than in *Pardalinum* and *Superbum*.

Under the head *Canadense*, Mr. Baker has in the above description, included both the Eastern and Western North American forms. We are inclined to consider them as distinct. The Eastern group, the true *Canadense*, is quite hardy with us, and widely spread in cultivation. It appears to have been one of the first plants introduced to European Gardens from America, and is figured in Parkinson's Paradisus in 1629. There are 3 varieties of this eastern form, one, the smaller, with an entirely yellow ground-work (the variety, *Flavum* of Kunth), a very pretty elegant Lily; another, with an entirely red ground-work, and much larger flower, the variety, *Coccineum* of Kunth, and *Pendiflorum* of Redoute, both figured in Bot. Mag., t. 800 and 858; there is a third intermediate form, which with the red variety, is figured in *Florist*, 1875, p. 157. For a figure and description of these bulbs, which are stoloniferous, *see* p. 110. The miniature buds of this form are triangular in shape, not rounded. Of the western analogous forms, mentioned by Mr. Baker; we have not grown var. 2, *Walkeri*, sufficiently to be able to speak confidently about it.

28 *a.* Var. 1, *Parvum*, we have cultivated for years, and find it very distinct, and one of the most beautiful of the small-flowering Lilies. The bulb is rhizomatous, and figured on p. 110. The plant grows 4 to 6 feet high, and bears in a raceme on long stalks, a great number of pendulous, small, yellow-dotted flowers, with broad blunt petals, scarcely at all revolute; foliage in whorls: until fully established, this Lily may attain only the small stature mentioned above by Mr. Baker, for it seems to be an especial characteristic of the Martagon group, that the first year after planting, they emit poor sickly looking growth, with feeble or no flowers, and so greatly disappoint cultivators; but afterwards, when fully established, they astonish the eye with their vigorous growth, tall stem, and multitude of richly coloured flowers. The causes seem to be, that early autumnal root-action is a necessity of growth, and this cannot always be afforded to moved or transplanted bulbs. We consider *Parvum* to be one of the most graceful and beautiful of the western forms, and regret that its rarity prevents it from being more frequently grown.

28 *b.* Var. 3, *Parviflorum*, as we have grown it, seems very closely allied to *Parvum*, but less tall and floriferous; the flowers are smaller, more reflexed and spotted with purple or dark brown.

Either the same or a closely allied species, recently described by Dr. Kellogg in the Proc. Calif. Acad., Sc. vi., p. 140, as *L. Maritimum* may here be introduced.

28 *c.* *L. Maritimum*, Kellogg.

"Leaves alternate, or rarely verticillate, chiefly clustered near the base, narrowly oblong-lanceolate, sub-obtuse narrowing into a short petiole, three nerved (intermediate or secondary nerves obscure), margins scarcely a little scaberulose, quite glabrous throughout, upper cauline successively diminishing to minute linear-lanceolate sessile leaves barely ¼ inch long; peduncles elongated-terminal. Flowers, few, 1—3, somewhat nodding, short, or equilaterally obconic-campanulate; segments, lanceolate, slightly revolute, equal; style, short, straight."

This differs essentially, according to Dr. Kellogg, from *Canadense*, its nearest kin, in the stamens being included. It is a small-flowered maritime Lily, found in low peaty meadows, exposed to the bleak, foggy climate of the coast of California, near San Francisco. The flowers are deep reddish orange brown, spotted dark purple inside.

We have grown this Lily for several years as a form of *Parvum*, but the flower is more campanulate, and the tips of segments more reflexed, while the colour is more richly tinted with crimson, and the spots numerous and darker than in that species. The bulb is said to be like that of *Columbianum*, and if so, this kind must be placed alongside of that species.

29. *L. Pardalinum.*—Kellogg, Proc. Calif. Acad., ii., 12, with a figure; Duchartre, Obs. 97.—Bulbs, *see* p. 112. (annual or biennial), shortly rhizomatous; scales, few, lax, lance-shaped, acute; stem, 3 or 4 feet high, terete, green, smooth; leaves, often arranged near the middle of the stem in 3 or 4 whorls of 9 to 12 leaves, the whorls distant from each other; upper leaves, few, scattered, oblanceolate, of a shining green, 3 or 4 inches long, acute, 9 to 12 lines broad in the middle, smooth, tender; lateral veins, sunk; flowers, 3 to 6 in number, arranged in a corymb or lax umbel; pedicels, elongated, nodding at the top; perianth, 2 to 2½ inches long, of a brilliant red, orange

at the base; segments, lance-shaped, bluntish, 6 to 9 lines broad in
the middle, deeply revolute, the lower half abruptly orange, covered
with large purplish brown spots, and slightly lamellate-papillose;
groove, deep, with smooth edges; stamens, shorter than the perianth
by one-third; anthers, red, 4 or 5 lines long; style, 12 to 14 lines
long, scarcely longer than the ovary; capsule, oblong, umbilicated at
the apex, with somewhat acute angles. California, W. Lobb, 249,
&c.

Var, 1. *Californicum*, hb., Lindley, Floral Mag, 1872, t. 33.—
Leaves, fewer, smaller, and in less regular whorls; flowers, 1 to 3
in number, longer, 3 or 4 inches long; segments, bluntish, 9 to 12
lines broad, the upper half, as in the type, of a brilliant scarlet, the
lower half abruptly orange, with large purplish brown dots; filaments
and style, 1½ to 2 inches long. California, Hartweg. I have seen
the original specimen in Lindley's herbarium, now at Cambridge.

Var. 2, *Pallidifolium*, Baker.—*Puberulum*, hort., Leichtlin, non
Torrey.—Taller, in our gardens the stem being 4 or 5 feet high,
green and smooth; leaves, 50 to 80 in number, oblanceolate, smooth,
pale green, firmer than those of *Pardalinum*, distinctly five to seven
nerved, the upper ones usually in regular whorls, the lower ones
scattered at the base, at the time of flowering; flowers, if more
numerous, in a loose raceme or umbel; pedicels, elongated, nodding
at the top; perianth, 2 to 2½ inches long; segments, more acute, 5
or 6 lines broad in the middle, deeply reflexed below the middle, of
a paler red on the inner surface than in *Pardalinum*, and more tinged
with yellow at the base, with fewer and smaller dots; stamens, shorter
than the perianth by nearly one-third. California, hort., Leichtlin.

Var. 3, *Bourgæi*, Baker, differs from *Pallidifolium*, in the few
specimens I have seen, by having narrower leaves all arranged in
regular whorls, and distinctly three to five nerved, the veins on the
lower part of the inner surface ciliated, and the dots more numerous
and larger, after the manner of *Pardalinum*. Banks of Lake
Winipeg, Borgeau. Very recently introduced into English gardens.

This is an extremely variable form, ued doubtless to locality as well as habit, see
pages 24 and 25. We recognise, in the main, 3 forms.

1. *Puberulum*, the pale tinted small spotted form, with short blunt frequent foliage,
crowded at base, whorled above.

2. *Pardalinum*, the medium tinted form, with large spots and reddish tips, with
long narrow pointed dark foliage.

3. *Californicum*, the richest tinted and finest form, with large spots, and scarlet
tipped perianth, foliage similar to that of *Pardalinum*.

But as to foliage, there is great individual variation in all three forms.

4. There is also another form described by Dr. Moore as "var. *Robinsonianum*," which
is simply a larger growing form, varying slightly. "In all the plants we have seen
cultivated under this name, the pale green stems, and *alternate* lanceolate leaves, have
been well marked features, while in the colour of the flowers, the tint of sanguineous red
pervading the upper half of the perianth segment is deeper, and the ocellate spots (dark
spots on yellow ground within the red portion) are more distinct." Dr. Moore, in
"*Florist*," Oct., 1875. For a good plate of *Humboldtii*, *Californicum*, and *Pardalinum*,
see that number.

30. *L. Superbum.*—L. Sp., 434; Bot. Mag., t. 936; Red. Sil., t. 103; Bury, Hexand., t. 36; Kunth, Enum., iv., 258; Flore des Serres, t. 1,014-15.—Bulbs (*see* p. 111), large, cæspitose, globose, perennial; scales, numerous, acute, closely imbricated, tinged with red; first leaves, firm, glaucous green; stem, 4 to 6 feet high, stout, tinged with purple; leaves often arranged in 3 or 4 whorls of 8 to 10 leaves, few or numerous scattered, narrowly lance-shaped, acute, somewhat firm, of a dull green colour, smooth, distinctly three to five nerved, the lower ones 4 or 5 inches long, 6 to 9 lines broad in the middle; flowers often 6 to 12 in number, sometimes 20 to 40, arranged in a deltoid panicle 9 to 12 inches broad, pedicels nodding at the top, the lower ones 3 to 5 inches long, divaricated; perianth, 3 or 4 inches long, brilliant orange red; segments, acute, lance-shaped, 6 to 9 lines broad, deeply revolute, with conspicuous claret - coloured slightly lamellated dots on the lower half; groove, deep, with

The Superb Orange Lily (*L. Superbum*).

smooth edges; filaments, 2 to 2½ inches long, very divergent; anthers, reddish, 6 to 7 lines long; ovary, 9 to 12 lines long, a little shorter than the curved style; capsule, obovoid, obtusely six-angled. From Canada to Georgia and Carolina, in woods and marshy places.

A very valuable, late, graceful Lily, in growth so like *Canadense*, that it is difficult to distinguish them, except by means of the immature flower buds, which are rounded in *Superbum*, but triangular in *Canadense*. Properly an eastern form, but stretching westward, and intermingling with the western varieties, so that it becomes difficult to separate the intermediate forms.

Var. *L. Carolinianum*, Michx., Flora, i., 197; Bot. Mag., t. 2,280; Bot. Reg., t. 580; Kunth, Enum., iv., 258.—*Michauxii*, Poir., Ency., iii., 457.—*Michauxianum*, Schult. fil., Syst., vii., 258. *Autumnale*, Lodd., Bot. Cab., t. 355.—Bulb, exactly like that of the type; first leaves appearing earlier, of a shining green, and thicker; leaves much fewer, broader, and shorter, often 5 or 6 in number, arranged in whorls near the middle of the stem, the others scattered; stem, 1 to 2 feet high, bearing one or few heads; perianth, exactly like that of the type, but the segments are sometimes broader and more obtuse. From Virginia and Carolina to Florida, flowering in our gardens in August, among the late flowering kinds.

Carolinianum or *Michauxii* is a form closely allied to *Superbum*, but really larger. It is called the Carolina Swamp Lily; it has broad obovate dark foliage, and bears a very richly tinted perianth, its bulb, however, is more like that of *Pardalinum*.

We may here introduce a description from Dr. Kellogg, of *L. Lucidum*, a new form as yet unknown to us, which seems allied to the preceding species.

31. *L. Lucidum*, Kellogg, p. 144.—" Leaves whorled, scattered below and above, lanceolate or ovate-lanceolate, very short, petioled or subsessile, pseudo tripli-nerved or somewhat three-nerved, smooth throughout, short peduncled. Flowers 4 (or 1—6) nodding, sepals sessile, lanceolate, strongly turbinate, revolute, thickened at the base; stamens and style exserted, about equal; style straight, thick; perianth light translucent yellow orange, the dark purple spots on the inside visible from without. June to August. Bulb spheroid or slightly depressed oblate spheroid, scales thickened, lanceolate acute, strongly incurved, and very closely appressed, whitish, with a yellowish green tinge 1½ to 2 inches in diameter, isolated, perennial; stem central, 2 to 3 feet high, quite glabrous throughout; shortish thick peduncles from axils of bracteoid leaves; lower and larger leaves, 1 to 1¼ inches wide, about 3 to 4 inches long, diminishing above; flowers 1½ inches in expansion, 1 inch deep; style ½ to ¾ inch long." A Lily from Oregon and Washington territory, long known, but also considered by authorities as a variety of *Canadense*. " Without recapitulating the isolated and peculiar bulb, the position of the stem, form and colour of flower surface, equal genitalia, &c., we take these to be constant characters. Indeed, the very revolute sepals remind us more of *Superbum* than *Canadense*, while the smaller closer flowers and thickened base are peculiar."— *Gardeners' Chronicle, vol.* 10, *p.* 627.

32. *L. Roezlii*.—Regel., Gartenfl., t. 667.—*Canadense*, var. *Hartwegii*, Baker, Gard. Chron., 1871, 321.—Bulb, perennial, rhizomatous; stem, 2 or 3 feet high, slender, smooth; leaves, in the specimens I have seen, 20 to 30 in number, a few of the upper or lower ones in whorls, or all scattered, ascending, firm, glaucous, narrowly linear, acute, indistinctly three to five nerved, the lower ones 4 or 5 inches long, 3 or 4 lines broad in the middle; flowers, 1 to 10 in number, if several in a corymb or raceme; pedicels, elongated, nodding at the top; perianth, 2 or 3 inches long, brilliant orange red: segments, acuminate, 5 or 6 lines broad in the middle, lower half yellow, with several purple spots, closely reflexed above the base; groove, distinct, with smooth edges; stamens, shorter than the perianth by one-third; anthers, 5 or 6

Roezl's Lily (*L. Roezlii*).

lines long; style, curved, twice as long as the ovary. I have not seen the capsule. Rocky Mountains in the Utah territory, introduced by Roezl into European gardens. California, on the Santa Cruz Mountains, Hartweg, 2,000. Easily distinguished from allied forms, by having narrow acute leaves, and perianth segments.*

33. *L. Columbianum.*—Hanson in hort., Leicht.—Bulb (*see* p. 113), *ovoid*, perennial, small white, acute, with lance-shaped scales; stem, 1½ to 2 feet high, slender, green, smooth; leaves, few, the lower ones in whorls of four or five leaves, the upper ones scattered, oblanceolate, acute, 1½ to 2 inches long, 5 or 6 lines broad in the middle; flowers, two or three in number, in an umbel; pedicels, slender, 2 to 4 inches long, nodding at the top; leaves, reflexed, bracted at the base, sometimes bracteolated; perianth; 1½ to 2 inches long, brilliant orange-red; segments, lance-shaped, closely reflexed from the middle, where they are 4 to 6 lines broad; inner surface covered thickly with purple dots; groove, shallow, smooth; stamens, shorter than the perianth by one-third; anthers, 3 or 4 lines long; style, scarcely longer than the ovary.—Oregon, W. Lobb, 350, hort., Leichtlin. It scarcely differs from *Canadense* var. *Parviflorum*,† except in the bulb not being rhizomatous.

A very graceful form, known as the Oregon Lily, found in dry sandy plains in that country and in British Columbia, 500 to 1,000 feet above sea level, with an ovoid bulb: from habit of growth and shape of flower, it has by many been considered to be a small variety of the next form *Humboldtii*, dwarfed by dry sandy habitat. It is, however, though smaller, a more elegant and graceful Lily, growing to the height of 3 and 4 feet, bearing numerous recurved pendulous flowers of a bright golden colour; and is one that seems easy of cultivation.

34. *L. Humboldtii.*—Roezl and Leicht., Duchartre, Obs. 105; Regel. Gartenfl., t. 724; Flore des Serres, t. 1,973-4—*Bloomerianum*, hort. Aug.—Bulb, large, 2 to 4 inches in diameter, oblique, perennial, not rhizomatous; scales, few, ovate-lanceolate, acute, 2 or 3 inches long; stem, terete, stout, 4 or 5 feet high, smooth or downy, green, with reddish spots; leaves, usually in four to six regular whorls of 10 to 15 leaves, oblanceolate, the lower ones 4 or 5 inches long, 9 to 12 lines broad above the middle, acute, firm, of a deep green colour, undulated; lateral veins, distinct, sometimes ciliated on the lower part of the inner surface; flowers, often six to ten in number, sometimes thirty to forty, in a deltoid panicle, which is a foot across when fully expanded; pedicels, divaricated, nodding at the top, the lower ones 3 to 5 inches long; leaves, oblanceolate, very much reflexed, bracted; perianth, 3 or 4 inches long, brilliant orange-red; greenish at the base outside; segments, acute, 9 to 12 lines broad in the middle, closely reflexed above the base, with numerous claret-coloured dots on the inner surface, slightly lamellate-papillose near the base; groove, distinctly excavated, with smooth edges; filaments, 1½ to 2 inches long; anthers, red, 6 to 8 lines long; style, 6 or 7 lines long, about one-third the length of the ovary; capsule large, obovoid, acutely six-angled as in *Martagon*. California, on the Sierra Nevada,

* We have no knowledge of our own, as regards this Lily.
† The form we have grown as *Parviflorum* is quite distinct from *Columbianum*. See our remarks on each species.

Roezl, in hort., Leichtlin.—*Canadense*, var. *Puberulum*, Torrey, Bot. Whipple, 90 (Hartweg 2,004), is a form of this species which has the stem and under-surface of the leaves puberulous.

This form, of all Lilies, has the largest and most peculiar bulb, sometimes globose, sometimes rhizomatous, often intermediate in form, with large long broad scales. We have had bulbs weighing as much as 1 lb. It is a very distinct, beautiful, and graceful form—graceful in whorled foliage, graceful in its spike of numerous pendent, golden purple-spotted flowers. Its reddish brown stem, bluish green smooth leaves, distinguish it even in early growth from all other Lilies. There is a good coloured figure given in the "Florist," 1875, p. 217.

Var. *Ocellatum*, Kellogg, Proc. Calif. Acad., v. 88, t. 4, from the Island of Santa Rosa, is a form with a yellowish perianth, marked on the inside with conspicuous purple dots.

This var., *Bloomerianum Ocellatum*, so called because each purple spot is (like a pupil) surrounded with a yellow circle; is a distinct form, with smaller bulb, not so vigorous in its growth, but with as large or larger flowers. *See* page 23.

Humboldt's Orange Lily
(*L. Humboldtii*).

Flower spike of Martagon Lily
(*L. Martagon*).

35. *L. Martagon.*—*Speciosum*, 435; Jacq., Austr., t. 351; Bot. Mag., t. 893 and 1,634; Red., Lil., t. 146; Eng. Bot., t. 279, edit. 3, t. 1,518 : Reich., Ic. Germ., t. 451.—Bulb, ovoid, 1½ to 2 inches long, yellowish, perennial, with very numerous narrow scales; stem 3 to 6 feet high, terete, smooth or puberulous in the upper part, green or spotted with purple; leaves, mostly in two to four whorls of six to nine leaves, the upper ones (rarely all) scattered, horizontal, oblanceolate, spathulate, sessile, tender, the lower ones 4 to 6 inches long, 12 to 15 lines broad above the middle, tender (with three to five distinct veins on each side of the mid-rib), smooth or pubescent; central internodes, 6 to 9 inches long; raceme, lax, elongated, containing from three to twenty flowers; bracts, small; pedicels, nodding when bearing flowers, the lowest ones 1 to 3 inches long; perianth, fragrant, claret-coloured, 15 to 18 lines long, pubescent on the right outside; segments, lance-shaped, very revolute, with numerous livid purple dots on the inside; claws, slightly lamellated (groove deep,

with papillose edges), hooded, thick, and puberulous at the apex; filaments, 8 to 10 lines long, twice the length of the anthers; pollen, red; ovary, 5 or 6 lines long, shorter than the very curved style by one-third; capsule, turbinate, acute-angled, umbilicated at the apex. Central and Southern Europe, to Siberia and Japan, flowering in our gardens at the end of June and beginning of July. For the forms of this species, *see* Parkinson, Parad., 31.

L. Hirsutum, Miller, Dict., No. 10 (*Milleri,* Schultes, Obs., 67), is a stout form with a puberulous stem.

*L. Glabrum,** Spreng, Syst., ii., 62, is a form with white flowers, a smooth stem, shining green leaves, and yellow pollen. There are also forms with claret and flesh-coloured undotted flowers.

Var. *L. Cattaneœ,* Visiani, Fl. Dalm., Suppl. 32, t. 3.—Segments of the perianth, thicker than in any other species, of a dark purplish-claret colour; dots, nearly obsolete. Dalmatia, Hort., Leichtlin.—

L. Marticum Dalmaticum, Malay, is a similar form, or the same.

It is the commonest wild European species, stretching from Spain and France through all Central and Southern Europe, and in Asia far into Siberia, but in the extreme East and Japan, appearing to be entirely replaced by *Hansoni,* which is confused with it in Ledebour's "Flora Rossica." It is the old original *Turk's-cap* Lily of the gardens, and is mentioned in Gerarde's list of the plants cultivated in 1596, but it has now given way to a large extent, as a popular favourite, to its allies with brighter coloured flowers. It is a very well-marked plant, not likely to be confounded with any other species, and, though so widely spread, it is very little liable to variation in its characters. *L. Martagon* is quite different from all other Lilies in the colour of its flowers.

I have seen a single specimen gathered by Bourgeau, in Piedmont, in which the whorls were entirely broken up, and the leaves scattered indiscriminately down the stem.

The *Martagon* group, stand alone in their peculiarities; they are remarkable for their whorls of broad dark-pointed foliage, for the peculiar mode in which the flower spike ascends, bearing a nodding, compact raceme of flower buds, hanging downward, which as the spike elongates, gradually unfold, and turn upwards one by one, till the branching spike, is symmetrically upright. (1 have never seen this peculiarity in any other group; but it is the normal, proceeding in the true *Martagon*). Lastly in the short, but very thick fleshy petals of the perianth.

Of the above named forms, *Album* is perhaps the most elegant and graceful; but *Dalmaticum,* the grandest and most superb: the stems of this exceedingly graceful plant rise with 5 to 7 whorls of broad pointed foliage, to a height of 6 to 8 feet, bearing a long symmetrical spike of from 20 to 40 flowers, varying from a light purple to a deep blood-red; sometimes spotted, sometimes unspotted.

36. *L. Avenaceum.*—Fischer, Maxim. in Regel., Gartenfl., 1865, 290, t. 485.—*Martagon,* Led., Fl. Ross., iv., 149, ex parte.—Bulb (*see* page 108), globose, small, perennial; scales, numerous, lance-shaped; stem, smooth, terete, 18 inches to 2 feet high; leaves,

* The well-known, very graceful, *Martagon Album.*

usually in a whorl of six to nine leaves at the middle of the stem,
a few scattered between the whorl and the raceme, seldom in two

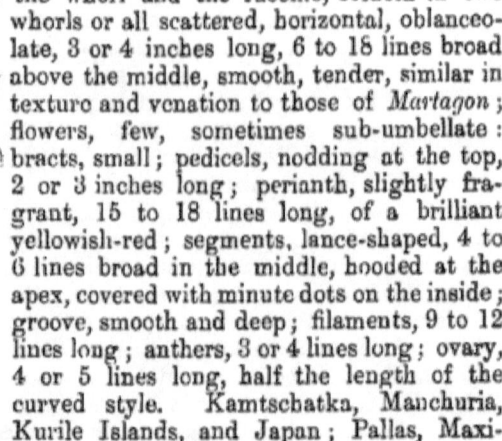

whorls or all scattered, horizontal, oblanceolate, 3 or 4 inches long, 6 to 18 lines broad
above the middle, smooth, tender, similar in
texture and venation to those of *Martagon*;
flowers, few, sometimes sub-umbellate :
bracts, small; pedicels, nodding at the top,
2 or 3 inches long; perianth, slightly fragrant, 15 to 18 lines long, of a brilliant
yellowish-red; segments, lance-shaped, 4 to
6 lines broad in the middle, hooded at the
apex, covered with minute dots on the inside;
groove, smooth and deep; filaments, 9 to 12
lines long; anthers, 3 or 4 lines long; ovary,
4 or 5 lines long, half the length of the
curved style. Kamtschatka, Manchuria,
Kurile Islands, and Japan; Pallas, Maxi-

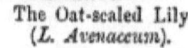

The Oat-scaled Lily
(*L. Avenaceum*).

mowicz, &c. It has the habit and foliage of *Martagon*, and the
yellowish-red perianth of *Canadense*.

This form differs from *Medeoloides*, in having drooping flowers with reflexed tips
(like *Tenuifolium*), unspotted, or but little spotted, and of a very variable tint; it is
found in the north of Japan, near Hakodadi.

It was first introduced in 1829, by Fisher, to the St. Petersburgh Botanic Garden,
but soon disappeared. Afterwards by Dr. Regel in 1856, and flowered; the colour of
the flower varies much from yellow to scarlet. In Hakodadi, the winter is very long,
8 or 9 months, and very severe; the summer, hot and brief. This Lily, might therefore,
be very properly introduced into Norway or Switzerland, with every chance of success.

The name *Avenaceum*, is given from the "oat-like" appearance of the scales of the bulb.

37. *L. Hansoni* (Leichl.)—Bulb (*see* page 109), like that of
Tigrinum, globose, perennial, compact, whitish; stem, 3 or 4 feet
high, slender, smooth, terete, stout, green; leaves, oblanceolate,
acute, green, tender, smooth, with three distinct, oblique, tender,
distant, lateral nerves, usually collected in a whorl of eight to twelve
patent sessile leaves at the middle of the stem, the others scattered,
4 or 5 inches long, 8 to 12 lines broad above the middle, gradually
narrowed from the middle to the base; flowers, 4 to 10 in number,
in a loose raceme, or crowded in an umbel; pedicels, erect-patent,
1½ to 2 inches long, of a brilliant reddish orange; segments, thick,
lance-shaped, 4 or 5 lines broad in the middle, deeply falcate-
revolute, dotted with purple on the lower half, inside; groove, long,
smooth, very deep; filaments, 10 to 12 lines long, yellow; anthers,
narrow, 4 or 5 lines long; pollen, yellow; ovary, club-shaped, deeply
channelled, 5 or 6 lines long, a little shorter than the style. Japan,
Hort., Leichtlin; coming into growth and flowering amongst the
earliest. This species is midway between *Martagon* and *Canadense*.

The figure of this Lily in *Florist*, 1874, p. 193, there miscalled *Avenaceum*, gives a
very inadequate idea of its beauty, and must have been taken from a plant not fully

established. When well grown, it throws up a spike from 4 to 5 feet high, with 12 to 30-flowers, of a much brighter tint than that given in the drawing above referred to.

It is a very early-flowering Lily, with well-marked whorled foliage ; the flowers are golden yellow, star-shaped, and spotted, like other true *Martagons*, has petals stout and fleshy in substance, broad and ovate, rather than long.

It was discovered by Maximowicz in 1860, in Japan ; we have had drawings of this Lily, with bulbs sent over to us thence, as far back as the winter of 1869-70, but we never flowered it till 1878. We consider it to be by far the most striking and graceful form of all the true *Martagons*.

38. *L. Monadelphum*.—M. Bieb., Flor. Taur., i., 267; Cent. Pl. Ross., t. 4 ; Gawl. Bot. Mag., t. 1,405; Kunth, Enum., iv., 260 ; Fisch. and Lall., Ind. Sem. Petrop., 1839, 57 ; Reich. Exot., t. 89 ; Regel,. Gartenfl., t. 723.—*Loddigesianum*, Schultes, fil, Syst. Veg., vii., 416 ;. Kunth, Enum., iv., 261 ; Lemaire, Jard. Fleur., t. 204 ; Paxt. Flow. Gard., t. 58.—*Szovitzianum*, Fisch. and Lall., Ind. Sem. Petr., 1839, 58 ; Kunth, Enum., iv., 674 ; Regel, Gartenfl., t. 436 ; Flore des: Serres, 507-9.—*Colchicum*, Steven.—Bulb, ovoid (*see* page 114), whitish,. perennial ; scales, numerous, lance-shaped ; stem, 2 to 5 feet high, stout, green, puberulous; leaves, 30 to 50 in number, scattered, ascending, linear lance-shaped, or oblanceolate, green, distinctly many-nerved, the central ones 3 or 4 inches long, 6 to 12 lines broad in the middle, pubescent on the back and edges; raceme, usually containing from 2 to 16 (sometimes 20 to 30) flowers ; peduncles, $1\frac{1}{2}$ to 2 inches long, nodding at the top; bracts, large, lance-shaped, in pairs ; perianth, fragrant, of a sulphur-yellow, $2\frac{1}{2}$ to $3\frac{1}{2}$ inches long ; segments, oblanceolate, falcate above the middle, 9 to 12 lines broad, tinged with purple at the base and apex, and having a few small blackish dots on the inner surface, not papillose ; groove, smooth and shallow; filaments, 18 to 21 lines long, green, flattened from the base, valvate at the base of the upper third of their length ; anthers, 5 or 6 lines long; pollen, red ; ovary, 7 or 8 lines long, half the length of the almost straight style ; capsule, obovoid, 18 to 21 lines long, obtuse-angled, umbilicated at the apex. The Caucasus, and northern Persia, flowering in our gardens in June, amongst the earliest. The original plant of Bieberstein is merely a form which has the filaments united below. This species recedes from the others of this group towards Eulirion, which it resembles in the form of the perianth, and in the absence of papillæ, &c.

Crimson-anthered Lily (*L. Szovitzianum*).

Var. *L. Ledebourii*, Baker ; *Pyrenaicum*, Lcd. Fl. Ross, iv., 151, non Gouan.—A dwarfer variety with narrower leaves (80 to 100 in number), linear, seven-nerved, 4 to 6 lines broad in the middle,. scarcely pubescent underneath ; segments of the perianth, 6 to 8 lines.

broad.   Caucasus, Güldenstadt, C. A. Meyer.   (I have seen it growing in Kew Gardens.)

This Lily, more generally called *Szovitzianum*, and sometimes *Colchicum*, is a most
beautiful and rather variable species ; not merely from the unusual (canary) colour of
the flowers, their large size, and contrast with the chocolate-brown anthers, but from the
symmetry of the pyramidal spike.   Each flower, (when well-cultivated), like an evenly
suspended bell, hangs with base parallel to the horizon.   In this respect the woodcut
above fails to do justice to the plant.   We have had in one season over 1,500 spikes in
bloom, from 4 to 6 feet high, with from 4 to 20 bells on each spike, some of them (the
flowers) 6 inches across, most beautifully coloured, scarcely any two alike, a sight of
beauty that falls to the lot of but few.

Among its many varieties, we have selected the following as especially worthy of
notice :—

A.—A fine broad petalled form with large bells of flowers, rather pale in tint, but
regularly and heavily spotted with about 4 rows of dark purple spots on either edge of
the petal.

B.—A very rich deep canary, almost citron coloured form, with very few spots.

C.—A pale lemon tinted form, few spots.

D.—Has a deep yellow centre and paler tinted edges.

E.—A peculiar pale coloured form, very regularly and richly spotted, with pale coloured
anthers of a light greenish tint.

F.—The unspotted variety, of a very deep citron colour.   We have been accustomed
to call this variety *Monadelphum*.   According to some Liliophilists, this form (*Monadelphum*) differs from the type in (a) having anthers covered with lemon yellow pollen,
instead of chocolate brown.   (b), in being earlier by three weeks to flower, and (c) in
shewing its flower buds directly it is above the ground, whereas, in the type, the buds
are concealed by the leaves till ready to bloom.   As regards (a), we have noticed anthers
bearing pollen of all shades, from a pale greenish yellow to a very rich red brown.   As
regards (b and c), we have noticed these differences, more especially in plants that have
been planted the previous autumn, and are not yet well established, but not with plants
like our own, that have been undisturbed through three winters.   Cultivators must not
expect to see this Lily in all its beauty, unless planted in a moist, loamy, or clayey soil,
and left undisturbed for at least two winters,—then it will be **magnificent**.

39.   *L. Polyphyllum.*—D. Don in Royle, Ill. Him., 388 ; Kunth,
Enum., iv., 677 ; Klotzsch, Reise Wald., 53.—*Punctatum*, Jacquem,
Duchartre, Obs., 76.—(For description of bulb, *see* pages 114 and 115),
stem, smooth, terete, 2 to 4 feet high ; leaves, 40 to 60 in number,
ascending, scattered (or the lower ones sometimes whorled, according
to Jacquemont), green, sessile, acute, smooth, minutely papillose on
the edges, resembling those of *Martagon* in their texture and venation,
the lower ones oblanceolate, 4 or 5 inches long, 6 to 9 lines broad
above the middle, the upper ones narrower and linear ; peduncle,
naked for 5 or 6 inches below the raceme ; raceme, lax, containing
from 4 to 10 flowers, branches often opposite ; bracts, in whorls ;
pedicels, nodding at the top when bearing flowers, the lower ones
3 to 5 inches long ; perianth, 18 to 21 lines long, fragrant, " of a
livid-yellow, with claret-coloured dots " (Jacquemont) ; segments,
oblanceolate, 2 or 3 lines broad, revolute from the middle ; filaments,
15 to 16 lines long ; anthers, 4 lines long ; ovary, 6 or 7 lines long,
one-third shorter than the very curved style ; capsule, obovoid, 12 to
15 lines long, sub-acute-angled.   Temperate region of the Western
Himalayas (Kunawar, Kashmir, &c.) ; Royle, Thomson, Jacquemont.
6,000 to 8,000 feet above sea level, also in Thibet.

This rare, but very beautiful Lily, was flowered by Mr. Geo. Maw, at Benthall Hall, in 1877, the flowers were then described of a pale cream colour, speckled internally with linear dark purple markings. We have also flowered it at Colchester. It is a beautiful and elegant form, colour yellowish, with purple lines and spots, resembling much in shape of flower the preceding form, *Szovitzianum*. For remarks about its culture, *see* pages 19 and 20.

40. *L. Ponticum.*—K. Koch, Linnæa, xxii., 234; Duchartre Obs. 22.—Bulb, ovoid, an inch in diameter; scales, numerous, lance-shaped; stem, 1½ to 2 feet high, slender, faintly pubescent in the upper part; leaves, 20 to 30 in number, scattered, lance-shaped, firm, ascending, 15 to 18 lines long, 4 to 5 lines broad, the upper one narrower; veins, numerous, distinct; lower part of the inside, and edges pubescent; flowers, 1 to 6 in number, nodding, 18 to 21 lines long, yellow; segments, oblanceolate, reflexed below the middle, where they are 3 or 4 lines broad, scarcely dotted; groove, shallow; filaments 3 or 4 lines long, half the length of the perianth; ovary, 6 lines long, a little shorter than the club-shaped style; capsule, 1 inch long, obovoid, obtuse-angled. Mountains of Asia Minor, at an altitude of 6,000 to 7,000 feet, K. Koch; the mountainous regions of Lazistan Balansa, Plantes de l'Orient, anno 1866, No. 1,531. It has the leaves and habit of *Monadelphum*; but is more slender, and the typical perianth of this species is more revolute. Regel's figure (Gartenflora, t. 436), which is referred by K. Koch to *Ponticum*, in my opinion represents the true *Szovitzianum*. In De Candolle's herbarium there is a narrow-leaved specimen from Lazistan, in which the leaves are more crowded, the lower ones 3 inches long, and 3 or 4 lines broad, resembling a variety of *Monadelphum*.

We cannot recognise this form as ought, but a variety of *Szovitzianum*, probably our variety. B. *See* preceding page.

41. *L. Carniolicum.*—Bernh. in Mert and Koch., Deutsch. Flora, ii., 536; Kunth, Enum., iv., 260; Reich. Ic. Flor. Germ., t. 990; Parl. Flor. Ital., ii., 404.—*Chalcedonicum*, Linn. sp. Plant., 434, ex parte; Jacq. Fl. Austr. Suppl., t. 20; *Martagon Pannonicum* sive *Exoticum Flore Spadiceo*, Parkins, Parad., 35.—Bulb (*see* page 113), perennial, ovoid; scales, numerous, lance-shaped; stem, 2 or 3 feet high, green, puberulous; leaves, thirty or forty in number, scattered, ascending, lance-shaped, or linear-lance-shaped, the lower ones 2 or 3 inches long, 6 to 9 lines broad in the middle, flat, distinctly many-nerved, and distinctly ciliated on the margins and the veins of the lower part inside; upper leaves shorter; pressed close to the peduncle; raceme, few-flowered; pedicels, 2 or 3 inches long, nodding at the top, sometimes bracteolated; perianth, 1½ to 2 inches long, of a brilliant yellow or vermilion; segments, oblanceolate, closely revolute, 5 or 6 lines broad in the middle, with numerous minute dots on the inner surface, papillose downwards; groove distinctly excavated; filaments, 8 to 12 lines long; anthers, 5 or 6 lines long; pollen, saffron; ovary, 5 or 6 lines long, as long as the club-shaped

style; capsule, 1½ inch long; obtuse-angled.　Lombardy, Istria,. Dalmatia, Illyria, and Bosnia; flowering in June.

We have received and flowered a variety of the above Lily without spots in the flower (*Unicolor*); we also have reason to believe that there is a white variety.

The Carniolian or Nodding Red Lily
(*L. Carniolicum*).

The Nankeen Lily
(*L. Testaceum*).

42.　*L. Testaceum.*—Lindl., Bot .Reg., 1842, Misc., 51, 1843, t. 11; Paxt. Mag. Bot., 1843, 221, with a figure; Kunth, Enum., iv., 673; Flore des Serres, t. 39; Regel, Gartenfl., t. 349.—*Excelsum*, Walp. Ann., xi., 110.—*Isabellinum*, Kunze, in Mohl. and Schlecht., Bot. Zeit., i., 609.—Bulb, globose, perennial; stem, 4 or 5 feet high, slightly downy, tinged with brown; leaves, sixty to a hundred in number, scattered, very close, linear, ascending, firm, dull, green, three to five-nerved, the lower ones 3 or 4 inches long, 3 or 4 lines broad in the middle, the margins covered with whitish down, the upper ones gradually smaller, 1 to 1½ inches long, pressed close to the stem, more distinct, being at some distance from the flowers; flowers, three to ten in number, in an umbel or raceme, fragrant; pedicels, erect-patent, 4 to 6 inches long, nodding at the top, bracted with small white-margined leaves; perianth, 2½ to 3 inches long, dull yellow; segments, deeply revolute, 9 to 12 lines broad, with a few small reddish dots near the base, slightly lamellate-papillose; groove, deep, with smooth edges; filaments, half the length of the perianth; anthers, 5 or 6 lines long; pollen, red; ovary, 6 to 8 lines long, about half the length of the curved style.　A garden variety, probably a hybrid between *Candidum* and *Chalcedonicum*; flowers in the end. of July.

This very graceful and distinct Lily is said to have been first noticed at Erfürt, in a. bed of seedlings, in 1846.　It has a most pleasant perfume, graceful appearance, and is a. general favourite.

It has been thought not to have a Japanese origin, because no bulbs of it have ever been traced as coming over from those Islands of the Western Sea, so productive of new and graceful forms; but, we have seen more than once, in Japanese drawings executed for us, years ago, by some of the best artists in Yeddo, as containing "all the Lilies of Japan," forms represented, bearing a very strong resemblance to *Excelsum*.　It is true that amongst these Lilies, there are some most wonderful forms and gorgeous pieces of colouring, such as would lead many to disbelieve in the veracity of the artist, but, on the other hand, we can point to other Lily forms which we know well, depicted therein with fair accuracy, while the birds and insects pourtrayed in some numbers, we recognise to have been truthfully delineated. Our own conclusion is, that as yet, we have scarcely touched the rich treasure of wonderful Lilies, which Japan will one day send to us.

43. *L. Leichtlinii.*—Hook. fil., Bot. Mag., t. 5,673; Ill. Hort., t. 540; Flore des Serres, t. 1,736; Belg. Hort., t. 11; Floral Mag., t. 509.—Bulb (*see* page 99), small, perennial, globose; scales, few, broad, acute, thick, closely imbricated; stem, 2 or 3 feet high, of a dark brown colour, slender, faintly covered with down, creeping at the base; leaves, 30 or 40 in number, scattered, linear, ascending, of a deep green colour, firm, flat, distinctly three-nerved, the lower ones 3 to 5 inches long, 3 or 4 lines broad, the upper ones lance-shaped and distant from the flowers; flowers, few, in a loose corymb; pedicels, erect-patent, 3 or 4 inches long, nodding at the top; perianth, scentless, 2½ to 3 inches long of a brilliant lemon colour, tinged with purple on the outside, and sprinkled from the base to above the middle on the inside with conspicuous claret-coloured dots; segments, lance-shaped, 6 to 9 lines broad in the middle, deeply revolute, callous at the apex, channelled, slightly lamellated near the

Max Leichtlin's Lily
(*L. Leichtlinii*).

base; groove, deep, with faintly pubescent edges; filaments, yellow, 2 to 2½ inches long, diverging widely: anthers, brownish red, 6 to 7 lines long; ovary, slender, 9 lines long, one-third the length of the curved style. Japan, Maximowicz. It flowers in our gardens in August, at the same time as *Tigrinum.*

Var. *Majus,* Wilson, in Journ. Hort., 1873, 371, with a figure, is a luxuriant form, 5 feet high, with leaves 6 or 7 inches long.—*Maximowiczii,* Regel, Ind. Sem. Hort. Petr., 1866, 26; Gart., 1868, 322, t. 596; Animad., 1873, 20, is a variety with brilliant scarlet flowers. Japan, Maximowicz.

A very beautiful form is *Leichtlinii*; it has one peculiarity not noticed above, that, apparently without reason, the shooting stem will run along beneath the soil for a foot or more before making its appearance, consequently, these Lilies are erratic in their nature, and unfit for pot culture.

With regard to the *Maximowiczii* mentioned above, we have always referred it to the later mentioned form, No. 45, *Pseudo Tigrinum.*

44. *L. Batemanniæ.*—Closely allied to *Leichtlinii* is another new Lily from Japan, which, through the kindness of Mrs. Bateman, a well-known Liliophile, and one of the first possessors of this kind, we have had the pleasure of calling *Batemanniæ.* It grows from 3½ to 4 feet high, and with suitable cultivation, might be expected to

N

attain at least 6 feet. It has a slender, light green, somewhat rough stem, inclined to bronze at the insertions of the lower leaves, which are crowded, alternate, long, and slender, arching downwards. The flowers are semi-cup-shaped, with spreading segments somewhat recurved, medium sized, of a deep apricot tint, and *unspotted* They are produced in umbels of from 4 to 8 or 12, not unlike in colour those of *Thunbergianum Venustum* (*Armeniacum*), but the plant, as to bulb, habit of growth, foliage, and time of flowering, resembles very closely *Leichtlinii* or *Maximowiczii*, to which it is closely allied. This new Lily first flowered with us in 1875, from some small bulbs obtained from Japan in rather poor condition; we were much puzzled by its nondescript appearance, for the flowers reminded us strongly of *T. Venustum*, while the foliage and habit were more like those of *Croceum*. As the plants were dwarf, weak, and poorly developed, we postponed, that year, any decision as to its character, till we could obtain stronger growth. Fortunately, in the winter of 1877—78, a large number of queer-shaped bulbs from Japan, under the name of *Talsta Juri*, made their appearance in the market: these were small, in shape and size much resembling those of *Leichtlinii*, having broad stout scales, with the front tier reaching nearly half way up the bulb. Bulbs of the *Umbellatum* section are in general large and flatter, with scales nearly up to the apex; those of *Thunbergianum* have more numerous, slender, and narrower scales, reaching vertically higher, up to the apex of the bulb. We purchased and planted a lot of these bulbs, which were new in shape to us, and, at first, during growth, comparing them with some of the true plants growing near, we thought we had got *Leichtlinii*, but, later on, a difference appeared in stems and foliage; the former were too rough and green, whereas, those of *Leichtlinii*, were smooth and dark coloured, the foliage was large, more crowded, and arching, whereas, in *Leichtlinii*, it was sparse, erect, and acute; lastly, the immature flower buds were blunt at the tip, marked with red, and arranged in an umbel: those of *Leichtlinii* were elongated, green at the tip, and arranged in the form of a spike. When the flowers expanded, we saw at once that we had again grown our old friend, which had so puzzled us in 1875. We have no doubt this form is a hybrid, it may be between *Excelsum*, which it much resembles in shape and substance of flower, and in being destitute of spots, and *Maximowiczii*, to the bulb of which its bulb is very similar; or it may be *Armeniacum*. Whatever its parentage, as an intermediate form it is most interesting; as a decorative autumnal form, it is floriferous, elegant, striking, and well worthy of a good place in the garden. A good plate of this Lily is given in *Garden, vol.* 15 p. 39.

45. *L. Pseudo-tigrinum.*,—Carrière, Revue Hort., 1867, 410, with a figure; Regel. Gart., 1868, 118; Animad, 1873, 21.—Bulb (*see* p. 100), ovoid, perennial; scales, acute, adpressed, moderately thick;

stem, 3 or 4 feet high, erect at the base, covered with whitish down, of a lurid green colour, faintly spotted; leaves, scattered, linear, 4 or 5 inches long, 3 or 4 lines broad, recurved-patent, revolute at the edges, when young covered with whitish cobweb-like down on the edges and base outside; raceme, loose, containing 4 to 6 flowers; pedicels, erect-patent, 2 or 3 inches long, nodding at the top; bracts and bracteoles, linear; perianth, 2 to 2½ inches long, brilliant scarlet, with numerous dark brown dots on the inside; segments, ovate-lance-shaped, 8 to 12 lines broad above the base, very revolute, and covered with numerous lamellate papillæ; groove, deep; filaments, 2 inches long, scarlet; anthers, 6 or 7 lines long; pollen, red; style, scarlet, 1½ inches long, very much curved, twice as long as the ovary. China. It flowers in our gardens in July and August.*

46. *L. Wallacei.*—Very closely allied to this form and *Leichtlinii*, is another form, to which we have given the name *Wallacei*. The bulbs, curiously enough, are small and cæspitose, at least, they have a great tendency to reproduction, and throw up numerous stems from the one bulb; the foliage and appearance are like those of a young Tiger, but with more crowded foliage; a Japanese form, and probably a garden hybrid between *Maximowiczii* and *Concolor;* the foliage is narrow, lanceolate, pointed, alternate, smooth; stem, light green, not pubescent; flower, of a rich vermilion orange, spotted at base and centre with numerous slightly raised small maroon spots; petals, stout, some reflexed; autumn flowering. It flowered with us first in 1877, having been introduced in 1876.

47. *L. Pomponium.*—*Speciosum,* 434; Bot. Mag., t. 271; Kunth, Enum., iv., 266; Reich. Ic. Germ., t. 991; Gren. Fl., France, iii., 181. —*Rubrum.* Lam. and DC., Gall., iii., 213.—Bulb, ovoid, perennial; scales, numerous, lance-shaped; stem, 2 to 3 feet high, thick, straight, channelled; leaves, 100 or more in number, deep green, scattered, narrowly linear, ascending, the lower ones 2 to 4 inches long, 1½ to 2 lines broad, three-nerved, with papillose and slightly revolute margins, the lowest ones 3 or 4 lines broad, the upper ones shorter and narrowly linear; peduncle, bare for 2 or 3 inches below the raceme; raceme, containing from 2 to 15 flowers; pedicels, nodding at the top, often bracteolated; perianth, fragrant, 1½ to 2 inches long, usually of a *vermilion-red,* furnished with numerous papillæ and black dots on the inside; segments, closely revolute,

* This Lily reminds one much of the Tiger group, which, indeed, it resembles in bulb, and flower, but differs in the fact, that it has an erect, smooth, less woolly stem, and does not emit bulbs in the axils of the leaves its foliage also is of a lighter green colour. It rejoices in various names, such as *Jucundum, Maximowiczii. See Florist,* 1873, p. 13.

It grows wild in Japan, on mountain slopes, and is very variable in colour, and spotting of the flower.

It may be regarded as a hybrid, between a Tiger (perhaps *Fortunei*) and *Leichtlinii.* It is a strong, erect, grower, 3—4 feet high, stem, more or less green; flower, in shape that of *Leichtlinii;* but in colour and marking more like *Tigrinum Fortunei;* flowers the end of August; is a fine acquisition to our hardy Lilies.

oblanceolate, 3 or 4 lines broad; groove, smooth, distinctly excavated. with smooth edges; filaments, green, 12 to 14 lines long; anthers, 3 or 4 lines long; pollen, vermilion-red; ovary, 5 to 6 lines long, a

Little Turk's Cap Lily (*L. Pomponium*).   Flower of The Little Turk's Cap Lily.

little shorter than the style; capsule, ovoid, 1½ inches long, umbilicated at the top, somewhat acutely six-angled. Northern Italy and the South of France. It flowers in our gardens at the end of June. —*Angustifolium*, Mill. Dict., No. 6, is a more slender form, with very narrow one-nerved leaves.

Var. *L. Pyrenaicum*, Gouan. Ill. 25; Red. Lil., t. 145; Reich. Ic. Germ., t. 992; Kunth, Enum., iv., 262.—*Flavum*, Lam. Gall., iii., 283. A more robust variety, with leaves a little broader and distinctly three-nerved, often extending to the base of the raceme; flowers, *yellow* and larger; bracts larger and style thicker. Pyrenees—*Martagon Luteum* non *Punctatum*, Parkins, Theat., 35, is a variety which has yellow flowers without dots.

Mention must also be made of a form called *Pomponium Verum*, collected by Mr. George Maw, 14,000 feet above sea level, in the Maritime Alps, and from Lantosca, near Mentone; it grows from 2 to 3 feet high, and is distinguished from the common garden form, by the bright scarlet tint of its flowers dotted over with linear arranged dots, and by its numerous, very slender, keeled, crowded, linear leaves; each leaf has a white edge and is somewhat sickle-shaped, with a spiral twist following the course of the sun: its foliage, therefore, has a very peculiar appearance, especially when just unfolded, resembling much that of *Tenuifolium*, but rather more white edged, like that of some Yuccas. It is a much more beautiful form than the preceding.

L. Albanum is a Transylvanian form, exactly like the yellow Pyrenaicum, but with a little larger leaves, and pollen of a different colour, the odour is sweet, like that of honey, whereas the savour of the garden form is rather nauseous; it occurs in quantities, near Verespatch; but the Macedonian plant from which Griesbach drew his description, referred to under head of Chalcedonicum, differs somewhat (Leichtlin).

48. *L. Chalcedonicum.*—Linn. Sp. Plant., 434, ex parte; Gawl., Bot. Mag., t. 993, non Jacq.—*Rubrum Byzantinum* sive *Martagon Constantinopolitanum*, Parkins., Parad., 34.—Bulb, ovoid, perennial, yellowish; scales, numerous, lance-shaped; stem, straight, downy, 3 or 4 feet high, green, tinged with purple; leaves, 100 or

more in number, ascending, very close, sessile, pale green, the lowest oblanceolate, the central ones linear, 2 or 3 inches long, 2 or 3 lines broad, three to five-nerved, covered with distinct white papillæ on the edges and on the veins of the lower part inside, upper leaves smaller and pressed close to the peduncle ; raceme, few-flowered ; pedicels, nodding at the top, often bracteolated ; perianth, scentless, 1½ to 2 inches long, usually of a brilliant vermilion red without dots (but sometimes having a few minute dots on the inside), seldom yellow ; segments, oblanceolate, closely revolute, 5 or 6 lines broad in the middle, with numerous papillæ ; groove, distinctly sunk, with smooth edges ; filaments, 12 to 14 lines long ; anthers, 4 to 4½ lines long ; pollen, vermilion-red ; ovary, 5 or 6 lines long, about the same length as, or a little

The Scarlet Turk's-cap Lily
(*L. Chalcedonicum.*)

shorter than the style ; capsule, obtuse-angled. Greece, and the Ionian Islands. It flowers in our gardens at the end of July and beginning of August, among the late blooming kinds.—*Albanicum*, Griseb. Fl. Rumel, ii., 385 ; Schur. Transyl., 662.

Pyrenaicum, Baumg, Transyl., 632, non Gouan, from the Mountains of Albania, and *Transylvania* is a variety found in the Mountain Woods with yellow, and usually solitary flowers.

Gracile, Ebel, Zwolf Tage auf Montenegro, 8, t. 1, from the Mountains of Montenegro (flower not described) is now said to be a *Fritillary*.

L. *Chalcedonicum* is a very favourite Lily, not merely for its tall, graceful spike, with pendulous scarlet bells, but because with *Candidum* and *Excelsum* it seems to have the happy knack of doing well everywhere, and in all soils, consequently, it is not an uncommon tenant in cottage gardens. The demand for it of late years, has been greatly on the increase, but cultivators must not be discouraged if the first year after planting, little or no growth above ground is apparent, *see* our remarks, p. 53, 54, & 174.

49. *L. Callosum.*—Sieb. et Zucc., Fl. Jap., ix., 86, t. 41 ; Kunth, Enum., iv., 262 ; Miquel, Ann. Mus. Lug. Bat., iii., 156.—*Pomponium*, Thunb., Fl. Jap., 134, non Linn.—Bulb (*see* p. 107), small, perennial ; scales, few, lance-shaped ; stem, 1½ to 3 feet high, slender, terete, smooth ; leaves, 30 to 40 in number, scattered, linear, ascending, smooth, firm, green, three to five-nerved, with narrowly revolute margins ; lower leaves, 3 or 4 inches long, 1 to 2 lines broad in the middle, the upper ones becoming gradually smaller ; raceme, narrow, lax, containing from 2 to 12 flowers ; pedicels, short, nodding ; bracts, in pairs, ligulate, thick, 4 to 9 lines long, obtuse at the apex, and callous (*hence the name Callosum*) ; perianth, always of a brilliant scarlet, 12 to 18 lines long ; segments, oblanceolate, spathulate, 2½

to 3 lines broad, hooded at the tip, and without dots of any kind on the inner surface; groove, smooth, deep, and with smooth edges; filaments, one-third shorter than the perianth; anthers, scarlet, 3 or 4 lines long; ovary, 5 or 6 lines long, of equal length with the club-shaped, slightly curved style; capsule, obovoid, 15 to 18 lines long, obtuse-angled. Japan and the Loo-choo Islands, Maximowicz, Oldham, 872; Buerger, &c. Introduced into Europe in 1840, indigenous to the mountainous regions of Japan.

The Callous Lily (*L. Callosum*).

After having handled several hundred bulbs of this Lily, we can hardly agree with the description above given of the bulb. For a more correct representation, *see* page 107, where a round bulb is given. If the elongated figure (?) in the annexed woodcut is intended to represent the bulb, it is utterly unlike those we have seen, and the fact that it is an article of food in Japan, points out that the bulb must be of a respectable size. No other Lily has the blunted thickened bracts, peculiar to this form, and shown in the woodcut, hence the name.

Var. *L. Stenophyllum*, Baker.—*Pumilum*, Hort., Leichtlin, non., DC.—Bulb, more ovoid; scales, fewer and broader; stem, stouter and taller; leaves, distant from each other, 1½ to 2 lines broad, three-nerved; perianth, 18 to 21 lines long; tube, longer and more cylindrical than in the type; segments, narrow and more ligulate. Eastern Siberia, Hort., Leichtlin.

The Var. *Pumilum*, from Mantchouria is (Regel) identical with *Callosum*.

50. *L. Tenuifolium.*—Fisch. Ind. Sem. Hort. Gorenk., 1812, 8; Schultes, fil., Syst. Veg., vii., 409; Kunth, Enum., iv., 263.—

Pumilum, DC. in Red. Lil., t. 378; Kunth, Enum., iv., 263: *Linifolium*, Hornem Hort. Hafn., i., 326.—*Puniceum*, Sieb. and De Vriese, Ann. Hort. Pays-Bas, 1861, 23.—Bulb (*see* page 106), small, globose,[*] annual (?); scales, numerous, lance-shaped; stem, 1 to 2 feet, very slender, terete, smooth; leaves, 40 or 50 in number, very narrow, scattered, ascending, the central ones 1½ to 2 feet long and ½ to 1 line broad, one-nerved, and with revolute margins; peduncle, bare for 2 or 3 inches below the raceme; raceme, loose, containing from 1 to 20 flowers; pedicels, 2 or 3 inches long, nodding at

The Slender-leaved Lily (*L. Tenuifolium*).

[*] We believe this statement to be correct.

the top; bracts, linear-subulate, in pairs; perianth, 15 to 18 lines long, of a bright pale crimson colour; segments, oblanceolate, 3 or 4 lines broad in the middle, very revolute, usually of one colour, rarely marked with a few small blackish dots; groove, smooth, distinctly sunk; filaments, pale red, 8 or 9 lines long; anthers, twice as long; pollen, scarlet; ovary, 4 to 4½ lines long, one-third shorter than the slender style.   Siberia, from the Altai Mountains to Amoor-land and Northern China.   Pallas, Maximowicz, &c.

An early flowering kind, as may be supposed from its habitat. The most elegant and graceful of all the dwarf Lilies.

CHAPTER X.
SUPPLEMENT TO THE SYNOPSIS.

SPECIES FORMERLY GROUPED WITH LILIES, BUT NOW PLACED AMONG
THE FRITILLARIES.

L. Nanum.—Klotsch., Reise Wald., 53.—6 inches high, downy, as far as the base of the leaves, one-flowered; leaves, linear, grass-like, bluntish, straight, erect, five-nerved; flower, nodding, small, bell-shaped, white; perigonous leaflets, oblong, obtuse, all sessile; stigma, thickened, three-angled, downy; filaments, subulate; anthers, oblong, obtuse, bluntly bifid at the base. Western Himalayas, Hoffmeister; Mount Gossain—Than, Nepaul; Gardner, Sikkim, 9,000 to 10,000 feet elevation, Dr. Hooker. Now known as *Fritillaria Gardneriana.*

L. Thompsonianum, now identified as *Fritillaria Macrophylla*, D. Don, Prod. Nep., 51 (1825)—*L. Roseum*—Wallich, Cat. No. 5077 (year 1832), Hook. in Bot. Mag., t. 4725.—*Lilium Thompsonianum*, Lindl., Bot. Reg., 1845, t. 1; Spae, Mon., p. 9.—*Fritillaria Thomsoniana*, D. Don, in Royle Ill. Him.,

p., 388, t. 92 (year 1839), Kunth, Enum., iv., p. 672.—A native of the Western Himalayas, extending from Affghanistan eastwards by way of Mussoorie and Kumaon to Nepaul. It has been gathered by nearly all the collectors who have visited those regions. In the eastern part of its range, the height which it attains above the sea-level appears to be from 5,000 to 8,000 feet. Figures will be found in the three publications quoted; that in the "Botanical Magazine" being the most recent and much the most satisfactory, both botanically and artistically.

L. Thompsonianum, Thomson's
Fritillary.

Royle's plant, called *Thomsonianum*, has flowers half as large again as those I have described, but differs in no other respect from Wallich's original *Roseum*. It seems to have been first introduced into cultivation by Loddiges, who flowered it in 1844. Captain Strachey sent it to Kew in 1853 from Kumaon, and it was from his specimens that the figure in the "Botanical Magazine" was drawn.

"It may surprise some to be told, that the plant of which the annexed is a representation, is sometimes a Lily and sometimes a Fritillary. It has been alternately referred to the genera Lilium and Fritillaria by different botanists, and even now, it is doubtful whether it has found a permanent resting place. It is one of those plants which puzzle botanists, and it illustrates the fact that it is often as difficult to characterise genera, as it is to define species. The plant was originally described by David

Don, as *Fritillaria Macrophylla*, and Mr. Baker, in his revision of the Tulipeæ (Linnean Society's Journal, vol. xiv.) retains this name for it, placing in it a sub-genus having the floral characters of Lilium, and the scariously coated bulbs and distinctly three-lobed style of Fritillaria. Messrs. Loddiges, imported and flowered it about the year 1844, and it was figured in the "Botanical Register" under the name of *L. Thompsonianum*. Mr. Baker's description, drawn up from a number of dried and living plants will aid in giving an idea of the general range of variability of this species. Bulb, ovoid, 1 inch thick, clothed with several scarious coats 2 inches thick, or more in length, striped on the outside, and bearing bulblets in their axils, stem, 1½ to 3 feet high, erect, round, and smooth, leaves, 20 to 30 directed upwards, narrow, bearing bulblets in their axils, lower ones crowded, 12 to 18 inches long, 3 to 4½ lines broad, upper ones looser and shorter; flower spike 12 to 18 inches long, bearing 6 to 30 flowers, flowers when expanded, 3 to 4½ inches across, lower ones nodding, upper ones smaller, half erect. A native of Afghanistan and the North West Himalayas."—*W. B. Hemsley, Garden, vol.* 12, *p.* 136.

Fritillaria Hookeri.—Baker, n. sp.—Closely allied to the last, but clearly distinct from it specifically. Bulb quite similar in shape and vestiture, but considerably smaller. Stem more flexuose, at most only a foot long, much more slender, not more than a line thick at the base, quite glabrous, like the rest of the plant. Leaves similar in shape and texture, but much fewer, not more than 6—9, all laxly scattered, not aggregated towards the base as in the other species, with 10—12 subequal nerves, the lowest 5—6 inches long. Raceme subsecund, 2—8 flowered, 3—6 inches long; lower pedicels ascending, 6—9 inches long; upper pedicels shorter, cernuous. Bracts, linear, 1—1½ inch long. Perianth, in the lower flowers, 15—16 lines, in the upper, about an inch long, so far as can be judged from dried specimens, just like that of *Roseum* in colour, direction, and texture; divisions, oblanceolate, bluntish, ¼ to ⅜ inch broad, narrowed gradually to the base. Ovary, clavate, ⅜—½ inch long; style, 7—8 lines long; stigmas linear, 1 line long. Capsule, oblong or obovoid, ½—¾ inch long, bluntly lobed. Filaments, very slender, nearly straight, 8—12 lines long; anthers, linear-oblong, 2 lines long.

Discovered by Dr. Hooker in the temperate region of the Sikkim Himalayas, at an elevation above the sea-level of 9,000 to 10,000 feet, in 1849.

It is figured in "*Bot. Mag.*," tab. 6385, also in "*Gard. Chron.*," 1871, p. 201, and is said to be restricted to the valley of Lacking, Sikkim. Flowers 3 to 8 in a lax raceme, perianth funnel-shaped, pale rose lilac, flowers from 1 to 1½ inch long. It flowered in 1877 with Mr. Max Leichtlin.

Sarana Kamskatchense, often called the Blue Lily.—*F. Kamtschatcensis*, Gawl., Bot. Mag., Sub., t. 1216; Regel, Gartenfl., t. 173.— A well-known and peculiar form, having an annual bulb, common in the northerly regions of Siberia, Asia, America, and Japan, bearing a small bell-shaped dark purple flower; it is rather a difficult bulb to flower, and very impatient of change of place; it has been well-flowered at the Edinburgh Botanic Garden by the late Mr. James McNab.

CHAPTER XI.

"FALLACIES" OF DUNEDIN (!)

PHYSIOLOGY OF LILY BULBS.

THE following peculiar views have been recently put forward in the *Horticultural Journals*, by a Veteran Lily grower, writing under the *nom de plume* of "Dunedin."

FALLACIES (?) OF LILY GROWERS.

§ 1. "There is hardly a situation in which Lilies will not thrive, and yet how rarely do we see them grown. This is true enough, but it raises the important question, who is to blame? Is it the buyer, or the seller, the amateur gardener, or the professional Lily grower? There are thousands upon thousands of amateurs in the suburbs of London, and other large towns, who could spare time for the interesting and healthy exercise of gardening in August and September; but who could not spare a day, or even an hour during the latter part of October, and yet, if they apply to nurserymen, they are told that Lily bulbs* will not be ready for lifting before the end of that month. If they apply to the Lily growers in Holland, the answer is even more fallacious, for they are told that Lily bulbs will not be harvested until the end of October, and that the best time for planting is from October to March. Others say, as an excuse for late planting, that Lily bulbs are not fully "matured" before the end of October. Now, this is a fallacy, most hurtful to both buyer and seller. No Lily bulb can be said to be fully matured, until it has advanced to a state of perfection, that is, until it is in full bloom,† this being its last and highest stage. In October, and onward through the winter months, Lily bulbs can only be said to be maturescent, that is approaching maturity. We are told by a writer on Lilies that a Lily will flower better the second year after planting than the first. This also is a fallacy, but why? Too late planting. The growth of the first year is checked, while the growth of the new, or successional bulb, is undisturbed, consequently, that bulb blooms well the following year, leaving the parent bulb to decay and die. In some Catalogues we are told that Lily bulbs should not be disturbed for

---

* Lilies have been obtained from the New Plant and Bulb Company, Colchester, for years past, after the 31st August, and even before that date, if specially ordered.

† Surely this is incorrect, no one ever heard of a *bulb being in full bloom*. Dunedin means evidently, that the whole plant is in a state of perfection, and fully matured at the season of flowering, and, that therefore, the bulb is also fully matured or ripened. Continental, as also English nurserymen, in using the word matured or ripened, apply it certainly to bulbs, but mean (which is quite another thing) that after flowering, there follows a season of rest, shorter or longer it may be, during which the bulb ripens, consolidates and matures its juices, plumps out its buds, and prepares, so to speak, for another effort, just as trees after loosing their leaves, put on internal growth, harden their wood, &c., during the season of rest, and this process of hardening and consolidation is what is generally known by the term ripening.

three or four years after planting, as patches that have been undisturbed, flower much better, and grow taller than those fresh planted. Why? For the same reason as already stated, too late planting in the first instance.

§ 2. "As regards the evils of late planting, it would be folly to attempt to transplant the White Lily (*L. Candidum*) in October, as it will then be making active growth, and if the roots be disturbed, it will have the effect of wholly, or partially, preventing its flowering next year. This remark holds good with regard to all Lilies,* with the exception of a very few late-flowering ones. We see the green tufts of leaves shooting up from the White Lily bulbs before October arrives, and we can therefore imagine the activity that must be going on beneath the surface of the soil. With regard to other Lilies, we cannot see this, but experiments can lay open the mysterious underground workings of Nature, as plainly as the green tufts of leaves can be seen by the naked eye. At the end of June, 1876, I lifted and transplanted a number of White Lilies; they bloomed well during the next summer, if not better than those which had not been disturbed. At the end of October in the same year, I lifted and transplanted a few bulbs, each of five different sorts, including the White Lily; only three stems out of all I had transplanted came up the following season, and even these did not show the slightest signs of bloom. So much for early and late planting. The method of reproduction is different in different plants, but, as a general principle, it may be stated that a parent bulb is charged with the function of liberating germs or seed-buds,† which vegetate as soon as brought into a condition fitted for their growth. And this is, in general, about eight or ten days after the flowers of the parent bulb have faded.‡ It is very soon after this time, that we are enabled, by experiment, to observe the phenomenon called "*the three generations in one*," that is, *the parent bulb, now destined by Nature to perish, the new bulb within it, which is destined to bloom next summer, and the seed bud within the new bulb, which is destined to flower the year after that.* From this, it will be seen that a Lily is not an annual, nor is it a biennial, but a part of both, two years comprising the period of its existence from birth to death; it is certainly not a perennial, as some have called it. These seed-buds, as soon as they can be discerned, even by the aid of a magnifying glass, can, by a simple, though necessarily protracted,

---

* Dunedin's assertion is a little too sweeping, much depends on the character of the season, whether fine or dry, wet or cold, early or late; we should prefer planting after the first autumnal showers had begun to soften the ground, and before the later and heavier rains had stimulated root growth. In some years, Lily planting may be done well at the end of August and September, in other seasons, a month or six weeks later will suit better. *L. Candidum* and one or two others are exceptions to this rule, they start in the autumn, and their foliage is persistent all the winter. The majority of Lilies push up their foliage in April and May.

† With Dunedin's use of the term seed-bud, I do not agree; germs, offshoots, bulbils, or bulblets are admissable, as applied to axillary or root-stock buds, but the term seed-bud is a misnomer.

‡ A good time to remove Lily bulbs. But I should not consider them to be properly matured and fit for removal, during the period of inflorescence. From a fortnight after the flowers have faded, to a month, if the weather be dry, is the best time; after that period, growth will ensue as soon as the first heavy rain-fall takes place.

course of experiments, be followed in their growth distinctly, until they become flowering plants, leaving no room, whatever, for those who are otherwise biassed or prejudiced, to theorize on the subject.

§ 3. "It is a *fact* which science[*] has placed beyond a doubt, that, if Lilies do not all bloom at the same time, they should not all be transplanted at the same time. Beginning, therefore, eight or ten days after the Lilies which flower first have shed their bloom, we go on lifting and transplanting from time to time, until October, during the most agreeable part of the year, and during a period, too, when amateurs have a good deal of spare time on their hands, which might be turned much to their own advantage, and, at the same time, to the advantage of our professional growers."

§ 4. "I know of no other plants, though there may be some, which we can compare in their underground action with the Lily. Of it there is undoubtedly an annual bloom, but not from the same bulb, though many who have not studied the matter sufficiently, believe it is. From what I have already said, it may be seen, that while one bulb is flourishing in its first and only bloom, another bulb within it,—mark these words, 'within it,'—not outside, or offsets of any description whatever,—another bulb, a new bulb within it,—is progressing in its growth, so as to be enabled to bloom next year, in the place of the one now blooming, which will then be dead, thus keeping up a yearly bloom from successional bulbs "ad infinitum," if properly cultivated. There is, therefore, no foundation whatever for saying that, the same (?) bulb goes on living and blooming for an indefinite period, and then dies of exhaustion, or old age. A greater fallacy than this could not be uttered; for the term of a Lily's existence, from the period of germination, till the final decay of the plant, is so designed by nature, as not to exceed two years. It is, thus, that every year witnesses a birth and death; that is the birth of the seed bud, and the death of the flowering bulb, being the youngest and the oldest of the 'three generations in one' the new bulbs being always intermediate between these two."—*Garden, vol.* 12, *p.* 557.

§ 5. "Some Lily growers call the bulb 'the root of the matter,' but this is incorrect. The bulb is a permanently abbreviated stem, clothed with scales, which are imperfect, and thickened leaves. The new bulb does not send up a stem during the first summer, but elaborates what it receives from the roots into organic or nourishing matter, and stores it up for future use in the core, and in the cells of the scales born on the core, which enlarge, and becomes more fleshy as the nourishing matter accumulates. When vegetation becomes active in the following spring, the new stem and the successional bulbule within the new bulb, fed by this stock of nourishment, grow with great vigour, and the stem produces leaves, and at last flowers. When the plant has continued in flower for some time, longer or shorter, according to the quantity of nourishment stored up, the stock will then become exhausted, and by using the microscope it will be

---

[*] Dunedin puts it rather too strongly, he omits to give chapter and verse for his "fact," and I cannot recall any reference. Nature is generally elastic and accommodating, and, as but little new root growth is made by any Lilies (except *L. Candidum* and its allies) in September, we really have August, September, and most of October for our operations, and we can choose the time which best suits our own convenience.

seen that the cells in the scales have become emptied of their contents, and are now soft and flabby, the old roots being dead or dying. The scales then dry up, and the parent bulb entirely perishes, leaving it to the successional bulb to go through the same course the next season."—*Garden*, *vol.* 13, *p.* 592.

CORE OR CENTRAL AXIS.

§ 6. "If we take a Lily bulb in the autumn, and cut it in two, right down from the apex to the base, it will be observed that it is composed of a core or fleshy part (*central axis*, *Baker*), more or less conical in the upper portion, and truncated below. This core gives rise, at its upper face, to fleshy scales, pressing one against the other, and to a central short stem (formed of leaves and rudimentary flowers), whilst from its lower face spring the root fibres. These root fibres, will be seen to emanate from the base of the stem itself and pass down through the core or fleshy part,* thus preserving a distinct connection between the stem and the roots, without interfering with the scales of the bulb, for these scales, if carefully picked off will be seen to have no connection whatever with the root fibres. The bulb itself, composed of the scales, is in fact, nothing more or less than the cradle, or nursery of the legitimate seed-bud, which imbibes its nourishments from the scales, through the core, until it has grown and become a fully developed bulb, capable of emitting a flower stem the next year."—*Garden*, *vol.* 13, *p.* 142.

§ 7. "I have in my garden, a bulb of *Croceum*, the progenitor of which I planted 35 years ago. During all these years I have watched this plant with more than ordinary interest, and, as I lifted and replanted it every year, I found that the fading flower stem was always attached to the fading parent bulb, and not to the new bulb, which appeared every succeeding year fresh, clean, plump, and crisp, with the scales firmly and closely set upon one another, while the scales of the parent bulb were discoloured, loose, and flabby. How far back the pedigree of this bulb could be traced, it is difficult to say, though, I believe, I could get evidence of 10 years more to add to the 35."—*Garden*, *vol.* 12, *p.* 557.

* This is surely incorrect, and would seem to imply that the central axis takes no part in the vital action, but that the roots proceed from the base of the stem through, and independently of the central axis, to collect nourishment for the leaves and flowers. We have pointed out before (page 4), that the upper set of roots formed in early summer at the base of the stem and above the bulb, provide support and nourishment for the stem, leaves and flowers, and that the lower set of roots emanating from the base of the bulb in autumn, provide nutriment for the bulb itself, and its requirements. Moreover, these last roots are active during the winter and spring months, at a time when the stem is in embryo; they are continued upwards throughout the central axis like the parietal divisions of an orange, and in spring when the stem is emitted, are continued upwards inside it. Such being the facts, we think impartial observers will consider the central axis or core to be the true *fons et origo vitæ*, emitting roots beneath, scales laterally, and last of all a stem above. This central axis we have always considered to be the centre of the life of the bulb; scales, roots, and stem, being adjuncts, and all capable of removal, and of reproduction by the action of the core itself. Whereas, in the absence of a core, neither roots or stem would live, and scales would have to reproduce an embryo bulb themselves, and perish in the act. But Dunedin, throughout his writings, discards the core from consideration, and if mentioned at all, as above, it is evidently looked upon as playing a very inferior part in the economy of bulb life.

§ 8. *Yearly Movement*—Elsewhere Dunedin has remarked.—" The bulb moves year by year in its new growth, or in the growth of the new bulb, further away in a direct line from the scars or sites of the growth of preceding years, unless unnatural growth interferes."*—*Garden, vol.* 14, p. 262.

§ 9. "There is another fallacy, which by long usage, has been so thoroughly engrained in the minds of many Lily growers, that I fear it will meet with much opposition before it can be completely eradicated. I mean the objection against annual lifting and transplanting. In order to solve the difficulty, it should be asked in the first place. Why annual transplanting is, at present, the exception, rather than the rule ? Simply because there is a very general belief that the first year's growth and bloom after transplanting are inferior to the second, and that consequently annual transplanting would simply be encouraging a constant repetition of this inferiority. And so it would, if late transplanting is persisted in, and I admit that it would be an act of great folly to transplant the general run of Lilies annually, if we left them in the ground until ' the end of October, or the early part of November,' as a cultivator, in a book lately published, directs. But it would be the very reverse, if the transplanting took place soon after the flowers have faded. In dealing with Lilies in this country, we should never overlook the fact, that here they are under artificial cultivation ; whereas, in their native places, nature has provided for them everything† that is requisite for their luxuriant and annual successional bloom. To those who may think that annual transplanting is an unnecessary trouble, or who may not care for superior bloom, the present system may be all in all. But, to those who would like to know that their favourites are doing well, and not left a prey to vermin, and, consequently, to retarded growth, the annual system is the best ; for too well we know, that a clump of Lily bulbs, left two or three years in the ground —the dead and rotten mixed with the living and growing—is in this country quite a paradise for grubs, slugs, and every other pest that is destructive to the growth and flowering of the plant. In order, then, to sweep all such enemies out of our way, let us, about 8 or 10 days after the flowers have faded, lift the plants, and in doing so, take care of the new bulbs that are connected with the stem that have flowered, and are within

* If these movement views of Dunedin are correct, the inference drawn, logically speaking, must be that Lily bulbs are *locomotive*, and every year advance in one particular direction. This identical bulb of Dunedin's, the progenitor of which was planted 35 years ago, would be now, if it had been left undisturbed, at least a yard, perhaps two yards distant from where its progenitor grew. Is this the fact ? My experience leads me to believe that Lilies are stationary, and that I shall find next year in the same spot, the plants (or if you will, their progenitors), that are now in bloom in my garden.

† Nature has in many places provided pigs and other long snouted animals to uproot the earth, &c., but I never heard it before hinted at that there was a gardening purpose in this operation, and that it was better for the bulbs to be thus uprooted and transplanted annually. Would Dunedin wish us to believe that as seeds are, no doubt, intentionally passed through the bodies of birds, and then deposited as dung in various new localities, and that thus plants are introduced into new regions : so doubtless bulbs or bulblets, passing through the intestines of pigs, are again deposited with their manure in new localities to perpetuate the race.

See also the opinion of our Indian correspondent, page 17.

the old bulbs, as that is the proof that these new bulbs are those which will flower next year. Let all other bulbs, large or small, be picked off and put aside for planting in a separate place until they also have flowered. Carefully examine the new bulbs, so as to make sure they are cleared of vermin, and when this is done, replant either singly or in clumps, in congenial soil, and leave the rest to nature. It is said by some writers that, 'Lilies are not ripe for lifting or replanting, until the growth ceases, and the stems and leaves die down,' but this is a fallacy which—whatever may be its value as regards Tulips, Hyacinths, and some other bulbous plants—is altogether inconsistent with the constitution of the Lily. I have cut down the stems when the plants were in full and fresh bloom, without in the slightest degree* affecting the growth of the new bulbs,

---

* Dunedin, here, pushes his theories too far.

Such Lilies as *Candidum*, *Excelsum*, *Martagon*, and in general all N. American forms, whose flower stems may be cut off, and yet leave ample foliage below for the requirements of the plants, would receive no damage from the operation of removing the flowers; but other kinds such as *Auratum*, *Umbellatum*, *Thunbergianum*, *Speciosum*, &c., whose stems are provided largely with foliage right up to the flowers, receive much injury by the ruthless cutting away of foliage, when removing the blooms for exhibition and decoration.

Compare on this head the remarks on pages 34, 47, and 87, also the following letters of Mr. Hovey, &c. :—

"We have found, after 30 years' constant experience, with thousands of bulbs of *Speciosum*, and its varieties, that the bulbs are injured or killed outright, just in proportion to the time at which cutting down is performed. If a plant be broken off in June, when 6—7 inches high, the bulb will die; if in July, the bulb will go off into divisions of small bulbs, and if in September, the bulb will be about half-size. Our autumnal exhibition always takes place about the middle of September, and we usually cut from 50 to 100 spikes, an operation which weakens the bulb so much, that they only produce a very few flowers the next year. In the case of any rare and choice kinds, we do not allow them to be cut on any account."—*C. M. Hovey, Garden, vol.* 13, p. 196.

"It does no more injury to cut away the flower stem of *Candidum*, when in full bloom, than it does to cut off the flower spike of a Hyacinth, or of a Gladiolus, the flowering shoot of an Amaryllis, or the bloom of a Guernsey Lily.

"The leaves are all left, and these are all that are needed to produce a sound and perfect bulb.

"If this were not so, it would have been discovered long ago; with Lilies, however, that have no leaves, only such as grow upon the flower stem, it is quite another, and a totally different thing. Nature points this out. If the flower stem of *Giganteum* be cut away, as soon as it makes its appearance, the leaves and bulb will increase in size; but if allowed to grow and bloom, it so absorbs the nutriment of both, that nothing but weak offsets, are the result.

"When the Hyacinth growers of Haarlem, tell us that the bulbs, are just as good, when the foliage is all cut off: or the Gladiolus cultivators of France, that cutting away the leaves does no harm or when the Amaryllis growers destroy all their leaves, I should believe that cutting down such Lilies as make no root or bulb leaves, does no harm. As to *Candidum*, when the flower stem is cut away, the bulb is greatly benefitted, just as removing the flowers or buds from any plant increases its growth and vigour; the leaves all remain, and it is these that nourish and sustain the root."—*C. M. Hovey, Garden, vol.* 13, p. 387.

But by the removal of the flowers only, and not the leaves, the exhaustion of the effort of producing the bloom, and of the production of seed, is avoided; consequently by leaving the foliage unmutilated, you contribute greatly to the growth and development of the new forming bulb. On this head compare the following remarks :—

"I find removing the flowers, throws the whole energy of the plant into the stem, and as a consequence, far finer bulbs are the result; this I discovered accidently, in 1865. Mr. Ray, the late Curator of the Dean Cemetery in Edinburgh, had a very fine bulb of

which, at this time, are themselves sending down roots,* by which they can gain subsistence sufficient to make them independent of the parent bulbs. Those who have carefully studied the connection that exists between the old and the new bulbs, will understand this. When lifting, I prefer leaving a portion of the stems in the old bulbs, as they make a convenient handle for moving the new bulbs about, without rubbing and breaking the scales with the hands. If this plan of lifting and replanting annually, were adopted, I will venture to say, that the result would be far better than by leaving the bulbs in the ground for some years undisturbed. It seems to me to require no science to tell us this. If we leave the bulbs in the ground for a few years, what can we expect? the offsets, instead of being removed, are growing and drawing the essential principal of life out of the expectant flowering bulbs ;† and these offsets, transformed into bulbules, will also generate offsets, so that all combined to the second and third generations, will be drawing vitality from the fully-developed or flowering-bulbs ; the very reverse of what we have in view in giving periodical supplies of nourishment in the shape of mulchings, top-dressings, etc."—*Dunedin, Garden, vol.* 13, *p.* 28.

§ 10. "Is a Lily an annual or a perennial, or is it between the two, a biennial? A Lily is not an annual, a biennial, nor a perennial. Then what is it? It may be said to be somewhat like two biennials joined together, but, overlapping one another in their growth ; that is, one portion blooming this year, while the other is growing, preparatory to blooming next year."—*Garden, vol.* 13, *p.* 385.

Auratum, which produced seven flowers — then thought something wonderful—and, according to the usual practice, he placed it, after blooming, under a stage, and allowed it to stay there until next March, when he determined to repot it. On examining it, he was surprised to find the pot full of new roots ; he gave it a good shift, without disturbing it more than he could help, but May came before there were any signs of a stem, and when one was found, it was only half as strong as that produced the previous year, and the top was deformed. This ultimately got broken off, when the stem began to thicken enormously, so that by autumn it was more like the stump of an Hollyhock, than that of *Auratum* ; besides, it formed a number of young bulblets at its base, and at the *axils of the leaves*, all indicating its great strength. It was allowed to remain undisturbed that winter, and next spring it threw up a magnificent shoot 5 feet high, and produced 35 perfect blooms on that one stem. This, which was thought something extraordinary, was noticed in all the Edinburgh newspapers, and visited by the late Mr. MacNab, and I may safely say, by hundreds of others. It really was magnificent, and even now, when I have seen hundreds of fine examples, I have never seen one which I have admired more than I did that one, or one more perfectly formed. It taught me that a year's rest from blooming, gives strength, and does no harm, and finally, that *bulblets on the stem, show signs of vigour, and must be considered to be a natural method of increasing the plant*."—*Edina, in Garden, vol.* 15, *p.* 82.

* Surely the tender ends of these new roots would be damaged and broken by the process of lifting.

† I beg again to differ. I have not found in the autumn, many offsets, either on the stem, or about the bulb, as large as a pea, without roots of their own ; these offsets, as soon as they are as big as a nut, which does not take many weeks, have 3 or 4 long roots of their own, and are quite capable of taking care of themselves, without drawing the vitality from the flowering bulb, which, according to Dunedin's views is one year old, and one year bigger than themselves, and must perish itself in the following autumn. How, then, can it be deprived of vitality by the 2nd and 3rd *generation?* Dunedin forgets his biennial theory ; the fact, is simply this (*see* p. 14), that bulbs when at home increase and multiply, so that every 3rd or 4th year, they must be lifted, separated, and planted again with sufficient room for each bulb. More than this is nonsense.

§ 11. "The origin of a Lily bulb is a germ or seed-bud.* Nature causes this to grow or vegetate the first year, to bloom the second year, *and then it dies, leaves, stem, scales, and roots, all perish.* Such is the short span of the existence of a Lily bulb. If a bulb that has flowered is taken up, say late in the autumn, and cut in two, vertically, it will be seen that it has, within itself, three distinct generations, that is, a portion of the parent *bulb,*† which has flowered, the whole of a new *bulb*, which Nature destined to flower the following year, and a germ or seed-bud, which was intended to grow up a full-sized bulb, and flower in the next year but one. At this time, the autumn, the seed will be so minute, as not to be perceptible without the aid of a magnifying glass, but, if a similar bulb be taken up in January next, and dissected, the seed-bud will then be perceptible to the naked eye, as it will be about the size of a canary seed, and will, if the scales are picked off carefully, be found in the axil between the inmost fleshy scale and the base of the new flower stem. In February, it will be six or eight times larger, and will continue to grow, until, in the next autumn, it will be found to be as large as the new *bulb* was, at the same time in the previous year. By a very simple experiment, it may thus be proved that the old *bulb* of this year, after having flowered, and after having all the sap absorbed from its scales for the nourishment of the new *bulb*, decays and dies. In like manner, its successor, the new *bulb*, flowers the next year, decays and dies. And so on, one generation following the other, year after year, all having emanated from germs or seed-buds. Then, how can it be said with truth, that " the bulb, which has flowered, has ever flowered before?" Or with what truth can it be said that "the bulb, that has flowered one year, will ever flower again?" I cut open a bulb last month (January, 1877); it is now considerably decayed by exposure, but still may be seen the seed-bud at the base between the scales, and a portion of the new flower stem. I have also a portion of a bulb I took up only two days ago (February): it is a very fine fresh specimen, as I was careful in picking off the scales. At the base of the flower stem, which was destined to flower this year, may be seen the seed-bud, eight or ten times larger than in the preceding specimen, showing the comparatively large increase in growth which it has made in only one month. This seed-bud was destined to become a full grown *bulb*, and flower in 1878.

§ 12. "The plan that I adopted in order to trace the progress of the seed bud as it grew up into a fully formed *bulb* was this. In October, 1873, I lifted some fifty thoroughly matured bulbs, and replanted them in a piece of spare ground. In January, I commenced by taking up two or three, cutting the bulbs vertically in two, and otherwise dissecting them for the

---

* For my objection to the term seed-bud, *see* page 187.

† Dunedin has here put a too limited meaning to the use of the word "bulb." Lily growers, and the public generally, in common parlance, when speaking of Lilies, or other bulbs, flowering year after year, include in the term "bulb" both old and new growths, roots, stem, if any, sometimes flower, in fact, the whole plant. It may not be strictly accurate, but it is the case. Dunedin, however, frequently restricts the meaning of the word "bulb" to scales only, excluding roots, stem, and rhizome.

I have, therefore, italicised the word "*bulb*" wherever, it seems to me, it is used in a restricted sense, and, if my readers will, in their own minds, there substitute the word "growth" for "bulb," I think Dunedin's meaning will be made more clear.

O

purpose of my experiments. In this month, I found the seed bud, as I have said, about the size of a canary seed. In this manner I continued to lift two or three bulbs every month up to the following October, in flower or not, as the case might be, and noticed the progress of the seed bud until it had grown up similar in size to the one I had cut and laid open for inspection in the previous autumn. By this simple experiment, it may be proved in the most satisfactory manner, that the parent *bulb* of this year, after having flowered, and after having all the sap absorbed from its scales for the nourishment of the new *bulb*, decays and dies. In like manner its successor flowers the next year, decays and dies; and so on, one generation following the other, year after year, all emanating from germs or seed buds."

§ 13. The annexed illustration is taken from a photograph, one of six skeletons, the bulbs for which purpose I lifted on the 1st of January, 1878, and dissected in the presence of a Lily grower, so that there cannot be any doubt of its being a genuine representation of the underground interior parts of a Lily, exhibiting plainly the phenomenon or mystery of three generations in one, to which I have alluded. By looking at the woodcut, it will be seen that the seat of the stem which has bloomed last summer is on the left at A; the mark underneath this part, at D, will show where the roots of last summer have been, but now, both stem and roots are entirely gone. In the middle, at B, is the new flower stem that was destined to bloom next summer; and on the right, at C, is the young seed-bud that was destined to grow up and flower the following year, that is, in 1879. The healthy, strong, and numerous roots, which spring from the new *bulb*, and are here truly represented as those of 1st January, ought to convince any one that it would be ruinous to their growth, and hurtful to the plant itself, if disturbed and checked late in the season by lifting and transplanting."—*Garden*, *vol.* 13, *p.* 143.

§ 14. In further illustration of Dunedin's views, I have, by the kindness of Mr. Robinson, included the woodcut on next page, and Dunedin's paper thereon:—*From the Garden, vol.* 14, *p.* 237.

Lily Bulb, from a Photograph.

A.—The seat of the stem that bloomed last summer.
B.—The new flower stem.
C.—The young seed bud.
D.—The mark where the old roots have been.

Want of space prevented the roots from being shown in their length and abundance, as in the photograph.

Through the kindness of the Editor of the *Garden*, we are enabled to make use of this woodcut, as illustrating Dunedin's ideas. Compare also the woodcut on next page.

"The accompanying woodcut is taken from a photograph, sent by me, of a bulb of *Candidum*, which was lifted out of the ground one month after it had bloomed in the present year, 1878. A, shows the scar on site of the stem of 1877; B, the old stem of 1878; C, the remains of the roots of the old stem of 1878; D D, the new *bulb*, having a large slice cut off it to lay open its interior formation; E, the roots of the new *bulb*; these were from 5 to 7 inches long, with fine, fibrous rootlets, but they were unavoidably broken off in the lifting; F, the radical leaves, peculiar to this Lily, being the precursors of the stem of the new *bulb*, which was destined to bloom in 1879. These leaves, springing up so early and so close to the remains of the old stem, now decaying, give rise to the mistaken idea that this Lily is an evergreen. G H I, are scales of the old *bulb* which were left in dissecting in order to show how the new *bulb* sits in the midst of them until they decay and wither off; K, shows the remains of the scales of the old *bulb* which were picked off to uncover the new *bulb*. As to early lifting and replanting, that is to say, early after blooming, I would direct attention to the progress which this Lily has made in only one month from the time when the flowers of the parent *bulb* had faded. The new roots had penetrated from 5 to 7 inches into the soil, and, as seen in the woodcut, the radical leaves had grown 2½ inches above the apex of the new *bulb*. Even at this early period the roots were broken in lifting the bulb out of the ground.

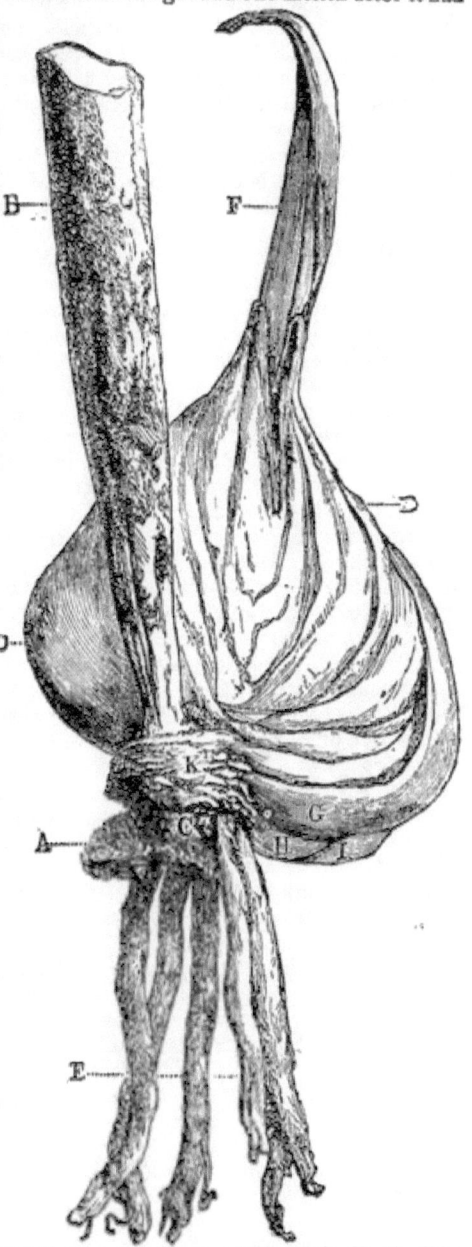

Old Lily Stem and Roots and New Bulb (*L. Candidum*).

§ 15. "Let me now add one or two remarks on the annual decay and death of the plant. M. Max Leichtlin says : (*see* page 205) 'If ' Dunedin ' has a correspondent in California who can send him a bulb of *Washingtonianum* carefully taken out, he will observe that his theory cannot be applied to that species, for he will find inserted in one long sideway-growing bulb the accumulated growth of eight or ten years.' Now, to me, there is nothing extraordinary in this, for the climate and soil of California are peculiarly favourable to the preservation of the phenomena alluded to. Compare the equable temperature of California with the land we live in. In this country we have the temperature of summer and winter differing by 50° or 60°, liable to great extremes, such as long and variable winters, and short, uncertain summers. Yet with all these disadvantages I have found Lily bulbs in my underground explorations with an accumulated growth of four or five years upon them. (? ?) As to the "sideward growth " of *Washingtonianum*, which seems to have struck M. Leichtlin as something remarkable, he will yet find, on close examination, that this is characteristic of all true Lilies.

§ 16. "Let your readers look at the woodcut (page 195). We have at A, on the left, the scar or site of the stem of 1877 ; on the right side of it we have B, the stem of 1878 ; and at C, immediately under K, the remains of its roots. On the right side of B and C we have D, the new *bulb*, which was destined to bloom in 1879 ; and if the new *bulb* were further cut away, we would find by microscopic observation, on the right, but close to the stem of the new *bulb*, the germ or seed-bud which was destined to grow up and bloom in 1880—all moving by a 'sideward growth' to the right, one year after the other, as M. Leichtlin describes *L. Washingtonianum*. Here, then, before us in that woodcut we have an accumulation of three years' growth presented to our view at one glance, the germ or fourth being unseen by the naked eye. Now let the reader picture to his mind what I have seen in my underground explorations, namely, an extension to the left of two more scars like A, being the sites of the old stems of 1876 and 1875. This would make in all five years' distinct growths, besides the germ, all moving in a 'sideward-growing' direction to our right. Before, however, the reader can realise this satisfactorily, let us examine the composition of that part of the plant which we see before us. The old stem B and the old scales G H I (the old roots being already gone) will shrink up and be entirely lost in our cold and damp soil before the spring comes round, leaving no traces behind but the site in the core of the old stem of 1878, as at A. Then, what becomes of the core itself ? This is, in reality, the question in difference between M. Leichtlin and myself. I need not explain, what the stem is composed of, as it can be seen, that during September, it has been fast hastening to decay, especially near its base, where it is greatly shrunk up. With respect to the old scales, the walls of the cells in which the sap has been stored being composed of what is termed cellular tissue, resist for a time, but even these have to give way in a very few months to the all powerful effects of decay, the commencement of which is easily recognised on the points of the scales.

§ 17. "We now come to the core. In the new *bulb*, the core has the appearance of a fleshy substance, but in the old *bulb* it resolves itself into a kind of woody fibre, and then it becomes almost fossilised, somewhat like the hardened root-stock of the Common Ginger. The scar A was left on the core in 1877, more than twelve months ago, but a double one I met with three weeks ago, in the presence of a friend, showed that the outer one must have been the scar of 1876, left there more than two years ago. If, then, in our own country, we sometimes meet with four or five years' growth ranged sideways—and this is the invariable rule with all Lilies—malformations excepted—is it anything to call forth wonder, that in a land so highly favoured as California, there should be found inserted in one long, sideward-growing bulb (successional *bulbs*) the accumulated (successional) growth of eight or ten years.*

§ 18. "There is sometimes more than one seed bud, which grows out of the new *bulb*, altogether independent of the parent *bulb*, and this gives rise to the phenomenon of what is properly called twin bulbs. As an illustration, I have a *Speciosum* bulb which I took up last October and cut in two. It is now shrivelled up by exposure to the atmosphere, but still I can see two finely formed twin *bulbs*, and behind, and entirely distinct from them, is the decayed stump of last year's flower stem. These *bulbs* are equal in size, and show each the rudiments of a new flower stem, and had the parent *bulb* been left in the ground or replanted, these bulbs would doubtless have both flowered this year. If the parent *bulb* had been allowed to remain in the ground, these twin *bulbs* would have been much larger than they are now, and the remains of the parent *bulb* in the ordinary course of nature, would have been dead and gone by this time. Then, how can it be said with truth, that the *bulb* that has flowered, has ever flowered before ? Or with what truth can it be said that the *bulb* that has flowered one year, can ever flower again ? I have said, that if a bulb that has flowered, be taken up late in the autumn and cut in two vertically, it will be seen that it has within itself, three distinct generations; to this it may be important to add, that at no other time in the year do such phenomena appear. If this, then, be steadily borne in mind, many points which at present, appear to be wrapped in obscurity, may easily be resolved. Hitherto, it has been the habit to call a bulb taken up in October, the parent *bulb*, but this is not, physiologically speaking, strictly correct. The parent *bulb* at that time is the new *bulb*, which is within the old one, as the new *bulb* has just then given birth to a young one in the form of a germ or seed-bud, while the old *bulb* itself is on the eve of dissolution. The old *bulb*, so often called the parent *bulb*, has no immediate connection with the young seed-bud ; the old *bulb* gave birth to the new *bulb*, and it is this new *bulb* that has given birth to the young seed-bud, which will grow up and flower the year after its own parent has bloomed. There is no genus in which the position of the seed-bud varies so much as

---

* It seems to me, here, that Dunedin contradicts himself. He has before, stated that the bulb after flowering disappears entirely, leaving a new bulb growing out from its centre to take its place. He here speaks of the accumulated growth of eight to ten years in California, and of four to five years' growth found in his own explorations, and in the woodcut figure he shows the core of the previous year 1877 ; and speaks also of those of 1876, and 1875, thus, clearly acknowledging that the core in part, at least, does not disappear every year.

My own views in full on these points are given on page 203.

in the Lily, the greater number originate low down in the centre of the new *bulb*, within less than a ¼ of an inch of the base of the *bulb;* some originate further down the centre, and others are formed at a distance from the parent *bulbs*, to which they are attached by an underground or creeping axis.

" All, however, spring from a familiar source, that is, from germs or seed-buds, and these in October, are of so delicate and tender nature, as to be in the highest degree liable to injury from drying, exposure, or other adverse circumstances.

§ 19. " Newly imported bulbs are not worth a tenth part of the value of bulbs ' freshly taken up ' out of a respectable nurseryman's grounds, and guaranteed by him as having flowered the previous season.   It is comparatively of little consequence what the quality of the bloom may have been, provided it was healthy, and that the leaves and stems decayed and died down gradually in the ordinary way, for it is the new *bulb* within the old one that is now to be depended upon, and that, and its successors, may go on gradually rising in the scale of perfection, through judicious culture.

§ 20. " Cutting off the roots is the source of more evil than can be foreseen or imagined ; in such a case, let me again remind your readers, that a Lily bulb, in the autumn, has, within itself, three distinct gene-rations, and that the third generation is the germ or seed-bud, which is intended by nature to bloom during the second season.   At the time for lifting and re-planting, the seed-bud, as I have shown, is very delicate and tender, and so minute, that it cannot be seen without the aid of a magnifying glass.   I have also shown, that in some bulbs, its position is within less than a quarter of an inch of the base of the *bulb*.   If, therefore, the roots, young as well as old, be cut off, the tender seed-bud is exposed to the drying effects of the atmosphere and other evils, the result of which is that, in nineteen cases out of every twenty, its vitality is destroyed. The new *bulb,* or second generation, may bloom, though not strongly, as it has to make fresh roots ; but any chance of future bloom in the seed-bud is completely gone.   It is thus that so many complaints have arisen about imported bulbs ; some bloom once, though weakly, and some do not bloom at all.   How can they, if kept dry all the winter, and planted as late as January or February ?"—*Garden, vol.* 11, *p.* 175.

§ 21. It will be seen from the subjoined extract that Dunedin not con-tent to apply his seed-bud theory to full grown bulbs, pushes the applica-tion of it to bulblet offsets, and seedling bulbs from the first year of their existence, contending that even these little bulblets perish every year, and are replaced by larger successional growths.   " There is not one in fifty Lily growers but believes that the same identical offset or seedling goes on year after year growing larger and larger, until it becomes capable of developing a flower-bearing stem.   Now, this is entirely erroneous, and clearly contrary to facts ; experimental researches have proved beyond a doubt that there is no such thing as a two or three-year-old offset or seedling, the existence of an offset being comprised within the first season of its growth, after which it decays and dies, having thus fulfilled what Nature had destined to be its office.   In the meanwhile, however, a successor is growing up within the original offset in the same manner as the legitimate seed-bud or bulbule is growing up within a fully developed adult bulb, with this exception, that, every season, Nature clothes the succcessional offset bulbule with new and more numerous scales, the original offset not having had a covering of more than some six or eight scales, according to the class of Lily to which it belonged. The first appearance from the offset above ground is not a stem, but generally one or two leaves attached to a long slender stalk or petiole. If lifted out of the ground, the offset will be found to be possessed of slender rootlets, these having been protruded from the base of the offsets before the leaf and its stalk began to rise, or, indeed, before there was the slightest appearance of their rising. The next season we see in a bed that has been originally planted with genuine offsets a very slight stem shooting up, furnished with a few leaves. This is a sign that a germ in the centre of the original offset has vegetated into a seed-bud ; for without the presence of a seed-bud there can be no real stem. The next season the stems will appear larger and more fully developed, and the bulbules, if dug up, will be found to be also larger, with more scales, and with new and more numerous roots—the site of the decayed stems and roots of the previous season being distinctly visible on all the bulbules. This process goes on year after year until the bulbule, which may now be called a fully developed bulb, produces a flower-bearing stem. All this is, to the Lily grower, worthy of the most attentive study, as the first thing that must strike the reflecting mind, is the harmony that exists, in what we are permitted to contemplate in the Lily, namely, the singular similarity in the organisation of all the kinds that are really true Lilies. With respect to the little bulbs, while only small offsets, they have by some been called side-buds by way of contra-distinction, and have also been called the principal reproducers of their class. Now, some of them may be called side-buds, though more properly small offsets, but they all differ widely from the true legitimate reproducers—the central seed-buds. The central or legitimate seed-buds are growing up, not at the side, but in the very centre of the parent *bulbs*, and will, most certainly, without changing their identity, flower the season after the parent *bulbs* have bloomed, unless something unforeseen should happen to them ; that is, they will germinate, grow up, bloom, decay, and die, all within two years ; while the side-buds or little offsets, which have no fixed place for their appearance at any time, will change their identity, by being transformed by a new creation every year, and will not take less than three or four years before they can, through their transformed successors, develop flower-bearing stems. These side-buds or little offsets are the means which Nature has placed in our hands for the purpose of propagating and multiplying the species, but not for the purpose of reproducing that which is lost, namely, the parent *bulb*, or the *bulb* of the previous season. The reproduction of that *bulb* is due alone to the central seed-bud ; for this bud, the instant it has germinated, is provided with all the organs of vegetation that the full-grown Lily possesses, and is, in fact, a miniature resemblance of an adult bulb. This should teach us that if we desire to ascertain whether a plant is a true Lily or not, we should carefully examine the organic interior structure of the bulb, as well as the flower itself. These side buds, though they have been made a great deal of by some writers, cannot be placed under any other category than that of 'adventitious buds,' for they present themselves without any order, and the exact spot where they may present themselves cannot be foreseen. It will, therefore, be seen that those who deal with the propagation of the Lily by seed, bulblets, or buds in the axils of the old scales entirely overlook the marvellous organ and its functions which Nature has provided for carrying on the hereditary reproduction of the plant, for the central seed-bud alone is all-sufficient to continue to reproduce annually the Lily and its bloom, even if seeds, bulblets, and all sorts of adventitious buds were never to have any existence. In fact, we every year see this result in our gardens, though we never dream of searching or looking for the cause.

" As a practical, and almost tangible, illustration of the truth of what I have said, I annex a photographic representation of the interior and reproductive organs of offsets, bulbules of one, two, and three years' growth, and fully developed bulbs, collected during the first two weeks in May last from clumps of a dozen or more distinct species of Lilium proper."—*See* paper and woodcut in *Garden*, *vol.* 14, *p.* 60.

REPRODUCTION OF LILY BULBS.

§ 22. " The act or process of reproducing that which has been destroyed is, with respect to the cultivation of the Lily, well worthy of the careful consideration of all Lily growers, more especially as we see at the present time that opinions differ most widely with regard to the wonderful operations of nature in the reproduction and increase of these deservedly popular plants. We are told that a new bulb, whether grown from seed or bulblets, takes not less than three years, under the most favourable circumstances, before it developes a flower-bearing stem. We are also told that raising seedling Lilies is a long process, as one must wait from three to ten years ere they bloom, and we are moreover taught to believe that it is this very same seedling or bulblet that grows year after year larger and larger, until it becomes a flowering plant, and that the bulb goes on then living for an indefinite number of years, sending up each year a flower stem from its centre. This may appear to many to be a very plausible doctrine, but how it has become the belief of so many Lily growers is difficult to understand. If we lift a clump of Lily bulbs we often find a whole colony of small bulbs, popularly, but without discrimination, called offsets. When we carefully examine them, however, we find they are not all real or genuine offsets, but that they consist of offsets and the offspring of offsets, properly called successional bulbules. A genuine offset is not furnished with all the characteristics of a fully developed bulb, but, though deficient in some respects, it is possessed of this important function, namely, the power of generating a successor in the shape of a bulbule or small bulb. With respect, therefore, to the powers of reproduction, it is important to bear in mind that no plants or animals come into existence without a parentage. An offset no larger

than a pea may during the ensuing summer send up above the soil a
slender stalk a few inches in length bearing what may be called a seed-
leaf, but this identical offset will never send up another stalk; this
becomes the duty of its offspring, the successional bulbule. Nature
causes this operation to be repeated season after season, each successional
bulbule growing larger than its progenitor, until a fully developed
flowering bulb is the result. If any of the successional bulbules be carefully examined it will be seen that the stalks or stems of the preceding
season did not emanate from them. De Candolle has said, 'If we desire
to know more of the plant life in its higher bearings, we must live with,
and observe the cycle of plant growth in all its stages, from the germination of the seed to the full development of the fruits.' For myself, I can
truly say, that I have almost literally complied with this injunction. For
many years I have lived with, and have been in the habit of watching the
underground life of the Lily, from the most minute seed bud, and the
smallest offset, to their full development as flowering bulbs, and even
after that. In order to do this satisfactorily, I have planted, from time to
time, in distant places, hundreds of offsets, as well as fully developed
bulbs, and have watched their progress, winter and summer, by taking
up a portion now and then for examination by dissection or otherwise.
*The result of this has been to me full confirmation that no individual offset,
bulbule, or fully developed bulb lives for another season after having once
sent up a stalk or a flowering stem.* Take a bulblet in the autumn,
that has been produced on a bulb bearing stem, and carefully cut
it open, at the very core will be found a seed-bud, in every respect
similar to one that will be found in a flowering *bulb*, in the axil
formed by the inner scale and the base of the flower stem. In the
case of the bulblet it will take more than three years before its successional bulbule is sufficiently developed to throw up a stem that will
bear even one flower. In the other case, the seed-bud, which is contained within the flowering *bulb*, will not take more than twenty months
before it blooms, possibly more perfectly than its parent did before it.
How is this? The seed-bud in the fully developed *bulb* is nourished by that
bulb as its parent, and its growth is consequently so stimulated that in eight
months from its germination it is shooting down strong healthy roots,
3 or 4 inches in length, mixed up with those of its parent, and through
these, its own roots it receives additional nourishment, while the parent
bulb continues still to nourish its offspring for some time longer. All
this time the little bulblet is left to starve or provide for itself. What
can it do, for it is still alive? In order to preserve its life nature directs
it to send down two or three slender feelers in the shape of thread-like
roots, in search of such food as the soil can supply, and such as is fit for it
in a young state. Its further progress, until not it, but its successional
bulbule, has arrived at a state of full development, I have already described
when treating of the progress of an offset, for an offset, if carefully dissected, will also be found to be possessed of a similar seed-bud. It is
from a careful study of this part of the subject that we learn that an
offset or bulblet has to go through a distinct and different stage or
transformation every year for a length of time, before it can arrive at the

stage of being a fully developed flowering *bulb*, whereas the seed-bud in the flowering *bulb*, which is graduated in the autumn, will in eight months be sending down strong roots, in two months more it will be nearly of adult size, and in six weeks from this time it may safely be detached from the decaying remains of its parent, and transplanted, if necessary, where it will bloom next summer. The rapidity of growth in the new *bulb* is not generally known, and has, therefore, given rise to very mistaken notions on the part of those who dip little deeper than the outward appearance of the bulb."—*Garden, vol. 12, p. 505.*

§ 23. "I cannot agree with Dunedin in all his views, yet considerable weight must be attached to the statements of a Lily cultivator, who, in his own words, ' has for many years, lived with, and been in the habit of watching the underground life of Lilies, from the most minute seed-bud and the smallest offset, to their full development, and even after that ; and who has planted, for this purpose, hundreds of offsets, as well as fully developed bulbs, and has taken up a portion, now and then, for examination by dissection or otherwise.' My own views are as follows ; that new growth (*see* page 14) takes place every year from a bud or buds at the base of the (flower) stem. I do not always find these situate in the exact place pointed out by Dunedin in his woodcut (*see* page 194).* I found, in March, in several bulbs of *Umbellatum*, the base of the old stem alive, and pink-coloured, and with a bud between it and the new stem, and, it is quite evident, that in many Lilies there must be numerous buds started into growth, as we frequently find three, four, and sometimes five, or even more, new growths starting from the centre of a bulb, numerous bulblets, arising from injured scales, and also from the side of the central axis, even to the number of fifty or more, and this always takes place, more or less, when a bulb breaks up, or in other words, happens when its stem-growth has been destroyed, either by cutting down wilfully, as 'Amateur' did (*see* page 57), or by accident, or by sharp spring frosts ; therefore, I cannot lay the stress that Dunedin does on the germ of the future growth being *always found in one and the same place* ; in fact, he states (page 197) that 'there is no genus in which the position of the seed-bud varies so much as in the Lily.' It is much to be regretted that Dunedin did not always state on what kinds of Lilies he had experimented. It is quite clear that *Martagon* growth is very different from that of the *Archelirion* group, to which latter, I should suppose his remarks chiefly apply ; while the growth of the Rhizomatous section, such as *Pardalinum* and *Superbum*, and that of the *Thunbergianum* section, have each special differences ; the habit of *Giganteum*, again, is peculiar. This Lily, *Giganteum*, either when grown from offsets or seed, builds up its bulb, year by year, larger and larger, making fresh internal growth until it arrives at a flowering size, in from three (from offsets) to five years (from seed) ; during the process of flowering, the old bulb then and there disappears, seemingly drawn up and absorbed in the gigantic stem-growth, leaving from 3 to 5 or more offsets, about the size of a large

* In *Garden, vol. 11, p. 260*, Dunedin writes "the true or legitimate seed-bud has a predetermined or settled position in the parent *bulb*, namely, on the opposite side of the old flower stem, the new flower stem being always between them."

walnut, clustered around its base, but, in November, the parent bulb has disappeared. *Canadense* and *Superbum*, on the contrary, present a different type; from a horizontal rhizome, a fresh bulb or bud-like growth is annually put forth (see page 82) to flower the succeeding year, and disappears the following (third year) quoad its scales; but I have not been able to satisfy myself that the rhizome dies then; I believe it puts forth new buds to form the successional growths, and this leads me to point out where I think Dunedin has overstated his case. We may lay it down as a general rule in Lily bulbs, that a fresh central scale growth occurs normally every year, starting probably from one or more central buds at the base of the flower stem; but that other lateral buds may likewise be developed and forced into action. This central growth, known by its fresh light colour, pushes and widens out the old scales, some of which, after a time, decay, or are fed off, or are detached and form new bulbs, or may be absorbed; within this new growth, is developed the flower stem of the succeeding year, and likewise the germs of future growth; and, so far I agree with Dunedin, that, without new growth in the preceding year, no flower can be expected. But—and Dunedin says nothing about this—what becomes of the central axis? The root stock or main axis, vertical in the case of the squamose perennial bulb, such as *Dalmaticum* and *Wallichianum*—horizontal in those of *Puberulum* and *Superbum*—oblique, as in those of *Humboldtii* and *Washingtonianum*, is an important factor in the problem; from Dunedin's statement (see page 196), I infer that he believes, that this perishes annually; my observations have led me to believe, that, whereas the scales may perish and are renewed from time to time, the central axis or root-stock is just that part of the Lily that maintains its growth for a much longer season, putting forth new buds each year, to perpetuate its form, but justifying the common remark, so strongly repudiated by Dunedin, that the same Lily continues to flower year by year.* In *Giganteum*, I think we may safely infer that root-stock life is limited; the prolongation of the bulb into that stout gigantic stem, seems to absorb the strength of the plant, and only a few lateral buds start into action; but, until the flower stem is thrown up (and I think that we may

---

* "Some Lilies, notably *L. Pardalinum*, are so markedly rhizomatous that, while the scales decay after one year, the root-stock and base of the decayed scales remain for at least three years (I have not observed this bulb for a greater length of time). In one instance the root-stock, growing horizontally, divided into two equal parts, the two ends clothed with scales being still joined by a fresh and succulent stem.

"This Lily then (*Pardalinum*), is neither a simple bulb nor does it die and renew itself entirely even in two years. On the other hand, only last week I found the young growth from a bulb of *Testaceum* actually growing up inside the decayed flower-stalk of last year, and blanched in consequence. This points clearly to the upward and unbroken growth from the core of last year, which was so exactly under the flower stem of last year as not to have swerved in the least from one side or the other. In this hybrid the scales of more than one season's growth are visible in autumn very distinctly, if a bulb be mutilated one year, and examined the next autumn. In a third instance there appears to be a total change both of scales and core in a year's time. The different ways of reproduction in Lilies are so marked that it alone would afford subject matter for endless remarks and controversy. I venture, therefore, to suggest that, in default of a better word, the term rhizomatous bulb might best explain the somewhat contradictory characteristics of what have been hitherto called Lily bulbs."—*E. H. Woodhall, in Garden, vol.* 15, *p.* 227.

say this also of all offsets and all seedling Lily bulbs), a continual growth of this axis takes place, and from it are developed fresh scales and buds; but that after flowering, the core degenerates more or less, and requires renewal. I do not, therefore, agree with Dunedin (*see* pages 198 & 201) that bulblets (even when seedlings) die year by year to be replaced by fresh growth, but, I hold that the centre of life resides in the axis, and that this developes scales and buds, growing year by year, till at length new growth has been developed strong enough to throw up a flower stem; at the base of this flower stem, the axis originates a bud or buds, clothed with scales, which, remaining connected with the axis, is developed into a growth, destined to prove the flowering crown of the succeeding year, and that this process is continued year by year, by the same root-stock, and, if this be true of the squamose type, I think it will be more plainly seen, as I have before hinted at, in the rhizomatous bulb of *Superbum*, and in the oblique bulbs of *Humboldtii* and *Washingtonianum*. I am also pretty certain that the old scales disappear at varying intervals in different Lilies, thus, in *Giganteum*, the old bulb scales are gone after flowering in the autumn; in *Superbum* and other rhizomatous kinds, they are to be seen there in March, and probably, for some months later; in *Speciosum* and *Auratum*, I have seen old scales in October and November; while, in the *Martagon* group, I have seen scales that were, in my opinion, certainly two years old. Therefore, I cannot accept, in all its entirety, as applicable to all Lilies, Dunedin's statement of a yearly renewal of the whole Lily bulb.

§ 24. I would rather again quote Mr. Baker's definition;—"Throughout the tribe the bulbs are strictly determinate and monocarpic, the main axis elongating into a flower bearing stem, and the bulb, the cycle of existence of which is from one to three years, either dying or remaining, but in either case developing a new bulb in the axil of one of its scales (or at the base of the flower stem). In a perennial squamose bulb the old scales remain, and a new bulb is developed into a flower stem in their centre, and all the numerous flattened scales of the bulb possess potentially, the power of developing new bulbs in their axils, and will do this in some species at any rate under cultivation. But in a state of nature there is only one new flower bearing stem developed each season from the centre of the bulb, and a few from the axils of the decaying outer scales. A new bulb, whether grown from seed, or from bulblets, developed in the axils of the above ground leaves of the floriferous stem, or produced in the axils of one of the bulb scales, takes not less than three years under the most favourable circumstances before it developes a flower bearing stem. After that, if nothing untoward happens, the bulb goes on living for an indefinite period, sending out each year a flower stem from its centre, and shredding off old scales with bulbs in their axils, more copiously in some kinds, less copiously in others, from the circumference all round."

§ 25. In concluding this subject, I beg to add M. Max Leichtlin's opinion as given in the *Garden*, *vol.* 13, p. 252, which seems to me to agree exactly with what I have previously stated:—

"*Lilies of various sorts* form their bulbs *very differently*, therefore, *no general theory can be applied to every species*. As to *Thompsonianum*, now classed among the *Fritillaries*, the old bulb annually dies, as I know from having carefully experimented upon it. On the other hand, it has no side bud at all ; but merely a central one. The leaves growing from that central bud, form each a scale of the newly forming bulb.*

"The scales outside are of a very watery consistence, and decaying, help to nourish the newly forming bulb. As to *Giganteum* and *Cordifolium*, I must openly say, I have made no dissections in regard to them ; but from studying these plants in the shape of hundreds of bulbs, so far as growth is visible, it seems obvious to me that these species do not produce annually a new bulb from a side bud, but that the old bulb is enlarged annually by the scales growing larger through the growth accumulating from a central bud, and that during summer, when vegetation is active,† another central bud is developed to grow next year. This goes on during five or six years, when the bulb arrives at mature age. It then flowers, and clearly dies, the entire bulb being exhausted by the flower stem which it has formed. In the meantime, the growth of the first and second year's existence of the bulb has decayed, either through pressure from the stronger scales of succeeding year's growth, or through general weakness. The year before flowering, one or more offsets make their appearance, which apparently spring from the *root stool*, and not from side buds in the interior base of the old bulb. If Dunedin can have sent him from California, a large bulb of *Washingtonianum*, carefully taken out, he will observe that his theory cannot be applied to that species, for he will find inserted in one long sideward growing bulb the accumulated growth of eight or ten years. As to the majority, or perhaps as to all Lilies of the 'Old World,' Dunedin's theory seems to apply exactly *as far as the formation of the next year's bulbs from side-buds is concerned, but not in relation to the entire decay of the old bulbs. Every year some scales decay, not those*

---

* Herein lies, I think, the explanation of all *normal* Lily scale growth, exemplified most simply in a bulblet or seedling Lily, or as in a full grown *Catesbœi*. The base of each leaf stalk is developed into a scale, and on the well doing of the leaf depends the vigour and health of that scale. Extend this rule a little further, and interpose a stem between the foliage and scales, and you find new scale growth developing at the base of the stem, continuously with the development of foliage, and I go further, and say, that experience shows me, that unless the foliage is healthy, the new growth will be scanty and stunted, and this, I think, may be taken as a reply to those who advocate cutting down Lily stems in full bloom, as not injurious. It is most decidedly injurious, in the way I have pointed out, viz., in checking new growth—unless it be done at a period when growth is nearly over—and unless at least two thirds of the foliage are left on the plant.

I say normal scale growth. *I have mentioned an exception amongst the Martagon group* (see p. 86), *but in these cases, my experience leads me to believe that new scale growth does not appear, but only the old growth of the last season is amplified and hypertrophied ; so that a larger heavier bulb is produced. I have also noticed, that in Auratum, Speciosum, and other kinds, if the flowering portion of the stem be broken off while in early bud, the leaves below, become much larger and broader as if to compensate for the damage done above.*

† I think here, Max Leichtlin theorises erroneously : not having dissected, he does not adduce any evidence to show that during the summer another central bud is developed to grow the next year. No stalk is developed in *Giganteum* until its time to flower is come, only a tuft of leaves ; and *Giganteum* will go on developing its one bulb till the flower stalk shoots up ; the root stock or central axis being the vital motive force in development.

*of last year's growth, but those of three or four years' of age. I AM OF
OPINION THAT THE OLD BULB DOES NOT DECAY EVERY
YEAR.* I cannot now, from want of careful investigation, say much
about the mode of vegetation of ther Rhizomatous group, but I may state,
that even among these, a different mode of vegetation takes place."—
Garden, vol. 13, *p.* 252.

§26. I cannot understand how—if it he true, as Dunedin asserts, 'that Lily
bulbs are all annual in growth, and that each year, the old bulbs disappear
entirely, and new bulbs succeed—large bulbs are built up.' We import
from Japan, every year, hundreds of bulbs, measuring 12 to 14 or 16
inches in circumference, many weighing a pound each. In many of these is
plainly visible a hole, wherein the base of the old stalk has been attached ;
this is generally situated, not in the centre, not outside the bulb, but
having, say, one-third of the bulb on one side, and two-thirds of the bulb
on the other, I can detect no difference in appearance in the scales, in the
majority of these bulbs, they all look equally fresh, plump, and healthy.
Is it possible, that these are entirely new bulbs, embracing—Mark ! not
lying to one side of—the old flower stem ; if so, how did the new growth
manage to encircle* the stem, and what has become of the old bulb ?
N. B.—The bulbs of *Auratum* which are imported into Europe, are dug up
in Japan, mostly in the months of October or November. The same
remarks will apply more or less, to the production of all large bulbs.

* Compare the figures of *Hansoni* and *Speciosum*, pages 109 and 110.

CHAPTER XII.

ON COLLECTING AND PACKING LILY BULBS.

The time to collect Lilies is when the flowering season is just over, the leaves then turn yellow and fall off, and the stems die down. It is true (*see* p. 9) that Lilies, even when in flower and full growth, may be moved carefully and safely from one spot to another; but then they must be planted at once, and encouraged to finish their growth; this might be safely done by collectors, if anxious to obtain decisive information as to any unknown species, by flowering a few roots more conveniently at a subsequent date; for in this way, bulbs may travel safely some distance, be replanted, and subsequently bloom. But it would not answer to collect Lilies thus in bulk, with a view to sending them a long journey; they might, perhaps, travel this way for a week without much damage, if carefully planted out afterwards and well watered; but a longer journey would endanger the flower, and probably do damage to the future growth.

Bulbs that are to be sent a month's journey and upwards, must be taken up when ripe as aforesaid, dried, but not to such an extent as to become flabby: the soil between the scales should also be dry, and therefore it is of importance, that the weather should be dry, when the bulbs are dug up; *they should be handled tenderly to avoid bruises, as these are a very fertile source of loss.* It is well also, to expose the bulbs to the sun for a few days only, thoroughly to ripen and dry them; they then acquire a tinted colour, varying from yellow to purple. The roots and stems should be cut off close to the bulb, and a dry material prepared for packing.

For a month's journey, sawdust, dry sphagnum moss, cocoa-nut fibre, or a mixture of these, with powdered charcoal, or other dry material will answer well, but for a two months' journey or upwards, this mode of packing is not safe. One object being to exclude light and air, and thus paralyse, so to speak, the bulb and deprive it of all vital action.

With this view, earth thoroughly dried (or charcoal) has been often used. A yellow volcanic earth has been much used in Japan by packers, but we prefer the cooler natural light soil, as we think the bulbs arrive in better order when packed in this. Charcoal has the objection of being very dirty, and of disfiguring the bulb greatly. We have unpacked bulbs in splendid order after two months' journey, which had been packed in coarse oak sawdust, smelling very strongly of tannin; but a second consignment from the same hand, packed in pine sawdust, finer in character, heated on the journey, and many of the bulbs were destroyed, the contents being quite hot when turned out.

Packing cases should be made of wood 1 inch thick. Cases 2 to 3 feet long by 12 to 18 inches wide and 12 to 16 inches deep, are preferred by Japanese packers, and will hold from 200 to 250 *Auratum* bulbs of moderate size; packed in balls of clay, they of course require a larger space.

It is a good plan to line the joints inside with paper, so as to prevent leakage, tier after tier of bulbs is then put in, and dry earth (or some other medium) poured in between, and the box well hammered to settle the earth thoroughly and tightly, it being a matter of great importance that there should be no empty space inside to allow of the bulbs shaking about and getting bruised: bulbs so packed will travel in safety for from two to two and a half months. If, however, one bulb be bad inside when packed, it will not only soon rot, but will affect the others, and in this way the whole contents on arrival may be a stinking rotten mass. Thus, during the season at Messrs. Stevens, Covent Garden, thousands of *Auratum* are frequently unpacked rotten, at a great loss to the importers. It is of importance at the end of a journey that not a day should be lost in opening the boxes and separating the sound bulbs; similarly it is important and even economical to choose the quickest route when forwarding bulbs, even if it be at first sight more expensive, since after two months, every day added to the length of the journey, deteriorates the bulbs and increases the number of diseased ones. In sending over new or unknown sorts, it is very desirable to send a drawing or dried flower by post, as a guide to the determination of the species. Lilies should be sent off as soon as possible after their stems have died down, and the bulbs are ripened. If bulbs have begun to grow before packing, there is great risk in sending them; better wait if possible another season.

In sending more sorts than one in the same case, it is well not to trust to partitions, as some of the Japanese packers do; the partitions often get shifted, and bulbs escape from one to another compartment. It is far better to pack each sort in a separate box, with a label, and enclose these separate boxes (slighter in build) in a large outer case. Small sized bulbs, such as those of *L. Concolor, Pulchellum*, &c., can be safely sent long distances by post, packed in tin or wooden boxes, with cocoa fibre or sphagnum, slightly moist; but, in this case, the Post Office regulations, as to weight, stamps, &c., must be strictly adhered to, and the sharp edges of the tin boxes protected by some kind of cover, otherwise they may be refused by the Post Office authorities as likely to damage the contents of their bags, and thus cause disappointment.

The overland route, viâ San Francisco, is far preferable to that viâ Suez Canal, if used before the month of December, when severe cold sets in.

But for large bulbs, by far the best mode of packing, yet discovered, is to seal hermetically, in lumps of mud or clay, each bulb, if large, or three or four together if small. Some years since, finding that our bulbs from Japan came over in bad condition, and learning that even Camellias and other plants in leaf had been sent out to the Cape and elsewhere with perfect success, having a coating of clay on each leaf and stem, we sent out instructions to our agents in Japan to make trial of this process, which, proving eminently successful, has now been universally adopted by the packers in that country. They prepare, in the autumn, a large quantity of soft puddled clay or mud, and coat each *Auratum* bulb with it, to a thickness of about ¾ inch, smaller bulbs, such as those of *Thunbergianum* and *Krameri*, with a thickness of a ¼ to ½ an inch, while of small bulbs, such as those of *Coridion* and *Concolor*, they put three or four in a lump; they then wrap up each lump in a piece of fine paper, to keep all together; and when slightly dried, which is soon effected by exposure to the sun in that country, they are placed in a case, and the interstices filled in with dried soil, sawdust, or other light material, the bulbs thus hermetically sealed, are kept cool during the journey, and remain in a quiescent state.

Nevertheless, it has been found that like all other modes before tried, this sometimes fails, and that rot invades the cases, spreading from bulb to bulb, till all are affected. And this leads me to another point, which is well worthy of further investigation. Bulbs invaded in this way by rot, turned out of the clay on arrival, and set apart, become covered in a few days with the Mycelium (growth), of a long silky-looking fungus, smell very disagreeably and rot rapidly. Similarly, bulbs *apparently sound and in first-rate condition*, when imported and turned out of their mud envelope, will, if left a few weeks unplanted, become covered with the same fungus, and be found in a soft rotten condition. This we have often experienced to our loss and discomfort, especially with bulbs purchased in the auction rooms for planting, and laid aside for a while, if the weather was too wet or frosty for planting, or our men otherwise occupied; we have likewise experienced grave complaints from our customers to whom we have sent bulbs, apparently sound, but which have rotted some time afterwards; and we have thus got into great disgrace, when the fault lay in the subsequent treatment by the purchaser, and not in our carelessness in selecting bad bulbs. We remember well, some years since, sending 50 bulbs to the Curator of a celebrated Botanic Garden, and receiving from him some months afterwards a demand to replace these, because, wrote he, "they had all rotted away, he had placed them," he said, "aside in a box, and watched them carefully,

P

every week some of them rotted, he wrote to tell us when the last was gone." Not knowing better then, we replaced the bulbs, but now we know that they were bound to rot under such treatment. *Imported Lilies must be planted as soon as possible;* if, owing to frost or wet weather, the ground is not in a fit state for planting, they must either be coated with mud, or kept covered in soil in a box, till they can be planted; air must not be allowed access to them, to dry them, or to permit the development of fungus.

It must not be forgotten that in collecting bulbs for packing and exportation their scales are more or less bruised, thus readily permitting the invasion of fungus germs; furthermore, that in all probability the collected bulbs will be massed in a heap in some outbuildings; that in Japan the packing for Europe is made a regular business of, and certain firms every year pack and send thousands of bulbs over to Europe and elsewhere, consequently bulbs coming in from the interior some miles, will be first jolted and bruised in the country carts, and then shot down in masses to wait their turn to be packed, and that this process goes on year after year in the same warehouses. What wonder, then, that fungus germs are rife on these premises.

Dunedin's remarks on this point fully coincide with my own suspicions.

" In my opinion the cause of so much loss in imported Lily bulbs is a parasitic fungus, constituting a kind of mould of foreign origin, of a most destructive character, and hereditary, descending from parents to offspring. The minute microscopic root-like filaments of the mould-like fungus that I have observed, insinuate themselves into the epidermis of the bulb, and, acting as parasites, draw nourishment from its tissues, and ultimately poison the plant. The minute germs of this fungus are dispersed everywhere throughout the atmosphere, and are ready to alight on any substance in which they can find a nidus. The tender scarf skin of the Lily bulb, freshly lifted out of the soil, is particularly favourable to their growth."—*Garden, vol.* 13, *p.* 142.

If, then, we are correct in attributing to a virulent fungus this rot of imported Lily bulbs we need not be slow in applying a remedy. The process of Antiseptic Surgery recently introduced by Professor Lister, with such remarkably favourable results, can easily be applied to the preservation of bulb life. This process consists in preventing the access of all poisonous and ferment germs (which are microscopic in their nature) to recent wounds, by, (1) washing in a solution of carbolic acid, of the strength of one part of acid to forty parts of water, all instruments, ligatures, &c., employed, likewise the hands of the operator; (2) in directing a current of spray of a similar solution during the whole of the operation over the part operated upon; and (3rdly) in covering the wound afterwards with lint, cotton wool, or gauze steeped in a similar solution, it being found impossible that fungus germs, can live or be propagated in these antiseptic solutions. Hence it is evident that if the Japanese would, just before packing, steep the bulbs in a bowl of water containing one part of carbolic acid to forty of water, the germs then attached to the bruised Lily scales would be either destroyed or rendered innocuous, and the bulbs would arrive safe. Similar treatment should be adopted on arrival. It is clear that the exclusion of air on the voyage by means of the mud coating is of material benefit in keeping the bulbs cool, and preventing fungoid growth during that period, but that it is not in itself all-sufficient, is evident from the fact that bulbs do decay on the voyage, and that rot, the result of fungus, probably contracted in the Japanese packing sheds, spreads from bulb to bulb and from case to case.* Even after arrival we have found the benefit of these mud envelopes, for whereas bulbs once turned out will not keep more than a very few weeks, even if covered with dry soil, kept unbroken in their mud balls we have found them perfectly sound two months after arrival. To carry this point further still, we recommend all buyers of imported bulbs to purchase only those which are still in their mud coats, or only just turned out, and to plant them at once, covered with several inches of the best antiseptic of all—mother earth. No fungus germs will then attack them; if left uncovered, they will rapidly deteriorate.

"I have dissected many imported bulbs, and have found colonies of little voracious thread-like worms, about ½ inch in length, feeding on the base of the young stems, so that subject to such attacks it would be impossible that these tender stems could live and thrive. I have put small fresh pieces of the stems into wine glasses, with seven or eight of these worms into each glass, and have found that they each consumed more in a day than was equal to the bulk of their own bodies. There cannot be a doubt that the parent insects (worms?) must have laid these eggs (?) on the bulbs during the ten to fifteen days they were exposed to the atmosphere before packing for exportation. I have also seen in many cases that these worms had consumed the young seed-buds; nothing else in my opinion can account for the wholesale destruction of bulbs, which is a common complaint, in consequence of the non-appearance of imported Lilies during the second season."—*Dunedin, in Garden, vol. 15, p. 83.*

The above remarks of "Dunedin" we are unable to corroborate, never having met with any worms in our *Auratum* bulbs. If, however, he refers to the thread-like worms (Gordius) found in this country in diseased potatoes and other decaying vegetable material, we can only remark that these worms do not attack healthy bulbs, but are found only in unhealthy and decaying roots and bulbs of all kinds, and are the "post hoc" not the "propter hoc."

* It is somewhat confirmatory of the correctness of these ideas, that we have as yet found in *no other bulbs, except in those coming from Japan,* evidence of this long silky fungoid growth, so destructive to bulb life.

CONCLUDING REMARKS.

It has been my object throughout this little work—

To obtain a correct nomenclature of all the Lilies, added to such descriptions as may enable amateurs at once to recognise the principal forms and varieties.

To give such instruction as to culture, both general and particular, as may enable Lily growers to contend successfully against the peculiarities of the soil and climate of their respective localities.

To impart such information about Bulbs, their reproduction, disease, and growth, as may enable and encourage cultivators to make further observations on points which are yet obscure, but which, when cleared up, will afford valuable assistance to Lily growers.

To encourage the collection and expedition to this country of new and rare forms, and the production of new varieties.

To attain their ends, I have thought it best not to put forward at length my own views and opinions, which, being formed from a few years' practice on the light and heavy soils of Colchester, must necessarily be somewhat limited, but rather to describe the modes of culture practised by numerous successful Lily growers in various parts of Great Britain and elsewhere, and to quote their opinions, interspersing a few remarks of my own, more especially citing the manner in which certain difficulties in soil, aspect, and locality have been evaded or overcome. Hence, though it will be remarked that the portion of the work which has been written by me bears but a small proportion to the whole, my excuse for this is, that as no two Lily growers have precisely the same soil and difficulties to contend with, they will be best instructed by perusing the varied experience and opinions, of a large number of observers, in many parts, and of learning the different views held by different authorities, rather than by being led by the *ipse dixit* of one individual.

I am under obligations, which I am glad here gratefully to acknowledge, (a) to Professor Baker, of Kew, whose valuable labours I am permitted to reproduce in the form of The Synopsis, chap. ix., by means of which any Lily may at once be referred to its proper group and place; and through whom the difficulties of incorrect nomenclature, which at one time seemed insuperable, owing to so many names having been given sometimes to one form, sometimes to another form, without discrimination, by popular authors, have been cleared up, and a clear chart left for us to work by; (b) to Mr. Burbidge for his valuable paper on Bulbs and their delineations, by means of which much light has been thrown on a subject, which to many was excessively obscure, but which now may easily be mastered, and by the help of the numerous woodcuts, made familiar to every cultivator; (c) to Dunedin (whoever he may be) for his "Fallacies," for though I cannot agree with all his remarks, and though I think he is often inclined to push his conclusions a great deal too far, cultivators must all feel greatly obliged to him for turning the light of his lamp on their practices, and compelling them to look at their doings through his spectacles, the result of which must be to make them walk more warily, to observe more closely, and get more correct views of Bulb life and reproduction; (d) to numerous Foreign Correspondents who have favoured me with so much highly valuable information as to the growth of Lilies in their native haunts, and the modes of cultivation practised in distant climes—the letters on Californian and Himalayan Lilies being especially valuable to us stay-at-home people; (e) also to Dr. Masters and Mr. W. Robinson, the respective Editors of the *Gardeners' Chronicle* and the *Garden*, for their kind permission to use many woodcuts, and to reprint various valuable communications.

Lastly, kind reader, excuse the many faults and omissions of this little work, most especially the unworthiness of many of the woodcuts to represent some of the most beautiful flowers in creation—take for example those of *L. Szovitzianum, Excelsum, Candidum,* &c.; to my mind most meagre and poor caricatures of the reality (stout tall stems, adorned with numerous flowers, fine, perfect, and symmetrical), as grown in full beauty by many a cultivator. Yet it is not easy, in the limited space at hand, to pourtray on paper, so as to convey an accurate idea, a Lily stem with numerous flowers; and it is more to the purpose faithfully to outline a stem, foliage, and two or three flowers, so that the chief characteristics are truthfully preserved, than to give a blurred heavy mass of foliage and flowers, beautiful perhaps as a whole, but too indistinct for precise identification.

If, reader, you have patiently borne with me thus far, one word of advice more before we part. Cultivate Lilies for their purity, gracefulness, and because they so abundantly reward the patience of the persevering cultivator with ever-increasing stateliness of form, and luxuriance of growth; and may this little work help you to enjoy to your complete satisfaction the fruits of your labour.

"In tenui labor, at tenuis non gloria, si,"
"ridet Fortuna."

CHAPTER XIII.

___

MR. BAKER'S
PRIMARY DIVISION OF THE GENUS LILIUM.

No one who will once take the trouble to master the characters of these five groups and thoroughly understand them by the aid of living specimens, will find any difficulty in referring any flowering specimen to its proper position.

___

SUB-GENUS I. CARDIOCRINUM.

Perianth,* funnel-shaped, with oblanceolate segments, falcate only at the apex.

Leaves stalked, heart-shaped, ovate—

> 1, *Cordifolium ;* 2, *Giganteum.*

SUB-GENUS II. EULIRION.

Perianth, funnel-shaped, with oblanceolate segments, which are falcate only at the apex ; leaves linear or lanceolate, sessile, or nearly so.

Tube scarcely widened from the base to the middle—

> 3, *Philippinense;* 4, *Wallichianum ;* 5, *Longiflorum ;* 6, *Neilgherrense.*

Tube gradually narrowing from the base to the neck ; leaves scattered—

> 7, *Odorum ;* 8, *Brownii ;* 9, *Krameri ;* 10, *Nepalense ;* 11, *Candidum ;* 12, *Belladonna.*

Leaves in whorls—

> 13, *Washingtonianum ;* 14, *Washingtonianum-Purpureum ;* 15, *Parryi.*

SUB-GENUS III. ARCHELIRION.

Perianth, open, funnel-shaped, with deeply spreading segments, which are broadest below the middle ; stamens diverging from the curved style.

Leaves sessile—

> 16, *Tigrinum ;* 17, *Oxypetalum.*

Leaves shortly-stalked—

> 18, *Speciosum ;* 19, *Auratum.*

___

* Perianth, for the information of my less learned readers, is the botanical term for the flower.

Sub-genus IV. ISOLIRION.

Perianth, erect, with segments, which are falcate in the extended flower, but not revolute; stamens diverging on all sides from the straight style.

Leaves in whorls—

20, *Philadelphicum*; 21, *Medeoloides*.

Leaves scattered—Style shorter than ovary—

22, *Concolor*.

Style longer than ovary—

23, *Bulbiferum*; 24, *Croceum*; 25, *Davuricum*; 26, *Elegans*; 27, *Catesbœi*.

Sub-genus V. MARTAGON.

Perianth, cernuous, with the segments very revolute; stamens diverging on all side from the curved style.

Leaves in whorls.

American species; bulbs, annual, bearing rhizomes—

28, *Canadense*; 29, *Pardalinum*; 30, *Superbum*; 31, *Lucidum*; 32, *Roezlii*; 33, *Columbianum*; 34, *Humboldtii*.

Old-world species—

35, *Martagon*; 36, *Avenaceum*; 37, *Hansoni*.

Leaves scattered.

Leaves lanceolate—many nerved—

Perianth, falcate above the middle—

38, *Monadelphum* (*Szovitzianum*).

Perianth, revolute to below the middle—

39, *Polyphyllum*; 40, *Ponticum*; 41, *Carniolicum*.

Leaves narrowly linear—with one or few nerves—

Segments of the perianth, from six to twelve lines broad in the middle—

42, *Testaceum*; 43, *Leichtlinii*; 44, *Batemani*; 45, *Pseudo-tigrinum*; 46, *Wallacei*.

Segments of the perianth, from three to six lines broad in the middle—

47, *Pomponium*; 48. *Chalcedonicum*; 49, *Callosum*; 50, *Tenuifolium*.

NOTE.—The *Notholirion* group (Himalayan Lilies), with tunicated bulbs, stigma cleft into three subulate hooked divisions, are now referred by Mr. Baker to the *Fritillarius*. See page 184.

FINIS.

THE NEW PLANT & BULB Co.,

LION WALK,

COLCHESTER.

LILIES.

The cultivation of this beautiful class of plants forms a speciality with us, and HOME GROWN bulbs of unusual excellence can be supplied. Our collection is the finest in Europe, and embraces all the known species in cultivation.

IRIS.

We have a splendid collection of the Iris family, which is now becoming as popular as the Lily family, and deservedly so. As with the Lilies, so also with the Iris, we have adopted the classification of Mr. C. G. Baker, so that our customers will be certain to get a correct nomenclature.

AMARYLLIDS, BULBOUS, AND TUBEROUS PLANTS.

Of these, besides a collection of the most showy and beautiful kinds, we have many splendid new and rare species, and we are continually receiving others from our correspondents in all parts of the globe.

Our Autumn Catalogue, containing a complete list of all the above named kinds, and of some others, is ready for distribution in the month of August, and will be forwarded post free to every applicant.

THE NEW PLANT & BULB COMPANY,
LION WALK.
COLCHESTER.

ORCHIDS.

This glorious class of plants also, form a speciality with us, especially those suitable for Cool House culture. Our importations are extremely large, and we can supply either newly imported, established, or semi-established plants, as required by our customers.

Arrangements have been made by us with GENTLEMEN RESIDENT in the United States of Columbia, Brazil, the West Indies, Borneo, Ceylon, the Himalayas, Assam, Burmah, various parts of Australia, The Cape, Japan, &c., to collect and forward to us at the proper time, all the most desirable and beautiful plant productions of these localities, more especially Orchids. These are at once offered to our customers, and as it is well known that Imported Orchids are mainly the produce of seeds self sown in their native countries, *purchasers of Imported Orchids have the best chance of obtaining new kinds and valuable varieties, at very low rates.* We would, therefore, respectfully advise all Orchid Growers, to favour us with their name and address, that we may communicate with them immediately upon the arrival of our various consignments.

Commencing with the early Spring months, our lists of fresh Importations are issued almost monthly, until Midsummer.

Gentlemen resident in new and unexplored localities, or in localities where valuable Orchids abound, are respectfully solicited to put themselves into communication with Dr. Wallace.

HARDY AND HALF-HARDY TERRESTRIAL ORCHIDS,
FOR OUT-DOOR AND FRAME CULTURE,

Form a speciality with us, and we lose no opportunity of adding to our collection from all parts of the world.

Catalogues post free on application.